POLITICS AND THE
SCIENCES of CULTURE
IN GERMANY

POLITICS AND THE
SCIENCES of CULTURE
IN GERMANY
1840–1920

Woodruff D. Smith

New York   Oxford
OXFORD UNIVERSITY PRESS
1991

Oxford University Press

Oxford   New York   Toronto
Delhi   Bombay   Calcutta   Madras   Karachi
Petaling Jaya   Singapore   Hong Kong   Tokyo
Nairobi   Dar es Salaam   Cape Town
Melbourne   Auckland

and associated companies in
Berlin   Ibadan

Copyright © 1991 by Oxford University Press, Inc.

Published by Oxford University Press, Inc.,
200 Madison Avenue, New York, New York 10016

Oxford is a registered trademark of Oxford University Press

Library of Congress Cataloging-in-Publication Data
Smith, Woodruff D.
Politics and the sciences of culture in Germany, 1840–1920
Woodruff D. Smith.
p. cm. Includes bibliographical references and index.
ISBN 0-19-506536-0
1. Politics and culture—Germany—History—19th century.
2. Learning and scholarship—Germany—History—20th century.
3. Germany—Intellectual life—19th century.   I. Title.
DD204.S58   1991
001.1'0943'09034—dc20
90-42623

1 3 5 7 9 8 6 4 2

Printed in the United States of America
on acid-free paper

Acknowledgments

I would like to thank the following individuals for assistance and advice at various stages in the preparation of this book: Ralph Austen, Ulrich Braukämper, Gary Cohen, Lewis Gann, Thomas Greaves, Arthur Knoll, Nancy Lane, and David Schneider. I want especially to thank Roger Chickering for his criticism of the entire first draft of the book and his suggestions for alterations, and my wife, Jane H. Smith, and my children, Anthony and Rebecca Smith, for their support and patience.

I would also like to express my gratitude to the National Endowment for the Humanities, which supported parts of the research with a fellowship and a summer stipend; the American Philosophical Society and the German Academic Exchange Service, which provided further grant support; the Shelby Cullom Davis Center for Historical Studies at Princeton, the Frobenius Institute of Frankfurt University, and the Hoover Institution at Stanford, all of which kindly provided facilities and other forms of assistance in the course of the study; the staffs of the libraries of the University of Texas at San Antonio, Frankfurt University, the University of Leiden, the University of London (Senate House), Princeton University, Stanford University, and the University of Texas at Austin; the British Library and the Library of Congress; and the staff of the *Bundesarchiv* in Koblenz.

I am grateful to Greenwood Press for permission to include some of the materials in chapter 9.

W.D.S.

Contents

POLITICS AND THE
SCIENCES of CULTURE
IN GERMANY

Introduction

In the nineteenth century, there appeared a new group of academic disciplines that took culture as a primary object of scientific study. These included anthropology in its many varieties, human geography, culture history, and branches of psychology that focused on culture. In other fields, the concept of culture became a significant part of the apparatus of interpretation. Bodies of theory about culture emerged, often overleaping the boundaries between disciplines. The development of these "cultural sciences" was an international phenomenon to which people of all major European nations and the United States contributed. But distinctive national approaches also revealed themselves, each largely shaped by the public context of intellectual life in a particular country.

This book is concerned with the cultural sciences in Germany between the 1840s and about 1920. During those years, German academia exercised its most profound influence on the rest of the world—an influence that is generally acknowledged in some cultural sciences, for example geography, but to which rather little attention is paid in others, such as cultural anthropology.[1] In the German intellectual setting, *Kultur* and *Kulturwissenschaft* came to have many meanings. Here we shall concentrate on cultural scientists who believed that they were practicing a nomothetic science (i.e., searching for the laws of human society as revealed in culture) and who regarded culture itself mainly in its anthropological sense. That is to say, they were interested primarily in the patterns of thought and behavior characteristic of a whole people rather than the intellectual and artistic activities of the elite, although their concerns could readily encompass the latter. Other forms of cultural interpretation developed in the nineteenth century, including the hermeneutic approach of the *Geisteswissenschaften*. But those featured in the present study constitute a relatively coherent set of approaches that can be contrasted with others in order to reveal some of the reasons cultural science evolved in Germany when and how it did.

That is the object of this study. Why did the concept of culture, which had been a secondary element of German social thought since the eighteenth century, rapidly become at midcentury the central feature of several new academic disciplines and several increasingly separate bodies of social theory? Why did cultural science, especially the *theories* of cultural science, develop thereafter in Germany in ways that diverged significantly from the patterns found in other countries? What relationship, if any, existed between the emergence of cultural science and the general explosion of creativity that occurred in German social science at the end of the nineteenth and the beginning of the twentieth century? What part did cultural scientists play in the debates over the nature of science that were so characteristic of the period and so productive of new theoretical directions? These are the questions with which we shall be mainly concerned. Although there are historical studies of individual disciplines and although the history of anthropology in particular has advanced an enormous distance in recent years, few have tried to investigate the cultural sciences as a whole, either in Germany or elsewhere.[2]

How do we go about answering these basic questions? Much of the historical work on the individual disciplines of cultural science—indeed, most of the histories of the social sciences in general—have taken a more or less traditional "history of ideas" approach. They have concentrated on how theories are constructed by individuals in the course of a kind of dialogue between those individuals and other thinkers, past and contemporary. For example, a major issue in the history of late-nineteenth-century anthropology concerns the nature of the intellectual debt owed by British social evolutionists to Charles Darwin.[3] In the German context, primary attention tends to be paid to the influence of Immanuel Kant, Johann Gottfried von Herder and the Romantic philosophers on later theoreticians of culture.[4] Other historians, still largely emphasizing the philosophical side of things, have portrayed the disciplines of cultural science as resulting from successive broad intellectual movements. Social science begins with the Enlightenment, interest in culture derives from Romanticism, and sciences of culture result, toward the middle of the nineteenth century, from the appearance of utilitarian and materialist philosophies.[5]

These varieties of interpretation have considerable merit, but they also have well-known weaknesses. They tend to exclude, or at least to downplay, influences on theory that arise in the social, economic, and political contexts in which thinkers operate. Although it may be that in some fields of intellectual endeavor, isolation from the rest of society is so pronounced that such an approach is entirely appropriate, this is certainly not true of the social sciences. It has become clear from recent research that even fields such as archaeology and cultural anthropology, which seem at first glance to be safely insulated against the currents of contemporary politics, are in fact not so.[6] Moreover, it has also become clear that interactions between academic theory and popular culture, which used to be viewed merely as a trickle-down process by which the great ideas of the intellectual elite are spread about in watered-down form for mass consumption, actually work in two directions and can have a profound effect on theory. To be more specific in the present case, my own interest in the subject of German cultural science arose from perceiving close connections between important turn-of-the-century political ideologies in Germany (certain versions of radical imperialism) and distinctively German anthropological theories (cultural diffusionism, for instance). These connections involved the exertion of intellectual influence, but the influence did not appear to move in only one direction: ideology affected theory and theory affected ideology. Although it is possible to refer to genealogies of ideas that influenced both ideology and cultural theory, these in no way explain why the particular forms of interaction that I thought I observed took place.[7]

The most obvious alternative to the various forms of the history of ideas would be a sociocultural or sociological approach—one that seeks to explain changes in ideas and modes of thinking by focusing on relationships among thinkers (either as individuals or as members of groups) and dynamic factors in their social environments. Typically, when such interpretations have been advanced in histories of social sciences, they have focused on the effects of class structure and class conflict. This is true not only of studies that are overtly Marxist, but of others as well. Some sociocultural studies also focus on generational conflict, but usually in conjunction with a class analysis.[8]

Again, this type of interpretation has yielded important results. The realization that class background can influence the theories of social scientists and that such factors as education, common generational experience, and the structure of careers can be as important in shaping theories as formal philosophies leads to explanations of considerable power. Sociocultural analysis can be used particularly to explain change in intellectual life by treating the latter as a recipient of influences arising in other areas of society: a general societal alteration (e.g., European industrialization) changes the conditions under which thinking occurs (in this example by creating a class conflict between bourgeoisie and proletariat) and, therefore, changes the structure of thought.

Just as the varieties of sociocultural analysis are many, so too are the difficulties inherent in using them. There is, for one thing, the problem of reliably deciding which of the myriad facts of social existence primarily account for particular intellectual changes. Usually, social theory is brought into play here. Marxian theory, by postulating the existence of classes in a conflictual relationship, tends to focus attention on the class consciousness of social scientists and to interpret particular theories as manifestations of their class interests. Although this approach can certainly reveal part of the basis on which theory is built, its fundamental assumption— that, one way or another, consciousness of class and of class conflict is the primary source of motivation in theory building—remains unproven. Attempting to force the idea of the primacy of class and the rest of the analytical framework that goes with it on the data can sometimes result in interpretations that do not work— especially in the many cases of social thinkers who manifestly ignore or oppose the interests of their own class. Various doctrines can be applied to cover such circumstances (false consciousness, for instance), but these often appear to be attempts to save the phenomena, to maintain the integrity of the theory, regardless of empirical evidence. As we shall see in later chapters, social-class membership, as usually conceived, is a rather awkward category for the analysis of cultural science theory.[9] And it does not help very much in trying to account for sharp differences over theoretical issues when the disputants clearly belong to the same social class. Even if one uses other ways to divide up the social environment for analytical purposes (e.g., into generations), the problem remains of showing how the categories one chooses directly affect the content of formal thought.

None of this, of course, precludes the use of sociocultural analysis for the purposes of this study any more than the weaknesses of the history of ideas exclude that approach. It does, however, suggest that some other way might be found to investigate the questions at hand, some way that would combine intellectual and social elements without necessarily giving primacy to either set. Could contemporary poststructuralist interpretive methods be employed, perhaps some form of discourse analysis?[10] To a certain extent they could. In the chapters that follow, considerable attention will be paid to the frameworks of meaning within which the construction of social and cultural theory took place in Germany. Although these will be discussed mainly in terms of their explicit and implicit idea-contents, modes of discourse will be very important to the analysis. But neither discourse analysis nor any other hermeneutic methodology will be adopted as the main approach here. There are several reasons for this, but the most important is that the aims of this study and those of most poststructuralist methodologies are to a substantial extent incompatible. This study, by focusing on the reasons for change in cultural science, requires an analysis of historical causes and effects that hermeneutic approaches—designed to promote "understanding" of historical phenomena rather than explaining processes—cannot readily provide.[11]

This is not the place for a lengthy discussion of other ways of dealing with the questions at hand and the reasons for declining to pursue them. (A Freudian psychohistorical approach is not taken, for example, because it would raise too many problems of circular treatment of evidence.)[12] The approach that *is* taken is based in part on the ideas suggested in the work of Thomas S. Kuhn (although important elements of Kuhn's analysis are discarded or severely redefined) and in part on the recognition that politics and political ideology seem to have been closely connected to the processes of change in cultural science.

Kuhn's account of the dynamics of scientific change, which emphasizes communities of scientists as the social structures within which scientific ideas are formulated and applied, seems at first glance to overcome many of the problems we have reviewed.[13] His concept of the scientific paradigm, which has become a commonplace in the philosophy of science during the past three decades, appears to provide exactly the kind of link between social context and theoretical change that we need. In addition, Kuhn's description of scientific revolution as a discontinuous process of intellectual change within a scientific discipline (turning on the rejection of the paradigms that have informed "normal science" in the immediate past) provides a model that appears to apply rather well to the social sciences.

Alas, nothing is that simple. Kuhn's legion of critics have raised innumerable objections to his methods, many of them so telling that Kuhn has had to revise his theories substantially since he first brought them out. One of the most important of these objections is that Kuhn is able to explain the effects of external context on scientific thought only because he defines the range of effective context very narrowly, limiting it to the practicing scientists within a particular organized discipline. The boundaries of the disciplines about which he has been talking have become narrower and narrower since his early work. It has become increasingly clear that Kuhn's explanation works best for narrowly defined disciplines in the physical sciences, ones whose subject matter is as far removed as possible from questions of conscious social concern.[14]

In fact, Kuhn claims that his analysis cannot be applied to the social or human sciences at all.[15] Kuhn's explanation for this is that the social sciences are, at least at present, "preparadigmatic"—that is, they do not display the high level of consensus about basic knowledge that the hard (real?) sciences do. This has worried many social scientists who have busied themselves with advancing paradigms in the ever-disappointed hope that all of their colleagues will accept them. It may be that the social sciences are, for the most part, permanently preparadigmatic because of their subject matter. Disciplines that take human behavior and society for their subjects probably cannot avoid reflecting the differences in interest and attitude that characterize humans and, therefore, in the long run cannot fail to display different interpretations of fundamental points. If this is the case, then why refer to Kuhn at all?

The reason is that, although we cannot employ the Kuhnian approach directly in the way Kuhn might apply it, say, to nuclear physics, we can still take from it some ideas that are valuable in analyzing change in the social sciences. The notion of discontinuous change, for instance, seems in general to fit the pattern we perceive in social science. We do not tend to think of social science as continuously aggregative. Clearly, however, Kuhn's general model, in which new insights are generated within a closed community of scientists by dissatisfaction with existing paradigms and are arranged into new paradigms, will not work for social science without substantial modification because we cannot postulate a community of scientists separated in their professional work from the outside world.

But what about the concept of paradigm itself? If we could not use the idea of paradigms, then it would be absurd to talk about borrowing from Kuhn at all, so central is the idea to his thought. If Kuhn himself thinks that the disciplines we are discussing are preparadigmatic, why bother?

Admittedly, Kuhn's primary definition of paradigm—a pattern of understanding shared, with almost no dissent, by the recognized practitioners of a scientific discipline—cannot be widely applied to the human sciences because of the lack of consensus within those fields. But Kuhn also acknowledges the existence of other underlying intellectual structures within scientific communities that are in some senses paradigmatic in character but that elicit much lower levels of agreement among practitioners. In his early work, Kuhn included these latter structures under the general term *paradigm,* but he later separated them conceptually from paradigms proper.[16] Paradigms, narrowly defined, specify for a discipline both a body of indisputable knowledge accepted by everybody in it (as the Copernican model of the solar system is accepted by astronomers) and a set of implicit rules, adopted with equal unanimity, that define the nature and boundaries of acceptable research. The broader, more loosely defined "paradigmatic" structures include such things as the general body of writings that must be understood by legitimate practitioners of a discipline, even if many of the practitioners disagree with some of them. These structures also include general notions (not always formulated in the same way) about what the purposes of the discipline and its objects of study are supposed to be and about how those objects are to be understood and approached. We can readily extend the category to include modes of discourse and vocabularies characteristic of a particular field. Unfortunately, these looser paradigmatic structures come in a great many forms; we cannot get from Kuhn a usable list that we can apply directly to the social sciences. But recognizing that such structures exist, that they perform functions within scientific disciplines similar to those of paradigms proper without necessarily being the sole shapers of theory, and that they do not imply total unanimity among scientists leads to the approach that will be taken in this study.

In our discussion, we shall examine certain structured sets of ideas widely shared by cultural scientists in nineteenth- and early-twentieth-century Germany. These sets of ideas (there were several, especially after the 1850s) each represented a partial consensus about the aims and methods of cultural study, about the appropriate behavior of scholars and scientists, about the kind of questions that were to be asked, and about the modes in which the questions were to be discussed. They incorporated basic assumptions about the nature of humankind, culture, society, and social change that served as foundations for theory building. None of the idea-sets was accepted unanimously within a single discipline. Differing schools of thought that featured different sets existed within each discipline and crossed disciplinary boundaries. None was therefore a paradigm in the strict Kuhnian sense, but each performed many of the functions of paradigms under conditions of imperfect consensus and substantial interaction with external social factors. These structured sets of ideas will be called the *theoretical patterns* of the cultural sciences. They were clearly not the only influences on the work of individual cultural scientists, nor do changes in theoretical patterns fully account for all change in cultural science, but they were important in both respects. We shall discuss the connections between the cultural sciences and their social context primarily in terms of theoretical patterns.

Identifying theoretical patterns does not automatically lead to an explanation of the causes of change in cultural theory—especially if the Kuhnian model of scientific revolutions generated within a scientific community is inapplicable to human sciences. Theoretical patterns do, however, provide a useful framework for exploiting the insight noted earlier: that there seems to have been a close connection between cultural theory in Germany and prominent ideologies in German politics and that political factors appear to have had a great deal to do with changes in the structures and the fashionability of particular theories. The present study began as an attempt to find parallels between intellectual structures in German politics and social science: ideological structures in politics that framed the programs of political movements, conferred legitimacy, and built consensus; paradigmatic structures in social science that performed the functions we have just discussed. Such parallels turned out to be quite abundant, affecting most recognized social studies (including the cultural sciences as they are defined here) in the nineteenth and early twentieth centuries. Links between the parallel structures also became apparent, especially the movement of elements of ideology into social scientific theory and the incorporation of ideas from social science in statements of ideology. In other words, by investigating the connections between ideologies and theoretical patterns, it became possible to focus on specific ways in which broader social forces and events, operating through the medium of politics, affected social science and encouraged changes in theory.

But the connections were not simple ones. Ideology acts in some respects as an aggregator of factors (especially factors derived from change) present in society in general.[17] But no ideology can be said to manifest the current array of significant social forces objectively. Comprehensive ideologies that have proven to be successful in politics in the past often have a very strong influence on the ways people perceive the social world and the changes that take place in it. Thus, ideology tends to organize social reality: to provide an important part of the framework of ideas that people use to understand the interactions of other people and the institutions around them. Looked at another way, ideology provides a large part of the vocabulary of people's social language and a fair amount of its syntax.

This is particularly true of intellectuals, especially ones with a professional interest in the study of society. Such people not only produce formal social theory, but they also provide much of the ideology of a political system. Obviously, they do not do so in a vacuum. In nineteenth-century Germany, it was the simultaneous engagement of certain intellectuals in politics and in academic social science that underlay the establishment of close parallels between ideologies and theoretical patterns. In responding to their perceptions of social forces present in a rapidly changing society as those forces impinged on the political system, academics helped to construct ideologies appropriate, as they thought, to new conditions. Ideologies also strongly informed (although they did not entirely dictate) theoretical work within the professional sphere of academics' lives. In this way, major political and social upheavals (such as the revolution of 1848) and longer-range socioeconomic changes provided much of the impetus to change in social scientific theory—even, as we shall see, in cultural sciences that had little apparent overt relevance to current social issues. At the same time, however, because the special role of academic intellectuals in politics derived from their ability to deploy the prestige of science in support of their ideological pronouncements, there was a strong tendency for them to apply social scientific theory to ideology: hence the complex passage of ideas and words back and forth between theory and ideology, and hence the creation of a partial community of discourse that incorporated both politics and social science. The phenomenon was not unique to Germany or to the period covered by this study. Here, however, we shall concentrate on Germany in the period from the 1840s to just after the First World War and on the cultural sciences, which we shall treat (as is appropriate for the nomothetic disciplines we examine) as a subset of social science in general.

The argument of the study can be briefly summarized. It focuses first on the connection between liberal ideology and social scientific theory in Germany before 1848. Because they arose from similar bodies of ideas and were developed by many of the same members of the academic elite, liberalism and social science were extremely closely linked—so much so that we can refer to a standard liberal theoretical pattern in social science. The liberal theoretical pattern was not the same thing as liberal ideology, of course, because ideologies and scientific theories are necessarily structured differently. Nor did all German liberal social thinkers accept the entire theoretical pattern. The pattern had many characteristics, but this study concentrates on three: its assumptions about the rational individual as the unit of social explanation, its central aim of discovering social laws, and its approach to social change and equilibrium. Starting approximately with the revolution of 1848, the liberal political movement in Germany experienced a protracted sequence of crises stretching to the end of the century, each of which caused liberal intellectuals in successive generations to question their allegiance to the movement and, by extension, to the intellectual structures with which liberalism was associated. Many other factors, of course, affected such reappraisals. Some derived from perceptions of ongoing socioeconomic change in an era of modernization, some reflected trends in philosophy, and some proceeded from the personal circumstances of individuals. But it was to a large extent political issues and a process of ideological construction that arose from the issues that shaped the context in which these factors interacted.[18]

The *cultural sciences* in Germany, like other social sciences, developed their particular theoretical patterns in part as a result of reappraisals of the liberal theoretical pattern. The concept of culture had been current since the eighteenth century in the kind of thinking that produced social science in the early nineteenth century. In the 1840s, it was for many liberal social scientists mainly a secondary means of correcting perceived weaknesses in their methodology, especially weaknesses deriving from rational individualism and liberal conceptions of social change. The revolution of 1848 and the crisis of liberalism in the 1850s brought the culture concept to the fore among many academics and journalists, who were seeking the causes of poor liberal political performance in the framework of ideas that liberals used to comprehend the social world. (At the same time, similar factors caused other academics to go in other directions—some to develop historical economics, a field with close connections to cultural science; others to focus on the "new" political history; and still others to adopt hermeneutic approaches to social understanding.) The 1850s saw an intellectual fad for cultural studies that was consciously viewed by its proponents as a response to 1848 and to the changes in politics occasioned by the rapid growth of the working class. To people such as Theodor Waitz, Adolf Bastian, and Rudolf Virchow, the scientific, empirical study of culture was to be a means by which the deficiencies *both* in liberal ideology *and* in social science would be corrected without dissipating the essence of liberalism. This was the origin of a "neoliberal" theoretical pattern in later cultural science. Others, for the most part former liberals like Wilhelm Heinrich Riehl, who had abandoned political liberalism but did not want to align themselves with reaction, turned to the study of culture in an effort to create a new conservative social science. Riehl's work resulted in the first of many similar theoretical patterns that were to emerge from succeeding generations of disillusioned liberal and ex-liberal academics.

A second cycle of fragmentation and innovation in German cultural science commenced with the remarkable liberal political recovery of the late 1850s and early 1860s—itself in part a political manifestation of rapid economic modernization. A generation of young academics entered political life in the 1860s, most of them as enthusiastic liberals who believed that science and reform went hand in hand and that great things were about to happen to Germany. What happened in the end was German unification under Bismarck's Prussia: a partial defeat for political liberalism that was followed by its organizational fragmentation, the rise of non-liberal parties in the new Reich, and the full manifestation of a social democratic political movement in the 1870s. The effect of all this on the young liberal academics was similar to that of 1848 on their predecessors, except that the generation of the 1860s was even more critical of the failures of older liberals and even more heterogeneous in its ideological and academic responses. The spread of

Darwinism and of the ideal of "apolitical" intellectual activity were signs of this generational discontent.

Between the late 1850s and the 1870s, most of the cultural science disciplines emerged as clearly defined academic fields, with geography acting to some extent as a model for others (especially ethnology).[19] The disciplines arose from diverse roots, but one of the most important was the neoliberal impulse among the post-1848 generation to plug the holes in liberal ideology and the liberal theoretical pattern. Starting in the 1870s, however, alternative theoretical patterns began to appear within the disciplines, theoretical patterns that cut across disciplinary boundaries. Many of these were advanced by members of the generation of the 1860s who were discontented with traditional liberalism and its theoretical cognates in social science. The newly emerging theoretical patterns were quite diverse, but several shared close relationships to agrarian, antiurban, and *völkisch* ideologies being developed (largely by disaffected liberals and former liberals) at the same time and that in the 1880s and 1890s came to be associated with the new radical nationalism in German politics.[20] Some individuals, such as the geographer Friedrich Ratzel, were prominent both in radical nationalist ideological construction and in the enunciation of new theoretical patterns (such as Ratzel's cultural diffusionism). These patterns were used by cultural scientists of Ratzel's generation to dispute the leadership of their disciplines with older elites of neoliberal outlook. Although the latter had their followers, the challenging patterns tended to appeal to still younger cultural scientists (ones who reached intellectual maturity in the Bismarckian and early Wilhelmian periods) who eventually became dominant around the turn of the century.

The argument thus far centers around cycles of crisis and partial failure in political liberalism as it faced the changes of the second half of the nineteenth century that resulted in the fragmentation of the liberal theoretical pattern in social science and the growth of alternative patterns (some neoliberal, some explicitly opposed to liberalism, and some ostensibly indifferent to political issues). Although the study concentrates on ethnology, human geography, and *Völkerpsychologie,* it also considers cultural history and other social sciences closely linked to cultural study (such as historical economics) in which similar developments occurred. It pays particular attention to the specific ways in which parallels between theoretical patterns and ideologies in the late nineteenth century were built on an actual exchange of ideas and vocabulary. This is seen especially in the relationship between various forms of imperialist ideology and cultural theory as well as in the effects of differing political perceptions of the "social question" on the ways in which cultural scientists dealt with the subject of societal change.

The last chapters focus on the political and intellectual upheavals at the turn of the century. These are best known in the history of social science for their effects on German sociology, but they also involved the cultural sciences. Among academics, as among politically active Germans in general, the period between 1890 and 1914 saw a rapid succession of ideological fashions and attempts at innovation in political organization and approach. Many of these were consciously aimed at combatting tendencies toward fragmentation in politics. One of their effects was to undermine much of what was left of the traditional function of liberalism as the framework of political reform, even though many of the participants in the process continued to think of themselves as liberals. These tendencies both affected and were influenced by parallel developments in the social and cultural sciences.

One of the most remarkable developments in the latter were attempts to create a broad, unified cultural science that would overcome the differences between competing theoretical patterns and disciplines and provide a basis for effective social policy. The effort to unify the cultural sciences was partly organized around a reaffirmation of the nomothetic orientation of the traditional liberal theoretical pattern, an orientation that had been maintained in many of the cultural sciences in part because of its utility in politics. The reaffirmation was felt to be necessary because of increasingly strong challenges to traditional nomothetic human science from the practitioners of *Geisteswissenschaft,* from the hermeneutic approaches of both Wilhelm Dilthey and the leaders of the German historical profession and, ultimately, from sociologists such as Max Weber and Georg Simmel.[21] The effort failed in part because it was unable to overcome the political differences that divided its adherents and to transcend the now-institutionalized boundaries between disciplines and between theoretical patterns. In any event, much of the ''nomothetic'' effort of early twentieth-century German cultural science came to be devoted to establishing elaborate cultural taxonomies rather than ''laws'' in a more traditional sense.

A final question that arises is why the nomothetic cultural sciences in Germany deviated in their theoretical approaches from their cognates in much of the rest of the world in the twentieth century, for example, in the continued domination of German ethnology by the diffusionist theoretical pattern. We shall focus on the connections between particular theoretical patterns and radical nationalist ideologies. The rise of the latter to great importance in German politics before and during the First World War enlarged the prominence of the former and, as we shall see in the case of the concept of *Lebensraum,* gave some ideas from cultural science considerable political significance. The identification of theoretical patterns with ideologies, however, also discredited these same ideas among social scientists outside Germany, especially after the victory of Nazism and the assimilation by the Nazis of the entire radical nationalist political tradition.

To begin our examination of these topics, we must go back to the first half of the nineteenth century, to a period when liberalism and social science were so closely linked that they were sometimes difficult to distinguish from one another.

1

The Liberal Theoretical Pattern
in Nineteenth-Century
German Social Science

The *Staatslexikon* stands as the most impressive symbol of the connection between German liberalism and the infant social sciences in the first half of the nineteenth century. A multivolume encyclopedia of matters pertaining to politics and policy, the *Staatslexikon* helped to shape German public opinion through each of three editions (1834–1843, 1845–1848, and 1856–1866).[1] Leonard Krieger has called it "the most influential organ of political liberalism in pre-March Germany." James Sheehan refers to it as "that paradigmatic expression of Vormärz liberalism."[2] It was also a broad-ranging compendium of the social science of the time. For this reason, we shall use the *Staatslexikon* as our main referent in tracing the outlines of the liberal theoretical pattern in German social science through the 1850s. Even though it did not encompass the social thought of all segments of German academic liberalism, it certainly was intended (and believed) to express the consensus of liberals interested in social science.

The editors of the *Staatslexikon,* Karl Rotteck (1775–1840) and Karl Theodor Welcker (1790–1869), were the acknowledged leaders of moderate liberalism in southwestern Germany before 1848 and, as professors of law and *Staatswissenschaft* at the University of Freiburg in Baden, preeminent academic proponents of gradual liberal reform based on a scientific understanding of society.[3] They set the goals and guidelines for the *Staatslexikon* according to their own political convictions, although they included among the contributors liberals ideologically to the right and left of themselves. In their introductions to the various editions of their encyclopedia, Rotteck and Welcker explicitly displayed the relationship in their own minds between political liberalism and the scientific study of society.

In the first edition, Rotteck announced that although the prime readers of the *Staatslexikon* would be "unimpassioned, moderate, thoughtful liberals" and that although the editors and contributors were themselves liberals, the main goals of the project were to increase the level of discussion among people of "good will" in both the liberal and the conservative camps and to promote "the greatest possible broadening or generalizing of sound political opinions and directions among all classes of society." The encyclopedia would educate the "active citizens of a *Rechtsstaat*."[4] Therefore, the first objectives of the articles must be scientific accuracy and manifest social utility, not special pleading for a particular party position. In the introduction to the third edition in 1856, Welcker admitted that a political bias was impossible to avoid but stated that he and Rotteck had intended from the start that "even our opponents, so we thought, could usefully read our finished products."[5]

Welcker and Rotteck were convinced that the presentation of an accurate scientific view of society was the primary means by which a liberal social order could be produced. Agreement among the "active citizens" to accept the conditions that made scientific social understanding possible would itself constitute the consensual basis of a liberal state. In his analysis of contemporary politics, Welcker warned that the states of Europe were being torn apart by fanatics of the Right and the Left.[6] He claimed that this threat could be averted through a public consensus in each country to establish a stable political system based on principles revealed by an impartial social science. Welcker thought that such a system would turn out to be a constitutional monarchy with representative institutions and organized as a *Rechtsstaat*. In other words, social science would reveal the desirability of political goals that Welcker sought as an active moderate liberal. And in order to make its maximum contribution to human progress, social science required the erection of a liberal social order. Social science and liberalism were thus logically (some might say tautologically) linked, but they were still seen as separate things, both as sets of ideas and as activities, with different, although mutually supporting, goals.

Liberals and Social Scientists

Part of the reason for the connection between social science and the dominant *Vormärz* varieties of liberal ideology lay in their similar intellectual origins, but another part derived from the social context in which they developed in Germany— a context that can be seen in the backgrounds of the editors and contributors of the *Staatslexikon*. As university professors, Rotteck and Welcker were civil servants employed mainly to teach prospective members of Baden's bureaucratic elite and to provide the government with expert advice on law and administration. At the same time, they were the leaders of the liberal opposition in the Baden legislature. (Baden was the most liberal of *Vormärz* states, but political liberals still constituted the opposition. Baden was not all *that* liberal.) This peculiar situation, which was replicated in other places, requires some discussion.

Before it became a political movement as a result of the French Revolution, German liberalism formed as an ideology from attempts in the late eighteenth century by officials and academics to weave together ideas that were the common property of the European Enlightenment with the German bureaucratic and university traditions in order to deal with problems of incipient modernization.[7] The French occupation of parts of Germany between the 1790s and 1814 can to some extent be seen as an acceleration of tendencies toward political modernization and thus as an acceleration of demands for change. Therefore, from its very start the intellectual and political tradition that became the moderate liberalism of Rotteck and Welcker was borne by people whose careers tied them directly to the state administrations. This situation strongly affected not only the development of liberal ideology in Germany (a fact that has been noted by historians),[8] but also the way in which social science evolved there. During the first half of the nineteenth century, German social science consisted in large part of attempts by a few academics and officials to put their moderate liberal convictions on a scientific basis, ostensibly in order to deal with the problems posed by socioeconomic change.

Widespread intellectual interest in Adam Smith and economic reform did not, however, in itself constitute a liberal political movement. The French Revolution, the French occupation, and the response in Germany to those events did that. The revolution created a programmatic statement of political liberalism that attracted many followers in Germany. The occupation established, in many areas, government structures committed to broad modernization that provided access to power for German adherents of reform. Most important, the French defeat of the German states, especially Prussia in 1806, created such disarray in the defeated governments that it brought reformers temporarily to office and generated a movement for national unity that was, to a degree, liberal in inspiration.[9]

Even after 1814, when the receding tide of French imperialism isolated its German collaborators and brought conservatives back into power in Prussia, liberalism remained. People who had tasted power under the French or under Freiherr vom Stein in Prussia, together with their academic supporters, formed the core of liberal opposition movements often partially located within state governments. The liberals attracted the support of many university students excited by new ideas and the drama of the revolutionary–Napoleonic era and by the liberal idea of the "career open to talent." The basis of the liberal movement between 1815 and the 1840s was thus firmly fixed in the *Bildungsbürgertum,* the class of people produced by the newly reformed higher educational system.[10] Liberals, of course, sought adherents elsewhere in society, but their core remained an educated elite. Although most liberals believed firmly that they belonged to a single loosely defined movement because they shared a desire for changes defined by liberal ideology, it is clear that by the 1830s they fell into various groups. One of the groups, however—the moderate, academic liberals of Rotteck and Welcker's type—provided most of the consistent leadership (although younger "radicals," typically university students or recent graduates, provided most of the excitement).[11]

University professors took an increasingly important part in the liberal leadership after 1815, inheriting much of the bureaucratic reformist tradition. They were subjected to less official harassment than liberals who were regular civil servants and, because of the prevalence of Wilhelm von Humboldt's views about educational policy, they enjoyed substantially more freedom of speech.[12] Although many bureaucrats were interested in reform, professors could speak most openly about it. Professors also had direct access to university students, the most enthusiastic advocates of change. Therefore, in the press and in the legislatures that survived the post–1815 conservative resurgence, professors, such as Welcker, Rotteck, and Friedrich Dahlmann, became the leaders of public, moderate liberal opposition to the policies of the governments that employed them. This required that they walk an ideological tightrope, eschewing any advocacy of violent or rapid change. It also required the erection of an understanding, a consensus, between themselves and their employers that defined the usefulness and the limits of their activities. The key to the consensus was what we would today call modernization.

Recent events had clearly demonstrated to the personnel of the German governments that, whether they liked it or not, most of the reforms instituted by and in reaction to the French had to be maintained. They also recognized that the economy of Europe was changing rapidly, probably in the direction pointed by Britain. It was necessary to keep up, or catch up, with these changes if Germany were not to remain a collection of backward economic dependencies of other countries. But if the German states were to do this, they required government personnel trained to understand and deal with the problems of modernization, and they required expertise in appropriate fields of study. It was primarily the universities—especially those reforming themselves according to the example of the new University of Berlin—and professors of such subjects as law, economics, and history who were responsible for meeting these needs.[13] Although alternatives to a theoretical framework closely connected to liberal ideology and professed by liberal academics did exist (the political models constructed by Friedrich Gentz and Adam Müller in their postliberal periods), none could be convincingly applied to the situation facing German governments. It was not that most government authorities necessarily *wanted* professors who taught political subjects to be liberals, even in Baden. It was rather that the authorities felt they had to accept liberal professors—and well-behaved liberals in general—because it seemed that the knowledge necessary to cope with the modern world lay in that quarter. Liberals were more readily (although not universally) tolerated as professors than as regular civil servants. They were even accorded a considerable amount of prestige, although they were usually kept away from positions in which they could exercise decision-making power. Throughout *Vormärz* Germany, for practically every case of a liberal professor being driven from his chair for his political beliefs, there was another case (often involving the same person) of nonliberal educational authorities competing with each other for the services of a liberal academic.[14]

These circumstances shaped the kind of social science that liberal academics developed and that Welcker, Rotteck, and their associates enshrined in the *Staatslexikon*. They took liberal political, social, and economic ideas (and some of the fundamental concepts on which those ideas were based) as the central points around which they constructed an ideology for political use *and* an approach to social science that paralleled and supported the ideology without becoming identical to it.[15] The generally nonrevolutionary tenor of their politics—a gradualist emphasis on educating governments and public opinion, on instituting free speech and representation as means of affording "progress," on the need for informed consensus— resulted not just from the moderation of their personalities and outlooks, but also from the occupational context in which they operated. It required the sanction of a science that could claim to be both objective and useful to governments regardless of those governments' ideological positions. As party leaders, liberal professors like Welcker and Rotteck also found it advantageous to be officially recognized as professional practitioners of a science, which gave what they said a degree of legitimacy few rivals could claim.

The leadership of *Vormärz* liberalism was not, of course, exclusively composed of professors. Nevertheless, until the appearance in the 1840s of an important group of liberal business leaders, most prominent German liberals were *academics* in the

German sense of the term: people with higher secondary or university educations who were qualified thereby for the professions or for executive service to the state. These were the people who referred to themselves as the *Bildungsbürgertum*.[16] Their numbers had expanded greatly in the early nineteenth century, faster than the number of jobs in the universities, gymnasia, government offices, and churches that they were traditionally supposed to fill. This meant that many young university graduates went into occupations requiring higher education but not conveying the status that the traditional career patterns did. These new occupations were widely regarded as temporary stops on the road to appropriate employment.[17] Politically, the most important of them was journalism.

Journalists attached themselves to all parts of the political spectrum, especially after about 1840 when governments and conservatives in general began to take the courting of literate public opinion seriously. Before 1848, however, most were probably liberals of some sort. Journalists made up a substantial proportion of the formulators, or at least the expositors, of liberal ideology, and many liberal journalists considered themselves to be social scientists. For present purposes, the important point about liberal journalists was their close connection to the university professoriate.[18] Not only did many journalists owe their credentials as social and political commentators to their educational backgrounds, but also some hoped eventually to be accepted as university teachers. Indeed, by the middle of the century, journalism had become a normal part of the early careers of even the most successful of academic social scientists. As a result, journalists tended to accept and propagate the intellectual fashions of the universities. They attacked and defended particular political ideas in the forms in which those ideas were expressed by professors. In other words, journalists on the whole accepted the intellectual and ideological ascendancy of the professoriate and cooperated with leading professors, as is demonstrated by the heavy journalistic participation in the *Staatslexikon*.[19]

As the professors were in charge of the actual task—higher education—that defined the *Bildungsbürgertum*, their influence over members of the other free professions (law, medicine, etc.) was also quite strong. The prestige they enjoyed as the supposed embodiment of the humanistic idea according to the Humboldtian notion of education reinforced this influence.[20] Even when businesspeople, such as David Hansemann and Gustav Mevissen, took over a large share of the liberal leadership in the 1840s, they were for the most part content to share the direction with liberal academics and to express their own views in modes consistent with academic conventions.[21] Although practical matters of policy important to businesspeople were touched on in the *Staatslexikon*, the encyclopedia tended to treat economic subjects within traditional theoretical structures supplied by law, history, and abstract classical economic theory.[22]

These were not the only factors that shaped the theoretical pattern of German social science as it developed in close connection with German liberalism in the first half of the nineteenth century, but they are the most important for the purposes of this study. The pattern reflected the political moderation of its adherents and the ambiguities of their roles as valued state employees and leaders of the political opposition. It also reflected the political advantages that liberal professors and journalists could obtain by discussing political issues from the standpoint of science rather than simply from partisan pleading. The liberal pattern of social science created a kind of consensual basis for the activities of the moderate liberal leadership, allowing them to respond simultaneously to several different kinds of demand placed on them.

Of course, all of this required that liberal social scientists make certain questionable assumptions and ignore certain difficulties. They had to assume that it was possible to create an objective science of society that could be universally recognized as such by (as Welcker said) liberal and conservative alike.[23] They had to assume that the liberal political movement could be kept from following a radical or revolutionary line that would compromise their positions. Most of all, they had to believe that the body of fundamental ideas that liberal ideology and liberal social science shared was coherent and did not contain debilitating internal contradictions. On the whole, up to 1848 these assumptions and beliefs, although challenged by political conservatives and by some liberal historians and philologists, could be maintained. The crisis of liberalism that commenced more or less with the revolution of 1848 changed all that. But before then, a paradigmatic theoretical pattern of substantial power and attractiveness had been erected alongside liberal ideology.

Liberal Ideology and Social Scientific Theory

For most practical purposes, a "liberal" of the first half of the nineteenth century could be identified by his subscription to most of a set of well-known political goals—goals to be achieved in a country like Germany or, having been achieved in a country like Britain, to be defended and universalized. Despite national differences and a wide range of opinions about particulars, liberal consensus about goals was remarkably broad and uniform.[24]

Almost all liberals believed that the rule of law, embodied in a rational constitution constructed in accordance with the natural laws of social behavior, should prevail. Law and government ought to be structured to protect such individual rights as equal access to justice and security of private property. Sovereignty should lie at least partly with the people, and the state should be in some (not always clear) way responsible to them. Although most liberals advocated some sort of popular participation in the state and an important role for representative assemblies, they disagreed, sometimes violently, about the ideal extent of participation and representation. Radicals generally gave a democratic interpretation of this aspect of liberal theory, arguing for widespread or universal manhood suffrage, whereas moderates, clearly dominant in the movement in Germany before 1848, wanted to maintain a distinction between Rotteck's "active" citizens (those of sufficient means and education to participate in decision-making), and the rest of the population. Radicals generally believed that the representative assembly should be the core of national government; moderates and right-wing liberals, including the editors of the *Staatslexikon*, thought that an assembly's main function was to review and check the administration of a hereditary prince.[25] Despite these differences, most liberals believed that their disputes with each other concerned details and interpretations, not fundamental issues.[26]

Liberals showed the same degree of consensus on economic matters. Governments should encourage economic change without excessively regulating its agents (private businesspeople). An economy should be based on individual private property; individual freedom to dispose of labor, capital, and income; the operation of free markets; and the enforceability of private contracts. There was, again, disagreement about particular matters: about the distinction between the public and private spheres and about the obligation (if any) of society to protect the losers in the free market and the game of economic progress. In Germany, radical laissez-faire ideas were never as important as in England—in theory, at least.[27]

One of the reasons most liberals thought that, despite differences, they belonged to the same movement and agreed on fundamentals was that the thinking embodied in their programs really did rest on a broad consensus about the validity of a set of assumptions, concepts, and inferences which they shared and about the appropriateness of a political language they all spoke. They used this conceptual set and this language to assign significance to events and ideas, to tie ideas together, and to frame the process of creating new ideas. The consensus thus constituted served as the intellectual core of liberal ideology and, in more specific and sometimes substantially altered form, also served as the core of the theoretical pattern that developed in German social science in the first half of the nineteenth century. There were liberal scholars who wrote on social and political questions—especially Wilhelm von Humboldt and other liberal Romantics whom he influenced—who rejected important elements of the body of assumptions that underlay liberal ideology and particularly liberal social science.[28] But as we shall see, their effect on liberalism and social thought was fairly limited before the 1840s, and their points of disagreement were not at first sufficient to lead to the fragmentation of German political liberalism or liberal social science.

It should not be assumed that this consensual core was so deep as to be subconscious. Liberal writers on social science, including the editors of the *Staatslexikon*, were quite aware of the nature of their conceptual apparatus, of its strengths and weaknesses.[29] They responded in a number of ways to their consciousness of the weaknesses. They assumed that the liberal framework, even if flawed, allowed a closer approximation to the "truth" than any existing alternative. They turned a blind eye to many of the less obvious sources of contradiction among their basic ideas and to the seriousness of conflicts among liberals;[30] and they made use of corrective concepts, of which the idea of *culture* was one. Part of the reason for the fragmentation of the liberal consensus after midcentury was the decreasing ability of many liberals to do these things conscientiously.

In the pages that follow, we shall focus on the composition of the liberal *theoretical pattern* in social science—that is, the consensual core of the kind of social science presented in the *Staatslexikon*. The consensus was not shared by all liberals, but it seems clearly to have been the dominant pattern among self-conscious liberal social scientists. The elements of the theoretical pattern were not identical, obviously, to the fundamental elements of the *ideological* core of liberalism in politics. Ideologies and social sciences are not, conceptually, the same things. But the overlap between liberal ideology and liberal social science was very extensive; significant points of intersection will be indicated throughout the discussion.

For purposes of summarizing the liberal theoretical pattern, we can classify its elements into four categories: classic presentations of theory, fundamental ideas and vocabulary, research goals, and guidelines for professional behavior. The second category will loom largest in this study, but the others need to be considered as well.

Classics

Among the classics of both liberalism and social science in Germany were the major works of the Enlightenment on social theory written by Locke, Montesquieu, Herder, and above all, Adam Smith, with an occasional reference to Rousseau by radicals. The articles in the *Staatslexikon* also refer to a host of secondary Enlightenment figures as contributors to the definition of *progress*.[31] The similarity of their early classic works was one of the strongest links between liberalism and mainstream German social science before 1850.

The classics of Enlightenment social thought were, appropriately, international in origin. But there were also peculiarly German inputs into liberal political and social discourse that greatly affected German social science. One of these was the heavy emphasis by many German *Aufklärer* on history and the study of development—an emphasis that can be seen especially in the works of Herder and that to some extent marks off the German Enlightenment from that of France.[32] When newly minted "conservative" (really former liberal) social scientists appeared in the 1850s, they attempted to annex this element of the liberal heritage for themselves and to identify liberal-oriented social science with a residue that they labelled "foreign" or (worse) "French."[33] This was a misrepresentation of intellectual history, one that has to some extent survived. In fact, as we shall see, the habit of placing social and political analysis in a historical context was a significant element of the *Vormärz* theoretical pattern in social science—as it was of German liberal political discourse in general. Liberal social scientists, such as Rotteck and Welcker, and more or less like-minded historians, such as Friedrich Dahlmann, influenced by the highly nationalist tenor of political liberalism in Germany after the wars of liberation, tended to follow Herder in arguing that the historical circumstances peculiar to a people needed to be taken into account in social and political analysis along with the general laws of social existence. On the whole, however, they did not follow the lead of Wilhelm von Humboldt toward a radical theory of hermeneutics and a radical historicism in which the uncovering of the particular and national predominated over the discovery of general social principles.[34] They *did* (together with the entire German academic profession) adopt the general idea of humanistic education as the proper training for a political elite that Humboldt and Johann Gottlieb Fichte developed at the beginning of the nineteenth century.

Mention of Fichte brings to the front the question of the relationship between theoretical patterns in social science and the major trends in German philosophy, both the classics of the late eighteenth and early nineteenth centuries and the changing fashions of the middle and late nineteenth century. The history of German social scientific theory is often presented as though it were primarily the story of the working of influences from philosophy on social thinkers.[35] This is, as we saw in the introduction, a perfectly acceptable approach. Social (and later cultural) scientists were for the most part widely read in philosophy and attuned to the intellectual fashions of their own times. Ideas presented by philosophers from Kant, Fichte, and Hegel through Heinrich Rickert and Wilhelm Windelband found resonances (in various ways) in social scientific thought. On the other hand, this kind of approach can clearly be misleading. For one thing, it tends to exaggerate the importance of the philosophical classics at the expense of other intellectual influences.[36] For another, it presupposes a pattern of influence that does not necessarily apply in all cases. Often a thinker will develop an idea in response to a number of different factors—the requirements of specific research, a relationship with another person, or (a matter of prime concern here) political perceptions and will then search the philosophical classics for the means to develop the idea more fully and within an already-legitimated framework of discourse. The present study deliberately puts questions of philosophical influence in the background so as to concentrate on the relationship between social science theory and political ideology. It does not seek to give a fully rounded picture of the development of the cultural sciences from all of their roots, but rather to emphasize one important and often-overlooked part of the process. In general, then, the influence of philosophical classics will be discussed when the occasion requires it, usually in the case of individual writers, and will not be a central focus of analysis.

The classic German philosophers of the late eighteenth century and the Romantic period with whom the authors of the *Staatslexikon* appear to have been most often engaged were (not surprisingly) Kant and Hegel, whose relationships to the liberal theoretical pattern in social science will be discussed later in this chapter. Fichtean idealism and Goethean *Naturphilosophie* can also be found. The classics of nineteenth-century political economy—Jeremy Bentham, David Ricardo, John Stuart Mill, and Claude-Frédéric Bastiat—are heavily featured. The attitude displayed toward Bentham in the *Staatslexikon* illustrates part of the function of a classic within a theoretical pattern. Hardly any German social scientists identified themselves wholly with Benthamite utilitarianism, which was held to be too ahistorical, too shallow, too rationalistic. But they recognized it as an exaggerated statement of a kind of thinking many believed to be legitimate; therefore, it was valuable as a means of clarifying ideas.[37]

Intellectual Content

The most important elements of a theoretical pattern are its assumptions, its basic formal ideas, and its characteristic imagery, vocabulary, and metaphors. Because theoretical patterns, like ideologies, tend to be structured as networks of ideas that supposedly support one another, it is often difficult to designate certain sets of elements as the most basic of all. In German social science before the middle of the nineteenth century, however, three linked aggregations of concepts, images, and words stand out—ones closely related to fundamental elements of liberal ideology. These aggregations are of crucial importance to the rest of this study.

1. The Rational Individual.   It is a commonplace that nineteenth-century liberals were individualistic in the sense that they took the individual human being to be the fundamental unit of social action and therefore of social analysis. They also generally believed that individuals, although different in many respects, resembled each other in possessing a potential for rational thought. In the political ideology of liberalism, individualism signified, among other things, that the state existed primarily to perform services for the "people," who were portrayed as a collection of individuals with more or less uniform characteristics of which rationality was the most important.[38] In liberal social science (in economics, for instance) it was assumed that predictable social behavior arose from the aggregated actions of similar, rational individuals.[39]

Few German liberals or social scientists in the nineteenth century believed that *real* humans were wholly rational or that perfect rationality was a practical possibility. They were entirely aware of internalized obstructions to rationality, of the existence of other springs of behavior than the human faculty for reason, of variations among individuals with respect to mental acuity, and of differences among peoples with respect to what was accepted as rational behavior.[40] Opinions differed about the extent to which reasoning abilities were distributed among a nation's population—a consideration closely tied to liberals' assessment of the feasibility of democracy. Many liberals of the Romantic era, such as Wilhelm von Humboldt, while remaining attached to the general notion of individualism, had attacked the tendency to identify the individual with rationality. But although aspects of this Romantic critique had penetrated both liberal ideology and liberal social science, yet mainstream liberal thought continued to hold that most people were at least capable of being educated to rational thinking and behavior.[41]

These and other familiar liberal ideas had important implications for the theoretical pattern that encompassed them. If rationality and the logical processes that manifested it were basically the same for all humankind, then it was possible to infer universal laws of society from the common possession of rationality.[42] Rationality was the primary means by which humans interacted with each other and gained control of their physical environments. Whatever particular liberals thought about the origins of society or the ratio of the reasonable to the unreasonable in real human behavior, most of them believed that embedded in society was a strong, common element of reason that arose directly from individual rationality and gave social institutions their purposes. To Welcker and others who were strongly influenced by Kant, this common possession extended to an innate moral sense closely connected with rationality.[43] Reason was most manifest in "advanced" societies, but it was implicitly and potentially present in all. "Progress" meant the process by which the latent rationality in a society was brought out and realized in its institutions. According to Welcker, the basic forms of social life were determined by individual consciousness, the rational element of which could be rationally understood.[44] Indeed, it *had* to be understood if humankind were to progress. Hence, a science based on rational principles that took individual human reason as its point of entry into broader social understanding was a prerequisite to progressive, liberal political action.[45]

Of course, there were problems. The obvious differences among individuals and societies could not simply be dismissed as insignificant—not in the wake of the Romantic attack on the Enlightenment. They posed, among other things, the problem of relating empirical evidence about human behavior, which was distressingly heterogeneous, to the postulates of a science based on the qualified presumption of uniform rationality. German social scientists of the second quarter of the nineteenth century could draw several approaches to this problem from the corpus of liberal thought, both German and international. They could follow Humboldt and, from the 1840s, the liberal historian Johann Gustav Droysen in downplaying the uniformity of reason and human nature and focusing on differences among peoples as revealed in their national states. But *Staatslexikon* liberals generally took a more traditional approach: they employed an abstract model of the rational individual. To correct the deficiencies of such an approach, recourse could be made to ideas about education and culture.

The "rational individual" in liberal social scientific thought was a deliberate abstraction: a fictitious person, clearly male, supposedly bearing the common characteristics of humanity—especially rationality. The use of such a model was far from new in Western thought.[46] Its capacity for laying bare fundamental regularities in human behavior was most impressive. Classical economics stands as a monument to its utility. But the heavy employment of the abstract individual model meant that, contrary to the claims of some early social scientists, their disciplines could neither be truly inductive nor truly empirical. They were founded rather on deductions from a limited number of propositions about what a rational person would do or think under certain circumstances.[47]

By the 1840s, when Welcker wrote his second introduction to the *Staatslexikon*, many questions had been raised about the abstract individual by liberals and critics alike.[48] To what extent did the pretense that humans were rational machines really reveal anything about human behavior, even as a hypothesis? How could it be objectively decided whether some forms of behavior and thought were rational and others not? Should social science take individual differences and irrational behavior formally into account? And if it should, how? Social scientists of Welcker's day tried to confront such questions *without* eliminating the model of the rational individual as a basic element of their theoretical patterns.

One way to do this was by trying to obtain empirical data about the human mind in order to augment the abstract model, which in theory would permit the exact delineation of the common features of minds and the exact relationships among brain, consciousness, and environment. This approach was one of the factors that led to the development of experimental psychology (a subject to which we shall return in later chapters) as a means of fleshing out the abstract individual.[49]

Another approach involved the use of statistics in social investigation. Although the most important models for quantitative study of social phenomena in the first half of the nineteenth century came from Britain, with its census and its tradition of royal and parliamentary commissions, statistical data collection emerged rapidly in Germany as well just before midcentury. The main centers of this activity were the state statistical offices, for the most part founded and led in their early years by liberal academic social scientists. Of these, the most important was Ernst Engel, head of the Saxon and then of the Prussian statistical office, a professor at the University of Berlin, and an active liberal reformer.[50]

Engel, like other contemporary statisticians, tried to fit his research into the dominant pattern of social scientific thought as a means of correcting some of its deficiencies. "Engel's law," which explained why rising wages often produced less rather than more labor, resulted from Engel's empirical research into the budgets of working-class families. He did not claim that he wanted to replace economic theory based on inference from the abstract model of the rational individual (which predicted that higher wages should increase labor availability), but rather to correct it in detail.[51]

The traditional liberal reaction to difficulties with individual patterns of explanation was to focus on *education* in its broadest sense. The most common response of the Enlightenment to the realization that individuals and peoples did in fact differ from one another in thought and behavior and that many, indeed most, people often acted irrationally by any standard was to point to the nature of the education individuals had received.[52] Differences were due mainly to variations in forms of education, whether experienced by individuals or characteristic of whole peoples. People learned differently how to apprehend the sense-data of the physical environment, to draw conclusions from them, and to reason from first principles. As there could only be one truth about something, differences must reflect varying degrees of error. The main reason that people did not display the full degree of rationality of which they were capable was that they were not educated to do so or in some cases (as with superstitions) educated not to do so.

Education was a cornerstone of most German liberal-reformist programs in the first half of the nineteenth century.[53] The concept of education was (and remains) a very useful means of social explanation. It underlay the dominant liberal modes of thinking about penology, the possibility of international peace, and ways of encouraging progress. It was extremely adaptable. It was able, in nineteenth-century Germany, to absorb the implications of Romantic attacks on the Enlightenment and the demands of Wilhelm von Humboldt that education pay due regard to sentiment, aesthetics, and character without serious diminution of its eighteenth-century emphasis on the development of reasoning capacities.[54]

But liberal *Staatslexikon* social thinkers were aware of some of the difficulties inherent in the concept of education, both as an aim of liberal policy and as a corrective to the model of the abstract individual. In the first case, the question of what kind of education people should receive was augmented by the question of who should receive it and how. Should education be selective on the basis of status or intellectual capacity, in which case some of the contradictions of liberal individualism were brought to the surface; or should educations be democratic, in which case the dangers of democracy as a political system arose. More important for our purposes was the realization that education was not a social phenomenon that could be understood by itself. Education was a part of the broader culture of a nation or people.[55] This realization played an important part in the emergence of the cultural sciences after midcentury.

The study of *culture*, which eventually came to engulf the study of education and a good deal else, can also be regarded as having been essentially a corrective to the model of the abstract individual before the 1850s—at least as far as liberal social science was concerned. (As chapter 3 shows, there were other ways of looking at culture, even among contemporary liberals.) The roots of the culture concept lay in the Enlightenment, with substantial development resulting from Romanticism and the growth of classical humanism in the early nineteenth century. Even W. H. Riehl—one of the leading figures in the attempt to create a cultural science with a nonliberal theoretical pattern in the 1850s—acknowledged the importance of Montesquieu and Herder as founders of the study of culture. However, as the former was a Frenchman and the latter too clearly associated with the Enlightenment traditions of liberalism, he treated them as forebears rather than creators of cultural science ostensibly because they were not sufficiently empirical in their work.[56]

Herder (1744–1803), following Montesquieu, had developed a theory of culture in order to confront problems that had arisen in Enlightenment social thought, thereby setting a precedent for the ways in which his nineteenth-century liberal successors would try to deal with problems of the kind that we have just reviewed. If humankind is fundamentally uniform and if one of the features of its uniformity is common potential for thinking and acting rationally, how can we explain the immense diversity of actual human thought and the manifold ways in which peoples throughout the world customarily violate what seem to educated Europeans to be self-evident rules of reasonable behavior? If differences in education account for this, how do we account for differences in education?[57]

These were crucial problems. Leading Enlightenment thinkers, living in an age in which the identification (or creation) of national identities was becoming a matter of political importance and in which a flood of information about alien cultures was reaching Europe, did not avoid them. In confronting them more comprehensively than anyone else of his era, Herder established the framework within which questions of national culture and cultural differences would be discussed in Germany until after the middle of the nineteenth century.

Although Herder occasionally used the word *Kultur* in its generic anthropological sense when discussing national character traits, he preferred the term *Volksgeist*.[58] Herder argued that each nationality, each *Volk*, possessed its own peculiar spirit that differentiated it from other peoples. This *Volksgeist* was embodied in customs, laws, folktales, personal behavior patterns, government and economic structures, and above all, language, which Herder and his followers believed to be not simply a medium of communication, but also the framework for higher human thought. The spirit of a people was largely the result of its interaction with its geographical environment over a long period of time. The manner in which the members of a *Volk* organized to confront their environment, the forms in which they became accustomed to perceiving their surroundings, and the stories that they invented to explain the world around them—all passed from generation to generation and made up a people's culture. Because each culture differed from others, the thinking of individuals sharing one culture would differ from the thinking of people sharing another.[59]

Because of their influence on Romanticism and on the new patterns in social science that appeared after 1850, Herder's ideas on these subjects have been taken as one of the the origins of a significant break with the Enlightenment tradition. This is only partly true. Herder's cultural theories are but a segment of a larger body of German Enligtenment thought about culture and history that included the works of Johann Christoph Gatterer, Johann Stephan Pütter, Angust Ludwig von Schlözer, and many others.[60] Neither these people nor Herder himself were aware of breaking with the main lines of eighteenth-century thought. Rather, their aim was to improve on a pattern of thinking common to the Enlightenment by solving some of the problems noted earlier.

For one thing, Herder did not dispute the fundamental sameness of human nature. His conception of the culturally defined *Volk* rested largely on inference from the assumed characteristics of abstract individuals confronted with varied environments over time. Herder used empirical ethnographical data about cultural differences, but not to question the assumption of the universality of reason and mental capacity among humans.[61] Environmental and historical variation may create major cultural differences among peoples and cause some to seem irrational in the eyes of others, but at a fundamental level of human behavior and cognition humans are sufficiently alike to understand each other fairly readily. The underlying processes that produce cultural differences are rational (the application of commonsense logic to the problems of a particular people's environment) and are therefore understandable if the members of one *Volk* will only apply reason and approach other *Völker* with as little prejudice as possible.

Herder's reputation in the nineteenth century was partly owing to his justification of German efforts to escape French intellectual domination and to his legitimation of political nationalism. But Herder's legacy was effective in these respects precisely because it was consistent with liberalism and the Enlightenment intellectual tradition. At the level of politics, Herder explained why each nation should follow its own genius in government and why generic political prescriptions based on inference from individuals had to be modified for each *Volk*—a point that Rotteck and Welcker would later emphasize.[62] An enlightened person had to be both a citizen of the world and a citizen of a particular country. Herder's political analysis was especially useful for liberals in early nineteenth-century Germany because it allowed them to separate themselves from the claims of revolutionary France that it was the bearer of universal progress for humankind.[63]

From the standpoint of the mid-nineteenth century, Herder's contribution to social science was to integrate the individualism characteristic of the liberal theoretical pattern into a structure of explanation that appeared to solve many of the pattern's main problems. Human differences and apparent irrationalities were accounted for through the effects of environment, and a wide variety of the actual phenomena of social life were taken under consideration. At the same time, the universality of the faculty of reason was not questioned. The culture concept, in other words, placed the individual in a convincing physical context as well as in a historical one. The work of Herder and other contemporaries ensured that culture—closely linked to a concept of history as a force in shaping culture and as a record of cultural change—would assume a respectable, if somewhat secondary, place in the liberal theoretical pattern of German social science in the early nineteenth century. The idea of culture appears here and there in the first two editions of the *Staatslexikon*, although the word culture is used in a variety of ways.[64] Herder's influence was manifested in other approaches to human understanding besides the theoretical pattern of social science. Some conservatives displayed it, and within the liberal spectrum of intellectual life it can be seen in the hermeneutic tradition of Wilhelm von Humboldt.[65] But the idea of culture as the central feature of a *social science* largely arose, as we shall see, out of its role in the liberal theoretical pattern.

2. The Nomological Mode and Nomothetic Empirical Science. Taken as a general European phenomenon, European liberal ideology in the first half of the nineteenth century contained a strong nomological element. Liberals usually assumed that human nature and human society, like the physical universe, obey rational laws that reflect a natural order underlying the varying appearances of things. Science consisted primarily of identifying laws and applying them to particular cases, while proper politics meant shaping political action in accordance with the laws of society. Behind this apparently simple idea, popularized by the Enlightenment, lies a complex set of concepts drawn from diverse sources: the natural law tradition, Newtonian physics, the Greek classics, and others. It was within this general nomological intellectual context that social science was formed. The idea that social science was nomothetic, that its primary function was to find and enunciate social laws, had obvious ties to the nomological outlook of international liberalism.

The classic nomological mode of political thought was not adopted by all liberals, least of all in Germany. Liberals such as Humboldt and Droysen preferred to focus on the peculiar characteristics of peoples rather than universal laws as the bases of political action, although they did accept the idea of an order or meaning immanent in particular societies. This kind of approach affected the intellectual context with which the *Staatslexikon* liberals conceived of social science, as did the substantial attention paid to history and historical change in the German Enlightenment tradition of social thought.[66] But the major tendency in German liberal social science up to midcentury was to maintain the nomological context and the nomothetic aim. This did *not* mean subscribing to a crude form of what would come to be called (or rather caricatured as) "positivism"—the belief that the methods of physical science could be applied directly to human phenomena and were sufficient for understanding. The complexities of the nomothetic element in the liberal theoretical pattern can be seen in the work of Karl Theodor Welcker.

To Welcker, the lawfulness and regularity of the social world depended on the rationality of individual humans—a fundamentally uniform rationality, which meant that when people were confronted with similar stimuli in their environments, they would behave in much the same ways. Therefore, social laws were not so much inherent in society per se as in the nature of the individuals of whom society was composed.[67] But how should one proceed from the regularities of human behavior to those of social action? Like most of the other contributors to the *Staatslexikon*, Welcker in theory rejected the approach taken by "the German philosophers" (presumably Kant, Fichte, and their followers) of the previous two generations. One could not simply infer social laws from prior assumptions about reason or human nature or universal morality.[68] It was necessary to argue from the individual to the general. If one knew exactly how the individual human mind functioned, one could draw valid conclusions about how humans function in groups. But *evidence* was needed, not only about the human mind, but also about how it manifested its presence in society. Nor could morality simply be postulated from abstract moral ideas. It had to be *found*—in both its current and its potential reality—in actual observed behavior. Otherwise, the observer was not a complete scientist; he was merely claiming universal validity for his or her own moral viewpoint. Only by avoiding subjectivity could *usable* social laws be formulated. As Welcker put it, "We seek laws, we seek the general, objective, practical laws of civil society."[69] These are to be found and demonstrated *both* logically *and* empirically. They are "logically, mathematically, and experimentally provable truths."[70] And as against what he called the general, a priori, subjective analysis of earlier (presumably Kantian) philosophers, Welcker recommended an approach that he rather inelegantly labelled "historical- (or more fully, anthropological-historical-) philosophical."[71]

Anthropological-historical-philosophical? If we ignore the hint of Polonius or Pangloss, we can see that what Welcker is doing is much the same thing—at the level of social analysis—that he and others did with respect to the individual: responding to obvious theoretical difficulties without threatening the basic pattern within which social science is conceived. For all its claims to grounding in the "real" world, Enlightenment thought had depended heavily on inference from abstract principles and models of society rather than systematic empirical observation. This was true not only of the rational individual, but also of abstractions such as liberty and property. Welcker did not deny that inferring from abstractions was essential to understanding society. Like most of his colleagues, he did it all the time. But the abstraction ought to be constructed, at least to some extent, on a foundation of empirical observation and the inferences ought to be tested by observation. This was what Welcker meant by "anthropological-historical." "Anthropology" referred generically to the empirical observation of humankind,[72] and as far more observational data were available from the past than from the present (and as only the past gave one a long-term perpective), anthropology had to be associated with history in building an empirical social science.

Welcker was far from the first to call for an empirical grounding for social science. Several *Aufklärer* in the eighteenth century had done so, and more recent Romantic criticism had led many liberals to look for an empirical supplement to their usual way of pursuing social regularities—something that can be seen in the *Staatslexikon*.[73] This did not, before the 1850s, lead liberal social scientists to subscribe to the Humboldtian hermeneutic approach or to the rejection of the nomothetic aim that was implicit, for example, in Leopold von Ranke's version of "scientific" history and his assertion that each past era was unique to itself. But it did lead to searching questions about how a law-finding social science, based on logical inference from fixed principles but incorporating an expanded empirical element, could be constructed.

The problems that lay behind these questions are illustrated by Welcker's difficulties with his own specialty, the law. Welcker believed that it was possible and desirable to make the legislated law of a state conform to the universal laws of society. Objective social science could uncover the latter. But apart from inference from general principles, universal laws could only be found by studying actual laws in operation. In that case, how could the universal elements of law be distinguished from the particular? Welcker never solved this problem. In practice, he continued to rely largely on abstraction and deduction.[74] He did recognize that a possible way out lay in the comparative study of laws and institutions, but even then, similar problems arose. Even if one could identify common features among different legal systems, how could one convincingly argue that these features corresponded to universal laws without recourse to some external standard? Rudolf von Gneist, one of Welcker's successors in the leadership of moderate liberal social science, made immense strides in creating a discipline of comparative law in order to solve this problem, but even he never wholly succeeded.[75]

Despite their awareness of the difficulties inherent in the idea, the leading German social scientists down to the middle of the nineteenth century (and beyond) continued to believe that the essence of social science lay in formulating laws that reflected the underlying regularities in social behavior.[76] Much of their thought was devoted to giving a valid empirical dimension to the process, and in so doing they exposed serious flaws in the enterprise of social science. The flaws were by no means fatal; important steps—including historical analysis and comparative legal studies—had already been taken to correct them. But radical new directions (especially broadening the definition of society to incorporate culture) awaited the partial breakdown of the liberal theoretical pattern after the 1840s.

3. Change and Equilibrium.   Although early nineteenth-century liberals on the whole strongly favored ''progress,'' the social scientific theories associated with liberalism treated long-term change rather inadequately.[77] Adam Smith, for instance, although he developed an implicit theory of economic change, was far more convincing with his explanation of short-term market adjustment—possibly because of his ambivalence about industrial expansion. The classical economists in general shared the same focus on the short run.[78] In Germany, more than elsewhere, this deficiency was often recognized by liberal social scientists, who were particularly concerned with questions of historical change. The Herderian tradition was very influential among liberal intellectuals, and the German Enlightenment in general had tended to view society in terms of historical progress operating according to social laws. Hegel, who worked to some extent in the latter context but added enormously to it, produced a theory of historical change that was well known, if not universally accepted, among liberal social scientists of the second quarter of the nineteenth century.[79] Even so, there remained through midcentury in German liberal social science an unresolved tension between models of social change that focused on *equilibrium* and others that were built around the concept of *progress*.

Most European liberal social scientists thought of society as existing normally in a condition of equilibrium or balance. The forces that compose society are usually in balance with one another. The balance reflects the regularities that underlie human action and is derived from the same sources as they are—especially human rationality. Laws of society are essentially laws of equilibrium. Social equilibrium was extremely important to liberal political thought and liberal social science. It provided much of the argument against absolutistic government: society does not need a regulator because, if left alone, society is normally self-regulating. It could be used to define the limits of individual freedom: freedom extends to the point at which it threatens social balance. It explained the nature of most social changes—as restorations of balance. The equilibrium idea was carried to a high point of abstraction in late nineteenth-century marginalist economics, but it was omnipresent in European liberal social science throughout the century.[80]

The idea of equilibrium, although perhaps less uncritically accepted in Germany than elsewhere, was very thoroughly established there, and not just in economic theory. It can be seen, for example, in Welcker's version of the *Rechtsstaat* concept.[81] The *Rechtsstaat* was an ideal form of government based on a self-regulating legal mechanism that preserved justice and stability through legislation that reflected the underlying equilibrium of social laws. The erection of a *Rechtsstaat* required that the principles of social equilibrium be identified (presumably by social scientists), that the principles be embodied in enacted laws, that state personnel be trained in both the principles and the laws, and that the people be granted a large degree of freedom. Like classical economics, the *Rechtsstaat* theory assumed that individual freedom maximized the extent to which real society could approximate its ideal condition of equilibrium. The essence of administration in a *Rechtsstaat* was the clearing away of obstructions to the exercise of individual freedom and the limitation of behavior that interfered with balance and liberty.

The equilibrium model is an extremely useful tool for envisioning short -and middle-term changes within certain kinds of systems. It has close affinities with models employed in natural science. Concepts of equilibrium have moved back and forth between social and physical science since the eighteenth century—for example, in the 1840s and 1850s when social equilibrium theory influenced the formulation of the laws of conservation of energy and Rudolf Virchow's theories of cell physiology.[82] These affinities do not necessarily imply that social scientists employing equilibrium models are simply practicing a crude form of positivism, but rather that similar theoretical structures have proven to be useful in both social and physical contexts.

Unfortunately, it is often difficult to apply equilibrium models to *long-term* change. In such models, changes usually appear as disequilibrium events. That is, some force (which must often be regarded as exogenous to make the explanation work) upsets the natural balance of a system, and the system readjusts itself to restore balance. Because in any complex system within a complex environment such events in fact occur almost continuously, change is practically continuous also. But this kind of change is not easy to correlate with fundamental revisions of the structure of the system, especially when the revisions appear to be generated *within* the system. Whence comes the impetus to fundamental change? Why are some disequilibria apparently *not* corrected? How, indeed, do we know that all systems—especially social ones—seek and maintain balance? Marx was only one of the mid-nineteenth-century critics who asked questions of this sort as they perceived fundamental social changes going on before their very eyes.[83]

Similar questions occurred to liberal social scientists who made use of the equilibrium model. One of the joint goals of liberalism and social science was *progress*. How could the fundamental changes that comprised progress be explained within a scheme of social dynamics that emphasized balance and stability? Some, like Friedrich List, a major contributor to the *Staatslexikon*, argued for relying less on equilibrium. List (1789–1846) was one of the precursors of the theoretical pattern of historical economics. He argued that irreversible economic alterations were basic facts of social life and that social sciences should concentrate on understanding them so that change could be directed.[84] The alternative—stability—for Germany meant stagnation and dependence on rapidly changing countries, such as England. Unfortunately, List was unable to propose a convincing theoretical alternative to equilibrium-based classical economics. His criticisms of liberal social science had the effect, not of changing social science, but of cutting him off from the mainstream of political liberalism.

German social scientists more often tried to encompass the idea of long-term change within rather schematic historical stage theories. The basic proposition of this approach, derived from an extensive tradition of the German Enlightenment and accepted by such forerunners of modern anthropology as Christoph Meiners and Gustav Klemm, was that human communities naturally undergo a sequence of stages of intellectual and social development, progressing from more primitive to more sophisticated manifestations.[85] The general pattern of stage change was, in principle, knowable, and the general character of each stage was predictable from the stage that went before. There was disagreement about what constituted the character of a stage in human history, but usually an array of intellectual, moral, and material factors was cited. Long-term change was treated as a movement toward the completion of the present stage and the realization of the next. A teleological element was at least implicit (and often explicit) in the approach. The work of Hegel, with its explanation of history as successive unfoldings of the idea underlying society, gave new impetus to stage models with teleological implications in the second quarter of the nineteenth century. Hegel's theory did not, however, follow a straightforward stage schema strictly speaking and does not seem to have been much used as a model by *Staatslexikon* social scientists.[86]

But there were problems with stage models, including a tendency toward circularity in the definition of the stages and the lack of a convincing explanation of the *social* mechanism of change from stage to stage. Circularity arose from defining each previous stage in the history of humankind (or of a nation) in terms of the theorist's perception of what was significant in the contemporary world. Previous periods were assigned characteristics that made them out to be imperfect, preliminary versions of the present—the failing of ''Whig history.'' Ranke and Droysen pointed out that this led to historical misunderstanding,[87] but it also meant that explanations for long-term change were reducible simply to descriptions of the ways in which the elements of the present stage grew ''naturally'' out of corresponding elements in the past—which was not explanation at all. The overly deductive nature of Hegel's analysis and his assumption of the primacy of ideas tended to make his approach unacceptable to social scientists of an empirical bent. Marx's alternative was not available until after midcentury; even then its political associations made it unacceptable to most social scientists.[88]

Often the dynamics of stage theories were supplied by metaphors and analogies. Welcker, for example, described the historical development of German society through stages of childhood (Teutonic tribal society), adolescence (the Middle

Ages), and adulthood, which began with the Reformation and was reaching completion with the emergence of the *Rechtsstaat*.[89] Living in optimistic times, Welcker
did not feel obliged to extend the analogy to encompass senility and death. By
arguing that society reflects the nature of the individual, he attempted to imply that
his analogy to the human life cycle had a real basis, but his argument was not
particularly convincing. It was, moreover, difficult to reconcile Welcker's account
of social change and others like it with the equilibrium model of short-term change.
One could assume that each stage had its own natural equilibrium, but change from
one stage to another had to be explained either through exogenous forces or through
internal changes that had somehow to be differentiated from equilibrium adjust-
ments.[90]

Recognition of this difficulty probably helps to explain why Darwin's theory
of natural selection was adapted with such alacrity to social analysis in the 1860s
and 1870s. In the realm of biology, Darwin's theory filled a gap that paralleled the
one in liberal social science. Natural selection explained how, in nature, mechanisms
that normally maintain balance also work to create new species, which in the long
run alter the context in which balance is achieved. Stages are largely heuristic
abstractions. Change is continuous and yet consistent with short-term, small-scale
balance: exactly what was required to bridge the dichotomy in liberal concepts of
social change.[91]

The liberal theoretical pattern in early German social science contained a great
many other elements, some of which we shall discuss later as the need arises. The
idea of *association*, for instance, was quite important both in liberal ideology and
in liberal social science and posed a number of inherent problems that midcentury
social thinkers attempted to solve with the use of the culture concept.[92] But the
three elements we have discussed thus far (rational individualism, the nomological
mode and nomothetic aim of empirical social science, and ideas of equilibrium and
progress) were fundamental, although not universally accepted by all liberal intellectuals.

Implications for Research

When it came to identifying the goals of social research, the *Staatslexikon* social
scientists took into account not only the implications of their theoretical pattern,
but also needs arising from their positions as commentators on government policy
and as liberal politicians. This required them to obscure the boundary that they
claimed to identify between politics and academic science and could easily entangle
them in circular patterns of reasoning. For instance, the existence of social science
was legitimated by its aim of increasing objective social knowledge that, in turn,
was justified by the contribution of such knowledge to the attainment of human
progress and freedom. But the identification of progress and freedom as human
goals, although sometimes considered to be self-evident, was in fact largely drawn
from liberal political ideology. Within that ideology, progress and freedom were
frequently represented as goals derived by science from natural law.

The kind of research sanctioned by the liberal theoretical pattern was thus
supposed to have a utility defined in terms of liberal ideology and good government.

This did *not* mean, however, that social scientists were supposed to concern themselves (as social scientists) primarily with detailed practical problems of government or politics. People like Welcker did pay attention to such problems, but they worked on the whole at a high level of abstraction and generalization. The "practicality" of their work lay in its contribution to the achievement of general, long-term ends through its demonstration of the underlying truths of social existence.[93]

In this sense, social research had several objectives that defined its conduct. In the first place, it was supposed to promote social amelioration and progress. Individual freedom was one key to progress; so, an important function of science was to demonstrate the utility and limits of freedom and to describe how society operated under conditions of freedom. But social science also had to contribute more directly to progress. Progress could be defined in several ways: as material improvements in technology and standards of living; as moral progress in behavior, government, and so forth; and as the realization of human potential. Most liberals assumed that all aspects of progress were ultimately consistent with one another.[94] Some, however, especially those influenced by the Romantic critique of the Enlightenment, suspected that material progress might interfere with the achievement of the other kinds. But before the 1840s, liberal doubts on this score did not result in a major questioning of the theoretical pattern of which the assumption of consistency was a part.[95] Fundamental rethinking required an additional set of stimuli.

Another objective of social science with implications for research was the political education of citizens. Here again, freedom played its role. Actual practice in the exercise of political freedom was the best educator as long as the practitioners knew how to analyze their own and their country's political experiences correctly. Social science had to provide knowledge about society and its laws as well as the *means* of assessing and applying such knowledge. According to Rotteck and Welcker, who thought that the average active citizen's political participation would be limited to elections and some involvement in local government, a general education, access to a free press, and such helpful compendia as the *Staatslexikon* would probably suffice.[96] It was different for those who exercised the authority of the people: legislative deputies and bureaucratic officials. They required more knowledge and more sophisticated means of understanding and using their authority.[97] These requirements were to be met by higher education and a civil service entrance system tied to the curricula of the universities.

The Prussian educational reform movement of the early nineteenth century had produced in the educational theories of Wilhelm von Humboldt the means by which liberal social scientists justified their scholarly work in terms of the training of officials. According to Humboldt, research was the central feature of higher education, not only because it increased knowledge, but also because research by students acquainted them with the true nature of knowledge and its uses. Research in any "pure" subfield of philosophy would perform the latter function.[98] Most academic social scientists accepted Humboldt's position, despite their disagreement with him about the nomological framework of social understanding. Humboldt legitimated the idea of research for its own sake and reinforced tendencies in social science toward abstraction.

Humboldtian ideas can be seen in some of the notions about culture that appear in liberal social scientific writings, including Welcker's introduction to the *Staats-*

lexikon. Welcker distinguishes between aspects of culture in terms of the state's personnel.[99] "Higher" culture, developed in part through research, is the possession of the *Gelehrtenstand* (the faculties of the universities and gymnasia), whereas "lower" culture is the aggregate of the normal activities of the uneducated part of officialdom. Educated officials are supposed to provide "harmonious or aesthetic" mediation between the two forms of culture by participating in both. Welcker's analysis illustrates one of the many ways the term *Kultur* was used in social scientific writing before midcentury—a way that attempted to make use of the ambiguity between culture as elite intellectual activity and culture in its anthropological sense. It also shows the importance of elite education in the definition of the research function within the liberal theoretical pattern.

Guidelines for Professional Behavior

Some of the rules supposed to govern the professional activities of social scientists are laid out in Welcker's introduction to the *Staatslexikon*. These rules were clearly not accepted by all liberals (especially by early advocates of historicist political analysis, such as Humboldt and Droysen), but they appear to represent the consensus among *Staatslexikon* contributors. If it is to be a science at all and if it is to achieve its goals, *Staatswissenschaft* must be objective.[100] Objectivity rests on the behavior of social scientists, who must employ rigorous logic and practice empirical observation, clear their minds of all bias, and follow truth wherever it leads. A familiar difficulty arises: What if pursuit of the truth leads away from basic liberal beliefs? In principle, the path must be followed, but Welcker hedges by assuming that the general outlines of social truth are already known and are embodied in the fundamental values of liberalism (freedom, human rights, etc.). Welcker also confronts another obvious problem: How can error and prejudice on the part of the researcher be prevented from interfering with the accurate identification of the truth? He gives the classic liberal answer: freedom and publicity. Social scientists have both the right and the obligation to publicize their findings. This benefits less-expert fellow citizens, and it allows colleagues to detect errors and identify biases. In other words, science is supposed to be a social activity. Social scientists have to present their work regularly both to the public and to their intellectual peers. Here was the legitimating basis for two important features of nineteenth-century social science: extensive journalistic activity by social scientists and the formation of societies for the presentation and discussion of research.

It followed that social scientists were *not* supposed to divorce themselves from politics, either personally or in their academic work. Social scientists did, however, need to maintain as high a standard of scientific objectivity as practicable in both, especially the latter. That this might be difficult to do, Welcker acknowledged, but he thought it both possible and socially necessary. That it was more difficult in practice than Welcker supposed, we shall see directly.

2

The Crisis of Liberalism
and the Emergence of
Cultural Science, 1848–1862

A host of factors converged in the third quarter of the nineteenth century to shake the dominance of the liberal theoretical pattern over German social science and to shape the evolution of the cultural sciences. This chapter and chapter 4 will show that the conjuncture of these factors—intellectual as well as economic, political and social—was stimulated to a large extent by the crisis of political liberalism that started around the time of the 1848 revolution and continued, in cycles, well into the period of the Bismarckian *Reich*. Although significant continuities linked the phases of the liberal crisis, it is convenient to divide the phenomenon into two periods: one that encompasses the revolution itself, the subsequent liberal eclipse and renaissance in the 1850s, and the first stages of the Prussian constitutional conflict; the other that lasts from the early 1860s until about 1885, including the unification of Germany, Bismarck's attempt to co-opt the liberals and their division over the appropriate response, the erosion of their voting base, and their further division over such issues as tariffs, social policy and imperialism. The present chapter deals with the first period; chapter 4 with the second period.

The argument of this chapter is that the events of 1848–1849 and the altered political circumstances throughout Germany in the 1850s led to significant changes in social science. Some social scientists questioned and rejected important parts of liberal ideology and therefore questioned and rejected parts of the related liberal theoretical pattern in social science. Others who retained a commitment to political liberalism sought to overcome perceived weaknesses in liberal social science and to buttress, without fundamentally altering, the liberal theoretical pattern in social science. In both cases, and in the many cases that fell somewhere in between, academically trained observers adopted new ways of looking at the social world. Many of them began to make much heavier use than previously of the concept of *culture* as a foundation for social analysis—a concept that was, as we have seen, already current in German social thought but that in the 1850s took on the character of an intellectual fad because of its apparent relevance to liberal ideology and social science. The fashion for cultural study of the 1850s set the stage for the more profound development of the cultural sciences in the period after about 1862.

The Revolution of 1848

Wilhelm Heinrich Riehl, about whom we shall have a great deal to say later, was one of those who turned to the idea of culture in the 1850s in order to create an explicitly nonliberal social science. Writing almost half a century afterward, he described the significance of the 1848 revolution in shaping his life and work:

> The year 1848 was decisive for me in this respect. This tumultuous year and the following one became the most important period of my education, and at the same time my test of fire. Others were torn from their paths by the Revolution. I was dragged back by it to my own path, to myself. I observed; I became acquainted with social and political life in its everyday appearance and filled my sketchbook with dozens of studies, of which I soon thereafter made use in my *Naturgeschichte des Volkes*. Having always possessed a conservative-leaning nature, I was for the first time made into a conscious conservative by the year '48.[1]

In this passage, Riehl displays a consciousness of the kind of connections on which this chapter focuses. A recent university graduate and a moderate liberal journalist at the start of 1848, Riehl quickly became disenchanted with the radicalism and violence that the revolution elicited; these he blamed on deficiencies in liberal ideology that could be traced, in turn, to deficiencies in liberal social theory. After 1849, while trying to move from a journalistic to an academic career, Riehl became an active "new conservative." He began a study of German folk culture in order to create the foundations for a conservative version of *Staatswissenschaft*.[2] In other words, the quotation from Riehl shows us a link between an individual's political experience of problems with liberalism (in this case, conflict between moderates and radicals in 1848–1849) and perceptions of a need to reexamine the basis *both* of liberal ideology *and* of liberal social science.

In general the effects of the 1848 revolution on German liberalism are well known. The failure of the revolution (that is, the failure of the liberal governments of 1848 to maintain themselves in power and of the National Assembly to unify Germany under a liberal regime) was clearly a setback to the liberal movement. On the other hand, few historians now argue that the revolution was in any real sense the beginning of the end for German liberalism, the reason for its less-than-impressive history thereafter. The liberals in fact recovered by the late 1850s, regained the political initiative in most states, and created a sufficient threat to the established order that Bismarck undertook the unification of Germany in large part as a response to liberal pressure. The revolution did expose many weaknesses in the liberal movement: its difficulties in maintaining a broad basis of support, the inapplicability of its ideology to the interests of many lower-class segments of society, the existence of splits within liberalism—the significance of which had not previously been understood. But most of these weaknesses were recognized immediately after 1848 and, although the movement fragmented in the wake of its first apparent failure, considerable thought was given to confronting them. The fact that the liberals were not ultimately able to build a unified state in Germany entirely to their liking after 1860 was the result of many factors, among which their performance in 1848 was probably not too significant. They greatly affected the structure of the Bismarckian *Reich* even after 1871.[3]

The rethinking of the foundations of German social science in the 1850s, which led to the development of cultural science, must be seen in this context—not one of absolute failure and disillusionment, but one in which problems inherent in liberalism, in its basic assumptions, in its relationship to the realities of a rapidly modernizing economy, and in its approach to social structure had to be confronted. We shall examine specific cases shortly, but we can begin by considering the general problems that the experience of 1848 revealed to liberals.

In the first place, they had learned very quickly that they were not ideologically united. Crosscutting differences between moderates and radicals, between regional outlooks, and between economic interest groups all manifested themselves in the formation of unstable, ill-defined parties in 1848. Liberals had always known that they harbored a substantial range of opinion, but most had assumed that with access to power and with free discussion of issues, the underlying consensus that bound them together would emerge. Some consensus *did* emerge, for example, in the compromises that allowed the National Assembly to frame the 1849 constitution. But factional strife and party divisions were what most liberals noticed, especially during the death throes of the revolution in 1849.[4]

Despite foreign evidence that partisanship was probably an inherent feature of a liberal political order, its presence in 1848–1849 surprised and disturbed most liberal intellectuals. Riehl's perception that factionalism and liberalism were fundamentally linked (and that factionalism begot radicalism) helped to drive him from the liberal ranks.[5] Radicals blamed factionalism for their own inability to force more rapid reforms on the state governments and the National Assembly and for the assembly's unwillingness to resist dissolution in 1849.[6] Moderate like Welcker bewailed factionalism and party spirit as sources of hatred and irrationality in the body politic that prevented the implementation of the objective solutions to social problems produced by social science.[7]

Recognition of liberal fragmentation and factionalism after 1848 held implications for the liberal theoretical pattern. It could no longer be taken for granted that free discussion and political participation would lead directly to consensus. Progress was not necessarily a uniform phenomenon. Rational people from different backgrounds could have different conceptions of what it was. The factors that led to such differences required empirical study, not simply dismissal as obstructions to rationality—a task for social science.

It was not only the fact of the liberals' fragmentation that impressed observers in 1848–1849, but also the content of the issues over which they divided. There was, for instance, the question of the exact structure of the political system that would result from successful liberal reform. Although practically all liberals agreed about the need for representation, constitutional government, individual rights, some form of *Rechtsstaat*, and so forth, radicals tended to favor democratic institutions and the dissolution of the monarchies—both were anathema to moderates like Welcker and Dahlmann. Such disagreements and the difficulties the liberals experienced in resolving them seemed more important in the wake of 1848 and more threatening to the intellectual consensus behind liberalism than they had previously.[8]

The issues revolving around the question of German nationality were even more perplexing. Nationalism was traditionally a major element of the ideological appeal of liberalism in Germany. It defined the sovereign *Volk* of liberal theory, and it gave coherence to the disparate assortment of groups whose support the liberals sought. Liberals often argued that only a liberal regime could successfully embody the national spirit of a people.[9] But when it came in 1848–1849 actually to creating a German nation-state and establishing its relationship to the culturally diverse *Länder*, serious problems arose. Some could be solved by compromise, as in the *kleindeutsch* solution to unification embodied in the 1849 constitution, but not to everyone's satisfaction. And as problems such as Schleswig-Holstein and the Polish question showed, other nationalities and ethnic minorities could define themselves as against the German nation and compromise German political and economic interests.

The issue of nationality and its cultural base was, of course, not new to German social researchers and theorists. Much of the study of linguistics and folk culture of the early part of the nineteenth century derived from attempts to identify and, in some senses, to create a German nationality within the context of political liberalism. But as late as 1848, liberal social scientists had neither developed a consensus on the major issues involved in studying the cultural foundations of nationality nor produced many solutions to the practical problems of nationality that arose with the revolution. This failure was noted by critics in 1848, especially those who saw that liberalism's near monopoly on nationalism as a political tool was being broken by nonliberal groups. One reason for the expansion of cultural science after midcentury was a perceived need to relate the study of national culture to the problems of politics.[10]

Another important problem that confronted liberals during and after 1848 was the difficulty of creating a support base outside the groups that had previously been their mainstays: the *Bildungsbürgertum*, progressive businesspeople, officials, and the like—a problem that contributed greatly to the liberal failure in 1848. To a considerable extent the fact that there was a revolution at all in the winter and spring of 1848 was due to the often-violent uprisings of urban artisans and apprentices and of small farmers. The leaders of the liberal movement had come to power in the wake of the uprisings—not always willingly. When it appeared that the moderate liberals had very different priorities from the articulators of lower-class interests, that the liberals favored market freedom over state protection of people disadvantaged by economic change, then the uneasy alliance between liberals, on the one hand, and workers and peasants, on the other hand, broke down in many areas, especially Prussia. Moderate liberals in Prussia acquiesced in the seizure of power by the king and the army late in 1848, partly for fear of workers' revolts. Radicals, especially in the southwest, attempted a full-scale revolution in 1849, but their belief that their democratic rallying cry would attract lower-class support was largely disappointed. They failed, and the revolution came to an ignominious end. Conservative parties and state authorities after 1849 made concerted attempts in many places to win peasant and artisan allegiance by emphasizing policies of social protection.[11]

Liberals in the 1850s responded to this problem in several ways. Many became interested in the "social question", that is, the problem of what to do about the segments of society exploited in the course of economic change. Social liberalism predated 1848, but it was the liberals' need to accommodate themselves to the concerns of workers, peasants, and *Kleinbürger* that made it an important force in the movement.[12] Some of the liberal intellectuals interested in the social question became quite conservative—for example, the influential economist Karl Rodbertus. Rodbertus's call for an active role for the state in ameliorating labor conditions and controlling the process of industrialization was very influential throughout the century among academics parting company with traditional liberalism.[13] Other liberals, such as the historian Droysen, simply downplayed the social question altogether, assuming that it would be taken care of as the Prussian state unified Germany and laid the groundwork for liberalization.[14]

Most of the social scientists associated with the *Staatslexikon* took other paths. Some, like Karl Biedermann, who had called for state protection of peasants and workers before 1848, now advocated rapid industrialization under conditions of economic freedom as the best means of improving both the standard of living and the education of the masses so they could understand that economic change was necessary.[15] A. L. von Rochau also became an advocate of rapid industrialization and national economic integration. Rochau insisted that liberalism and liberal social science become more empirical in orientation, that they deal with social realities and political power rather than theories. This orientation Rochau dubbed *Realpolitik*, a term later used by Rochau and others to show why Bismarck's policies were consistent with an improved version of liberalism.[16] Welcker responded to the problem of weak lower-class support by showing an increased interest in questions of culture, focusing on the legitimate cultural reasons for resistance to revolutionary changes.[17]

The responses of liberal social scientists to the lack of consistent popular support for liberalism in 1848 were thus quite varied. Certain general (although not universal) themes did, however, emerge. One that came naturally to a person like Welcker but that can be found in the writings of people as different as Rodbertus, Biedermann, and the radical democrat Rudolf Virchow was a recognition of the need to understand the cultural bases of politics.[18] This recognition had obvious implications for the reevaluation of liberal social science. It was the main source of impetus to an intellectual fashion for cultural studies that emerged in Germany in the 1850s—a fashion advanced mainly by liberals and former liberals anxious to explain, in different ways, liberalism's poor performance in 1848–1849.

In the rest of this chapter, the paths taken by four prominent people toward cultural study will be examined. We shall look at each person's political and intellectual positions before 1848, the various factors that led each one to reevaluate those positions, and the results of the reevaluation in the 1850s and 1860s. In each case, the discussion will be framed in terms of what each individual came to think about the three major content elements of the liberal theoretical pattern discussed in chapter 1: the model of the rational individual, the nomothetic view of social science, and the linked ideas of progress and equilibrium.

W. H. Riehl: Cultural Science
as a Rejection of Liberalism

Wilhelm Heinrich Riehl (1823–1897), the first major star of the fashion for culture in the 1850s, has had an uneven reputation. His influence peaked before 1860 when his new discipline of *Volkskunde* attracted wide attention in Germany and some interest even in England, where it was favorably publicized by George Eliot.[19] His reputation waned considerably thereafter, partly because he came to be considered a crackpot by many academics and partly because the new generation of cultural scientists produced by the 1860s tended not to acknowledge their debts to their immediate predecessors. He retained some popularity, however, as a public lecturer. At the end of his life, his intellectual stock rose again, mainly because of the growth of radical forms of conservatism with which his thinking was very compatible. Today, Riehl is more often regarded as an early *völkisch* ideologue than as one of the more innovative figures in nineteenth-century social science.[20]

Riehl was the son of a senior domestic servant of the duke of Hesse-Nassau. According to his (rather unreliable) reminiscences published at the end of his life, he was subjected to crosscutting influences in his youth from his freethinking father and a deeply religious maternal grandfather.[21] However these influences interacted in Riehl's youth, it is quite clear that when he went to the universities of Bonn and Marburg in the 1840s he intended to study for the Lutheran ministry and that he already inclined toward moderate liberalism. His inclination was reinforced by the popularity of liberal politics among the students and by his favorite teachers: the historian Friedrich Dahlmann and the old hero of the resistance to Napoleon, Ernst Moritz Arndt. In later years, Riehl claimed that Dahlmann's limited, historically oriented constitutionalism and Arndt's vision of a liberal nation built on a self-conscious German *Volk* were fundamentally conservative notions, but in *Vormärz* Germany they were both clearly aligned with moderate liberalism, and so was Riehl himself.[22]

So interested had Riehl become in politics that he dropped his intention of becoming a village parson and instead studied history, *Staatswissenschaft,* and related subjects. He ceased to be an orthodox Protestant, although he remained greatly interested in religion all his life and, like many other cultural scientists with strong Lutheran backgrounds, in the relationship between personal religious sentiment and the social context of morality.

When he left Marburg in 1845, unable to afford further pursuit of an academic or bureaucratic career, Riehl had no profession. He took the customary path, therefore, into journalism. He was holding down a minor editor's job in Karlsruhe when the 1848 revolution gave him his great opportunity. Riehl was called to Wiesbaden to be editor of the mouthpiece newspaper of the Hessian moderate liberal faction in its struggles with the radical left and the reactionary right.

In this capacity, Riehl took an active (indeed, a hyperactive) part in the intellectual and political life of the year of revolution.[23] He generally adhered to the faction in the National Assembly at Frankfurt led by his teacher Dahlmann and by Heinrich von Gagern, the leader of the Hessian moderate liberals. Like his patrons, he increasingly decried the danger to public order posed by the "radicals"—a category into which he put everybody to the left of the Dahlmann–Gagern faction, including those who accepted the use of violence to accomplish change and those who sought a republican form of government. He wrote a manifesto for a "democratic-monarchic" party in Wiesbaden to counter the appeal of the radicals. In the manifesto can be seen Riehl's continued adherence to important liberal ideas, but also his movement toward the right in response to the disorder of 1848.[24] The princely governments, he wrote, ought to be maintained in the German states because the German people were insufficiently "partisan" and "brazen" for fragmented republican politics. The princes should be regarded as the representatives of the sovereignty of the people (whatever that might mean). They would be restrained from arbitrary rule by their realization of their representative function. Riehl's party favors a form of state that "without forcible destruction of existing relationships, . . . secures the rights of the people," makes taxes "as light as possible," and provides maximum protection for personal freedom and property. There should be a free press and a monarchy "where the people take part in the administration directly through the deputies." (Details of the last arrangement are not provided.) Although to modern ears this sounds like a betrayal of liberalism, in fact it manifests sentiments widely shared by moderate liberals in 1848.[25] Like many others, Riehl was frightened by the disorder and violence of revolution and, as can be seen in his hatred of radicals, dismayed at the fragmentation in liberalism that the revolution had revealed.

The end of the revolution, which meant the end of effective party politics, left Riehl without a job. Within a year, however, he had been taken under the wing of the Stuttgart publisher J. G. von Cotta, with whose help he had developed a new career plan—to move from journalism to academic social science—and a new, overtly conservative political orientation. Riehl had come to the conclusion that the reason the 1848 revolution had failed, in fact the reason there had been a revolution at all as opposed to a gradual reform, was that the liberal leadership had not understood German society, had permitted the movement to fragment, and had allowed the initiative to pass to the radicals. The radicals, Riehl believed, had attempted to apply to Germany a body of foreign (mostly French) political doctrine entirely inappropriate in Germany. This failure was not so much a failure of good intentions as it was one of knowledge. If society was to be reformed, reformers needed to know the specific social materials with which they were working. A set of abstract theories was insufficient. Riehl thus laid the blame for the upsets of 1848 firmly at the doorstep of liberal social science.[26]

Riehl's thinking in this regard was neither unique nor completely selfless. Apart from other liberals who were having second thoughts, there were also many people, some of them very important in postrevolutionary politics, who had never been liberals but who accepted the need for some kind of reform and were distressed by the attitudes of reactionaries in power in the years after 1849. Such reformist conservatives tended to be more sensitive than most liberals to the distress among peasants and artisanal workers caused by incipient economic modernization.[27] The problem was that they had no acceptable models of moderate reform that they could use to articulate their positions except liberal ones, which they were loath to adopt.

It was this kind of sentiment to which Riehl, the journalist who wanted to be an academic social scientist, intended to appeal.

With Cotta's help, Riehl decided to undertake a campaign of empirical research into the ways Germans in their various classes and regions lived, spoke, and thought—in a word, their culture. The project was of course suggested by the earlier folktale collecting of the Grimms; although Riehl acknowledged the legacy, he went about his work in a different way. He believed himself to be a scientist and systematically built up the empirical data base of a science of the *Volk,* a cultural science in which philological concerns played only one part among many. He acknowledged also that his science had been suggested earlier by Herder and his successors, but Riehl faulted them for relying on inferences from intuition rather than from facts and for maintaining untenable Enlightenment notions of human nature. Finally, he acknowledged the influence of his teachers Dahlmann and Arndt for their insistence on the importance of specific national cultures in understanding politics.[28] The procedure Riehl established was, however, entirely original. He created a format for data collection that was supposed to elicit information about all aspects of life: daily schedules, modes of organizing work, childrearing, home furnishing, religious beliefs (formal and informal), political outlook, consciousness of the physical environment, folktales, modes of speech, and so forth. He took trips into different regions to interview people at all levels of society. His system became more refined as time went on. Although it was not equivalent to modern anthropological field research (Riehl seldom spent more than a few days in one place and apparently collected much of his information while hanging around taverns), Riehl's methodology was, by almost any standard, far in advance of his time.[29]

Although Riehl had not really completed his project even by the time of his death nearly half a century later, he began to issue the results of his work in 1851 with the first volume of his *Naturgeschichte des Volkes.*[30] Having judged his market very nicely, he won almost instant acclaim. King Maximilian II of Bavaria, in accordance with his policy of trying to enliven the intellectual life of his kingdom while pursuing enlightened conservative social reform, invited Riehl to become professor of economics at the University of Munich in 1854. Riehl remained there for the rest of his days. In 1859, after he had organized his own discipline of *Volkskunde* around his methodology, he had that subject added to his pedagogical title.

Riehl's published work in cultural science is too varied to be summarized here. Important elements of it will be discussed in more detail in chapter 7. The work suffers from a number of general defects: lack of system in presenting data, a tendency to romanticize the lives of certain classes (especially the peasantry), and a constant harping on political issues. This last Riehl did not regard as a defect at all. His cultural science, his *Volkskunde,* was consciously intended to support a conservative (although not a reactionary) approach to politics and policy-making.[31] In 1858, Riehl also claimed that as a result of his efforts, "an entire system of *Staatswissenschaft* is developing organically on the basis of *Volkskunde.*"[32] In other words, he thought he was presenting what earlier liberal social science had promised but not delivered: an empirically grounded science of society that could serve as the basis for accurate policy-making and limited reform. He was doing this as an avowed conservative, having rejected the more "radical" strains of the liberal and Enlightenment traditions and redesignated the ones that were more agreeable to him as "conservative." And he had used the study of culture as the key to the whole approach.

If we look at what Riehl did with the basic elements of the liberal theoretical pattern, we can see the extent of his break with the pattern and also the utility of the culture concept in making the break. He rejected the model of the rational, abstract individual almost completely, arguing that abstraction was the worst sin of liberal social science, that rationality was neither uniform nor universal, and that the individual was not the appropriate unit of social analysis. Instead, it was necessary to focus on the *groups* to which the individual belonged. These groups were not the voluntary associations emphasized by the *Staatslexikon* liberals that reflected rational individual aims, but rather "natural" collectivities that shaped such aims. It was groups that interacted over time to produce particular ways of acting and of looking at things; it was groups that unconsciously developed consensus about values; and it was groups that passed on attitudes, values, and behavior patterns from generation to generation, thus reinforcing and further defining culture. To a very large extent, individuals were who they were because of the culture of the group to which they belonged. Political behavior was group behavior. It was not, to any significant degree, reducible to individual behavior, but it could be understood in terms of culture. Thus, politicians who wanted to deal with the real world and reformers who wanted to improve it had to take the cultures of the natural groups in society into account. This was what the liberals had failed to do in 1848, assuming, for instance, that peasants whose cultures were actually very different from their own bourgeois backgrounds would, with proper education, see the advantages of liberal reforms.[33]

One of the strongest aspects of Riehl's analysis, and the one that was probably most attractive to intelligent contemporaries, was his insistence that different kinds of groups had different cultures and that national cultures, although they existed, were but layers laid atop equally valid regional and class cultures.[34] Each region of Germany had its own distinctive culture (derived, as Herder had suggested, from its peculiar environment and history) that limited the extent to which it was possible to generalize about, for example, peasants. Saxon peasants differed from Bavarian peasants, and both differed greatly from French ones. In addition, classes (Riehl preferred to call them *Stände*—corporate estates) had distinctive cultures as well.[35] In the Germany of the 1850s, according to Riehl, there were three *Stände* with fully developed cultures: the aristocracy, the bourgeoisie, and the peasantry. Each culture was different and each contributed something useful to the whole society. There was also a fourth *Stand*, the urban working class, which was not yet fully formed or self-conscious. Riehl's analysis of the social question revolved around the policies required to acculturate the working class to playing a respectable, positive role in society.[36]

Riehl also addressed himself to the nomothetic element of the liberal theoretical pattern. As an overall aim, Riehl accepted it completely. The job of a scientist, which Riehl claimed to be, was to discover natural laws. He rejected the practice of reasoning from universal human nature and accused liberal social scientists of failing to emphasize sufficiently the need for empirical research into culture.[37] Culture, for Riehl, was not an abstract entity, but a concrete one. It was what people actually thought and did and what an observer perceived them thinking and doing. In essence, Riehl defined culture as the appropriate—and in some senses the only—object of social research.

Riehl dealt with the third major element of the liberal theoretical pattern by devising a theory of social stability and change—a theory intended to provide a conservative alternative to the existing liberal ones. He held that no society was a uniform entity. A society was an aggregation of *Stände* in constant tension with each other, each possessing a different culture. Each *Stand* featured distinctive principles and forces. *Stände* could be classified in terms of whether their basic principles were primarily ones of "movement" or of "conservation." Stability— essentially a cultural stability—was maintained when the forces and principles balanced each other in society. Change occurred when new *Stände* emerged or when existing ones decayed, requiring one or more of the others to assume its functions. The aristocracy had to some extent decayed by the mid-nineteenth century, forcing the peasantry to take over much of its job of conserving the social order (hence the need to protect the peasantry against dissolution through economic change). The urban working class was also emerging, rivalling the bourgeoisie as the embodiment of the principle of movement or change.

Riehl thus presents an important example of a social scientist who altered his theoretical orientation—who created a new theoretical pattern—partly in response to the crisis of liberalism that he perceived in the 1848 revolution. Many important elements of the older liberal theoretical pattern lingered in his work, especially in his claim to being a scientist in search of social laws. His emphasis on real empirical research was a break with past practice rather than theory. But his radical rejection of individualist assumptions constituted the basis of something like a paradigm break. Like many others in similar circumstances, Riehl simultaneously claimed originality for his insights and attempted to create a legitimizing pedigree for them. At the same time that he was putting together a genealogy for his brand of non-reactionary social conservatism in politics by reclassifying earlier moderate liberals as conservatives, he also pointed back to precursors who had combined opposition to radical change with a cultural approach to social analysis. Justus Möser, an eighteenth-century figure who had been very much a part of the liberal tradition in German social thought, was the most important of the predecessors Riehl associated with his conservative social science.[38]

Riehl was, for a while at least, a very significant figure in German social thought. The connection between his movement from moderate liberalism to self-conscious conservatism and his decision to study culture illustrates vividly the effects on German social science of the beginnings of the crisis of German liberalism. Riehl's challenge to the liberal theoretical pattern resulted in his establishment of an alternative pattern, the first of many that shared similar characteristics, including an alignment with conservative political forces. Riehl displays one aspect of the general process of fragmentation in social science. Other people followed similar, although not identical, courses.

Carl Theodor Andree: Journalism, Geography, and Politics

Carl Theodor Andree (1808–1875) was a figure of secondary importance compared to Riehl, but he had some influence on the formation of cultural geography and he reveals, like Riehl, connections between a personal reappraisal of political liberalism, journalism, and a movement toward cultural science.

Andree was half a generation older than the other people featured in this chapter.[39] He was born to a family of artisans in Brunswick. Recognized early as a child prodigy, he was sent to the local gymnasium and to various universities where he studied history and *Staatswissenschaft*. His activities as a radical liberal student leader excluded him from an academic career after he took his degree in 1830 and forced him into professional journalism. He took at first a radical democratic line, which led the police in several states to keep him from getting a toehold in academia. From about the late 1830s, Andree began to tailor his politics to the lines taken by the newspapers that employed him, moving toward the moderate side of the liberal spectrum and becoming interested in economic development as he became acquainted with liberal industrialists. By 1846, when Andree was chased out of Cologne by the police during a time of unrest on the basis of his old reputation, he had lost his last trace of radicalism—partly because he was older and presumably tired of police attention, partly because of the nature of his profession and its peculiar tendency to make its members confront political questions directly and to search for answers acceptable to their public and their employers.

Journalism also helped to interest Andree in social science. As a student he had known the founders of academic geography, Alexander von Humboldt and Karl Ritter; but it was his involvement with the emigration question as a journalist in the late 1830s and the popularity of his travel pieces that brought him into contact with the geographical publishing firms of Saxony and the network of academics that centered around them. He turned his hand to writing textbooks in this field and read widely in ethnography. By the late 1840s, Andree had acquired a reputation as an informed geographical writer.

When revolution came in 1848, Andree took a position similar to Riehl's (except that Andree was much more pro-Prussian). He attacked the violence and radicalism of his former allies on the democratic Left and, without cutting his ties to moderate liberalism completely, he directed his criticism at the intellectual foundations on which liberalism was built. Like his contemporary Rochau, Andree claimed that liberalism was based on assumptions that were too narrowly defined, too abstracted from reality, and, under the guise of universality, too foreign to be applicable to German politics. Liberalism had a tendency to fragment because of the intransigence and intellectual rigidity of the Left. Like Rochau, after 1848 he aligned himself with the far Right of the liberal movement and with the views of businesspeople and industrialists whose support he sought.[40] Unlike Rochau but like Riehl, he decided that the study of culture was the best cure for the ills of liberalism and also the best avenue for an academically trained journalist to seek success under new political and economic circumstances.

In the 1850s, Andree moved more strongly into geographical writing and editing. The result of his efforts was his two-volume 1859 book *Geographische Wanderungen*.[41] The theoretical part of the book, which shows the strong influence of Alexander von Humboldt and Ritter in its emphasis on the environmental shaping of culture, was never very influential because it had to compete with more solid works, like those of Theodor Waitz, that came out at the same time. It is interesting, however, because it proposes a cultural science that Andree calls *Völkerkunde* as the proper foundation for *Staatswissenschaft*. Unlike Riehl's *Volkskunde*, which focused on the empirical study of German regional and class cultures, Andree's science was to be comparative ethnology on a worldwide basis.[42] Only by comparing factors that caused people throughout the world to think and act differently was it possible to understand how one's own people thought and acted.

Andree did not actually obtain an academic position. Instead, he became an entrepreneur of geographical and ethnographic publishing. With the backing of Saxon-Thuringian publishers, he founded several journals. The most important of these was *Globus*, one of the first and most successful journals to bridge the gap between scientific ethnography and geography, on the one hand, and the lucrative field of popular travel literature, on the other. Andree also took part in organizing German geography and anthropology as a founder of the important *Verein für Erdkunde* of Dresden and as a fund-raiser for overseas expeditions. In politics, he was active until his death in the right wing of the National Liberal party, supporting unification, Bismarck, and a national policy of commercial and industrial expansion. He was one of several publicists and academics who oriented geographical organizations toward imperialism in the 1870s.

Although Andree shows many similarities to Riehl in the way in which his politics and his approach to cultural science were related, his rejection of liberalism was not as extreme as Riehl's and his theoretical break with liberal social science not as significant. Nevertheless, in a rough spectrum of post–1848 cultural science, Andree and Riehl probably belong fairly close to one another. There were, however, others who turned to cultural science without parting company as drastically either with liberal ideology or with liberal social science. One of these was Theodor Waitz.

Theodor Waitz: Education, Psychology, and Culture

Waitz (1821–1864) came from a family of parsons and teachers in Gotha.[43] Another child prodigy (in mathematics), he took his doctorate in philosophy at Leipzig at nineteen, habilitated (see p. 74) at Marburg at twenty-three, and became *extraordinarius* there at twenty-seven in 1848. All through his brief career, he was widely regarded in German academic circles as a multitalented genius. He never had to struggle for a reputation the way Riehl and others did, and although his political convictions retarded his professional career somewhat in the 1850s, his academic place was quite secure. He engaged in journalism and politics not out of necessity, but out of personal concerns born largely of scholarly pursuits and a deep sense of morality, possibly linked to his origins in a Lutheran parsonage. Waitz is not much remembered today because of his early death and because many of his contributions were rendered obsolete just afterward, but in the 1850s and 1860s he was a formidable figure with an international reputation.[44]

Waitz's interests originally lay in ancient philosophy, particularly in the classical writers on ethics. His professional concern with ethics appears to have led him to contemporary social thought, and the liberal political climate at Marburg in the mid–1840s directed his attention to liberal political theory. Waitz was also swept up in other related intellectual currents of the time. At Marburg, he came under the influence of his colleague Karl Ludwig, one of the pioneers of the contemporary revolution in physiology and a vigorous proponent of scientific materialism. Waitz was philosophically inclined toward idealism and had done his early work within the Kantian tradition, but he found it impossible to deny the successes of materialism in physical science and the great potential for its application to the understanding of human behavior.[45] Like many others, he sought to reconcile these competing philosophical approaches by focusing on psychology—the study of the realm in which the ideal and the material confront one another directly.

Waitz's early attempts to create a psychology that would provide a firm basis for ethical and social understanding fit fairly securely into the framework of the liberal theoretical pattern.[46] Waitz did not doubt that the prime focus of psychology, like the focus of ethics, was the individual. Nor did he doubt that the purpose of studying humans was to uncover laws of thought and behavior. He agreed with Ludwig that one of the weaknesses of contemporary human studies was its too-exclusive reliance on deduction from assumed first principles—a reliance that needed to be lessened by empirical research in psychology. But at the same time, he argued that if one wished to understand the full range of human mental activity, one could not concentrate exclusively on the individual or depend solely on experimentation. Most of a person's ideas are derived from education (i.e., from other people). Experimentation with individual perceptions could never reveal the process by which such derivation occurred.

Up until about 1849, Waitz's thinking about psychology was caught up in these and other unsettled issues. Thereafter, the issues resolved themselves in Waitz's mind within a complex theory of mental operation he developed—a theory that called for a detailed examination of the cultural aspect of thought. One of the key factors that led Waitz in this direction was the revolution of 1848 and its aftermath.[47]

Before 1848, Waitz's political involvements had been fairly casual; but during the revolution, he emerged as one of the foremost liberal spokespersons for educational reform as a concomitant to the erection of a liberal society. When conservatives returned to power in 1849, Waitz was branded by the local authorities as a suspicious character. Although he did not lose his job, he had to forego promotion to full professor until 1862, despite his international reputation. He did not renounce liberalism. Rather, he increasingly oriented his scholarship around the solution of problems that confronted liberalism as a reform movement and as a model of social understanding. This, in turn, led him in the early 1850s to transform his psychology by connecting it to the anthropological study of culture.

This linkage between post–1848 liberal politics and Waitz's movement toward cultural science can be seen in his involvement with education. In 1848, Waitz had called for massive national reforms in educational organization, financing, and curricula. He had argued for a completely secular, free primary school system with instructors trained and selected according to rigorous standards; for increasing the number and variety of secondary schools; and for revising the operations of the universities. He justified all of these reforms by citing the need for an educated citizenry in a liberal society.[48]

After 1848 and the apparent failure of liberalism, Waitz's interests in education changed. He was still concerned with structural reform, but he focused his attention elsewhere, toward the reasons that people rejected liberalism, despite its obvious connection to progress and its rationally and morally attractive program of reform. The most immediate cause was the inadequacy of people's educations—the old liberal excuse. The uneducated needed to be trained in reason and moral judgment, whereas the *Gebildete* needed to be better grounded in these things than they had been. But the main stumbling block to better education was not so much superstition imposed by interested parties as it was deficiencies in the psychological theories on which instruction was based.[49] These deficiencies were characteristic not only of older theories, but also of most of the newer ones associated with liberal educational proposals (including Waitz's own). A new psychology was needed as a foundation for better education and as a precondition for progress and reform.

Waitz's new psychology turned out to be extremely complex. It cannot be discussed here at any length, but it bore distinct similarities to that of Wilhelm Wundt, which we shall examine later.[50] Not surprisingly, it focused on the inadequacy of the various models of the rational individual current in educational theory. Like the post-Kantian idealist psychologists of the previous generation and in contrast to the associationists and materialists, Waitz argued that the human mind was not simply the central feature of a sensory mechanism that reflected on the stimuli it received. Human rational capacity was more than just an ability to discover the order inherent in the external world through the mental manipulation of stimuli, and it was certainly not the only, or necessarily the most important, capacity people possessed. On the other hand, he accepted the argument of materialists like his friend Ludwig that ideas could not be discussed as entities completely separate from external realities and sense impressions. Following the lead of Johann Friedrich Herbart (1776–1841), Waitz downplayed the distinction between the ideal and the material. He identified a wide range of capacities the human mind possessed of itself, presumably as a result of its physical constitution: reason, judgment, moral sense, and the like. These capacities served to advance or restrain motives that arose from other characteristics of the mind, including feeling and will, that determined the basis of perceived self-interest. But these characteristics and capacities provided only the framework for psychic activity. They required organization and focusing, even to permit humans to deal with simple sense impressions. The organization of psychic activity centered around the formation and employment of *concepts*, which were a continuously developing array of mental phenomena that arose from interaction among the various elements of the individual's mind and between the mind and the external world.

On this basis, Waitz advanced an influential theory of pedagogy that emphasized the harmonious development of mental capacities and the proper formation of concepts in pupils.[51] More significantly for our purposes, Waitz recognized that most of an individual's concepts are not really products of personal experience of physical reality and unique reflection on the patterns that lie behind it. Rather, the individual *learns* most concepts from other people, occasionally contributing to the general pool. Because of this interaction, a group's shared set of concepts changes while maintaining continuity. Not only is the individual mind furnished, therefore, with concepts drawn from a dynamic culture, but the external reality with which the mind deals is itself primarily a cultural construct.[52] Individual thought and motivation, although still at the center of Waitz's analysis, plainly cannot be understood without a consideration of culture. In other words, Waitz has promoted culture from being (with education) a corrective to the model of the rational individual to the status of an entity that defines much (although not all) of both education and the individual mind.

But in what way does one go about understanding how culturally determined minds function? How does one differentiate what is universal in mind and culture from what is specific to a certain people? These are crucial questions not only for education, but for politics and all other rational social activity. The possibility of general social laws, the uncovering of which Waitz regarded as the aim of social science, depended on the existence of uniformities (or at least mental commonalities) among people. To Waitz, convinced that predecessors like Herbart had paid too little attention to the need for empirical research, the universality of a common human nature amid cultural diversity was not a fact to be assumed, but rather a hypothesis to be tested. And it could only be tested by systematic comparison of available data about all aspects of human culture throughout the world. From liberal reform in education, Waitz had proceeded to a psychology that contained a constructive critique of the assumptions of liberal social science and from there to comparative anthropology.

Waitz devoted himself almost entirely from the mid–1850s until his death to compiling from secondary sources a vast compendium of ethnographical information, organized (except for the first volume) by continent but always tied overtly to the solution of theoretical questions of direct importance to his psychological theories and to issues of liberal politics. Waitz's six-volume *Anthropologie der Naturvölker,* which started coming out in 1859, was for many years regarded as one of the foundations of modern ethnology in Britain and the United States as much as in Germany. It was cited extensively by E. B. Tylor and the Boasians; the English translation of its opening volume (1863) was the first publication issued by the Anthropological Society of London.[53] It was not the first such compendium. The works of the German scholar Gustav Klemm (1802–1867) preceded those of Waitz, but the latter's work was vastly more systematic and influential. Unlike Klemm, who was interested mainly in material culture, Waitz emphasized religion, politics, and mythology—in other words, the concepts on which his psychology depended.

One of the reasons for the impact of Waitz's anthropology was that it was overtly addressed to political and moral issues of great concern to liberals (especially issues about which liberals were divided), but it considered those issues as scientific questions to be answered by research in comparative anthropology. For example, Waitz presented the first volume of his *Anthropologie* as a discussion of whether or not all human groups could be regarded as belonging to the same race. This was a hot issue in the late 1850s and 1860s. Early ethnology in England had grown up around the defense of human unity, but the development of physical anthropology in the previous few years, which had given a new, physical, and scientific dimension to the question of race, was widely believed to have established the validity of polygenism: the idea that each human race had a different origin.[54] Apart from the general implications of scientific racism for liberal assumptions, the issue was particularly germane to the political question of slavery—a question that divided liberals. Waitz took the issue very seriously. If humans did not belong to the same race, then perhaps slavery was justified; if they did, then on moral grounds it was insupportable. He carefully reviewed the evidence from physical anthropology, brilliantly summarizing the progress the discipline had made to that time, and he announced that on physical grounds alone the issue was undecided. He then demonstrated through cultural comparisons between "advanced" peoples and the so-called *Naturvölker* (primitive peoples) that, regardless of somatic and cultural differences, all peoples showed approximately the same basic mental capacities and so, for practical purposes, had to be considered part of one race. A moral and political question, therefore, was capable of being answered by cultural science.[55]

Waitz's reconsideration of elements of the liberal theoretical pattern—especially the rational individual model and the methodological problems of a nomothetic human science—had led him to a revised psychology and to anthropology. These, in turn, led him to a consideration of the question of change. Waitz adopted a vaguely evolutionary position in the sense that he agreed that different peoples had attained different levels of culture and that the more advanced peoples, the *Kulturvölker*, had once existed at the level of the less advanced, the *Naturvölker*. But the actual range of cultural phenomena was too great to be encompassed within this simple scheme; by itself, it gave no explanation of why cultures changed. Waitz developed a theory of cultural change that was essentially diffusionist, that was consistent with his ideas on the relationship between society and culture, and that preserved the liberal notion of the fundamental unity of humankind.

Waitz argued that ethnographical and archaeological evidence discredited the idea that some people were, because of their mental or physical makeup, inherently superior to others and for that reason the biologically-designated vanguard of progress. Environmental factors played a role, but they could not explain why peoples in similar environments develop quite different cultures. Waitz focused his explanation on gifted, innovative individuals, who appear (he said) with about the same frequency in all societies.[56] These individuals introduce new ways of thinking and of doing things, which are first adopted by their own people and then transmitted to others by various means. Certain peoples are better situated geographically to receive such influences than are others, which helps to explain relative differences in apparent innovativeness. But in any case, a particular innovation is not the same when it has been transmitted. It receives part of its meaning and significance from the culture into which it is fitted, which helps to explain the enormous diversity of human culture. Waitz's diffusionism would later be replaced by other, more elaborate diffusionist theories. It was not a very comprehensive response to the need for a liberal theory of change, but at least it was consistent with key elements of the liberal theoretical pattern in its emphasis on individuals, on progress, and on human unity.

Waitz's work can be interpreted from a number of perspectives. His work fits nicely into the history of post-Kantian idealist philosophy and (through the influence of Herbart) psychology. He can be seen as one who attempted to bridge the intellectual gap between idealism and materialism. But clearly one of the most important ways to interpret Waitz is as a social scientist who attempted to develop cultural science as a support for political liberalism and for what he believed to be valid in the liberal theoretical pattern. Like Riehl and Andree, Waitz was deeply interested in political questions, especially ones susceptible to treatment by cultural science. Waitz, for instance, was a convinced abolitionist, ostensibly on the grounds developed in his *Anthropologie*. Andree, on the other hand, ostensibly on the basis of his own cultural and social analysis, was a supporter of the South during the American Civil War.[57] In remaining within the fold of liberal politics and liberal social scientific theory, Waitz was not alone. A similar pattern can be seen in the career of Rudolf Virchow.

Rudolf Virchow: Medical Science and Liberal Cultural Science

Virchow (1821–1902) was an intellectual giant of the nineteenth century, one of the founders of several scientific disciplines: pathology, cell physiology, public health, physical anthropology, archaeology, and last (and certainly least in terms of his contributions) ethnology. He is also remembered today for his opposition to, among other things, the theory of natural selection and to microbiology. The growth of Virchow's interest in cultural science parallels that of Waitz in some respects, but it also shows how the connection between liberal politics and cultural study extended into the natural sciences and into the radical end of the liberal political spectrum.

Virchow belonged to the same generation as Waitz and Riehl. Like them, he came from a decidedly nonelite background: a lower-middle-class family in rural Pomerania.[58] After showing early promise, he was accepted into the Prussian army medical school in Berlin. In Berlin in the 1840s, he joined the brilliant group of Johannes Müller's physiology students, including Hermann Helmholtz and Emil Du Bois-Reymond, who were attempting to link physiology to chemistry and physics and to reorganize science radically on a materialist, experimentalist basis in reaction to the tradition of *Naturphilosophie*. Virchow's radicalism extended to politics as well. At the start of the 1848 revolution, Virchow—with a reputation for brilliance (and arrogance) in medicine and an appointment at Berlin's teaching hospital— became one of the most outspoken leaders of the democratic Left in Berlin. He remained, however, a liberal. Although he advocated government action to ameliorate working-class living conditions, Virchow opposed socialists of all descriptions—as he continued to do to thereafter.[59] His radical reputation was due more to his youthful political enthusiasm and his acceptance of democracy as both the logical implication of liberalism and the appropriate solution to social problems than it was to disagreement with moderate liberals on fundamental assumptions.

Just before the revolution broke out in March 1848, Virchow undertook a government-sponsored investigation of a typhus epidemic in Silesia. The resulting report, like a similar report on health conditions in the Spessart that he delivered to the Bavarian government in 1852, was a major contribution to the literature on public health. The two reports also reveal at an early period some of the factors that linked Virchow's political views to his medical work and led to his interest in culture.[60]

Virchow's typhus report placed his statistical description of the outbreak and his case studies in the context of the geography, society, and culture of the region. He argued that diseases and treatments could be analyzed by focusing exclusively on individual cases, but not an epidemic. An epidemic was a disease raised to the level of a social phenomenon by the conditions of poverty and ignorance in an area, which encouraged the disease's spread, and by the inability of the local power structure to respond to the disease by limiting its extent or changing the conditions in which it appeared. In Silesia, a potentially rich country, poverty and ignorance arose partly from political and economic factors: the agricultural labor system, overcrowded dwellings, an unsympathetic Prussian administration. But to an even greater extent, they were *cultural* in origin. They arose from the backwardness, superstition, and conservatism of lower-class Polish culture and the unwillingness of the Silesian elite and Prussian bureaucracy to change things. The long-term solution was simple: "full and unlimited democracy."[61] Political pressure emanating from an enfranchised people would lead to social and economic changes that would reduce the incidence of epidemics. But democracy would not work if the majority of people remained imprisoned by a backward culture and resisted modernization. A policy of cultural change was therefore needed in Silesia, but not a crude or authoritarian one. The educational system had to be modernized and Germanized, although the German language should not be imposed lest it elicit Polish resistance. Most of all, the Prussian state should reduce the role of the Catholic church (the main prop of "superstition") by assuming its social and educational functions.[62]

Virchow's Silesian report and his similar (although less anti-Catholic) report on the Spessart show that Virchow did not strictly differentiate between natural or medical science and social science. Their basic methods were generically the same, although specific applications might differ. The reports also show how his brand of liberalism impinged directly on his scientific work. Most important, Virchow's public health studies give an early clue to his interest in studying culture systematically. In order to modernize societies like those of Silesia and the Spessart, to raise living standards, prevent disease, and pave the way for democracy, it was necessary to overcome the obstacles posed by traditional culture. It was inexpedient to do so by force, and it was unrealistic to assume that merely modernizing certain sectors of the economy would automatically alter local culture for the better. Traditional culture had to be studied so that its modification could be effectively undertaken.[63]

Virchow lost his teaching position during the conservative purge of 1849. He was saved by a call to the University of Würzburg from Bavarian educational authorities anxious to hire a potentially world-famous physiologist as part of King Maximilian II's program of upscaling Bavaria's intellectual life. Maximilian insisted on a promise from Virchow not to engage in politics, which Virchow grudgingly gave.[64] It was during his seven years at Würzburg, while he was making his most important contributions to cellular pathology, that Virchow began to take an amateur interest in the study of culture—especially in physical anthropology and archaeology, but also in other fields as well. By the 1860s, he was a contributing researcher in practically every field of cultural science; by the 1870s, he spent more time on these studies than on any others.[65]

By that time, Virchow was back in Berlin. So successful had his research in Würzburg been that the Prussian authorities swallowed their pride and offered him a chair at the University of Berlin in 1856. Virchow returned in triumph. With his limitless energy and overbearing manner, he soon became a consummate academic politician, with strong connections in business and the Prussian bureaucracy. He also reentered liberal politics, helping to lead the liberal revival that began in 1858.[66] Although still a democrat, he had learned the value of cooperation among liberals of all stripes, just as he had learned the value of not offending the authorities too much. His experience of 1848 and its aftermath had also convinced him of the futility of revolution as a tool of liberalization. Much of the considerable political power he wielded after 1858 as one of the founders of the Progressive party (*Fortschrittspartei*) and as a long-time member of the Prussian Chamber of Deputies was due to his ability to present a comprehensive liberal ideology that did not compromise basic liberal principles (e.g. constitutional government and legislative responsibility) but allowed for substantial differences of opinion among liberally-oriented politicians. This permitted Virchow to maintain good working relations with the Prussian bureaucracy all through the 1860s at the same time that he was one of the leaders of the liberal opposition during the Prussian constitutional crisis and one of Bismarck's main opponents.

Virchow's major contributions to cultural anthropology were as an organizer rather than as a theoretician or researcher—although in physical anthropology and archaeology he was a good deal more. We shall discuss his theoretical outlook and the significance of his organizational activities in chapter 5. For the moment, the important thing to recognize is that Virchow did not strictly separate his politics from his science. He used his scientific reputation to speak authoritatively about a range of political issues, and he frequently used ideas from political theory to visualize and explain biological phenomena. (E.g., he thought of a multicellular organism as a "republic" of cells.)[67] Although Virchow believed it was necessary for a scientist to be objective, he did not find anything anomalous about a science of society directly applicable to politics. Moreover, apart from obvious differences in subject matter, sciences applicable to physical matter, to living organisms in general, and to humankind were to him all basically the same enterprise with the same rules. He did not share with his great colleague Hermann Helmholtz the belief that *Naturwissenschaft* and *Geisteswissenschaft* had necessarily to be quite different activities—although as he modified his radical materialist position later in his life, his view of what activities could be encompassed under the "scientific method" broadened.[68] As a social scientist, then, Virchow clearly upheld an important part of the traditional liberal theoretical pattern, just as he upheld the standard elements of liberal political ideology. In each case, however, he adopted a radical posture: positivist and (at least initially) materialist with respect to social science, democratic with respect to ideology.

Links between Virchow's political position (both ideological and practical) and his interest in cultural science can be found at all stages of his very long career. Just as his experience with the typhus epidemic at the time of the 1848 revolution showed him the necessity of understanding the cultural factors that retarded reform and modernization, so also the failure of the revolution and the various setbacks experienced by the liberal movement in attempting to gain broad support in the following decades showed him the need to understand how cultures maintain themselves and resist change and how cultural change actually takes place. Virchow's deep interest in archaeology may have been related to this sort of concern. It has been noted that in the 1850s and 1860s in Britain, archaeological interests were often tied to a desire to understand the processes of sociocultural change with direct application to the current politics.[69] Virchow's involvement in the *Kulturkampf* of the 1870s, in which he supported Bismarck's efforts to curtail the activities of the Catholic church in Prussia, was presaged by the attitude toward Catholicism shown in his typhus report. The Catholic church was an obstacle in the path to the eventual liberalization of German society because it maintained obsolete cultural patterns through its control of the education of Catholics. It was Virchow, in fact, who coined the term *Kulturkampf*, which fairly indicates the nature of his interest in attacking Catholicism.[70] Virchow also saw a connection between the difficulties the liberal parties were having in retaining working-class support in the 1870s and 1880s against the growing Social Democratic party (SPD—*Sozialdemokratische Partei Deutschlands*) and the need to acculturate the industrial proletariat to liberal, capitalist society.[71] In other words, one of the things that continually drew Virchow to cultural study, starting with the 1848 revolution, was his involvement with liberal politics and with its problems.

The examples we have discussed give some idea of the relationship between the politics of liberalism in the 1840s and 1850s and the sudden growth of interest in cultural science after about 1850. In each case, to a greater or lesser degree, a perception of crisis in liberal politics contributed to a reevaluation of the liberal theoretical pattern in social science. The nature and consequences of each reevaluation varied, although we can speak loosely of two broad categories: those that resulted in a substantial break with the theoretical pattern as part of breaking radically with liberal ideology and those that led to modifications of the theoretical pattern as part of an attempt to buttress the framework of liberal ideology. In either case, the results were a fragmentation of liberal social science and a tendency to turn toward the concept of culture as a means of accomplishing the break or the modification. As we shall see later, a similar tendency to emphasize the culture concept appeared at the same time among the leading *Staatslexikon* social scientists.

This process continued into the period of national unification and the *Kaiser-*

reich. Before we trace it further, however, we must stop for a moment and consider various other contexts in which German cultural science developed. The political crisis of liberalism was certainly not the only factor that affected the new prominence of cultural studies after midcentury in Germany.

3

The Contexts of Cultural Science

When people like Riehl and Waitz became interested in cultural science after 1849, they were not, of course, moving into terra incognita. Not only were various ideas of culture a part, albeit a secondary part, of the theoretical pattern within which their ideas of social science had originally been framed, but the outlines of what would become the disciplines of the cultural sciences had begun to form in Germany and abroad. Ideas about culture had also been developed outside the liberal theoretical pattern, although their impact was as yet limited. Moreover, the larger contexts of academic organization, public opinion, political and social structure, and the economy within which the cultural sciences would emerge in the second half of the nineteenth century were forming as well.

Thus far, we have been concerned mainly with laying the foundation for central themes of this study: the development of cultural science from the fragmentation of the liberal theoretical pattern at midcentury and the relationship between that fragmentation and the crisis of political liberalism in Germany. We shall return to these in the next chapter. For the moment, however, we shall step to some extent outside the flow of the discussion to consider some of the intersecting contexts within which the developments we are examining took place. These contexts—intellectual, structural, and socioeconomic—are, of course, arbitrarily delineated. Any of them could, in another study, be considered not as context but as the central feature of the interpretation, and the political aspect on which we are concentrating could be relegated to its place. But because the main direction of the analysis is as it has been laid out, the most economical way of maintaining that direction while indicating the significance of other factors in the emergence of the cultural sciences is to treat these other factors as context.

The Intellectual Context

Many currents of thought—native and international—joined together in various ways after 1850 to form the intellectual context of cultural science in Germany. If we were to concentrate (as several historians of particular cultural sciences have) on the main recognized philosophical movements, we would see that major Enlightenment trends, post-Kantian idealism, Hegelianism, Comtean positivism, British political economy and utilitarianism all lent elements to the cultural sciences.[1] Some of these have already been discussed in the earlier analysis of the liberal theoretical pattern. Here, rather than considering these movements directly as influences, we shall see how some of them were taken—together with other sets of ideas—into the aggregations of concepts, modes of discourse, and personnel that eventually formed the organized *disciplines* of cultural science. We shall concentrate on academic fields that looked at culture primarily in its anthropological sense as opposed to culture as the product of higher sensibilities or education, although the distinction was not always clear in some of the disciplines.

Geography

Along with comparative philology, the cultural discipline that had obtained the firmest academic standing by midcentury was geography, a field in which Germans had made major contributions. From the beginning of the Age of Discovery, German mathematicians, cartographers, and geographical publishers had been in the vanguard of geographical science, and German naturalists had taken part in major voyages of discovery in the eighteenth century. The real foundations of geography as an academic discipline were laid in the first half of the nineteenth century, and a large part of those foundations were laid by Germans. The disciplinary structure of geography that had emerged by the 1860s not only produced a substantial amount of cultural research of itself, but it also acted as a model for other fields, particularly cultural anthropology.[2] The significance and the intellectual breadth of German geography in its formative years can be traced through the careers of three very different people: Alexander von Humboldt, Karl Ritter, and Wilhelm Perthes.

Alexander von Humboldt (1769–1859; the brother of Wilhelm) was the Napoleon of nineteenth-century natural science. Through his travels and writings, Humboldt added vast amounts of data about the earth and its inhabitants to general European knowledge. He served as a model for generations of explorers and travel writers, and he contributed significantly to the establishment of geology, physical geography, and meteorology as sciences.[3] His greatest influence on cultural science arose from his attempt to create a comprehensive intellectual structure within which all the phenomena of natural existence—the entire cosmos—could be explained. Physical geography—the relationships among geological formations, ocean currents, atmospheric and climatic conditions, and the like—constituted the framework within which living beings (including humans) played out their roles. These relationships could be comprehended only by understanding their totality. In his multivolume book *Kosmos*, which began to appear in 1845, Humboldt attempted to lay out his geographical science of totality.[4] He linked broad, often impressionistic generalizations to immense amounts of data about physical phenomena throughout the world. *Kosmos* was widely read and admired by cultural scientists at midcentury—in spite of the fact that, in terms of Humboldt's intentions, it was clearly a failure. His vision of the interconnectedness of all natural phenomena did not actually yield basic, underlying laws of natural existence, as Humboldt had claimed. It did not even lead to testable hypotheses on which a comprehensive natural science could be built.

Although Humboldt's attempts to define principles and interpretive techniques for geography were mostly dead-ends, his notion of the role of geography as the matrix into which the other sciences could be worked acquired almost paradigmatic status.[5] Geography was to be the science of the whole, the study of the natural environment that gave significance to the other disciplines. Geography's own method was to assemble the findings, deductive and empirical, of all relevant sciences; to delve into their interconnections; and to arrive thereby at grand statements of natural regularities or laws. All of this depended on accepting Humboldt's belief in the harmony of all things.

The Humboldtian "method" had important sources in the Enlightenment and was, to some degree, consistent with philosophical idealism, with *Naturphilosophie*, and with the empirical tradition of natural history. Its many intellectual connections gave it a very broad appeal, although from the standpoint of the increasingly accepted idea of science as hypothesis testing through experimentation, it also had many obvious deficiencies. Yet it was possible to make Humboldt's idea of geography as framework compatible even with rigorous sciences, such as physics, by considering the latter to be specialized contributors to knowledge, the overall pattern of which could only become apparent through the synthetic, partly intuitive methods of geography. This view was rejected by many cultural scientists, but it strongly influenced others in the latter part of the nineteenth century, especially Friedrich Ratzel.[6] Theories in which interactions between individuals or groups and their environments played an important role, including those of Herder and Darwin, were particularly easy to reconcile with Humboldtian geography.

Karl Ritter (1779–1859) was to all intents and purposes Germany's first professor of geography, although his chair at the University of Berlin was theoretically in history.[7] He was mainly responsible for organizing geography as an academic subject with its own curriculum and for regularizing the methods of geographical research according to German academic convention—in other words, for turning geography into Kuhnian "normal" science. His theoretical work was of secondary importance. Although as a follower of Herder, Ritter was interested in the relationship between human history and physical environment, most of his work was devoted to laying down, more systematically than Alexander von Humboldt had, the descriptive groundwork of physical geography in the form of what he called the comparative anatomy of the earth's surface. He proposed that differences between human societies could be explained systematically by differences in their physical environments. His aims, not his achievements, made him a cultural scientist. Several of his students saw their task, from the 1850s on, as the extension of Ritter's approach into the study of human society. Ritter left geography a small but accepted discipline in Germany's premier university.[8]

Wilhelm Perthes (1793–1853) was neither explorer nor academic, but he was an essential figure in the development of German scientific geography just the same.[9] He was the son of the founder of the large Gotha publishing house of Justus Perthes. Shortly after taking over the firm in 1816, Wilhelm made the decision to publish the *Hand-Atlas* of the cartographer Adolf Stieler, an expensive undertaking that made the reputation of his firm in geography. Perthes set another example by developing close relations with Ritter and other academic geographers and by encouraging travellers to publish accounts of their journeys with his firm. He began the process of developing ties also with other geographical publishers in Thuringia and Saxony, a process that created, after his death, an informal cartel dominated by the Perthes firm. The cartel facilitated the undertaking of expensive cartographical projects. It also created a major regional foundation for the expansion of geography as a science. Perthes and the other firms participated in the establishment of geographical societies, attracted writers like Andree and cartographers like August Petermann to direct such new geographical journals as *Globus* and *Petermanns Mitteilungen*, contributed to expeditions that the societies organized, and became crucial parts of a wider geographical and ethnological network, developed in the 1870s, that linked the publishers to the Saxon government and to the University of Leipzig.[10] More will be said about this network in later chapters.

By the late 1850s, then, German geography had the outlines of a theoretical pattern, incorporating a notion of its function (Humboldt's) and of its ultimate object of study (human culture, according to Ritter.) It had its founder-figures; it had a recognized, if minor, academic status; and it had the initial elements of disciplinary organization inside and outside the universities. But it was still merely the platform on which a science could be erected. The real work of theory building, of systematizing professional training, and of laying out boundaries around and within the field had yet to be done.

Ethnology

Ethnology was a barely recognizable discipline in Germany in the 1850s. Interest in it was advanced by the enthusiasm for cultural studies that appeared during that decade and because of the expansion of the field as an amateur intellectual enterprise in Britain and France.[11] It remained for some time a stepchild of geography. Major figures in the field, including Adolf Bastian, often considered themselves to be primarily geographers, and much of the early ethnological work in Germany was done in the context of Humboldtian holism.[12]

By the 1850s, much of the vocabulary associated with the comparative study of culture (the central activity of ethnology) had emerged, although the particular meanings of words in the vocabulary had not yet been fully fixed. We have discussed the multiple definition of *culture*—a word that did not become notably clearer in meaning in ensuing years. As is the case with most disciplines, the very existence of ethnology depended to some extent on practitioners' willingness to be somewhat vague about the exact delineation of what they were studying. The term *anthropology* could still be used, as we have seen, to refer to any empirical study of humankind. Mainly because of its usage in Britain and France, however, there was a tendency for the word to be employed particularly to refer to physical anthropology and its implications for culture.[13] The term *ethnology* was only a little more specific. It usually appeared at midcentury in its most common British usage—to refer to studies, like Waitz's, concerned with determining whether humans belonged to one or to many species and also where and when particular societies had arisen. It could also be used more broadly to refer to any study of exotic peoples—a connotation that anthropology did not yet possess. In either case, ethnology might include not just analyses of social, religious, and intellectual phenomena, but also the results of archaeology and physical anthropology.[14] Only gradually did the term come to refer to sociocultural studies only, and then mainly because of the adoption of particular names for other subfields. The word *Ethnologie* continued to be preferred, although not exclusively, by people adopting the theoretical pattern maintained by Virchow, Adolf Bastian, and the other pillars of the Berlin anthropological establishment after the 1860s—in other words, by adherents of what we shall shortly call neoliberal cultural science.[15] Increasingly, however, other people preferred the German word *Völkerkunde* for comparative cultural anthropology on an international scale. (*Völkerkunde* should not be confused with Riehl's idiosyncratic *Volkskunde*, which focused on the regional cultures of Germany.)[16]

Germans, without colonies to explore and govern, had played a subordinate part in the early history of ethnology, but not a negligible one. Alexander von Humboldt and, in the 1850s, Heinrich Barth (1821–1865) had become major figures in European exploration.[17] Barth's travels in northern Africa attracted attention among young university graduates of his generation eager for adventure, notoriety, and the scarce professorships that successful exploration might acquire for them. In addition, German-speaking scholars from the eighteenth century onward had contributed to comparative cultural study. The historian Christoph Meiners (1747–1810), for example, had proposed a universal history of humankind based on a comparative analysis of culture, in which "wild and barbarous" peoples as well as civilized ones were to be considered. Meiners did not, however, suggest how the needed information was to be collected and he did not complete his project.[18]

It is customary to perceive the actual beginnings of German ethnology in the work of Gustav Klemm.[19] In a series of books that he commenced publishing in the 1840s, Klemm assembled an immense amount of data about the material cultures and social patterns of peoples throughout the world. Although based on travellers' accounts, not field collection, Klemm's books remained major sources of data for many later ethnologists, including Waitz and E. B. Tylor.[20] His theoretical contributions were minor. He produced a stage theory of human cultural development that could be applied to contemporary peoples (his stages were savagery, domesticity, and freedom) and that figured among the set of such classifications that influenced later theories of social evolution. Otherwise, his theoretical constructions were important mainly because they gave later German cultural scientists something to attack. Klemm's approach to culture history was essentially racist. He argued that some physically defined races were active, others passive. The former were the originators of significant cultural advances and the latter were imitators. The most important of the active races was, not surprisingly, the Germanic.

Klemm's stage theory and his racism were far from unique in the 1840s and 1850s, as scholars interested in culture history attempted to bring together the findings of physical anthropology and philology.[21] Klemm's theoretical statements were in fact confused and not very convincing, but the general thrust of his analysis, backed by a large array of data, was clear enough. It was a direct challenge to the idea that people are basically the same; as such, it was something that people like Waitz, determined to maintain as many liberal assumptions as possible, had to counter with their own arguments, even while acknowledging the usefulness of Klemm's data.

Thus, although ethnology did not have a recognized organizational structure in Germany until 1869 (somewhat later than in Britain and France), it did have an intellectual existence, a vocabulary, and a body of literature which was in part German. Until the fad for culture studies of the 1850s, however, its role in intellectual life was quite minor. It was not the forgotten Meiners nor the ponderous Klemm who created effective ethnology in Germany, but people such as Waitz and Bastian.

Philology and Folklore

Outside the natural sciences, the discipline that developed most rapidly in Germany in the middle decades of the nineteenth century and that had the greatest impact on European thought was philology.[22] It was also the discipline that was most commonly identified as distinctly German in origin. The fashionable area of philological studies at midcentury, comparative philology, arose from the classical philology and biblical criticism of the eighteenth and early nineteenth centuries. These were fields that continued to follow a separate path of development in their own right—acting, among other things, as a major source of inspiration for the hermeneutic approach to understanding human intellectual life later associated with Dilthey.[23] But most of the cultural scientists whose work we shall examine opposed the hermeneutic approach. To them, comparative philology remained a science of the same generic sort as all others.

One of the reasons that philology emerged as a major academic field in the early nineteenth century was its connection to the educational reforms in Prussia after 1806. The ideologist of the reforms, Wilhelm von Humboldt (1867–1835), was himself both a classical philologist and one of the founders of comparative philology.[24] He insisted that humanistic higher education include a thorough grounding in the scientific study of language. Comparative philology also became popular because of its association with German nationalism during the war of liberation against Napoleon. Taking a cue from the discovery by William Jones of a linguistic connection between European and Indian languages, German philologists, such as Wilhelm von Humboldt and Jacob Grimm (1785–1863), worked out a linguistic identity for the Germanic languages as part of a more general process of identifying a German nationality. A close link between liberal nationalism and comparative philology existed throughout the first half of the nineteenth century as a series of brilliant German scholars, especially Franz Bopp (1791–1867), turned comparative philology into a major science in its own right.[25]

This link is most obvious in the work of Jacob Grimm and his brother Wilhelm (1786–1859), who not only laid the groundwork of Germanic philology but also began the systematic study of folklore (under the influence of Herder) by collecting and collating folktales in northern Germany.[26] The Grimms's work was quite explicitly nationalist and political in inspiration; they were attempting to recover the essence of German culture—and therefore of the *Volk*. Jacob Grimm was a moderate liberal throughout his career. He was one of the "Göttingen Seven" dismissed from their university teaching positions by the king of Hanover in 1837 for protesting the king's revocation of the Hanoverian constitution.

The development of folklore studies was, of course, an important element of the Romantic intellectual movement and a significant influence on the cultural sciences after midcentury. At least as important an influence, however, was the central discovery of German comparative philology: the Indo-European or Aryan language group. Working from Jones's original insight, the German philologists systematically uncovered the relationships in words and grammar between the Indo-European languages of Europe and Asia and inferred from them general rules of linguistic change.[27] From this it was only a step to inferring the existence of bearers of the Indo-European languages, an Aryan people whose prehistoric movement throughout Eurasia was suggested by the distribution of Indo-European linguistic traits. This movement could be correlated with the known migrations of peoples such as the Celts and Germans, in classical and postclassical times.

Not only did the philologists' discovery appear to offer a means of understanding previously unknowable portions of history and to provide a body of data against which broad theories of human cultural development could be tested, but it also contributed to the intellectual foundations of German nationalism. The international prestige German comparative philology attained rubbed off on the rest of German academia. Moreover, linking the German language (and by extension, German culture) to a larger family that also included Greek and Latin, and placing all of them in a historical sequence of presumably similar migrations, put the classical, Romance, and German cultures on the same basic plane. One could revere the memory of Arminius and reject French cultural snobbery while still subscribing to the classical enthusiasms of early nineteenth-century German humanism. Both the intellectual appeal of the Aryan hypothesis as a means of tying historical loose ends together and its political appeal to academic nationalists guaranteed for it a major place in the array of ideas popular among German intellectuals at midcentury.[28]

The methods of philology also contributed to the formation of a model of analysis and interpretation increasingly employed by cultural scientists later in the nineteenth century—a model according to which the regularities of human mental activity were seen to be immanent in the histories of peoples and in their frameworks of thought and expression.[29] Even among cultural scientists who did not adopt the hermeneutic approach, the model of philological analysis helped to modify and ultimately to replace stage theories of human development.

Archaeology and Prehistory

The study of the physical and structural remains of earlier humans was an intellectual enterprise that boomed—at first more as a hobby than anything else—throughout the Western world in the middle of the nineteenth century.[30] The antecedents to most of the major branches of archaeology and prehistory go back, of course, to the eighteenth century, but it was only in the middle of the nineteenth that they began to form themselves, like the other cultural sciences, into organized disciplines. For the most part, up until the 1850s, the major work in these fields was done in other countries: Britain, France, Italy, and the United States. But during the 1840s and 1850s, the Germans came into their own. As in Britain, so in Germany enthusiasts for regional history and for excavation of old sites put together local organizations. They were rewarded in 1857 by a discovery crucial to the establishment of human antiquity: the bones of Neanderthal man, which would probably not have been properly assessed a few years before in the absence of widespread knowledge of the interpretive problems of prehistory among educated people.[31]

In the 1850s, archaeology and prehistory also began to attract some of Germany's foremost minds, particularly that of Rudolf Virchow.[32] Virchow's interest—like that of other academics who began to involve themselves in archaeology at about the same time—was probably attracted by several different things. There was the fascination of discovering the origins of the world we know in the remains of worlds that we cannot know except from odd clues. One could say that this fascination was awakened by Romanticism, but if so, it was a general spirit common to large numbers of people in the modern world, including people as unromantic as Virchow. The same interest was enhanced when, again mostly in the 1850s, the results of early archaeology in exotic places like Mesopotamia, Egypt, and Middle America were presented to the educated public in a spate of illustrated books. But there was also, as we have seen, a political angle, in a very broad sense. Many of the leaders of archaeological thought in Britain, France, and Germany were deeply concerned with the question of human progress—what it was, how it took place, whether or not it was inevitable.[33] These were, of course, obvious questions to be asked in a rapidly changing society in which the problematic qualities of change itself were revealing themselves exactly at the time that "progress," in a material as well as moral sense, was being enshrined as the self-evident goal of social action. But they acquired particular importance at midcentury because of political issues centering around the question of progress.

In the specific case of Germany, the conditions under which archaeology developed included the aftermath of the 1848 revolution and the growth of ideologies in the 1850s and 1860s—some arising from liberal roots, others from political positions to the left and right of liberalism—that questioned the necessity and desirability of progress as liberals defined it. People such as Riehl, Rodbertus, and Marx, although they did not deny the inevitability of change, cast doubt in different ways on the liberal assumption that change in society was normally an improvement. Because such views were attached to positions in politics of real or potential strength, it was impossible to avoid them. As in other countries, liberal scholars and amateurs in Germany, including Virchow, were brought to take an interest in archaeology partly as a means of examining empirically the question of progress in the hope of demonstrating human advancement and explaining declines from earlier high points of civilization on grounds that were consistent with the liberal assumption of the overall improvability of humankind.[34] Because the evidence of archaeology cannot be interpreted by itself and requires the imposition of a theoretical framework, it was relatively easy to fit the data of early archaeology into a framework consistent with generic liberal ideas of progress. When the fashion for Darwinian theory appeared in the 1860s, Darwinian ideas could be readily adapted for the purpose. Civilizations and cultures in the past rose and fell because of their relative fitness in competition with others, but the overall progress of humankind was upward, toward material control of the environment, higher levels of personal morality, and freedom.[35]

Physical Anthropology

This study is concerned primarily with the self-consciously "cultural" sciences and therefore avoids much discussion of fields such as physical anthropology and racial studies whose practitioners considered themselves mainly to be natural scientists. In reality, of course, the line between physical anthropology and the disciplines that focus directly on culture is very finely drawn and hardly existed at all in the middle of the nineteenth century. Some of the most important figures in German anthropology, especially Virchow, worked in physical anthropology at least as much as in other fields and saw no clear distinction setting off the former. Others, including Waitz, who were not physical anthropologists still paid close attention to the field.[36]

They had good reason to do so. The development of systematic physical anthropology in the 1840s and 1850s and its close connections with the booming intellectual business of physiology represented a strong potential challenge to the assumptions of liberal ideology and of the liberal theoretical pattern—a challenge that could be enormously effective because it came from within a realm of physical science that many liberals held to be archetypal and legitimate.

The systematic classification of human skeletal remains, especially skulls, had made it possible to identify distinct physical types among the world's population. Although the existence of skeletal categories was subject to varying interpretations, there was a strong tendency in the middle of the nineteenth century to correlate the types with the language groups that the philologists had discovered in order to to produce a general racial picture of the distribution and early history of the world's population. Before the 1840s, although the concepts of race and racial difference had figured strongly in some social theories, the notion of race itself had been rather difficult to define. Now, however, the comparative anatomy of humans seemed to provide a definitional base stronger than any depending on skin color, social organization, or even language by itself.[37]

There appeared a number of systems of racial classification, first of Europeans and then of other peoples, which employed cranial categories (longheaded, broadheaded, etc.) as designators of central tendencies in the populations of people speaking languages of particular types. It was not difficult to progress from such systems to theories of prehistory. For example, both longheaded and broadheaded people with white skin could be found currently speaking German, the longheads clustered on the northern plains, the broadheads toward the Alps. One could easily hypothesize that the longheads were present as a result of the prehistoric migration of Aryan people who settled in the north and formed the Germans proper, whereas the broadheaded Germans resulted from intermarriage and the diffusion of language in the mountainous southern areas of Germany from which the original broadheads had not been dislodged. Physical anthropology seemed to offer a scientific way of discovering human prehistory and tying it up into neat packages. Moreover, if racial types were identified with particular arrays of cultural accomplishments and if it were assumed that different physical types had different mental capabilities, it was possible to arrive at a racial explanation for human progress. Some races, for reasons associated with their physical and mental characteristics, were more capable of advancement than others. Some races (not surprisingly, usually the Aryan ones) were thus the bearers of progress.[38]

These ideas became extremely important, especially for liberals, in the middle of the nineteenth century. They were superficially consistent with the liberal pattern of human science. They focused on the characteristics of individuals and they related those characteristics directly to the histories of the larger groups to which individuals belonged. They identified a group (the race) that was itself defined by measurable central tendencies in the traits of individuals; if those traits were held to include rationality, the race became almost the ideal collectivity of discrete individuals. Physical anthropology also fitted liberal notions of nomothetic science because it proceeded from empirical observation to classification and measurement to the drawing up of laws that related race to social behavior. Even before the advent of Darwinism, the idea of race inferred from physical anthropology had led to theories of social and historical change.[39]

Yet the conclusions reached by physical anthropologists profoundly disturbed many liberals because they challenged the validity of widely held theories about humans and society and the specific assumptions on which the theories were founded. Physical anthropology, for instance, was often taken to support a polygenist view of human origins, the view that the human races were separate species with separate ancestors. Its overt materialism greatly bothered liberals like Waitz who believed in the moral autonomy of individuals, which could only be maintained by postulating some sort of basic nonmaterial element in the composition of individual humans.[40] But even more disturbing were the political implications of physical anthropology.

The question of slavery, a crucial issue for liberals throughout America and Europe in the 1850s and 1860s, became directly connected to questions of physical anthropology. If the polygenetic implications of physical anthropology were correct, a scientific basis existed for the enslavement of "inferior" races by "superior" ones. This kind of argument was widely employed by apologists for slavery in the United States. Waitz, as we saw, confronted polygenism by weighing the evidence of physical anthropology, finding it not wrong but inconclusive, and holding up against it his ethnological interpretation of the evidence about human culture to demonstrate the unity of humankind.[41] Confronting the descendant of the scientific argument for slavery as justification for racial discrimination in the United States many years later, Franz Boas attacked the basic assumptions that made social inference from physical evidence possible by arguing for the radical mutability of human anatomy under changing social and environmental circumstances—in other words, for the primacy of culture over anatomy.[42] These were not simply forays into anthropology by people interested in knowledge for its own sake or intrigued by the interpretive problems posed by physical anthropology. These were the reactions of liberals concerned about the political consequences of interpreting physical anthropology in a certain way.

Slavery was probably the most important political issue (even in Germany) on which the findings of physical anthropology touched in the 1850s and early 1860s, not only because of its significance for the future of the liberal political experiment of the United States, but also because it displayed potential contradictions in liberal ideology. But other issues became important, especially in the dual context of Germany's unification and the spread of Darwinian ideas in the late 1860s and 1870s. The tendency to equate nations with races and to identify the resulting conflated entities with the active units of natural selection produced a bewildering array of theories of international relations, the main effect of which was to provide "scientific" bases for arguments in favor of nationalist aggression (or, as in the case of France after 1871, explanations for military failure.)[43] Extreme nationalism was a serious problem for liberalism in its competition with its ideological rivals from the 1860s onward, again in part because the basic notions of nationalism arose within the liberal tradition itself. Antiliberal politicians who favored the hereditary nobility or the autocratic state could use extreme nationalist arguments to attack parliamentary and participatory government on the grounds that these weakened Germany in her competition with other races. Rudolf Virchow, as we shall see, was moved to perform some of his most spectacular work in physical anthropology by disgust at political uses that had been made of the discipline (especially by Frenchmen attacking Germany) in the 1870s.[44]

The employment of racialist ideas in German politics in the late nineteenth century continued to produce problems for liberals and for social scientists. We shall consider these matters in later chapters, although the emphasis will continue to be on cultural science, not on physical anthropology or on the racialist theoretical patterns that continued to develop from the 1850s.[45] To some degree, most of the cultural scientists with whom we shall be dealing considered themselves to be opponents of racialism, that is, of the attempt to assert the primacy of biologically defined race as the organizing principle of social and historical understanding. On the other hand, most of them continued to show the utmost respect for physical anthropology, in part because it was more obviously classifiable as a science in the sense of physical science than almost anything else that touched on cultural studies. And they were quite clear that what they practiced was science.

History

One of the most profound intellectual influences on cultural science in Germany—indeed, one of the most profound influences on social studies throughout the world in the nineteenth century—was the emergence of professional "scientific" history and its various subdisciplines. Later chapters will give considerable attention to two of these subdisciplines—historical economics and cultural history—but a brief overview of the whole field is needed here.

Systematic or scientific German historiography did not spring full grown from the head of Leopold von Ranke (1795–1886), neither did the idea that history was the context within which society must be understood. The German Enlightenment possessed a significant historical element, one that was greatly enhanced by the Romantic enthusiasm for history in the early nineteenth century.[46] Although conservatives often accused liberals of being ahistorical, in fact the idea of careful historical research into primary sources that grew up in Germany in the early nineteenth century was found as widely among liberal historians as it was among any others. And although Ranke, the most influential formulator of the rules for the scientific use and citation of primary sources, was an avowed conservative, many of his predecessors and students were liberals. Moreover, the Rankean revolution in historiography was not the only significant development in the field in the early and middle years of the nineteenth century. Other developments, such as the study of legal history, also cut across political lines. Liberal social scientists, such as Welcker, frequently employed historical arguments as bases for their theoretical assertions.[47]

Vormärz liberal historiography can be illustrated by one of its most distinguished practitioners, Friedrich Dahlmann (1785–1860), the teacher of W. H. Riehl and a leader of moderate, constitutionalist liberalism in northern Germany before 1848.[48] Like Jacob Grimm, Dahlmann was one of the "Göttingen Seven" of 1837, and he eventually served as a leader of the right-wing liberals at the National Assembly in 1848. His historical work clearly revealed his political concerns. His specialty was constitutional history, and his major books on the French and English revolutions, published in the 1840s, were intended to demonstrate the virtues of limited, constitutional monarchy for the German states. But Dahlmann's academic work was not simply an extension of his politics. He devoted much of his life to the identification of primary sources for German history in the belief that accuracy in research was essential to making history applicable to the solution of contemporary problems. Dahlmann was interested in the cultural peculiarities of nations. He argued that laws could not be entirely the products of rational lawgivers working from the universal principles of human behavior. The laws of a nation had to recognize, alongside universal rights and characteristics, the particular geographical, economic, and cultural circumstances of a nation. The most effective way to understand the elements of a contemporary society was to study its history.

The differences between Dahlmann and Ranke, or for that matter between those two and other leading historians of the period 1830–1860, did not lie in disagreements about the importance of basing research on the systematic analysis of accurate primary data. They lay instead in differing conceptions of the meaning of history and the purposes that historical research was supposed to achieve—purposes that were sometimes, although not always, delineated by politics and that were more sharply defined in response to political and social change from the late 1840s onward.

For Ranke, an avowed conservative, history provided some inkling of the will of God, which could be obtained by studying every historical period as the equal of all others. The Rankean view tended to counter liberal ideas about inevitable progress and about comprehending change in the human condition through understanding natural law—although Ranke did actually take something like a nomological position. Even if the plan for humankind were not entirely knowable and did not reveal itself in Hegelian fashion through the unfolding of human reason, the plan still existed and could be partly perceived.[49]

For Dahlmann, history provided an understanding of the broad context of modern politics and legislation, thus allowing correct decisions to be made. Dahlmann, although in general a believer in the eventual progress of humankind, was not as insistent about tying his historical research to a progressive framework or a stage theory of history as, for example, Welcker was. Finding social laws in history was much less important than applying them to discrete problems of political interpretation. Within an intellectual framework closely connected to the liberal theoretical pattern in social science, Dahlmann emphasized the nomological aspect of the pattern more than the nomothetic.[50]

Other historians and social scientists took positions on history that corresponded to the liberal theoretical pattern. Welcker, for instance, had never believed that society, law, and politics could be understood without reference to history. Much of his own work was historical. He did, however, more than Dahlmann and much more than Ranke, accept the idea that the laws of society and of historical progress could be understood through empirical research and inference from human rationality. One of the purposes of historical study was to identify these laws and thereby to predict the future. To Welcker, as to Dahlmann, history was an intellectual activity that enhanced both political liberalism and social science—for instance, by accounting for political differences between peoples.[51]

All of these viewpoints—those represented by Dahlmann and Welcker that were closely linked to liberalism and to liberal social science as well as the more conservative view of Ranke—had profound influences on the emergence of the cultural sciences, as we shall see in later chapters. Although Ranke, Dahlmann, and Welcker all concerned themselves strongly with politics and international relations as key subjects of historical research, none of them ignored the importance of the broader social structure and culture within which politics operated. Dahlmann influenced Riehl in the 1850s. People interested in correcting perceived deficiencies in liberal social science could look to Dahlmann for a model of how to place historical and cultural factors in a context that explained individuality in political history. Ranke's influence was more complex. He advocated techniques of research and analysis that could be used within practically any academic theoretical pattern regardless of political affiliation.[52] Historically oriented cultural science later in the century adhered, on the whole, scrupulously to Rankean rules of evidence. But Ranke's own concern for cultural factors in relation to politics was generally lost from view by much of the historical profession—especially by the self-professed liberals who founded the Prussian historical school in the middle decades of the century.

Prussian-school historians, like Droysen, followed the lead of Wilhelm von Humboldt in casting doubt on the nomothetic possibilities of history (although, like Dahlmann, they accepted the assumption that history was patterned in some rational way). In this, they laid the groundwork for a hermeneutic view of human studies that was profoundly antagonistic to most of the cultural sciences that emerged from the reexamination of the liberal theoretical pattern in the years after 1848. The Prussian historians focused narrowly on politics as the arena of free human action, largely unencumbered by cultural context. When the hermeneutic approach was broadened under the influence of Dilthey and others in the last quarter of the century in order to encompass a wide range of cultural factors, there was a gap between Dilthey's kind of *Kulturwissenschaft* and the disciplines with which this study is mainly concerned.[53]

Another development in historiography that affected all the social (and later the cultural) sciences in Germany was the approach to legal history established by F. K.

von Savigny (1779–1861).[54] Savigny, from 1810 professor of Roman law at the University of Berlin, attempted to demonstrate that laws are not created by reasoning from abstract principles but rather form over time from the activities of the people who comprise a nation. Basic legal principles can be derived from studying earlier laws (e.g., Roman law), but only if the particular circumstances that gave rise to those laws are understood through accurate historical research that encompasses a wide range of cultural factors. Savigny helped to explode the traditional view of Roman law as the objective foundation for rational, universal law. At the same time, Savigny refused to worship past precedent as immutable. Rational change was possible and often desirable, but it had to be undertaken on the basis of systematic, scientific historical research. Savigny was even more insistent than Welcker and Dahlmann about the need for basing social science on history and about training officials in historical research. The rigorous examination of the past was the bridge between empiricism and deductive rationalism in social science.

Although Savigny took part in the reform of the Prussian educational system, he generally stayed out of politics. His most renowned successor, Rudolf von Gneist (1816–1895), on the other hand, was one of the major leaders of right-wing liberalism throughout his career.[55] Gneist added a comparative dimension to Savigny's notion of historical scholarship as the basis of legal understanding and reform. He also deliberately structured his scholarship as an elaborate defense of moderate liberalism, supporting the ideas of gradual progress through individual freedom, constitutional monarchy, and representative institutions. Gneist was one of the founders of the National Liberal party and was probably its most consistent and influential ideologist throughout the Bismarckian period. Together with his mentor Savigny, he helped to maintain the orientation of German social science toward history.

Two other fields of history—historical economics and cultural history—became major subdisciplines in the 1850s in large part through the work, respectively, of Wilhelm Roscher and the Swiss Jacob Burckhardt. Historical economics became the most important approach to economic science in Germany and was closely connected to developments in the cultural sciences. Although its relationship to other cultural sciences was in some ways ambiguous, cultural history, nevertheless, affected and was influenced by them. Both fields rejected the narrow focus on politics that characterized the Prussian historical school. We shall discuss these subdisciplines in chapter 10.[56]

Culture Around 1860

In its third edition, the *Staatslexikon* for the first time included an article on "*Cultur*."[57] The article was written by the prominent Saxon liberal journalist and politician Karl Biedermann, presumably as a result of his growing interest in the concept of culture as a tool of social understanding. Biedermann was by no means a practicing cultural scientist and contributed nothing original to any of the cultural disciplines, but he was an intelligent amateur whose social thinking was shaped by the liberal theoretical pattern and reshaped by his experience of politics from 1848 to the time he wrote the article in the late 1850s. His article can, therefore, serve as an indication of the state of thinking about culture among educated, liberally oriented laypeople at the end of the first period of enthusiasm for cultural science.

Biedermann starts by making a categorical distinction between the realm of nature and that of culture. Nature is the physical universe, ruled by blind, necessary forces that are understood by humans as regular repetitions of phenomena. Culture, on the other hand is "everything . . . that is created by the higher spiritual powers of humans."[58] Laws in the cultural realm are many-sided and ever-changing. Humankind lives in both of these realms; it has created culture to tame nature. Human ability to do this is the result of unique psychological endowments: people can think and, therefore, can draw general laws from their perceptions. Because of their capacity for speech, humans can cooperate with each other in many complex ways, which is how they are able to create culture and shape nature. "Without speech, there would be no culture, no progress of the human race and without it no history, for history is the transference of steady cultural progress from race to race."[59] Culture adjusts itself to geographical circumstances because those circumstances represent the specific conditions of nature with which culture works.

Thus far, Biedermann has managed to combine several different approaches of midcentury cultural scientists and has (perhaps unwittingly) revealed some problems and inconsistencies in them. He has differentiated between the subjects of physical and cultural science without dealing with the implications of the difference for methodology. He has tried to integrate the Herderian emphasis on geographical adaptation as the key to culture with a claim, like Waitz's, that culture is universal among humans, progresses continually, and is passed from one people or another. He has, in other words, tried to combine elements of what would shortly be called diffusionism and evolutionism without confronting the logical incompatibilities between the positions. The same sort of problem is present in Biedermann's adherence to the notion of universal human rationality and its manifestation in language. How can this notion be made compatible with the idea of culture as adaptation to geographical circumstances?

Biedermann's distinction between nature and culture seems to suggest the position taken later by Dilthey and the advocates of *Geisteswissenschaft*—a position already formulated by the physicist Hermann von Helmholtz and one that would be rejected by most cultural scientists in the disciplines on which this study concentrates. But Biedermann does not in fact go that far. He uses the vocabulary of natural science ("law," "regularity," etc.) to refer to the study of culture. What the term *law* can mean in a sphere of existence characterized (according to Biedermann) by individual freedom and the ability of peoples to change in various ways is never clarified, but Biedermann seems to assume that laws in each sphere, although specifically different, have some sort of generic similarity. On the whole, the cultural scientists of the latter part of the nineteenth century, although they also frequently made use of the nature–culture distinction in one form or another, were equally unwilling to follow its logic in the direction of radically separating cultural studies from physical science. One thing that does seem to be clear at the start of Biedermann's discourse is that he is using the term *culture* in its anthropological sense. According to Biedermann, both the "highest" and the "lowest" accomplishments of humans find their places in culture.[60]

But no, even this clarity is soon dispelled when Biedermann, following a vaguely evolutionist argument, says that in a "narrow sense" one can differentiate *Kultur-völker* from other peoples if one defines culture as the highest of activities of the human mind (science, art, polite social life, etc.). He takes it as given that these traits are inherently "higher" than others and that the extent to which they are present among particular peoples can be immediately detected by observers.[61] Nevertheless, Biedermann also says that in a "broader sense" all people have culture. It is merely that *Naturvölker* (presumably those people who are not *Kulturvölker*) are at the "lowest levels" of cultural life. This definitional confusion could perhaps be accepted (because it mirrors a familiar linguistic confusion in the use of the word *culture*) if Biedermann could state clear criteria for assessing relative advancement in culture among peoples, thereby using his two categories of peoples as end points of a classificatory or evolutionary continuum. But in fact Biedermann cannot. He rejects the notion that high culture equates to the presence of abstract idealism in a people's philosophical thought, he indicates that progress can take radically different forms among different peoples (partly for environmental reasons but also because humans, being free, can make collective "mistakes" that influence their development), and he opposes the tendency (which he associates with Hegel) to impose an a priori pattern on the process of cultural change.[62] The best he can do, however, is to suggest a few a priori patterns of his own when he tries (as a liberal) to show that the most advanced cultures are those that have developed around concepts of individual freedom, which thus becomes both the criterion and the end of cultural development. Biedermann—a convinced nationalist—also claims that the most advanced cultures are those belonging to the German *Volkstum*.[63]

Biedermann's article, which also discusses a number of the emerging subdisciplines of cultural science, is interesting as a summary of current views of culture. It includes some basic ideas that would remain part of the theoretical equipment of the cultural sciences (the *Kulturvölker—Naturvölker* distinction, for instance) and some of the theoretical problems with which cultural scientists would wrestle for the next century.

The Structural Context

Patterns of ideas exist and develop in contexts that extend beyond the realm of intellect—perhaps beyond even the exchange of ideas between individual persons through language and symbol. Apart from the broad social context of class, generation, sex, and ethnic group, there is also a more specific context of institutions, patterns of day-to-day and life cycle behavior defined by institutions, and the organized exercise of power that strongly influences the thinking of individuals. We can call this the *structural* context. One specific aspect of structure—politics— is of special concern to this study, but for the moment we shall consider a range of aspects of the structural context in which cultural science developed in nineteenth-century Germany.

Academia

Most of Germany's leading cultural scientists were academics. That is, they were employed in universities or university-related institutions or else they were qualified to be so employed and, in many cases, wanted to be.[64] Other university-educated people participated (usually as amateurs) in scientific organizations and collected data in many fields of cultural science, but the core of the enterprise consisted of university academics. It is necessary, therefore, to focus on the setting in which the latter spent their lives.

In the nineteenth century, the German universities attained a position of enormous prestige throughout the world. They showed great flexibility in responding to new currents of thought in intellectual life; they generated many new disciplines and modes of inquiry; and, for better or worse, they largely created the institutional ethic that continues to surround the academic profession.[65]

There was a certain hierarchy among German universities, partially determined by the reputations of their professors and by the extent of state support. The University of Berlin, founded early in the nineteenth century as part of Prussia's recovery from the shock of defeat by the French, was generally the best-supported university and quickly became the most prestigious as well as being, certainly in the first half of the century, the most significant locus of intellectual and academic innovation. The seminar, in its classical form, was largely pioneered there. Older universities, Prussian and non-Prussian, sooner or later followed the lead of Berlin.[66]

The universities continued to retain their traditional division into faculties of theology, medicine, law, and philosophy. The first three generally maintained a large degree of coherence between their organizational structures and what they taught, despite arguments over theory. But the philosophical faculties—still supposedly colleges of general philosophers with, at most, specialties in particular fields—were the focal points of the disciplinary explosion of the nineteenth century and of the consequent fragmentation of knowledge. Although they still functioned as administrative entities by the end of the century, they had largely broken down as contexts of scholarly exchange and identification. They were not replaced by departments, as in America, but the individual disciplines that emerged within the philosophical faculties build up a bewildering array of organizational fixtures: seminars, institutes, laboratories, and the like. In some ways, this probably contributed to maintaining the flexibility, and thus the innovativeness, of German academia. A professor, once appointed to a philosophical faculty, was free to experiment, to move around from field to field, to follow an interest in a new area by becoming a specialist in it—thereby introducing it to the university curriculum. Many of the cultural sciences emerged in this way.[67]

The fragmentation of the philosophical faculties and of the idea of a single generic "philosophy" was widely decried within the universities, no less by many of the people doing the fragmenting than by others. Apart from a natural distaste for change within a tradition-minded institution, the main reason for this negative view of what was going on was the general acceptance within the universities of a legitimating ethic for philosophical study that seemed to be threatened on all sides—by the idea of technical education as well as by disciplinary fragmentation.[68] The core of the ethic was Wilhelm von Humboldt's theory of liberal education. In addition to his focus on philology, Humboldt had combined a justification for a general education in classics and philosophy (the traditional function of philosophical faculties) with an advocacy of research in a particular subject as a device for educating the intellect and character. He saw all of these as means of producing the cultured individuals who ought to rule society. Professional training in the other faculties was supposed to build on prior humanistic education and was, even within those faculties, supposed to follow the same general principles by emphasizing the well-rounded individual and the educational value of research.[69]

As we have seen, Humboldtian humanism had immense appeal for intellectuals and was fairly readily adaptable to a variety of ideological stances—especially nondemocratic forms of liberalism that emphasized freedom of intellect and political careers open to *Bildung* and talent. It could be set against rule by the masses or by hereditary elites without alienating either group because humanistic education was supposed to be available to everyone of ability, regardless of birth.[70]

The almost-universal adoption of the Humboldtian ideal as the legitimating ideology of the universities had significant effects. It identified the philosophical faculties as the conscious centers of university life and it made the fashions that appeared in them the trendsetters not only for the rest of the university faculties, but also for the intellectual world in general. The ethos of university humanism was brought by former students with them into the "real" world. Those graduates who hoped eventually to qualify for university chairs maintained an especially close allegiance to the humanistic ideal in their other activities, such as journalism. It was also incumbent on people trained in the natural sciences to adopt a proper appreciation of the virtues of classical education. This, as we shall see, affected the writings of such a significant figure as Friedrich Ratzel, who lacked a humanistic education and bent over backwards to try to make up for it.[71]

Later in the century, with the growth of the industrial economy's demand for managers, technicians, and engineers, the humanistic ideal in education came to appear increasingly out of touch with social reality. Not surprisingly, the academic guardians of the ideal tended to become defensive and bitter about social reality. It became fashionable after about the 1860s for the opinion leaders in the philosophical faculties to adopt a kind of Romantic antimodernist position on economic and social change, decrying the threat of industrialization and mass society to the values inherent in Western civilization and German culture. Nietzsche and Paul de Lagarde were but the best-known exponents of this view. Because the antimodernist fashion was so predominant, even university faculty members who worked in fields entirely compatible with modernity (such as the physical sciences) tended to adopt the fashion at least to some degree. This was especially true of people in cultural or other social sciences that were not too firmly established and needed legitimation in the university setting.[72]

Given the structures of the German universities, it was almost inevitable that the people who developed the cultural science disciplines were viewed initially—indeed, viewed themselves—as specialists in other fields who extended their efforts into cultural studies. We have seen that Karl Ritter, although in fact the first real professor of geography at a German university, was officially a professor of history and commenced his career teaching historical and philosophical subjects.[73] Waitz taught in a wide variety of fields at Marburg, arriving at the study of culture only comparatively late in his short career. Virchow belonged to the medical faculty;[74] so did Wilhelm Wundt initially. Wundt took his transfer to the philosophical faculty on moving to the University of Leipzig very seriously and regarded himself as a philosopher rather than a psychologist.[75] The presumption that the cultural sciences were organizationally as well as intellectually linked with other fields remained strong even when geography, anthropology, and culture history started to present themselves as separate disciplines with their own students.

Two significant consequences arose from this situation. First, the task of defining the cultural-science disciplines as autonomous fields could not be as effectively undertaken in the universities as it could outside through the creation (largely by academics) of membership organizations that extended well beyond academia. Once identified in this way, disciplines could be fairly readily recognized within the universities. Equally important was the second effect: the tendency for strong links between cultural sciences and their mother disciplines to be maintained and to influence the directions taken in cultural theory. One of the reasons that German cultural science acquired a strong historical cast was the fact that some of the major figures in the development of the cultural sciences were historians. History also, of course, as we saw earlier in this chapter, occupied a high place in the intellectual pecking order of the philosophical faculties. The constant reference by cultural scientists to classical philosophy shows, among other things, their continued sense of continuity with their academic origins.

By the second quarter of the nineteenth century, a distinct career pattern for university professors and aspirants had developed, a pattern that was largely uniform but that involved special twists for people who followed new fields, such as the cultural sciences.[76] After taking their doctorates in one of the faculties, would-be academics would begin a lengthy, unpaid apprenticeship as they prepared their first major postdissertation scholarly work. Like predoctoral studies, studies for this second educational stage (*Habilitation*) usually involved considerable movement from university to university. In a new or controversial field it was sometimes necessary to find a faculty that would agree to accept the *Habilitationsschrift*. Furthermore, in order to explore a new field (such as anthropology), it was necessary to work with some of the relatively few professors who taught the subject. There was, therefore, apart from the obvious factor of varying state support for new subjects, a strong tendency for certain universities to attract most of the senior students and postgraduates interested in such subjects.

Regardless of where a person had been "promoted" to his doctorate or where he had found a faculty to habilitate him, he was almost certain to have spent time at one or more of the recognized centers of his discipline. In the cultural sciences with which we are concerned here, that meant Berlin or Leipzig. Often, of course, the people who moved into cultural-science fields did so because they had been studying something else at one of the main centers of cultural science and had, by talking to other students or attending lectures out of curiosity, become fascinated with questions of culture.

Probably only a minority of the people who started to study a cultural-science subject with the intention of making an academic career actually habilitated. Intellectual burnout, lack of talent, changing interests, the need to make a living quickly, all played their parts. Following habilitation came a lengthy period in which candidates who were lucky or able enough to receive university appointments (which were very few in cultural-science fields until late in the century) had to teach without official salary. The unpaid habilitation period and the unsalaried apprenticeship of the *Privatdozenten* meant that unless prospective academics had private means, it was unlikely that they could even hope for a regular income until well into their thirties. The prospect was too discouraging for many, who left the university to teach school or to seek nonacademic jobs.

The nature of this academic career pattern had a substantial effect on shaping the cultural sciences—indeed, on shaping the social sciences in general. The fierce competition for a small number of university positions encouraged aspiring academics to try to make names for themselves—sometimes by taking unorthodox positions in scholarly disputes (which involved the danger of offending established scholars) and sometimes (in anthropology and geography) by field research in exotic places (which involved the, perhaps, equally serious danger of early death). Cornelia Essner has demonstrated that a large proportion of the famous German travellers in Africa during the second half of the nineteenth century—including Heinrich Barth, Georg August Schweinfurth, and Gerhard Rohlfs—were people motivated initially by a desire to make an academic career.[77] This was significant because field research did not become a prerequisite to an academic career in anthropology in Germany. The need of some impecunious young anthropologists to make a splash in public helped to bridge the gap between the theoreticians and the field ethnographers. From the late 1870s onward, it also meant that explorers sought to make the most of the political prominence that the growth of imperialist enthusiasm thrust upon them.

Journalism

The uncertainties of young academics' prospects also pushed many of them into journalism. In the first half of the nineteenth century, writing for periodicals was still largely an activity undertaken by educated people for educated people. In 1848, there was a sudden burgeoning of more popular political journalism, and although this had diminished in the 1850s, the period from the 1860s onward saw a proliferation of the types and levels of journalistic activity.[78] The newspaper business could be very profitable, and although most of the profits went to the owners, educated university graduates with appropriate credentials and something to say could make a living by writing newspaper articles, pieces for monthlies, and popular books without sacrificing their academic reputation. For junior academics trying to eke out a living while waiting for greater things, it was a way to get by and get ahead. The habit of journalism was difficult to break, and many continued to be active journalists long after they had established themselves as professors.[79] Some, such as Max Weber and Friedrich Ratzel, thought it gave them power. For others, those who could not stick the academic course, journalism was an alternative career.

The link between academia and the public world created by journalism was a factor in the change of theoretical patterns in the social sciences. By engaging in journalism, academics were inevitably drawn to politics and to political issues, which were the meat of the kind of middle-class-oriented journalism in which they were engaged. Involvement in politics opened their thinking to a broader array of influences than they had experienced as students. They found it necessary to adjust their expressed opinions to the editorial positions of the periodicals for which they wrote. They found it expedient to take into account ideas that would appeal to large groups of readers and to powerful sponsors. At the same time, they might believe, in turn, that they were influencing such people with their own higher perceptions of things. They had to pay attention to the systems of images, words, ideas, and beliefs within which politics were framed—in a word, to ideology. The most successful academic journalists were those who could take the existing elements of ideologies and shape them to the needs of the moment, revising them in the process. Such people were extremely useful to the active personnel of political parties, economic interest groups, nonpartisan political organizations—even to governments and state ministries. In other words, journalism as practiced by academics and would-be academics created a structure within which ideas, images, and assumptions could, and naturally did, travel back and forth between the realm of the university and the realm of politics. Although the central role of academics in the leadership of political parties diminished substantially in the second half of the nineteenth century, that decline was balanced by the vast extension of middlebrow journalism.[80]

The journalism practiced by academics in the social and cultural sciences often involved questions of theory, for to the reading public and to editors, the whole point of articles by certified academics was to apply academic expertise to issues of current significance—an expertise defined primarily as knowledge of the theoretical framework within which particular questions could be placed. Even when academics were writing outside of their particular area of expertise (e.g., on the international situation), they could assume the right to pronounce authoritatively on the grounds of their acquaintance with the ideal or theoretical nature of social phenomena in general.[81] This meant that theories in the social sciences had a strong tendency to be deployed for political analysis and argumentation, and they were often modified in the process.[82] In addition, ideas from the world of politics and ideology could readily be transmitted through journalism to the world of theory construction, especially in the social and cultural sciences. During the first half of the nineteenth century, such transmission tended to be structured by the liberal theoretical pattern. After the middle of the century, however, as liberalism faced its continuous political crisis and the liberal theoretical pattern fragmented, the situation became much more complicated.

Extra-academic Organizations

For the reasons previously discussed, it was often necessary for a new discipline to have achieved some sort of definition at least partly outside the universities before it was accorded complete faculty acceptance. In the case, for example, of cultural anthropology, although lecture courses in aspects of the subject were given in the late 1850s at some universities, the full emergence of the discipline had to await the formation of regional and national anthropological associations in the late 1860s and early 1870s. We shall see an example of this in chapter 5 when we discuss the formation of the *Berliner Gesellschaft für Anthropologie, Ethnologie und Urgeschichte* and its attendant network of anthropological interests extending deeply into the University of Berlin.[83] The activities of the network and the political standing of its leaders were largely responsible for the appointment of regular professors of anthropology at the university in the 1890s. A similar process occurred at the University of Leipzig, where the involvement of the university in the sciences of culture arose partly from the formation in Saxony and Thuringia of a network of disciplinary organizations with contacts in government and business.[84]

The establishment of both formal organizations and networks of people concerned with the study of culture was one of the reasons that certain disciplines survived more or less intact, whereas others changed or disappeared. The disciplines embodied in the *Berliner Gesellschaft für Anthropologie, Ethnologie und Urgeschichte* (physical anthropology, ethnology, and archaeology) were defined as separate sections of the general anthropological enterprise, and so they remained. *Völkerpsychologie*, however, although it had its own journal, did not have its own interest organization at the national level. It eventually was swallowed up, or rather torn apart, by the burgeoning discipline of psychology and the better-organized field of ethnology. The fact that archaeology in Germany remained allied with anthropology rather than with history stems in part from the accidental circumstances of its extra-academic organization, not from its position within the structures of universities where, as parts of the general subject "philosophy," the fields of ethnology, archaeology, and history could have formed any number of relationships.[85]

Government and Politics

Political institutions are, of course, central to the subject that this study addresses because they are the organizational frameworks within which ideologies develop and operate. Because of the massive changes that occurred in the structures of government and politics in Germany in the nineteenth century and because the subject is so vast in any case, it is impractical even to outline this element of the structural context of cultural science. Specific connections between aspects of cultural science and particular political circumstances are discussed throughout the following chapters. A few general remarks are, however, in order, some of which extend well beyond midcentury.

The links between academics and the state administrations continued after 1848 to be shaped by ambiguities similar to those we have already observed. University instructors were state employees and had to give some thought (especially if they were junior) to how their writings would be received by educational authorities. At the same time, bureaucratic oversight of the professional activities of academics, and even over their political activities, was less oppressive than it might have been.[86] Both academics and government officials really did take seriously the idea of academic freedom. There were limits. In the latter part of the century, it was almost impossible to be a member of the Social Democratic party and pursue an academic career.[87] One could, however, be almost anything else short of a socialist.

The connection to the state governments could work in the opposite direction. After the 1840s, the role of social science professors as the prime experts in policy fields diminished somewhat (in part because the universities had produced so many fully-qualified civil servants who could do their own thinking). But interaction between professors and state officials remained significant. They shared similar backgrounds and outlooks, and members of each group had something to gain from serious association with the other. Professors achieved influence on policy, and officials could arrogate to themselves some of the prestige of the intellectual elite. The economist Gustav Schmoller, founder of the *Verein für Sozialpolitik*, was the acknowledged master of this game from the 1870s, but there were many other fine players, including Rudolf Virchow.[88]

The relationship between social scientists and extragovernmental political organizations (parties, interest groups, etc.) was vastly more complex and individualized than the relationship to government, and it changed more drastically after Germany's unification. Some academics—many more of them after the 1860s than before—avoided partisan politics altogether, although as we shall see, many of these in fact adopted a well-defined political stance even in their nonpartisanship.[89] Most of the important German cultural scientists before the 1880s were at some time involved in politics, and although political interest probably diminished thereafter, it did not disappear. We have already discussed political participation through journalism, which remained the major way in which academics were led to take ideological positions and to relate them to current issues.

Academics were also active in political parties, even though after the 1840s their domination of the liberal movement came to an end. As more or less modern parties were organized in the 1860s and 1870s and as nonliberal national parties appeared, the unique role in political life played by liberal academics naturally was reduced in scope, and many academics felt the loss.[90] But especially in the National Liberal, Progressive, and Center parties, the professoriate was still a significant element of the leadership group—in part because of its enormous prestige, in part because those parties remained rooted in local organizations dominated by people distinguished in nonpolitical fields. Some professors, such as Rudolf Virchow, exercised substantial power at the national level. We shall see, however, that the tendency in the late nineteenth century was for professors and other academics increasingly to look, not to the regular parties, but to new extraparty political organizations as places where they could exercise leadership. Within the parties, they increasingly played the secondary roles of giving speeches during elections and elucidating, in the proper vocabulary, the ideological underpinnings of parties' positions. These roles also had some bearing on theoretical work in social and cultural science.[91]

The Socioeconomic Context

The cultural scientists of nineteenth-century Germany, like other people, lived out their lives in a social context defined by class structure, class conflict, and massive economic change. Much of the historical work that has been done in recent decades on German politics, ideology, and social science has interpreted specific developments in these areas in terms of the grand events of Germany's socioeconomic history: rapid industrialization, the rise of increasingly conscious and structured antagonisms between bourgeoisie and proletariat, the disaffection of social classes disadvantaged by the process of change, and so forth. Cultural scientists, like other intelligent observers of social phenomena, were quite aware of these events and responded to them, among other ways, in their professional writings.

Nevertheless, to try to interpret cultural science solely as a direct response to socioeconomic change would be misleading, especially if the response is treated as a class response alone. Perceptions of society as a whole and of the causes and effects of social change are hardly ever immediate in any meaningful way. Rather, they are constructs, resulting (among other things) from the mediation between individuals and the social environment of the kinds of structure we have been discussing: theoretical structures, such as ideologies, theoretical patterns, and disciplinary orientations; organizational structures, such as universities and political parties; and, of course, class and generational structures. Ideally, all of these factors should be considered together as interactive elements of a general social context. To do so in practice, however, even if possible, would require too much time and space. The approach taken in most chapters of this study is to focus on key individuals and to pursue relationships among their professional thinking, their political outlooks, and the broad social factors revealed in their social backgrounds. Here, we shall do something more general, although still along the same lines. Instead of rehearsing the well-known outlines of social and economic change during the era of German industrialization and suggesting its effects on cultural scientists, we shall undertake a modest collective biography of German cultural scientists and attempt to relate central tendencies in their backgrounds and careers to changing aspects of their social environment.[92] This will require us to extend our focus beyond the middle decades of the nineteenth century.

The collective biography is based on a sample of forty-seven cases of Germans prominent in some way or other in the cultural sciences in the nineteenth and early twentieth centuries. The cases were selected in a fairly informal manner. A list was drawn up of names prominently mentioned in leading histories of the individual cultural sciences, in the major cultural science journals of the day, and in the lists of directors of the leading disciplinary organizations. An attempt was made to obtain a fairly even coverage over time and to include individuals from all the appropriate academic disciplines as well as journalists, explorers, and amateurs. From this list, the sample was chosen mainly on the basis of whether or not sufficient biographical information was readily available, with the further provision that most of the people who figure significantly in the rest of this study be included.[93]

In order to obtain an appropriate time dimension, the subjects in the sample were distributed among five generational categories: ten in each of the first four, and seven in the fifth. (The people in the fifth group figured only at the very end of the period under study; much of their careers lay outside it.) Rather than arbitrarily defining the boundaries of categories at a fixed number of years for a generation, the groups were established on the basis of shared, important political experiences of people at certain crucial periods in their lives. These groups turn out to be consonant, in most cases, with age-cadres identified by contemporaries.

The first age category consists of people born before 1820—in other words, those who had already reached their late twenties by the time of the 1848 revolution and who may have perceived it differently from those still in the process of forming their political opinions and deciding on careers. The second group is made up of people born between 1820 and 1832. These are the ones who experienced the 1848 revolution during what are often considered to be the most impressionable years, intellectually and politically (between the ages of sixteen or seventeen and the late twenties). The third group includes subjects born between 1833 and 1853. These are the people who lived through some part of the crises of the 1860s and through unification during the same formative period of their lives—the "generation of the 1860s."[94] The fourth group is made up of people whose political experiences in their formative years occurred in Bismarck's Reich. They were born between 1854 and 1873. And the final group consists of those born after 1873, those who came of age intellectually after Bismarck's fall and became professionally important in the twentieth century.

First, we need to look at the relationship between the cultural scientists in our sample and the social or class structure of Germany. As is usual in such analyses, we shall use occupation or profession as the main clue to class, from which further inferences can be made. If we look at the occupational status of the fathers of the members of the sample and infer class membership from that, we find that the families of cultural scientists were (not surprisingly) overwhelmingly bourgeois. The occupations of forty-one of the fathers of the forty-seven people in our sample are readily available. Of these, twenty-one, or fifty-one percent, clearly belonged to the *Bildungsbürgertum*, especially university professors, senior civil servants, doctors, and lawyers. Only two were Protestant clergymen—a circumstance that differentiates cultural scientists markedly from German historians and philosophers. The proportion of cultural scientists coming from such families remained essentially the same through the first four generations and then fell off in the fifth—possibly the result of greater educational opportunities for children of poorer families toward the turn of the century. Ten other subjects had fathers who were well-to-do business owners or senior managers. Half of these were concentrated in the fourth generational group (born between 1854 and 1873). This may be testimony to the impact of the era of industrialization. In any event, seventy-six percent of the people in the sample whose family occupational backgrounds can be ascertained came from these two bourgeois groups, as opposed to seven percent from traditional elite families (military, noble, and large-scale landowning); fifteen percent from lower-middle-class, master artisan, domestic servant, and peasant families; and two percent from working-class families. It is true that some of the most important figures came from these last two (poorer) categories (Friedrich Ratzel, Virchow, Riehl, the elder Andree), but it is also true that overall, cultural science corresponded in its social-class origins to the standard pattern of German academia as a whole: it was bourgeois.[95] How significant that may have been in shaping theoretical consciousness is a matter for discussion, but at least *one* of the common factors influencing the thought of cultural scientists was probably their bourgeois background.

The cultural sciences, like all other academic disciplines in Germany before 1914, were also overwhelmingly male. Not only was every person in the sample a male, but only one member of the much larger pool from which the sample was taken was female—and her ethnological activities were noted only because they were mentioned in the sources along with those of her husband. Not enough information was readily available to include her in the sample, which would in any case have been skewed in terms of gender had she been added.[96]

If one looks at the specific occupations of the subjects themselves on reaching maturity, the dominance of professional academics in cultural science is very obvious. Twenty-nine became university professors or held academic positions of equivalent rank (such as museum director), and three others held academic appointments without reaching the rank of full professor—for a total of sixty-eight percent of the sample. Of the rest, seventeen percent were "bourgeois" amateurs (people in other professions with an interest in cultural studies or else middle-class persons with private incomes); four percent were members of the nobility or higher civil service with a cultural science hobby; nine percent were professional journalists not in academic positions; and two percent were working missionaries. Bourgeois dominance is again in evidence, but the most striking (and perhaps most expected) factor is the preeminence of professional academics, which remains at about the same level throughout the period covered by the sample. The important role of amateurs that is noted in, for example, British anthropology is not reproduced in German cultural science.[97]

It is also interesting to look at the areas of specialty within cultural science of the people in the sample. This is somewhat problematical because individuals often had interests in several areas, but if one attempts to identify each person's prime field of activity, the distribution appears to be something like this: thirty-four percent ethnology, eleven percent physical anthropology, and eleven percent geography. Nine percent of the subjects were amateurs whose concentrations simply could not be determined, and the rest consisted of smaller numbers of archaeologists, psychologists, economists, historians, and so on. The predominance of ethnology grows steadily over the period covered, the percentages of geographers and amateurs decline, and the physical anthropologists are present in significant numbers only in the second and third generations (born from 1820 to 1853). The last point probably reflects the popularity of physical anthropology in the third quarter of the century and its subsequent tendency to separate itself from cultural science. In general the distribution supports Virchow's perception that ethnology was the core of the cultural sciences.

There are few surprises with respect to education. Although the precise type of secondary school the subjects attended can be easily determined in only twenty of the forty-seven cases, there is no reason to think that the rest of the sample would show a markedly different pattern. Seventy-five percent of the subjects attended a classical Gymnasium, regardless of the later degree they took. The others went to *Realschule* (technical secondary schools), seminaries, and so on. The *Gymnasia* maintained their dominance throughout the period. Despite exceptions like Ratzel, most cultural scientists were brought up in the humanistic environment of the prime institutions for preparing the *Bildungsbürgertum*.

Eighty-four percent of the sample completed university education by receiving doctoral degrees, and another thirteen percent attended university without receiving a degree. The majority (sixty out of the eighty-four percent) of those with doctorates took them in the philosophical faculty or took two degrees, one of which was the doctor of philosophy degree. Most of those with doctorates in other fields had medical degrees. It was in the second and third generational groups (born from 1820 to 1853) that the medical cultural scientists were most numerous. Earlier, the generalized philosophy degree predominated, and afterwards the majority of the sample had specific fields in cultural science disciplines. The process of professional specialization associated with modernization clearly extended into cultural science.

The geographical makeup of the sample can be described in two ways: in terms of the regions in which the subjects were born and in terms of the kind of environment in which they grew up. Thirty-four percent were Prussians by birth, thirteen percent were from southwestern Germany (Baden and Württemberg), eleven percent were Saxons, and another eleven percent were from Hanseatic states. Four percent were born outside the Reich. The Prussian predominance tended to grow slightly over time, more or less in accord with the growing proportion of the German population that was Prussian. At no time, however, did the proportion of native Prussians in the sample equal or exceed the proportion of Prussia's population to the rest of the Reich.[98] However, judging by the addresses at which persons in the sample lived, in *later* adult life the number living in Prussian cities probably matched the distribution of Prussians within the German population fairly closely—a tribute mainly to the attractiveness of Berlin. With respect to environment of origin, thirty-six percent of the sample came from big cities, twenty-three percent from substantial towns, and forty percent from small towns and rural areas. Despite the high rate of urbanization during the years covered by the sample, the ratio of subjects originating in big cities to that of cultural scientists from rural environments did not change very much from period to period.

The adult religious affiliations of the sample did not closely reflect the distribution of affiliations within Germany as a whole. For fifty-seven percent of the sample, no religious allegiance was listed in the sources. This could mean, for individual subjects, either conscious disavowal of religion or accidental noncitation, but even in the latter case it may well indicate that religion was insufficiently important to them as adults to be listed in autobiographical notices. In the third of the generational periods (the generation of the 1860s, in which the enthusiasm for scientific materialism was at its height), seventy percent of the sample had no reported religion. Thirty-six percent of the total sample were Protestants of one denomination or another. The number of acknowledged Protestants diminished over time. Catholics made up only six percent of the sample and appeared only in the last two generations (mostly reflecting the development of German Catholic missionary anthropology). There were two people in the sample born to Jewish families but who did not practice religion as adults. Although the family religious backgrounds of only some of the people in the sample can be determined directly, inference from place of origin supports the impression that, whatever their religious leanings as adults, the vast majority of German cultural scientists were Protestants— mostly Lutherans—as children.

We cannot tell for sure whether the large proportion of cultural scientists not reporting religious affiliation reflected the situation of the *Bildungsbürgertum* as a whole, but it seems likely, judging from a comparison with nineteenth-century

German historians (whose backgrounds have been exhaustively examined by Wolf-gang Weber), that it did not.[99] Cultural scientists as adults appear to have been much more indifferent to religion than the average recipient of a humanistic edu-cation. And although presumably most of them had a Protestant upbringing, the omnipresence of the Lutheran *Pfarrhaus* that has been remarked in the backgrounds of so many German philosophers and historians is not replicated in the case of the cultural scientists with whom we are concerned. It is quite possible that the tendency of cultural scientists to follow particular theoretical patterns in their work and not others (to retain, for instance, the nomothetic definition of social science rather than pursue hermeneutic approaches favored by many historians) was correlated with their relationship, as a group, to religion. The form of the correlation, however, is not entirely clear. It is not unlikely that nomothetic science and religious indif-ference (or unbelief) were related concepts in many people's minds, and that what-ever led individuals to choose one position as adults led them also to adopt the other—but it is difficult to say whether one position was causally prior to the other. Several important cultural scientists (e.g., Ratzel and Wilhelm Roscher) were sin-cere, practising Protestants. We shall consider later the part that religion may have played in their theoretical work.

It is not difficult to postulate a direct connection between acceptance of her-meneutics and an upbringing in a Protestant pastoral family such as Dilthey and Droysen had. One could suggest that a group of scholars not led by people with such backgrounds (focusing intellectually on intuitive understanding of the meaning of scripture through close textual reading) would be less likely to see the point of the hermeneutic approach. On the other hand, Karl Lamprecht, one of the two people in our sample who *did* have such a background, became at the end of the nineteenth century a leading opponent of hermeneutic social science. Lamprecht was the "positivist" most despised by the historical profession. But Lamprecht's predilections have been explained by one scholar as a *rejection* of his background, represented by his father.[100] This, of course, illustrates the difficulty of identifying and interpreting such correlations.

Most of what has been noted thus far consists of factors of social background. Categories referring to voluntary professional and political activities are somewhat more difficult to quantify. Judging more or less impressionistically from the bio-graphical sources, it appears that fifty-three percent of the subjects were very active in professional organizations devoted to cultural science, whereas forty-seven per-cent were only moderately active or not active at all. There is a fairly strong correlation between a high level of activity and amateur status, but that is an artifact of sample selection. (The amateurs would not have been in the sample had they not been prominent in organizations.) Marginally more interesting is the change over time. The proportion of people active in organizations increased from ten percent in the first generational period to fifty percent in the second to eighty percent in the third, and then diminished somewhat thereafter (sixty percent and seventy-one percent in the fourth and fifth periods). The generation of the 1860s thus seems to have been unusually enthusiastic about voluntary organizations.

As far as the key factors for the rest of the study are concerned—those that relate cultural science to politics—a few points can be made. A *minimum* of sixty-six percent of the sample were actively engaged in journalism at some stage of their careers. Involvement with journalism was most pronounced earlier in the nineteenth century (at around eighty percent in the first two generational groups), diminished slightly in the third and fourth generations (sixty percent), and fell to slightly below fifty percent in the last group—perhaps as a result of the growing security of an academic career, perhaps because the increasing professionalization of journalism reduced opportunities for part-time or temporary work for budding academics. The figures do clearly reflect the observations made earlier about the close connection between journalism and cultural science.

Measuring political activity presents difficulties because of the multiplicity of forms that such activity can take. It becomes even more difficult if ideological leanings are taken into account because, as we shall see later, these were by no means consistent with membership in organizations, especially in the latter part of the nineteenth century. Just over forty percent of the total sample were, at some point in their careers, active in self-consciously liberal political parties or clearly supported such parties, as evidenced especially in their political journalism. Liberal political commitment was, however, strongest in the earlier generations. In the first generational group, seventy percent of the cultural scientists can be clearly identified as active liberals, as can fifty percent of the second generational group (not counting Riehl, who started as a liberal but became a conservative). In each of the next three groups, however, the active liberals comprised only between twenty and thirty percent of the sample. Moreover, it is necessary to include as "liberals" people such as Friedrich Ratzel, who remained an active member of the National Liberal party but who espoused political ideas that varied substantially from the liberal norm. There were self-proclaimed conservatives in most of the age groups, although there were none in the first and one only in each of the other groups.

The most obvious political tendency over time was not in the direction of traditional conservatism (support for the established social and political order, opposition to most aspects of the liberal program, etc.), but rather toward an apolitical posture—at least with respect to political parties. The apolitical posture was, as we shall see, partly associated with a new ethic of professional human science in the late nineteenth century, but in many cases it was itself an ideological statement not completely divorced from the traditions of liberal social science. Fully seventy percent of the people in the third generational group were or became apolitical together with approximately sixty percent in the fourth and fifth groups. Individuals in the sample were active in colonialist, imperialist, and radical nationalist organizations in all five generations: ten percent in the first; twenty percent in the second, third, and fourth; and fourteen percent in the fifth. Some of these people were self-conscious members of liberal parties; some were conservatives; and some were apolitical in the sense of supporting no party. No clear correlation emerges from the sample. What the numbers cannot indicate is another tendency for the political ideologies accepted by cultural scientists (including the liberal ones) to fragment greatly in direction and content in the younger generational groups. We shall consider that phenomenon in later chapters.

It is necessary to caution against relying too heavily on these figures. They are not based on an analysis even remotely approaching the work of Wolfgang Weber on German historians in detail and in breadth.[101] The sample is small, many of the categories are necessarily problematic, and the process of selection is rendered questionable by the lack of definition of the disciplines under study throughout much of the period covered.

Nevertheless, important information about relationships between cultural scientists taken as a group and the socioeconomic structure of nineteenth-century Germany does emerge. It is no surprise that cultural scientists should be overwhelmingly bourgeois in social origin, like all groups of German academics. Because, as academics, they remained essentially bourgeois throughout their careers, it would not be surprising to find them taking characteristically bourgeois attitudes toward issues arising from social change. Nor is it unexpected that cultural scientists' social origins should be concentrated among the *Bildungsbürgertum*—the subsection of the bourgeoisie to which they belonged as adults.

The peculiar relationship of this subclass to the process of socioeconomic modernization has been taken, in many important studies of political and intellectual life in imperial Germany, to be a matter of great significance. Some have focused on the incongruity between the humanistic outlook of the elite of education and the circumstances of the modern industrial world, and they have developed explanations of the tendency of the group to antimodernism and "illiberalism."[102] Others, although focusing on incongruities, have seen the position of the *Bildungsbürgertum* as similar to that of the educated middle classes in general—not so much out of step with modernization as with a social order that perpetuated the power of obsolete elites and augmented the power of new elites not qualified by education or intelligence. At the same time, it seemed that the most likely alternative to the existing power concentration was the rule of the masses through a socialist version of democracy, which was also not acceptable.[103]

We have, in the cultural scientists, a sample of the *Bildungsbürgertum*—people who, although their specific academic fields ostensibly took them away from current social and political concerns, in fact displayed (albeit in diminishing numbers) a close interest in politics and social issues and who, through the evolution of their theoretical patterns, indirectly dealt with current issues in their work. The fact that some of the leading figures in the field did not come from bourgeois families must be taken into account, as must the relatively high proportion of cultural scientists who came from families belonging to the business bourgeoisie. We shall see that although the similarities among cultural scientists with respect to social origin and relationship to socioeconomic change did constitute a significant part of the context of their politics and their academic work, it does not easily explain the *differences* among them, either in ideological perspective or in subscription to particular theoretical patterns.

4

The Crisis of Liberalism and the Emergence of Cultural Science, 1862–1885

The failure of the 1848 revolution did not lead to a permanent decline of liberalism in Germany, nor can it easily be shown (contrary to what many historians used to believe) that the collapse of the revolution infected the liberal movement with germs that would later weaken it beyond recovery.[1] Liberalism in Germany in fact recovered its strength after less than a decade, and although it was a changed liberalism, it was in most ways a stronger, more realistic, and more effective political movement than ever before. Taking advantage of the wealth-based franchise system established under the new Prussian constitution and the shift of income that occurred during the economic expansion of the 1850s, the Prussian liberals gained control of the House of Deputies by the end of the decade. By 1862, they had engaged the Prussian government in a constitutional struggle that had the potential for producing responsible representative government. Liberal resurgences had also occurred in other states. Although some of the intellectual leaders of liberalism, especially radicals, had left Germany or became politically inactive, there was a compensation in the attraction that restored liberalism had for large numbers of students and young academics in the 1850s and 1860s.

Liberals were better organized than before. The *Nationalverein* (founded in 1859) gave them the semblance of a national organization, and the founding of the Progressive party during the Prussian constitutional crisis gave them an effective parliamentary and electoral structure. On the whole, liberals throughout Germany had been fairly successful in expanding their voting base and appealing to segments of society that favored political change. In the absence of many of the leaders of the old radical wing, the liberals were mainly led by antirevolutionary moderates, many of them businesspeople. This may have made them less decisive, but it also made them less divisive—at least for a while. The business liberals could exercise substantial influence on governments. There were problems: more sophisticated conservative ideologies among their opponents, near hysteria among conservative aristocrats with army support, fewer bureaucrats sympathetic to political liberalism, and, in the 1860s, the beginnings of an antiliberal working-class political movement led by Ferdinand Lasalle. But in general things seemed to be going the liberals' way by 1862.

Despite the growing importance of business leaders in the liberal movement, academics and intellectuals still played extremely important leadership roles. Some, like Ludwig Rochau, made close alliances with the new business leadership. The business boom of the 1850s had encouraged this development and so had the growing acceptance among many intellectuals of capitalist conceptions of material progress. At the same time, some liberal intellectuals like Karl Rodbertus grew increasingly distrustful of industrial capitalism and began to decry its excesses, calling for protection of workers and of part, at least, of the old social order. Although they agreed in general on the need for political reform, liberal academics were beginning to display the divisiveness on social and economic questions that would be one of the sources of the continuing crisis of the whole movement from the 1860s onward.[2] This potential for fragmentation was hidden, however, beneath agreement about the need for reform in general. Liberals also agreed about the desirability of rapid national unification, which most still saw as a necessary part of the triumph of liberalism in the German states. The aggressive tone of confident liberal nationalists of the 1860s, such as Treitschke and Rochau, may have disturbed some liberals, but liberal optimism was such that it probably bothered only a few.[3]

These circumstances changed very quickly in the 1860s. Although liberalism was to have its ups as well as its downs for the rest of the century, it never regained the confidence, the political momentum, or the impression of unity that it possessed early in that decade. Instead, German liberalism experienced a series of crises, most of them marked by further fragmentation, loss of popular support, the migration out of liberalism of many intellectual leaders, and an overall decline of confidence in the coherence of the basic tenets of liberalism among those who remained. Although by the early twentieth century there were still many liberals in Germany, although liberals had had a substantial effect on the shaping of imperial society, although collectively the several liberal parties were a force to be reckoned with and were experiencing a modest revival, political initiative was by then clearly in other hands.

How did this come about? The problems of German liberalism in the late nineteenth century have been the subject in recent years of a considerable amount of research that has corrected, although not entirely replaced, traditional interpretations by linking political events to changes in political, economic, and social structures.[4]

We can focus on liberalism's confrontation with Bismarck and his version of German unification. Bismarck, appointed minister-president of Prussia to resolve the constitutional dispute in 1862, tried various expedients to deflect the threat of a liberal takeover. Several of these expedients—state support for economic unification and modernization to attract business interests, an attempt to exploit the divisions that were becoming obvious among the liberals, and Bismarck's willingness to compromise on certain political reforms not affecting the real locus of political power in Prussia—more or less accidentally came together into a coherent policy as Bismarck had to deal with a series of foreign policy crises. Bismarck realized that he could undercut the liberals' position by representing Prussia's actions in these crises as part of a program of national unification—as long as Prussia in fact undertook to lead such a program. The story of how Bismarck used the conflicts with Denmark in 1864, with Austria in 1866, and with France in 1870 to accomplish this purpose is well known and need not be repeated.[5] The Prussian state, in other words, took up and achieved a political aim that was central to German liberalism, thereby taking wind out of liberal sails. This was a pattern that was to be repeated in the future, as liberals saw many, although not all, of the changes they desired built into the structure of the new German Empire, but within an overall institutional framework that, whatever it was, was not liberal.

The effects on the liberal political movement of Bismarck's success in unifying Germany by Prussian arms and overcoming the Prussian constitutional crisis by unification were serious but not catastrophic. The Prussian liberals divided after the 1866 war over whether or not to surrender on the constitutional question and to accept Bismarck's invitation to cooperate in Prussia's establishment of the North German Confederation. The Progressive party, including Rudolf Virchow, maintained in general their position of opposition, whereas the National Liberal party decided on cooperation in the hope that the confederation would pursue a liberal economic policy and that the institutional structure of the confederation would be conducive to eventual liberalization. The result of this cooperation, constitution of the confederation, became the constitution of the *Reich* in 1871. It made unreformed Prussia dominant within a federal Germany in order to achieve Bismarck's aims of preserving the Prussian monarchy while augmenting it with sovereignty over the empire, extending the scope of the Prussian administrative structure by giving it federal functions, and protecting the special privileges of the Junkers in Prussia— all essentially illiberal goals.[6] At the same time, it did provide the apparatus for enhancing economic unity in Germany and thus encouraging economic modernization, it did make Germany a great power not subject to bullying by other countries, and it did provide, among other institutions, for a national legislature—the Reichstag. All of these were consistent with liberal aims, even if the national government was explicitly not made responsible to the Reichstag and the Reichstag's powers were formally limited.

Most of the moderates who dominated the National Liberal party would have preferred a stronger national legislature with members elected indirectly by property-qualified voters rather than Bismarck's weak assembly chosen by universal manhood suffrage, but most also believed that the Reichstag was, together with the Prussian House of Deputies, a base from which they could work to modify the national political system along lines of which they approved. The National Liberal party, which extended its organization to all of Germany in the late 1860s and early 1870s, continued to cooperate with Bismarck in the new *Reich* and became his main supporter in the Reichstag.[7] For a while, the National Liberals flourished because they could influence national policy, especially on economic matters, and because they attracted the support of many liberals and liberally minded voters, particularly young ones, who had been caught up in the enthusiasm of the Franco-German War and excited by the reality of a united, powerful Germany. The Progressives maintained themselves as the party of liberals who thought that the compromise with Bismarck had given too much away, but they also sometimes found it expedient to cooperate with Bismarck, most obviously during the *Kulturkampf*—Bismarck's attempt to reduce the autonomy of the Catholic church in Prussia in the 1870s. Both parties, but especially the National Liberals, were very loosely organized. They were built upon autonomous local associations and led by notables, few of whom were full-time politicians, who were notoriously difficult to discipline when parliamentary deputies.[8]

By the early years of the *Kaiserreich* in the 1870s, it was clear that the German liberals were divided in more than organization and attitude toward Bismarck.[9] They were also divided ideologically, and many of their divisions cut across party lines. In particular, liberal positions on issues arising from Germany's rapid industrialization varied widely. The business-oriented National Liberal leadership and the doctrinaire former radicals who led the Progressives favored free enterprise and passive government support for business. Each party had, however, elements that called for a more active role for government in promoting economic expansion or protecting segments of society disadvantaged by industrialization. Divisions over these matters became more pronounced and individuals migrated from one party to another or out of the parties altogether in the late 1870s and 1880s as some of the other parties, especially the Free Conservatives and the Catholic Center, adopted positions that had formerly been exclusively liberal and as the question of what to do about the Social Democrats grew more serious. Ideological fragmentation increased in the late 1870s when the National Liberal party split over the issue of Bismarck's proposed tariff increases and the chancellor ceased to view the party as his main ally.

Apart from tendencies toward fragmentation, the liberal parties at both the national and the local levels discovered in the 1870s and 1880s that their voting base was uncertain and deteriorating.[10] The National Liberals did well in Reichstag elections in the 1870s and the Progressives put on a good showing in the early 1880s by attracting migrating National Liberal votes, but the liberals quickly lost control of the Prussian House of Deputies. They also became aware, even before their electoral strength began to diminish drastically later in the 1880s, that they could no longer be sure of drawing the votes of people who were simply discontented with the existing system for whatever reason. New parties had appeared—some representing peculiarly regional interests; one, the Center party, represented a Catholicism politicized by the *Kulturkampf*; another, the SPD, attracted the support of discontented factory workers and artisans. People in business who had previously voted liberal as a matter of course now felt the attraction of more conservative parties as their social aspirations rose and as the liberals increasingly appeared to be unable to influence economic policy after the late 1870s. Most of all, the economic depression of 1873 and the series of cyclical downturns that followed, by exacerbating the problems of workers, small businesspeople, farmers, and people in traditional manufacturing trades, also exacerbated the difficulties the liberals had in deciding on approaches to the social question.[11] The liberals' hesitancy and fragmentation in the face of the problems of rapid industrialization and depression cost them votes among the people most directly affected and led those people to seek a voice in other parties or outside the party system altogether.

Another of liberalism's problems in the *Kaiserreich* was generational: its inability to retain the support of large numbers of young, educated Germans who had flocked to liberal reformism in the early and mid-1860s and from whose ranks a generation of future liberal leaders should have been drawn. The generation of the 1860s experienced substantial political disorientation that resulted from Bismarck's brand of unification and from the dissonance between the complexities of imperial politics and the liberal formulas to which they had subscribed in their youth. The wars of unification excited their enthusiasm and achieved goals that had previously been associated mainly with liberalism. But Bismarck, for all his links to the National Liberals, was clearly no liberal. The image of divisiveness and inconsistency the liberal parties presented while operating in the parliamentary arena, an arena that liberalism insisted was a necessary part of a modern polity, did not build confidence in the coherence or correctness of liberal ideology. Large numbers of educated Germans, including many in the social sciences, who had started their political careers as liberals found themselves from the late 1860s onward questioning liberal assumptions and the whole ideological and intellectual edifice built upon them.[12]

Their questioning did not lead to a new consensus. Some continued to adhere to ideas traditionally associated with liberalism, whereas others, staying for the most part within the liberal organizational fold, gradually altered their interpretations of liberal ideas—sometimes radically. Still others moved to other parts of the political spectrum altogether. Many academically qualified people, whatever their formal political affiliations, increasingly took the position that the problems and opportunities presented by modern society required a politics that rose above interest and party strife—a politics of *Unparteilichkeit* (nonpartisanship).[13] By implication, *Unparteilichkeit* was the political position most conducive to enhancing the influence of the academic elite on policy-making because academics could see themselves as the possessors of the broad vision that should replace narrow party perspectives. The idea was not inconsistent with the tradition of liberal political thought represented by Welcker. But the generation of the 1860s could not easily agree with Welcker that liberalism or a social science closely associated with liberalism embodied objective social truth. Liberalism as a political movement and liberal social science as an intellectual framework for social action were demoted by many to the status of a partisan phenomenon.

The political crisis of the 1860s generation was not entirely a matter of private conscience. Some of the intellectual leaders of the generation conducted their political conversions in public, especially through their journalism. The historian Heinrich von Treitschke (1834–1896) started the decade as a Saxon liberal, became an enthusiast for Prussia in 1866, and by the 1870s was a National Liberal Reichstag deputy, a strong supporter of Bismarck, and one of the earliest of the "radical nationalists" in German politics.[14] Others, including people important in cultural science, followed similar (although seldom identical) patterns. The aggregate result was a weakening of liberal leadership not only intellectually, but also quantitatively. An examination of the birthdates of Reichstag deputies belonging to liberal parties at the turn of the century, for instance, shows a severe underrepresentation of the generation that came to adulthood in the 1860s and early 1870s—a phenomenon not found in other parties.[15]

In the remainder of this chapter, some connections between politics and changes in the general intellectual context of cultural science between the 1860s and the 1880s will be discussed in terms of the picture of liberalism in crisis that has just been presented. This will set the stage for the more specific discussions of particular theoretical patterns that follow in later chapters.

Darwinism

The most famous intellectual controversy of the 1860s and 1870s swirled around Charles Darwin's theory of natural selection and its implications. The controversy spread from the natural to the social and cultural sciences, to the public, and eventually to politics. In German social science, it took the form of a generational dispute with a political dimension.

Historians of Darwinism sometimes portray the theory of natural selection as embedded in the larger social and intellectual context of Darwin's times.[16] This context included politics. Darwin himself acknowledged his employment of Malthusianism and other elements of classical liberal theory as a paradigm for individual competition and species change.[17] But in Germany as in England, the affinities between positions on Darwinism and particular contextual factors were complicated and seldom clear-cut. For example, many of the early German Darwinists were philosophical materialists to whom natural selection, with its purely material mechanism of biological change, was a useful banner behind which to rally in attacking the remnants of *Naturphilosophie,* vitalism, and the influence of religion in education.[18] But not all of the people who undertook this attack accepted natural selection (Rudolf Virchow, for instance), just as some of them (including Waitz) were not thoroughgoing materialists. Similarly, many of the early adherents of Darwinism were radical liberals in politics, often for conscious reasons connected to, say, their reasons for being materialists, but obviously not all liberals, even supposedly radical ones like Virchow, accepted Darwinism.

Interpreted in a liberal sense and extended to society by analogy, Darwinian theory could be used to provide a scientific justification and framework both for liberal ideology and for liberal social science. Darwinism asserted that change was a fact of nature; liberal reform could be represented as a human dimension of universal processes of change. Furthermore, Darwinism offered a pattern for overcoming incompatibilities between elements of liberal notions of change. It convincingly connected the idea of self-regulating equilibrium as the framework of change to the idea that progress was continuous, permanent, inevitable, and generally unidirectional. Natural selection depended on the free actions of individuals, but related those actions in a lawful manner to the structure of the environment. At its heart was a model, apparently compatible with liberalism, of the relationship between the individual and the collectivity in which the individual was the active agent. And best of all, natural selection seemed to be firmly based on empirical observation.

Several young German scientists with an interest in politics, including the biologists Ernst Haeckel and Friedrich Ratzel, made the implications of Darwinism for liberal reform explicit in the 1860s.[19] In his first book, a popular summary of Darwinian theory published in 1869 when the recently graduated zoologist was twenty-five, Ratzel announced that the purpose of the book was to encourage general progress in a liberal direction by displaying the biological need for radical political and social change.[20]

It was relatively easy for people like Ratzel and Haeckel—both trained scientists and, at that time, materialists and radicals—to see a link between their enthusiastic advocacy of Darwinism and their desire for political reform. Other liberals, however, some scientifically qualified and at least nominally radical, refused to accept Darwinism in the way Haeckel and Ratzel did. These included Adolf Bastian and, most notably, Rudolf Virchow.

Virchow formally opposed the enthusiasm for natural selection on the grounds of reasonable objections to the theory.[21] The starting-point of natural selection, natural variation, was not accounted for in Darwin's theory. It was merely assumed on the basis of experience to be a characteristic of living things. As far as Virchow was concerned, this was inadequate in a theory making such comprehensive claims. Virchow also argued that natural selection could not be accepted as more than a hypothesis until the process of species change had actually been observed occurring in nature (as opposed to manipulated breeding of animals by humans). He claimed to have no objection to the use of natural selection as a source for hypotheses to frame scientific research by professionals, but he did object to propagating it as received truth. These were legitimate criticisms of Darwin's theory, taken seriously by Darwin himself.

But the violence of the disputes over Darwinism in German academia, in which Virchow and his ex-student Haeckel brought themselves into a classic (and very nasty) confrontation with each other in the 1870s and in which Haeckel conducted a personal attack on Virchow's ally Bastian, clearly transcended the bounds of a formal disagreement on the status of a scientific theory.[22] On the anti-Darwin side, Virchow was deeply disturbed about the danger of extending the Darwinian model beyond the question of natural species change to encompass human society— precisely the thing that pushy young scientists like Haeckel and Ratzel did so readily. In the absence of a convincing empirical demonstration of the biological reality of natural selection, which Virchow claimed not to see, and without a clear causal link between species change and social phenomena, against which Virchow, as a physical anthropologist, said the evidence was strong, the application of natural selection to society could only be regarded as a source of loose, suggestive analogies. There was nothing inherently wrong with this, but Virchow and others correctly foresaw that, when transferred into the sphere of social science and thus of politics, the looseness of the analogies would be forgotten. The almost-infinite flexibility of Darwin's theoretical categories would allow many different, often obnoxious, political ideologies to clothe themselves in the garb of science.

Even if people who used Darwinian theory in social science or politics did so with full knowledge of the actual complexities of the theory, the implications of natural selection for social thought could be disturbing to a liberal social scientist like Virchow. Using natural selection to identify the underlying laws of society threatened the belief that a firm correspondence existed between basic social laws and the principles embodied in morality and enacted law—unless morality was interpreted simply as affording evolutionary survival value, which seemed to bring into question traditional liberal ideas of moral progress. In addition, it was very easy to misinterpret Darwinian theory (which postulates competition between *individuals* in which species change appears as a by-product) and to apply the framework of the theory to humans as though the basic units were collectivities, such as the *Volk,* the race, the state, the class, or the nation. On this basis, early "social Darwinists" in the 1870s and 1880s were already arguing that struggle between nations and classes was an inevitable fact of life, a notion wholly repugnant to most traditional liberals.[23] It is not surprising that people like Virchow often came to see Darwinism not as a support for their conception of social science, but as a potential danger.

Haeckel, Ratzel, and many others, although they saw many of the same implications of Darwinism for politics and social understanding and although they started in the 1860s from a similar political background, did not perceive these features of natural selection as a danger but rather as a means of building a new, tougher, more accurate science of society. A large part of the difference appears to have been generational. Many of the leading liberal anti-Darwinists, including Virchow and Bastian, came of age in the 1840s and 1850s, whereas many leading scientific partisans of Darwinism as a social and intellectual model (especially Haeckel and Ratzel) belonged to the generation of the 1860s. During the bitter conflicts over the teaching of Darwinism in schools in the late 1870s, partisans of Haeckel's side made it clear that in attacking the anti-Darwinism of Virchow, Bastian, and others they were attacking the domination of out-of-date people and views over the academic and, by extension, political worlds.[24] Virchow gave as good as he got, explicitly linking the need to restain the excesses of the Darwinists with the need to safeguard the tradition of liberal reform through accurate social science.[25] By the late 1870s, Virchow had convinced himself that much of the younger generation of academics had become socialists or conservatives (or both) and were threatening thereby the very foundations of standard liberalism and liberal social science.

By the 1880s, then, the question of whether or not natural selection was an adequate theory of biology had been extended into the issue of whether or not natural selection was an appropriate paradigm for understanding society. The latter issue was debated widely within the social sciences, including the cultural sciences. The main combatants were people such as Virchow and Ratzel who were also trained natural scientists, but others took part as well. There was a more or less straightforward scientific dimension to the dispute that focused on the evidential status of Darwinian theory, and there was a tendency for Darwinian approaches to appeal to those who were theoretical materialists. But one of the most important aspects of the conflict, the aspect that seemed to give it a peculiar sharpness and to bring together all of the others, had to do with politics and age. Although Darwinism was in many ways consistent with liberal approaches to society, it also lent itself readily to informing a sharp reevaluation of the assumptions underlying liberal political theory and traditional liberal social science. This made Darwinism unwelcome to liberal social scientists, especially those of an older generation, who saw the intelligent defense of liberal assumptions as one of their main tasks. At the same time, it gave Darwinism an appeal to a younger generation whose members, in the 1870s, were trying to reassess the political assumptions they had made when coming to maturity—assumptions brought into question by the politics of Bismarck's Germany and by rapid socioeconomic development. It also served as a convenient banner behind which members of a generation eager to make their own careers in the academic world could rally to assert themselves against an intimidatingly impressive generation of predecessors—a generation that occupied the senior academic positions.

It is true, as we shall see, that members of the generation of the 1860s often later repudiated part or all of the theory of natural selection. Ratzel, for instance, changed his mind about basic elements of Darwinism, both as a biological theory and as a paradigm for cultural understanding.[26] But Ratzel in his area of work, like Haeckel in his, continued to acknowledge the importance of Darwin in influencing his mature thinking and in structuring the break with his intellectual predecessors.

Nationalism and Imperialism

Nationalism—the body of doctrine that presented the ethnically defined nation matched by a corresponding unified national state as the proper unit of politics— was by tradition closely linked to liberalism in Germany. By the middle of the nineteenth century, there were few wholly internationalist German liberals. Before 1866, the assumption that the liberalization of Germany had to be accomplished by a national state attracting the enthusiastic support of the German *Volk* was as characteristic of the moderate liberals of the *Staatslexikon* as it was of radicals like Virchow and right-wing liberals like Dahlmann.[27] The connection between liberalism and nationalism often created difficulties—as it did, for instance, in 1848 over German liberal attitudes toward the national aspirations of the Poles. Should the legitimacy of these aspirations be recognized if they threatened to awaken nationalist feelings among Prussia's Poles? Were Prussian Poles part of the German *Volk*? In fact, who composed a *Volk*? This last question, so vital to defining a national liberal state, was exceedingly difficult to answer and attracted the attention of many liberal social scientists interested in culture.[28]

But nationalism did not remain the sole property of the liberals. From the beginning of the nineteenth century, some writers not in sympathy with liberalism and reform had tried to appropriate nationalism, although not with enormous success. In the second quarter of the century, state governments began to supplement their traditional appeals to loyalty to the ruling dynasty with appeals to identity with the country and its history, thus taking a leaf from the book of liberal nationalism. Cultural scientists like Riehl could be called into service for this purpose. In Prussia in the 1850s and 1860s, the attempts of nonliberal governments to broaden popular support through the educational and military-training systems followed similar lines, which was taken by moderate liberal historians like Droysen as evidence of Prussia's capacity to merge traditional Prussian state loyalty with German nationalism.[29]

From that point it was only a step to attempts by bolder conservatives, such as Bismarck, to appeal to German nationalism rather than territorial loyalty. In his efforts to undercut and split the Prussian liberals in the 1860s, Bismarck recruited formerly-liberal nationalists like Lothar Bucher to write nationalist propaganda in support of his successful attempt to create a united Germany that would preserve the peculiarities of the territorial states. The unification of Germany represented the association of German nationalism with a political system that Bismarck hoped would retard the growth of liberalism.[30] With the growth of the Social Democratic party in the 1870s and 1880s, nationalism became closely connected with the effort to foster consensus, cooperation, and political obedience among other classes by attacking the SPD and the political dangers supposedly arising from the working class.

But, of course, Bismarck, his supporters (including the National Liberals), and his successors had to face the same problems that had confronted the liberals earlier. How do you define the nation? If you define it in cultural terms, you immediately have a problem not only with linguistic minorities, but also with religious ones—especially the Catholics, whose organizational loyalties extended beyond the national state. With liberal support, Bismarck attempted to deal with this last difficulty through the *Kulturkampf* and failed miserably.[31] The problem of the large (and growing) Polish minority in eastern Prussia took on important social and economic dimensions in the 1880s and led to the Bismarckian state's first comprehensive attempt at ethnic discrimination—an attempt that caused far more problems than it solved.

Then there was the problem of foreign policy. The appeal to nationalist sentiment had been essential both to Bismarck's diplomacy and to his domestic politics during the period of unification, and it remained at least as important to him in the 1870s and 1880s as a means of overcoming political opposition. But it involved dangers. An aggressive foreign policy brought with it the possibility of diplomatic isolation and war, yet the most effective way of winning diplomatic victories (and thus gaining popular support for the government) was by assembling violent nationalist sentiment behind such a policy and using the threat that such sentiment would force a war as a ploy to encourage other governments to back down. But when, after deliberate appeals to nationalist feelings, aggressive initiatives were followed by compromise solutions to international issues, it could easily appear that national expectations had been betrayed, that the government had backed down. Bismarck experienced some of this as early as 1875, and his successors after 1890 did so more frequently—culminating in the public backlash against the government after the settlement of the 1911 Moroccan crisis.[32]

The problems that resulted from the employment of nationalism by the *Reich* government in the conduct of diplomacy were only part of a more complex set of political phenomena.[33] In the years after 1871, rapid socioeconomic change in Germany created demands on the national political system. The country's constitutional structure (designed for purposes other than flexible response to changing social circumstances) was not very well suited to meet such demands. Bismarck (like everybody else in politics) was forced to improvise—short of undertaking major revisions in Germany's constitution, which the very complexity of the power balance among interest groups and the nature of Bismarck's political system largely precluded. Politics came to center around the attempt to create consensus among at least some of the significant groups into which German society was divided so as to afford the basis for consensus among the parties operating in the Reichstag and the state legislatures. Thus Bismarck turned to a policy of protective tariffs in 1879 partly to unite the interests of heavy industry and big agriculture (both then beset by depression and foreign competition) behind him and thus obtain the permanent support of the Conservatives, Free Conservatives, and some of the National Liberals in the Reichstag and Prussian House of Deputies. As was the case with every other similar attempt by Bismarck to create consensus and a basis of support, protectionism failed to attain its political aim. The "league of rye and iron" proved to be an uncertain, often-fragmenting, foundation for political action.

This general problem was not Bismarck's alone; it was shared by all major participants in the political process, including the parties, the growing array of economic interest groups, and government departments competing for appropriations. All required political support and some degree of favorable consensus within an ill-defined body politic, and all experienced much difficulty in finding these things. This, in turn, made the political system and its major operators appear ineffective and contributed to growing disenchantment with traditional models of government (including liberal ones) among educated people. Politicians were driven in the 1870s and 1880s to seek ideological means of affording consensus and appealing to the disenchanted. Many of them turned to nationalism and its offspring, imperialism.

The image of a united citizenry bound together by ties that transcended class, region, religion, and even traditional ideology was a powerful one, legitimated by generations of liberal writers and now adopted by most political groups that wanted to affect national politics. There were ideas as well as images, including the idea that the nation was the natural unit of politics, the framework within which individual freedom was properly exercised. Progress could be equated with nationhood. These ideas were fairly easy to interpret in ways that suited particular interests. Thus, when the heavy industrial lobby campaigned for tariff protection in the 1870s, it naturally portrayed a threat to the nation as a whole arising from the importation of foreign manufactures.[34] Consumers should accept the higher costs that protection might cause out of loyalty to the nation. Hundreds of other interests made similar arguments.

But for parties and interest groups, nationalism was a two-edged sword. A party that made nationalist noises could find itself forced to decide between either supporting proposals made by the government or another political party that were offensive to it but successfully dressed in nationalist colors or having its nationalism called a sham. This happened to the Progressives in 1884–1885 when Bismarck seized a colonial empire in the name of nationalism and with the support of the National Liberals. By sticking (with equivocations) to their traditional opposition to colonialism, the Progressives paid the price of being labelled unpatriotic by the new imperialist organizations.[35] Almost any political organization could subscribe to imperialist aims, but having done so, it became vulnerable to someone else's demands for an even more aggressive imperialist policy. This could be highly embarrassing and, for the German government, dangerous because imperialist thinking soon lost contact with the realities of international politics. Especially after the advent of radical nationalist and imperialist organizations, such as the Pan-German

League in the 1890s, it became increasingly difficult for parties that had committed themselves to imperialism—and, indeed, for the government itself—to take a pacific public line on imperial issues even when the international situation clearly demanded it.[36]

Social and cultural scientists concerned themselves directly with all aspects of the role of nationalism and imperialism in politics. Ever since the beginning of the nineteenth century, academics had considered themselves the particular exponents of German nationalism. It had primarily been academics who had invented German nationalism in the first place; liberal academics who had worked out the main lines of nationalist ideology before 1848; and academics and academically trained journalist, like Treitschke and Ratzel, who had taken the lead in advancing the use of imperialism in the politics of the *Kaiserreich*.[37] Some social scientists, especially Max Weber, were later led by their own experience of the attractiveness of nationalism and of its problematic character to reassess the motivations that underlay political behavior.[38] Cultural scientists, both as students of humankind and as participants in German politics, gravitated to the role of attempting to define the nature of the group that comprised the nation—that is, the *Volk*. This problem had exercised liberal social scientists before midcentury. It remained a matter of central interest to cultural scientists in the fragmented ideological context of the *Kaiserreich*.

We shall see in later chapters that some of the same factors that created theoretical divisions among cultural scientists over issues such as Darwinism also informed their disagreements over questions arising from the politics of nationalism and imperialism. Virchow, for instance, oriented his most important anthropological research project (a study of the physical characteristics of Prussian schoolchildren) around his desire to discredit the argument that the *Völker* of particular nations were racially defined.[39] The dispute over Darwinism between Virchow, Bastian, and other members of the anthropological elite of their generation, on the one hand, and the pro-Darwinians, such as Ratzel, on the other (a dispute that had ethnological consequences) paralleled the dispute between the two groups over the desirability of a German colonial empire. Virchow and Bastian, although not averse to a limited amount of economic imperialism, opposed large-scale colonial acquisition—at least in part because of their fears that the adoption of imperialism by younger academics like Ratzel would endanger liberalism as a political force.[40] In general, as nationalism and imperialism became more prominent in politics and as their links to traditional liberalism dissolved, they helped to change the ways cultural science interacted with ideology.

The Critique of Economic Modernity

One of the most notable features of German politics during the late nineteenth century was the appearance of an antimodernist ideological tendency, especially (but not exclusively) among the members of the elite of education. *Antimodernism* has been ascribed to many factors: to the failure, particularly of traditional liberalism, to provide immediate solutions to the social problems created by economic change;[41] to the search for popular support by conservative elite groups and the parties they represented;[42] and to the perception of humanistically educated people that socioeconomic change was making their training and values irrelevant.[43] Antimodernism contributed to the emergence of the parallel (and equally heterogeneous) phenomenon of *radical nationalism*, although they were not exactly the same thing, for not all radical nationalists opposed modernity.[44] Both antimodernism and radical nationalism had important roots in earlier liberal ideology, even though both explicitly opposed traditional liberalism as a model for current politics. Both strongly, and disastrously, affected later German politics.

Cultural scientists helped to define both antimodernism and radical nationalism. This involvement will be examined in later chapters when the relationship between cultural science and the politics of the Wilhelmian period are discussed. But the involvement arose earlier than the 1890s. Cultural scientists like Riehl and Ratzel, in attempting to construct alternatives to the liberal theoretical pattern that would correspond to the new directions in political ideology, established the foundations for a cultural critique of contemporary society.[45] This type of critique, although partly antimodernist, was by no means absolutely so. It differed from similar approaches to modern society taken by contemporary intellectuals (e.g., Nietzsche) in that it was based on cultural science and therefore employed an anthropological definition of culture.

Not all cultural scientists took part in the critique of modernity. The lines of cultural thought that held most firmly to the original liberal theoretical pattern adhered also to the notion of progress that underlay liberal conceptions of modernity. But even in those cases, the prejudice against industrial society that became fashionable in the universities and among intellectuals in the last third of the century ensured that younger cultural scientists, mindful of their careers, seldom adopted the largely progressivist approach to culture that predominated in Britain and that can be seen both in British cultural evolutionism and in its successor, functionalism.

The difficulties liberalism as a movement and ideology experienced after 1862 thus had profound effects on the enterprise of German social science. As in the 1850s, the faltering of liberalism encouraged social scientists to seek alternatives to the liberal theoretical pattern—or at least to look for ways of shoring the pattern up in support of a modernized liberalism—in the further development of the culture concept and of the cultural sciences.

The continuing crisis of liberalism had a more profound effect as well. It constituted a central political focus around which the social concerns of a multitude of groups could be oriented and given meaning. Concerns about the costs and benefits of industrialization, for example, found expression in debates over the efficacy of the liberal social vision. In such debates, some people defended traditional liberal views, some wanted modifications, and some demanded radically different alternatives—alternatives that were, however, largely defined by the specific rejection of elements of liberal ideology. In this way, liberalism framed the ideological context in which the problems occasioned by economic change, social conflict, and political modernization were perceived and discussed. This process was reflected in academic social science partly by the expansion of cultural science. Concepts of cultural seemed to offer a means either of adjusting the liberal ideology or of constructing an alternative. The following chapters will examine various attempts to do one or the other, attempts that revolutionized the sciences of culture in Germany and had important effects on German political life as well. We shall start with theoretical patterns in ethnology and psychology that had a neoliberal orientation and then move on to others that broke more radically (although seldom completely) with the liberal theoretical tradition.

5

Berlin Ethnology as
Neoliberal Cultural Science

The Formation of the Berlin
Anthropological Establishment

In September 1869, the Congress of German Natural Scientists and Physicians met in Innsbruck. Included in its program was a section devoted to anthropology and ethnology.[1] The section was organized and, in the event, dominated by Rudolf Virchow who had for the past several years been spending increasing amounts of his professional time on anthropological subjects. At one point, the discussion turned to the fact that practically every other major European country except Germany possessed national associations for the advancement of physical anthropology, ethnology, and related subjects. Undoubtedly, this discussion was affected by the nationalist political climate of the late 1860s, by the formation of the North German Confederation, and by the prospect of Germany's impending complete unification. The section issued a call for the establishment of a German Society for Anthropology, Ethnology and Prehistory—in part for the reason that if other countries had such organizations, Germany ought to have one as well. The society was envisioned as being German in a *grossdeutsch* sense—incorporating members from north and south Germany and from Austria. It was intended to support research in the three general areas indicated by its title, and it was supposed to coordinate the activities of local societies devoted to those subjects.

In 1870, thanks to the efforts of Virchow, Adolf Bastian, and other prominent people throughout German academia who were interested in cultural studies, something resembling such a society was in fact organized. It functioned for many years as the German Anthropological Society, held annual meetings, and contained members representing all currents of German anthropological thought. But the German Anthropological Society was never, in itself, a very active or important force in German cultural science. The leadership of the anthropological disciplines was seized from the start by a second, theoretically local and subordinate organization that also derived from the Innsbruck meeting: the *Berliner Gesellschaft für Anthropologie, Ethnologie und Urgeschichte.*

When Virchow and Bastian returned to Berlin after the Innsbruck meeting and began to try to implement the plan for a national association, they found the process a good deal slower than they had expected. The reasons for this are unclear, but it is possible that the network of geographical scholars and publishers centered in

Saxony and Thuringia was not as eager as the Berlin cultural scientists to link itself to a national organization for fear of domination by Berlin. Within a few weeks, Virchow, Bastian, and a number of other people—academics and interested amateurs—had decided to form a Berlin society with the same breadth of intellectual coverage as the planned national association. When the latter was finally formed, the *Berliner Gesellschaft* was supposed to become its local affiliate. As it turned out, the Berlin society became the permanently active driving force in the anthropological disciplines.

To a significant extent, the society was an extension of its prime founder, Virchow, who devoted an extraordinary amount of time to it as he withdrew from active research in physiology. Virchow was regularly elected president of the *Gesellschaft's Vorstand,* except every fourth year, when someone else (usually Bastian) would be chosen in accordance with the society's constitution.[2] Regardless, Virchow generally ran the show, although he was not the organization's sole shaper. Bastian was very active (when he was not out travelling), as were a wide assortment of academic physical anthropologists, archaeologists, and ethnologists. Virchow and Bastian also cultivated the society's large amateur membership. Virchow, as a leading academic politician, was careful to involve prominent government officials and businesspeople in the *Gesellschaft's* affairs.[3]

The *Berliner Gesellschaft* quickly proved itself to be what Virchow had hoped the German Anthropological Society would be but never was: an active promoter of anthropological investigation, organizing support for research projects, building public awareness of cultural science, and helping to create an empirical science of anthropology based on an organized network of amateur data collectors and academic analysts. In addition to publishing the proceedings of its annual meetings, the *Berliner Gesellschaft* also began to publish the *Zeitschrift für Ethnologie*, which became the leading anthropological journal in Germany and one of the most important in the world. Control of appearance in the *Zeitschrift für Ethnologie* was one of Virchow and Bastian's major sources of power in the anthropological community. Their power was far from complete, but it expanded greatly in the 1870s as publishers specializing in travel and geographical literature (including the older Saxon-Thuringian houses, such as Perthes) turned to the leadership of the *Berliner Gesellschaft* for editorial advice.[4] The *Gesellschaft* also assembled a library and a collection of artifacts.

The artifact collection soon outgrew the space available for it, which provided Virchow with the excuse to use his political influence as a member of the Prussian House of Deputies and his contacts with the Prussian and Berlin governments to push for the establishment of a government-sponsored ethnological museum. As early as 1873, the Prussian Education Ministry indicated that it favored the idea, and eventually, in 1886, the government established the Royal Museum for *Völkerkunde,* of which Bastian became the director.[5] (*Völkerkunde* was replacing *Ethnologie* as the general term for cultural anthropology, in part because it was a uniquely German word and in part because it was tied to no traditional theoretical stance.) The Royal Museum, although state supported, was thus intimately linked to the *Berliner Gesellschaft.*

In addition, close connections developed among the museum, the *Gesellschaft,* and the University of Berlin.[6] Several professors, including Virchow and the physiologist DuBois-Reymond, figured among the *Gesellschaft*'s founders. It was mainly *Gesellschaft* members who insinuated *Völkerkunde* as an independent subject into the philosophical faculty. Bastian became an adjunct lecturer at the university, teaching, apparently, the first full-scale course of ethnological study in Germany.[7] When he was made museum director, Bastian also assumed an honorary university professorship. The lecture offerings in his field expanded in the 1880s and his assistants began to do the teaching (a good thing because Bastian was a very poor teacher). The *Berliner Gesellschaft* was a major force behind the Prussian government's decision to appoint regular faculty in ethnology and related fields in the 1890s. It worked with the Berlin branches of the German Colonial Society to encourage the transformation of the university's Seminar for Oriental Languages into a comprehensive training institute for colonial officials, featuring many courses on anthropological subjects.[8]

The *Berliner Gesellschaft* sponsored particular projects in ethnography and archaeology, although it directly supervised very few major expeditions because its resources were limited. More typically, the *Gesellschaft*'s leadership (especially Virchow and Bastian) used their influence to seek private and government funding for explorers, archaeologists, and academic ethnographers they had taken under their wing, and they gave such people an opportunity to find future support by publishing the results of their work. The most famous instance of this kind of sponsorship, however, involved recognition rather than funding: Virchow's championing of Heinrich Schliemann and the latter's work at Troy and Mycenae. Several of the best-known German explorers of Africa just before the partition of the 1880s (including Schweinfurth and Gustav Nachtigal) obtained support through the *Berliner Gesellschaft*'s leadership.[9]

By the mid-1870s at the latest, then, the *Berliner Gesellschaft* had emerged as the central institution of a highly complex and wide-ranging establishment in German anthropology. The *Gesellschaft* was to maintain this position well into the twentieth century, although the Berlin establishment was to receive serious challenges to its dominance of anthropology from the 1880s onward, both from cultural scientists working in other parts of the country and from within the Berlin-centered network itself. To understand the nature of some of these challenges we must turn from the structure of the Berlin establishment to the ideas and the theoretical pattern associated with it.

Neoliberal Anthropology

Virchow, Bastian, and other longtime leading members of the *Berliner Gesellschaft* had a fairly clearly defined strategy for cultural science in mind, a strategy in which the *Gesellschaft* played a vital role. In the first place, they sought to prevent disciplinary fragmentation as the fields of cultural science expanded and took on particular identities. All of the fields advertised in the *Gesellschaft*'s title received attention, although the leadership openly treated ethnology as the most important because it was central to the theoretical enterprise of cultural science. Virchow particularly emphasized this point, even though his own research was primarily in archaeology and physical anthropology.[10]

Behind Virchow's emphasis was an intent that transcended the immediate purpose of maintaining intellectual coherence. One of the dangers Virchow recognized in a physical anthropology that diverged from ethnology was that it might develop a racist logic that subordinated both culture and the individual to skull type and brain capacity in explaining social development. Although Virchow paid a great deal of attention to physical characteristics as an influence on human culture and although he believed that there were such things as degenerate races, he consistently maintained that a people's capacities and achievements were primarily functions of its culture, which was itself a complex entity not solely determined either by racial type or by environment. For most peoples, culture was something that attained meaning through the thoughts and actions of individuals who were fundamentally similar. In any event, as Virchow concluded after his famous survey of the physical characteristics of Prussian schoolchildren, all peoples (especially the Prussians) are biologically mixed, which makes it impossible to isolate physical or racial effects on society.[11] Part of Virchow's resistance to uncritical acceptance of Darwinism derived from his opposition to simplistic sociocultural explanations based on somatic inference.

In insisting on the centrality of ethnology—the study of culture—in human science, Virchow was in essence attempting to maintain liberal assumptions and liberal values against the threat of a racialism based on physical anthropology. Both human science and progressive liberal politics (as Virchow understood them) depended on accepting such assumptions as the fundamental sameness of human individuals; the capacity of individuals to realize a potential for intellectual development that was, despite qualifications, universal; and the ability of a society maximizing individual freedom to improve people. Like Waitz, Virchow thought that an empirical human science of culture could, by demonstrating the validity of these assumptions beneath the varieties of culture, prevent the use of physical anthropology and racial studies to support what he regarded as antiliberal ideas: the assertion that there are no universal political ideals because there is no commonality among human races and peoples and the belief that class differences based on differing levels of inherited intelligence are inevitable.[12]

There were other elements in the Berlin establishment's strategy. Bastian particularly emphasized "salvage anthropology"—that is, the recording of as much data as possible about the cultures of primitive peoples before those cultures were altered permanently by the onslaught of modernization and European imperialism.[13] The *Berliner Gesellschaft* generally subscribed to Bastian's view, if not to his obsession with it. Bastian's concern followed directly from his conception of the function of anthropology, which will be discussed in chapter 6. The fundamental operations of the human mind could only be revealed by comparative analysis of "primitive" thought as manifested in the cultures of *Naturvölker*. If evidence about those cultures were lost, humankind would lose its only hope of understanding its own "real" mental self. But the *Gesellschaft*'s subscription to salvage anthropology also displayed some of the motivational ambiguities felt by liberals throughout the Western world in the era of the "new imperialism." On the whole believers in modernity, progress, and change, they could, nevertheless, hardly help but regret—presumably not always for the academic reasons that they cited—the passing of premodern societies. As supporters of individual freedom of choice and opponents of tyranny, they had to be repelled by the methods through which the most obvious agent of cultural change—imperialism—operated. The growing tendency toward formal cultural relativism in their thinking after the 1860s both arose from and strengthened their belief that items of value from premodern non-Western cultures had to be preserved as those cultures changed.[14]

Virchow and Bastian both publicly opposed (with reservations) Germany's expansionary colonial policy in the 1880s, but both, as leaders of the Berlin anthropological establishment, were willing to cooperate with the colonial authorities after the decision for colonies was finally made. They recognized that a colonial empire would bring new opportunities for government support of anthropology.[15] This reveals yet another facet of their strategy: the creation, from whatever materials were available, of an efficient system for the conduct of cultural science. By 1900, using opportunities such as Germany's new colonial empire, they had put together a wide but loose network for cultural research that involved a substantial division of labor.

The core of the network was a small cadre of professional academic specialists: the professors, *Privatdozenten,* and students of anthropological subjects, mainly at the University of Berlin. Bastian took primary change of creating this nucleus when he acquired professorial status and became director of the Royal Museum for *Völkerkunde.* The latter afforded him museum assistantships to give out to potential academic anthropologists. In the 1880s, Bastian recruited the first generation of Berlin-trained professional ethnologists—such great lights as Franz Boas and Karl von den Steinen as well as decidedly lesser luminaries like Felix von Luschan.[16] Bastian did not inspire his recruits with his teaching or (in many cases) with his specific ideas, but rather with his enthusiasm and example. The students, in turn, attracted and trained a second and third generation of anthropologists in Berlin and at other universities, including those places where Boas taught and worked in America. A second center of anthropological study arose at the University of Leipzig, but until after the turn of the century, Berlin was the capital of academic anthropology.

It was never intended that academics should take over all activities of the discipline. Rather, they were to be its general staff and high command, succeeding the less specialized pioneers who had founded the *Berliner Gesellschaft.* They were to collate data and material artifacts acquired from around the world, and they were to use them to formulate and test hypotheses about culture. The modern idea that fieldwork was a *necessary* component of anthropological training and that data collection and theorizing had to be undertaken by the same people did not enter into the plan. Many Berlin students did in fact travel for ethnographic purposes, and their spiritual father, Bastian, spent a large part of his life abroad. But it was never considered essential that an academic anthropologist do so in order to achieve his doctorate or habilitation. Indeed, as anthropology became more professionalized after the turn of the century, it became increasingly possible to make a career in anthropology (especially ethnology) as a theorist alone, leaving data collection to others.[17] Some of the very best students who became connected to the Berlin establishment in the 1880s—von den Steinen and Boas—did indeed conduct full-scale programs of fieldwork as junior academics. Later on Boas, in America, was to help create the modern view that fieldwork was essential to the development of the theorist as a scientist. But this was not why they were sent out, Boas to the Canadian north and von den Steinen to the Amazon. They were sent on specific missions to collect artifacts for the Berlin Museum and ethnographic data that could be presented in journals—in both cases for other people or the collectors themselves, once they got back, to analyze.[18] Bastian talked some of his students—those with little apparent potential as theorists but with adequate private incomes—into acting as travelling collectors and ethnographers who regularly sent materials back to Berlin. One such was Arthur Bässler, who apparently accepted with equanimity his role as wealthy collector of artifacts for the perusal of more esteemed professional colleagues.[19]

For the most part, however, the Berlin anthropological establishment expected that data, both artifacts and recorded ethnographical observations, would come from amateurs—from the "explorers" and travellers with whom the Victorian world abounded, from colonial officials, and from missionaries. Bastian and Virchow made these people as welcome as possible in the *Berliner Gesellschaft,* partly in order to encourage them, but partly also to train them—to make sure that data collection would become less occasional and haphazard, more systematic, and more closely adjusted to answering the theoretical questions with which the anthropological elite concerned itself.[20] We shall see later how the Berlin establishment set about developing the ethnographical capacities of colonial officials from the 1890s onward. Even earlier, they had tried, with varying degrees of success, to do the same thing with the explorers they took under their wings.

Part of the appeal to such people was, of course, the possibility that their work would appear in print—*if* it met the standards of the Berlin establishment. At the same time, amateurs and most of the fieldworkers were not encouraged to move too far into the realm of theory building and theoretical controversy. Efficient science required an intellectual division of labor, and theoretical work was the function of the academic centers, of specially trained and gifted people. Virchow in particular was very concerned lest comprehensive ethnological theories be prematurely advanced by people unqualified to advance them. This may partly have been due to his experiences with the Darwinists and to a certain crankiness he displayed as he grew older, but (not surprisingly) Virchow explained it differently. Anthropology was just at the beginning of its development as a science. It was necessary that its methods be systematized, its organization perfected, and an adequate body of reliable data be acquired before substantial theory building could be performed. Virchow regretted his colleague Bastian's tendency toward broad generalization, and he certainly disapproved of theorizing by just any overgrown adolescent who had tramped through some seldom-visited part of the world.[21]

Virchow's position on theorizing and his notion of the division of anthropological labor also derived, however, from much more fundamental concerns than these. They were in fact basic to his view (and that of other founders of the Berlin establishment) of the function of cultural science as an intellectual activity. These views can be represented in various ways, but they can be seen most coherently as manifestations of a theoretical pattern derived primarily from traditional liberal social science. Virchow, Bastian, and other founders of the Berlin anthropological establishment saw their version of cultural science as a means simultaneously of extending the basic thrust of the liberal theoretical pattern into new areas of inquiry and of using the study of culture to correct some of the defects in the traditional pattern that were discussed in earlier chapters. As we have already seen, this perception was colored, although not entirely dominated, by considerations of liberal politics in Bismarckian Germany.

The "neoliberal" theoretical pattern developed by the Berlin anthropological establishment encompassed positions on the three major elements of the older liberal pattern: individualism, the idea of nomothetic social science, and notions of social change and equilibrium. With respect to the first, Bastian advanced a complex view of human psychology in its relationship to culture.[22] (See chapter 6.) Briefly, he saw comparative anthropology as a way of identifying the elementary ideas common to the psychic activity of all humans that lay beneath the differing patterns of thought that signalled the differences among peoples and cultures. These elementary ideas, once identified by empirical research, could be used to build a substitute for the the abstract individual of traditional human science and to construct a model of the basic mental processes that in the past had been too glibly categorized as "reason."

Virchow, as a physical anthropologist, approached the problem of the individual somewhat differently. Like Bastian and Waitz, Virchow perceived the questions of human unity and the relationship of individual, *Volk,* race, and species at least ostensibly as empirical problems. Rather than simply postulating an underlying human similarity, he took very seriously the possible implications of the physical differences among races, the classification of which had made physical anthropology a major science. He argued that certain physical differences did affect the capacities of various races to adapt to particular environments—and therefore affected the cultures that arose from environmental adaptation.[23] Cultural, social and technological progress could improve the adaptability of a race, but not infinitely—as Virchow argued in trying to show that European populations could not be transplanted successfully to tropical climates because they could not maintain adequate reproduction rates there, regardless of the ability of individual Europeans to find ways of surviving. (Significantly, Virchow's motive in advancing this argument was largely political: he used it to oppose a policy of German colonialism, or at least colonial settlement in Africa, in the 1880s.)[24]

But allowing for these and other points, Virchow claimed that, on the whole, anatomical and physiological evidence supported the idea that humans were fundamentally the same. It should, therefore, be possible to reason inferentially about all humans on the basis of an ideal-typical individual if the type were described accurately from reliable empirical evidence. In order to account for human groups that, from such evidence, seemed to be inferior to the common run of humankind, Virchow argued that there could exist degenerate races which preserved some sort of physical or psychological deformity. This would account, he thought, for groups such as the pygmies of Central Africa. On the other hand, even degeneracy often dissolved on closer, impartial examination. In 1875, at Virchow's instigation, the *Berliner Gesellschaft* brought a number of Lapps to Berlin for interview and observation. Virchow, who had accounted the Lapps a degenerate race, admitted that there was no obvious deficiency of mind or body among them—that what at a distance had seemed inferiority owing to degeneracy was more likely a cultural difference due to adaptation to environment.[25]

Virchow was confident that, in time, comparative ethnology of the sort pioneered by Bastian would reveal the psychological foundations of common humanity beneath the differences of culture and within the parameters imposed by variations in physical environment and anatomy. This would replace the inadequate model of the abstract individual as the basis for making general statements about the thought and behavior of humankind.[26] But what about real individuals? One of the appealing features of the traditional abstract, universal model of the individual in social thought was that it could be linked (however tenuous the logic of the linkage might be) to the individual of liberal political and legal thought—an individual with whom liberals believed real people could identify. If the abstract individual were reduced to a disembodied collection of psychological traits perceptible only after exhaustive anthropological comparison among cultures, what would that do to the sense of reality, the feeling of identity between real individuals and the abstraction upon which liberal social theory was based and upon which liberalism as an ideology depended?

One answer, of course, was to merge the individual entirely into the group or classification—the race, the *Volk*, the cultural type. Real people could then perceive themselves as members of groups, as exemplars of the German nation, the white race, and so forth. A great many cultural scientists did this. But one of the essential features of the neoliberal approach to culture as taken up by the Berlin anthropological establishment was an unwillingness to accept that answer, possibly because it would have been too destructive of the intellectual basis of the liberal ideology to which they were committed. Instead, their anthropology tended to focus on the relationships among what was universal in the composition of the individual, what was learned by the individual from his or her culture, and what was unique to a person. Hence, neoliberal cultural science strongly emphasized the usefulness of comparative ethnology as a means of making valid statements about individual psychology.

Bastian developed the outlines of a theory of cultural diffusion in part as a way to understand the structure of these relationships.[27] The transmission of cultural traits from place to place and their accumulation in certain combinations among certain peoples, together with the effects of differing environmental circumstances, accounted for the differences in cultural characteristics of peoples and, at the same time, provided a means of preserving the notion of human uniformity. Bastian's view of diffusion also provided scope for the actions of particularly creative individuals because the invention, transmission, and acceptance of new cultural traits (ideas, material objects, words) all require such actions.

Like practically all cultural scientists with whom this book is concerned, Virchow and Bastian accepted the nomothetic aim of human study, considered themselves to be scientists, and refused to acknowledge a categorical distinction between physical and human science—although they readily admitted that the methods of cultural science had often to be different from those of the natural sciences.[28] For the reasons that have already been discussed, both were convinced that the essence of cultural science for the moment was the systematic, accurate recording of data and the building up of inferences from the data. To Virchow in particular the postulating and testing of full-blown theories was something for future generations of anthropologists. For the present, the main aim was to clear away unsound older theories about human behavior and history not grounded in empirical research in order to combat the tendency to pursue premature, dangerous, and factually unsupported ideas, and to collect the material on which real theories could be built.[29]

Because Virchow had made his own reputation in physiology by advancing theories substantially in advance of the evidence, this position seems at first glance to be surprising. It probably reflects a degree of intellectual conservatism that came to Virchow with age as well as his position as a leader of several intellectual and political establishments. (His adherence as a Progressive party leader to traditional liberal ideology in the face of new ideas—for instance, those about social welfare— was just as pronounced).[30] It also represents a not ill-founded suspicion of the implications of new cultural theories that began emerging in the 1870s and 1880s and that overtly challenged many of the elements of the traditional liberal theoretical pattern that Virchow wanted to preserve. We shall pursue these matters later.

Bastian was less hesitant than Virchow about theorizing and about prescribing abstract methods of doing cultural science. He did in fact present several rather wide-ranging theories about cultural development, diffusion, and psychology, and he developed his own "comparative-genetic" ethnological method.[31] But Bastian regarded these as only necessary first steps toward a fully developed cultural science, and he agreed with Virchow about the primary need for systematic data collection. In fact neither Bastian's theories nor his method survived him intact, even among those followers he most influenced.

In other words, neoliberal anthropology did not, in its period of greatest dominance in Germany, actually produce characteristic theories of culture or laws of the sort that science was supposed to discover. Its founders, although acknowledging the nomothetic aim of their discipline, kept it from proceeding rapidly in that direction and bequeathed to it a suspicion of universal theorizing and a bias in favor of making limited statements deriving directly from collected data—a suspicion and bias that can be seen most profoundly developed in the work of their most distinguished descendant, Franz Boas. Lack of a theory, however, did not mean the absence of a theoretical pattern. Virchow's deliberate avoidance of theorizing and the rationale for his position in themselves constituted a distinct element of the neoliberal pattern that distinguished that pattern from others that grew up to challenge it.

Like all German approaches to cultural science, Berlin anthropology concerned itself deeply with the question of social change. As we have seen, one of the most pronounced motives behind the widespread interest among liberals throughout Europe in ethnology, archaeology, and prehistory during the second half of the nineteenth century was the desire to use insights from these fields as means of understanding the problematical features of change in modern society.[32] German scholars associated with the *Berliner Gesellschaft* were fully cognizant of the main lines of theoretical dispute about change among anthropologists in Britain and elsewhere: the arguments of the degenerationists with the advocates of progressive development, followed by the disputes between the diffusionists and the famous British cultural evolutionists Sir Henry Maine, E. B. Taylor, and Sir John Lubbock. Many of the same arguments found their way into the discussions of the Berlin ethnologists.[33] Nevertheless, professional discourse about change developed differently in Germany than it did in Britain, in part because the proponents of all of the major positions on culture change in Germany took history (the source of factual knowledge about change) seriously as a complex, problematical subject of empirical study. They were less likely than their British counterparts to regard history as a simple, uniform pattern of change that could be inferred from theory and applied universally.

The idea that cultural study should be placed in a historical setting was something of a novelty in British anthropology in the mid-nineteenth century, one partly imported from Germany. It was essentially absorbed in a general pursuit of broad patterns of cultural explanation. East of the Rhine, however, historical orientations had long been an accepted part of social theorizing (although they became even more significant in social analysis in Germany as the century went on).[34] Furthermore, the concepts of "culture" and "history" were conventionally linked together in Germany to a larger extent than they were in Britain. The idea of stages of development was part of the liberal theoretical pattern in German social science. Therefore, when German social science fragmented from the 1850s onward and when the major theoretical patterns of cultural science arose from the fragments, many of these patterns, including Berlin neoliberalism, displayed strong historicizing tendencies.[35]

The predominance of this concern for historical development in Germany was partly due to the absence of a clear-cut liberal victory in politics. To some extent, concern on the parts of social and cultural scientists with the possible nuances and complexities of change in history reflected a political situation in which the specific direction of change was uncertain, in which there was real cause to doubt, especially after the 1860s, that the liberal model of social and political organization would ever be entirely realized. In Britain, on the other hand, liberal social thinkers after about 1850, even though they might be perplexed by unexpected aspects of socioeconomic change, nevertheless could be completely sure that their own society was fundamentally liberal—and convinced also that their society represented the highest attainment of humanity to date.

Even without the Darwinian model to give a specific set of forms to their thinking, the leading British anthropologists would probably have come to the same general consensus on cultural evolution that they did, along the lines suggested by Herbert Spencer before the publication of *The Origin of Species*.[36] On the basis of the fundamental uniformity of the human species and the limited array of possible human responses to environments, a more or less uniform course of human social and cultural development could be postulated. Some peoples or races were thought to have followed the course faster than others, whereas others were arrested in their development. The mechanisms of progress were many, but the British evolutionists on the whole emphasized individual invention in a context of competition. The evolutionists did not at all neglect the possibility of the diffusion of inventions, but they made parallel invention, not diffusion, the central feature of their thinking.[37]

Neoliberal anthropology in Germany displayed many similarities to evolutionism in Britain, not only because of the substantial exchange of ideas between German and British anthropologists, but also because of similarities in ideological outlook. Both groups were essentially liberal, and liberal in what was by the 1870s a traditional sense: preserving liberal ideas against attacks from all ideological directions.[38] The ideas of progress and social evolution were generally accepted by the German neoliberals; indeed, it had been a significant part of the theoretical pattern of their intellectual forebears. But few of the Germans were as certain as their British counterparts about the inevitability of uniform, or at least generically similar, social evolution among peoples. The Germans had to confront more directly the question of differences in patterns of sociocultural change, of variations that called into question the assumptions that underlay evolutionary anthropology in Britain. They were living through a process of rapid modernization in their own country that might or might not be comprehensible through patterns observed in the earlier modernization of Britain. They had adopted an approach to culture and to the task of finding the laws of culture that made it difficult to take the kind of a priori position that the British evolutionists did. The differing intellectual and political contexts in which intellectuals of a liberal persuasion confronted these circumstances in Germany and Britain led to differences in emphasis between the establishment anthropologies that emerged in the two countries.

Having said what view of change did not emerge in Berlin anthropology, it is rather more difficult to describe exactly what view did present itself. In part the problem is the same as the one mentioned previously: the anthropological establishment's (especially Virchow's) reluctance to theorize, and sometimes even to hypothesize, in advance of the evidence. Part of it is also due to the absence of a clearly defined idea of the mechanism of change among people unwilling to adopt Darwinian analogies as models. What emerged was an attitude rather than a full-blown theory. It was universally agreed that anthropology, whether ethnology, physical anthropology, or archaeology, had to be developed in a historical dimension with a view of all aspects of societal change over time.[39] If there were laws of humankind that could be reliably identified amid the data that were being accumulated in increasing amounts from around the world, they would most likely be developmental laws. The question of whether or not these laws would correspond to the laws of physical nature and thus could be used for prediction was generally answered in the affirmative, although it was seldom considered to be worth asking. Only with the growing attention paid to hermeneutics and idealist approaches to social understanding by the academic community in the 1880s and 1890s did it become necessary to deal with the issue at length.[40]

The leaders of the Berlin anthropological establishment considered themselves to be scientists. To them the essence of science was accurate data collection, the careful construction of hypotheses, and the equally careful testing of the hypotheses. Because insufficient data were as yet available, it was premature to do more than frame tentative hypotheses—or, in the case of Bastian, it was premature to regard cultural theories as much more than hypotheses. Hypothetical statements about human social and cultural development could take many forms: they could be evolutionary, diffusionist, even on occasion, if the data seemed to demand it, degenerationist. Indeed, they could easily combine all three. The most important of them, however, had to be in some sense historical or at least to have historical implications: to tend toward explaining, if not necessarily where humankind was going, at least how it had arrived at where it was.

Because of the general array of ideas and attitudes out of which establishment anthropology grew, its intellectual framework was built around notions of the cultural superiority or inferiority of different peoples or cultural forms. Such notions were inherent in the outlooks of nineteenth-century Europeans and were fundamental to the idea of progress incorporated in liberal thought: progress was change in the direction already laid down by the most "advanced," thus superior, peoples. The distinction between *Naturvölker* and *Kulturvölker* obviously depended on the same kind of thinking. It was not uncommon to explain cultural superiority through the biological superiority of certain races, although the leadership of the Berlin establishment resisted biological racism.[41] The spread of popular Darwinism, however, helped to propagate racist interpretations of neoliberal doctrine toward the end of the century.

In the 1870s and 1880s, there also appeared a tendency within the framework of neoliberal anthropology toward cultural relativism—a tendency that became a basic principle of theory in the work of the most important of the second-generation neoliberals, Franz Boas. The tendency arose in part from the general pattern of traditional liberalism with its emphasis on the uniformity of basic human nature, which is probably the most significant source of modern cultural relativism. In part relativism in Berlin anthropology also arose from the difficulty professional anthropologists experienced in fitting all the data from particular cultures into a simple continuum of superior and inferior elements. People who appear primitive in some ways are not always primitive in others, no matter what criteria one applies. But the full implications of cultural relativism for comprehending the possible aims of cultural science and the nature of its methodologies were not recognized by the leaders the Berlin establishment in the nineteenth century.[42]

The Heirs of Neoliberalism

The Berlin establishment did succeed in creating a cadre of professional anthropologists to carry on the program of neoliberal cultural science. Naturally enough, teaching and research positions at the University of Berlin and at the Royal Museum were mostly filled in the late nineteenth and early twentieth centuries by students of Bastian and students of Bastian's students.[43] Moreover, the success of the Berlin establishment in allying itself with the colonial administration gave the new professional anthropologists opportunities that their predecessors did not have: state funding for teaching positions in part intended for the training of colonial officials, some limited funding for research, a close association with the state that amplified the "established" character of Berlin anthropology.[44] Berlin-trained anthropologists also obtained teaching jobs in other universities. The *Berliner Gesellschaft,* despite the founding of other, often more specialized associations in the cultural sciences, retained its position as the premier anthropological society in the country, and the *Zeitschrift für Ethnologie* remained the nation's leading anthropological journal.

But even before the passing of Virchow and Bastian at the turn of the century, Berlin anthropology had ceased to be the source of creativity, of new directions in German anthropology. There were several reasons for this. The Berlin establishment showed all of the standard tendencies of establishments everywhere, except perhaps that it did not confront intellectual opposition by banning or ignoring it. Although Berlin University produced some outstanding anthropologists, only a few of these reached the top of the academic career ladder at Berlin. On the whole, the people who got professorships at Berlin from the first professional generation (and even more so from the second) were mediocrities like Felix von Luschan—people whose limited talents were noted by their own students.[45] The successful establishment politicians, as opposed to the most creative scholars, reached the top. There was nothing novel about that, of course, but it worked against the long-term dominance of Berlin anthropology.

Even more important, however, was the fact that Berlin remained attached to the theoretical pattern laid down by the founders of neoliberal cultural science. Supposedly, the essence of this pattern was the idea that theories would grow naturally out of increased data collection. But they did not—at least not theories of sufficient scope and content to catch broad public attention or to impress themselves on students. Novelty there was, in the sense that public interest in the exotic was as keen as ever and even dull and pedantic articles on, say, head-hunting could find a nonacademic audience, especially if accompanied by pictures. The Berlin anthropologists did not neglect the popular geographical press. But they did not produce the kinds of ideas that would allow them to compete, in the overheated intellectual climate of the late nineteenth and early twentieth centuries, with more comprehensive presentations of human fate and history, including some that were appearing within their own profession. Even excellent research by Berlin anthropologists like von den Steinen and Paul Ehrenreich did not have the same public impact as diffusionism and other approaches to holistic cultural science emanating largely from other academic centers.[46]

Apart from the undramatic character of Berlin anthropology, it also suffered from being tied to what were coming to be regarded as old-fashioned approaches to science and politics. Increasing numbers of students, young academics, and the intellectual community at large came to think of the Virchow–Bastian style of cultural science as obsolete, inadequate to meet new demands on social science for understanding the human condition. The same sort of criticism appeared all through the human sciences in the last years of the century. Without a dominant personality to defend the neoliberal approach after Virchow, Berlin anthropology was left vulnerable to assault from newer directions in cultural science.

The assault had been building since the 1880s, but it breached the walls of the Berlin establishment in 1904, shortly after Virchow and Bastian's deaths. At a meeting of the *Berliner Gesellschaft,* two junior ethnologists, Fritz Graebner (1877–1934) and Bernhard Ankermann, (1858–1943), presented classic papers that reviewed diffusionist interpretations of cultures in Oceania and Africa.[47] These papers were published in the *Zeitschrift für Ethnologie* and became the central canon of the diffusionist movement in German anthropology. Diffusionism (examined in later chapters) was structured consciously to be an alternative to neoliberal cultural science of the Berlin type, and now it had been legitimated as a theoretical pattern at the very center of the Berlin establishment. Ankermann went on to become a professor at the University of Berlin; although the neoliberal pattern did not disappear, diffusionism became the dominant approach to anthropological theory in Germany—Berlin included.[48]

The neoliberal theoretical pattern did produce long-term results. Many of the basic tenets of the neoliberal approach were brought into the twentieth century by linguistic anthropologists such as Diedrich Westermann and by Richard Thürnwald, the founder of German functionalism. Although the pattern lost much of its linkage to political liberalism, the connection did not entirely disappear—as the career of Westermann shows. But on the whole, diffusionism became the characteristic form of German anthropology, which was one of the reasons that Germany moved apart from much of the rest of the world in that area.[49]

The greatest long-term impact of German neoliberal anthropology was felt not in Germany, but in the United States—in the work of Franz Boas (1858–1942). To describe Boas simply as a product of Berlin anthropology and to trace his approach to ethnology to that source alone would be absurd.[50] Boas reflected a large number of influences and was extremely eclectic in his thinking about culture. From the 1890s onward, he operated both physically in the United States and intellectually in the Anglo-American world, although this second aspect took some time to become predominant. Moreover, Boas was only in Berlin for a short time at the end of his formal training (which was more in physical science than in anthropology). Although his first fieldwork took place under Bastian's wing, it is by no means clear that Bastian regarded him as a particularly promising scholar. That Boas decided to make his career in the United States may have been due to fear that anti-Semitism would keep him out of one in Germany, but it may also have been that Boas had no particular reason to expect that the leaders of the Berlin establishment favored him.

Yet, not only did Boas continue to play an active part in theoretical discussions in German anthropology, but he also showed in his own work the permanent impress of neoliberal cultural science. He was, for one thing, a lifelong liberal. It is true that his liberalism, finding a more congenial political home in America, adapted itself to American conditions—as the political thinking of thousands of other nineteenth-century German immigrants had done. It retained, nevertheless, a generic quality; clearly, Boas regarded it more as a practical manifestation of social truth than as just an ideology to which he happened to subscribe. On this basis, Boas did not hesitate to marshal his scientific forces to engage in political controversy—if the controversy was significant and broad enough.[51] His research into the psychological and physical characteristics of American Blacks in order to support the idea of racial equality in the early twentieth century (and incidentally to attack the politically oriented racism that had previously dominated much of American anthropology) was the most famous instance of Boas's marriage of science and politics, but there were others. And in Boas's emphasis on accurate data collection, on resisting the temptation to theorize too early, on treating anthropology as a science like others, and on understanding the psychology of the individual as the chief aim of cultural science can be seen reflections of the theoretical pattern within which Boas was trained. Boas went well beyond the boundaries of neoliberal cultural science—for example, in fostering the idea of fieldwork as intellectual training for the anthropologist and in working out the implications of cultural relativity for ethnological method—but most of his work was at least consistent with the neoliberal approach.

6

Völkerpsychologie

Most of the cultural sciences examined in this study still exist, even if the theoretical patterns connected with them have changed. *Völkerpsychologie* is dead. It did not, in any real sense, survive the 1920s, and it never achieved full recognition as an independent discipline outside of the German-speaking countries. Even in its heyday, during the last third of the nineteenth century, it was rather difficult to separate its central concerns from those of cultural anthropology as that discipline was defining itself. Nevertheless, German *Völkerpsychologie* was widely respected, if not imitated, among cultural scientists throughout the world.[1]

Völkerpsychologie was the comparative study of the characteristic mental patterns of different peoples, with particular emphasis on the historical development of those patterns. Although its concerns would today be considered almost wholly anthropological, in the nineteenth century it was usually regarded as a complement to the emerging discipline of experimental psychology. *Experimental* psychology? Strange as the connection may seem to us, it appeared perfectly natural to people like Wilhelm Wundt, one of the fathers of experimental psychology and also Germany's foremost practitioner of *Völkerpsychologie*. Experimental psychology was a form of *empirical* psychology; *Völkerpsychologie* was essentially empirical psychology without laboratory experiments.[2]

The history of *Völkerpsychologie* would be worth examining as a case study of a deserted science. We shall in fact consider some of the reasons that the discipline did not maintain itself, but our main concern will be with *Völkerpsychologie* as a cultural science, particularly with its relationship to the traditions of liberal social science. *Völkerpsychologie* started out in the 1850s as (among other things) a response within the framework of the liberal theoretical pattern to the crisis of liberalism and of social science. From the 1860s until close to the turn of the century, it was connected with neoliberal anthropology, at least to the extent of sharing a similar theoretical base. As time went on, however, and especially from about the 1890s, the connection to neoliberalism increasingly broke down as the adherents of *Völkerpsychologie* tried to develop alternatives to a pattern that many of them no longer believed to be effective. They were unable to do so—at least not to the satisfaction of the rest of the academic community and the public at large—and in the end their science disappeared. This chapter is not a comprehensive history of *Völkerpsychologie* or a description of its disciplinary structure.[3] Rather, it concentrates on the contributions to *Völkerpsychologie* of two of its major figures: Adolf Bastian and Wilhelm Wundt. Both are remembered as founder figures of

115

other disciplines, but both believed that their most lasting impact would be felt in the field of *Völkerpsychologie*.

Adolf Bastian: *Völkerpsychologie* as Neoliberal Cultural Science

Völkerpsychologie was identified as an independent field of human studies in the 1850s. It was a outgrowth of the fashion for cultural studies of that decade and, like most other cultural sciences, was created by scholars whose recognized disciplinary affiliations lay in various areas. By the end of the decade, it had its own journal and courses of lectures at some universities, although the lectures were usually gives as sidelines by instructors employed mainly to do other things.[4]

One of the founders of the discipline was Theodor Waitz, whose path through psychology to cultural science in the 1850s we have already traced. Distressed by the unwillingness of the mass of people to act rationally and to support the erection of a liberal society and disturbed also by the apparent inability of current educational methods to produce the citizens of a rational liberal state, Waitz decided to look deeply into the factors in human psychology that produced these circumstances. This led him to a consideration of the mental and behavioral differences among individuals and to the question of the extent to which the groups to which individuals belonged accounted for the differences. As we saw in chapter 2, Waitz eventually came to the conclusion that it was necessary through the comparative study both of human physical characteristics and of cultures throughout the world, to try to demonstrate empirically what was universal and basic in human psychic life and what was historically and culturally conditioned.[5] Only then would it be possible to create an effective system of education (and by extension an effective essence of politics) that would realize liberal aims. What Waitz advocated was a connection between psychology—with its traditional focus on the individual and its characteristic method of reasoning from the psychologist's introspection—and comparative cultural study—with the investigator as objective outsider. The was the essence of *Völkerpsychologie*.

Waitz was only one of several people who came to similar conclusions in the 1850s about the need to link psychology to comparative ethnology. Waitz's *Anthropologie der Naturvölker* was a major contribution to the process, but Waitz died too early (in 1864) to shape the resulting discipline. More significant in the latter respect was Adolf Bastian (1826–1905). We have already met Bastian as one of the founders of ethnology in Germany and as a pillar of the Berlin anthropological establishment. He was also a founder of *Völkerpsychologie* and a strong proponent of the neoliberal idea that psychology should remain close to the core of all social and cultural study.[6]

Bastian came from a well-to-do Bremen commercial family.[7] Although he trained as a physician at Würzburg (under Virchow, among others), he only practiced medicine briefly. In the early 1850s, while at the university, he was caught up in the general enthusiasm for cultural study. After taking his medical degree, he embarked on a five-year round-the-world trip as a ship's doctor. From then on,

Bastian regularly took extended tours of different parts of the world to observe customs and behavior and to collect artifacts. Because he enjoyed travel, possessed an independent income, and did not marry, he never became purely a sedentary scholar. By later standards (which Bastian helped to develop), his field methods left a great deal to be desired, and the one elaborate ethnological expedition he organized was pretty much a disaster. But his wanderings by himself—often un-planned—gave him a direct experience of other cultures equalled (if at all) only by that of Alexander von Humboldt. In the periods between his travels, Bastian pro-duced mountains of publications on geography, ethnology, comparative psychology, and other subjects—some theoretical, some descriptive, and some journalistic. The theoretical works were, in truth, badly written, confusing, and repetitious, although some of the ideas they contained influenced students and scholars in all of his fields.[8] The journalistic and descriptive pieces were more gladly and widely read. Although essentially a free lance for most of his career, he was active, as we have seen, in the *Berliner Gesellschaft*. From the 1870s, he lectured on ethnology at the University of Berlin and in 1886 became the first director of the Royal Ethnological Museum in Berlin.

We know less about Bastian's early intellectual development than we do about that of Waitz or Virchow, and still less about his early politics. We do know that at least from his middle twenties, and probably before, Bastian was a political liberal of the same general type as Virchow and that, although only occasionally active in politics, he remained loyal to the orthodoxies of midcentury liberalism in much the same way Virchow did. It is also evident from his writings—particularly on comparative psychology—that Bastian attempted to adhere as much as possible to the traditional liberal theoretical pattern in explaining human behavior, using the concept of culture as a means of supporting both the theoretical pattern and liberal political ideology. He was, therefore, a neoliberal.[9]

Like almost all post-1850 cultural scientists in the fields we are examining, Bastian believed that the object of human study should be the uncovering of laws. Because of the variety of cultural forms according to which people lived, however, such laws could be discovered only by the direct observation and comparative analysis of a worldwide sample of human phenomena. It was not enough to devise simple patterns of correlation between certain types of physical environment and certain cultural forms in the tradition of Montesquieu and Herder. Such thinking often led to generalizations that broke down on careful application (e.g., the ra-tionality of peoples from cold climates as opposed to the passion of peoples from hot ones). Bastian suspected that a wide variety of influences, including but not necessarily dominated by environmental ones, were processed by the human mind in such a way as to produce different forms of consciousness, different ways of thinking. These were transmitted between generations (and places) as culture. If one wanted to understand human behavior, it was necessary to understand these psychological processes through examining their workings in different cultures—a fundamental insight of *Völkerpsychologie*.[10]

Bastian had a fairly clearly defined framework within which to conduct com-parative analyses of the ethnographic data he collected. His framework displayed many of the characteristics of the neoliberal theoretical pattern. It was built around the idea of the uniform individual—not, however, in its traditional form as an abstract model from which inferences could be drawn, but rather as a hypothesis that, at a certain level of human mental activity, corresponded reasonably well with common human experience—or at least with Bastian's experience as a world traveller. Despite the great differences in thought and behavior between individuals from different cultures, an observer still had the feeling that beneath the differences existed a psychological foundation that was the same in everyone. Bastian referred to this foundation as the "psychic unity of mankind." Like Waitz, Bastian understood the ideological implications of psychic unity. If psychic unity could be empirically demonstrated and if the mental capacities that were uniform in humankind could be shown to be of a sufficiently high order, then most of the propositions of liberalism that were based on the presumption of common individual rational capacity could be maintained against attacks from the Right and the Left.[11]

But how was psychic unity to be demonstrated? Some neoliberal cultural scientists, including Waitz and Virchow, set great store by showing, on the basis of physical anthropology, that human individuals display far more similarities in physical form than they do differences and that anatomical differences that do exist between peoples or races seem to bear little relation to individual mental abilities. Bastian realized that this could never be a decisive argument. It could always be claimed that mental differences between peoples so extensive as to rule out psychic unity might exist and yet not be correlated with anatomical differences. Bastian decided to pay relatively little attention to physical anthropology and to focus on the relationship between individual mental capacity and culture.[12]

Bastian developed a structural model of the mind—one that, like Waitz's, had both material and psychic elements. Mental phenomena were the combined results of material circumstances (brain physiology, the impingement of the environment, etc.) and immaterial entities (mostly ideas) in the mind. Some of the latter were innate and some (the more complex) were acquired by acculturation. Just as the most important of the material elements of the mind—brain anatomy and physiology—were essentially uniform throughout humankind, so too the basic structure of ideas on which the rest of human thought was constructed was uniform as well. Bastian called this basic structure the "elementary ideas" of the species. What the exact relationship was between elementary ideas and the other varied forms of mental activity, between elementary ideas and brain physiology, and between elementary ideas and behavior Bastian could not say without extensive empirical research. But the most important thing that had to be demonstrated was the existence and the nature of the elementary ideas themselves because simply postulating them was obviously not convincing.

Identifying elementary ideas was not easy. According to Bastian they were not overtly present in conscious thought but rather lay hidden behind consciousness. Consciousness itself was given its general shape by elementary ideas, but its specific forms and most of its content were provided by culture. Culture varied with different peoples' historical experiences with their environments as well as with their levels of social and intellectual development.[13] Although Bastian was not a thoroughgoing evolutionist and did not believe that there was a single pattern of progress by which "primitive" peoples became "civilized" (unless civilization were imposed on them), he did retain the general distinction between *Kulturvölker* and *Naturvölker*.

The latter, although they possessed cultures that could be regarded as morally equivalent to those of the former, did not have as elaborate sets of cultural patterns to transmit from one generation to the next, nor did they have as complex institutions through which to transmit them. Therefore, among *Naturvölker,* especially the most primitive, "elementary ideas" were likely to be more evident, less overlaid with cultural differences than among other peoples. One could not, however, penetrate directly to the elementary ideas by studying just one people, no matter how primitive. All peoples have a substantial cultural overlay. But by comparing cultures with each other, it would be possible to isolate the elementary ideas common to all and to show the general process by which the cultural superstructure is built on them. The collection of data for this purpose had, however, to be done quickly, before the worldwide expansion of European culture eliminated the others that were essential to Bastian's strategy. To find their real selves, Europeans had to look abroad—and soon.[14]

Bastian's theoretical work extended to other areas, some of which we have already discussed and to some of which (especially his ideas about cultural change and diffusion) we shall return later. But elementary ideas, their relationship to variable cultural superstructures (which he generally called *Volk* ideas), and the use of comparative ethnology as a means of uncovering universal psychological processes constitute Bastian's main contribution to *Völkerpsychologie.*

There were problems, both with the results of Bastian's research and with the psychocultural model he devised.[15] He never convincingly demonstrated the existence or the identity of any elementary ideas. Furthermore, his general approach prevented him from establishing a basis of cultural comparison. Both his feeling that all cultures were morally equivalent and his strategy of comparing elements of culture at all levels throughout the whole world meant that he could not, as evolutionists in Britain did, take his own culture as the absolute standard of comparison, as an array of cultural traits in relation to which the traits of other cultures could be meaningfully interpreted. Although the religious ideas, say, of aboriginal Australians could be understood by an evolutionist as characteristics of a certain stage in the progress of humankind toward a future defined by Victorianism, to Bastian they were primarily data to be compared with religious data from other cultures in order to reveal the features of universal psychology that underlie religious behavior. Although even identifying these data as "religious" implies the imposition of some sort of ethnocentric classificatory framework, Bastian, aware of the dangers of ethnocentrism in interpretation, tried to keep more formal impositions of this sort to a minimum. So do modern anthropologists. The difference is that modern anthropologists are not trying to reveal universal laws of mental behavior, to find the key to common humanity in diversity. Bastian's ultimate goals were universalist; the material with which he worked was particular and immense in volume, and if he rejected the use of his own culture as the conscious standard of comparison, he had no other to replace it.

This is the main reason that Bastian's theoretical works are so infuriatingly diffuse and confusing. His cross-cultural comparisons bounce around from one place and culture to another.[16] Every comparison suggests others, each of which suggests still others. And in the end, the patterns that emerge are neither very clear nor very convincing. Bastian's model of elementary ideas and *Volk* ideas was not a sufficient substitute for an effective framework for comparing cultures. Indeed, it is difficult to see how any basically psychological model could fill the role, which may be one of the reasons that *Völkerpsychologie* did not survive. Many of the most important theoretical patterns in later anthropology—functionalism, for instance—can in part be seen as attempts to establish a framework for cultural comparison that depended neither on the overt designation of modern European culture as the standard nor on psychological models. Bastian was still too closely tied to the kind of thinking embodied in the neoliberal theoretical pattern, which continued to emphasize individual psychology as part of any social theory, to be able to go far in this direction.

Bastian's version of *Völkerpsychologie* also suffered from the fuzziness of his basic concepts—elementary ideas and *Volk* ideas—and the relationship between them. Probably, Bastian thought he was just laying down the outlines of these concepts and that empirical research would lead to sharper definitions. Despite his close association with Rudolf Virchow, Bastian never really worked the modern idea of hypothesis testing into his approach to mind and culture. He presumed the existence of elementary ideas and set about finding them rather than regarding them as hypothetical constructions that might account for certain human phenomena and that ought to be subjected to conscious testing for explanatory capacity. In other words, the kind of *Völkerpsychologie* advocated by Bastian, like his theoretical work in general, was not entirely satisfactory to people educated in the modern approach to experimental science that became dominant during the third quarter of the nineteenth century. One of these people was Wilhelm Wundt.

Wilhelm Wundt: *Völkerpsychologie* and Experimental Psychology

Wundt (1832–1920) was one of the founders of modern psychology. He was born in Baden to a family accustomed to producing distinguished scholars.[17] The young Wundt's own performance at the *Gymnasium* did not hold out much hope of academic distinction, which was the reason that his family used connections at the University of Tübingen to enroll him as a medical student. He would have preferred to study philosophy. He continued his medical studies at Heidelberg, where he showed unexpected talent, and decided on a career as a researcher—in part, because it allowed him to attach his medical studies to the generalized pursuit of philosophy.

Wundt's rather slow path to eminence began in 1858 with his appointment as Hermann von Helmholtz's assistant at Heidelberg. Originally under Helmholtz's direction and then by himself, Wundt began to study psychological phenomena, starting with perception. Wundt was strongly influenced by the new approach to scientific method that was sweeping the intellectual world in the 1850s and 1860s— an approach based on hypothesis testing through experimentation that Helmholtz, Virchow, and others had advanced in the closely related fields of physiology and physics. Wundt perceived the desirability of treating psychology at least in part as a physical science in the same way. The brilliant intuitions about the sensory system that had already been advanced by Gustav Fechner and others now had to be supplemented by systematic empirical research. After breaking with Helmholtz, Wundt created an international reputation for himself by conducting perception and reaction-time experiments and by publishing a number of classic synoptic texts on psychology. He continued this work when he transferred first to Zurich and then, in 1875, to Leipzig. It was at Leipzig that Wundt established the permanent psychological laboratory that became the training ground for two generations of the world's leading psychologists and that gave Wundt his reputation as the founder of modern experimental psychology.

Yet, while all this was going on, Wundt himself was at least as interested in aspects of psychology that he believed could not be subjected to laboratory experiment. He saw his experimental work mainly as a preparatory study for a much more elaborate investigation of the human mind and its relationship to the universe.[18] Although Wundt insisted on treating psychology as a science according to the strictest standards, this did not mean that he rejected the idea of psychology (or of physical science in general) as a branch of philosophy. He claimed to be strongly influenced by major philosophers whom he frequently cited. Like Bastian, Wundt had a habit—possibly born of insecurity about his own status as a "philosopher"— of hunting around among current and classical philosophical ideas until he found some that could be used to legitimate ideas that he had already formed. Nevertheless, his aim of using psychology as Waitz had wanted to do, to bridge the gap between the philosophical materialism associated with the science he had adopted and the philosophical idealism he deeply respected, was quite genuine.[19] This aim could only be achieved, Wundt thought, through the creation of an accurate *Völkerpsychologie* backed by an accurate physiological psychology.

Both the importance of *Völkerpsychologie* in Wundt's thought and some of the factors that led him into it are indicated in Wundt's autobiography—a book published in the year of Wundt's death—which is, although fascinating in places, unfortunately also rather unreliable in specific details. Its meandering style is defended by Wundt as a reflection of the way the human mind works. Recollections are not stored in the mind as discrete, unaltered impressions of perceived realities, but as the results of frequently changing, mostly conscious interactions between sensations and inner feelings that create long, parallel trains of memory—not necessarily chronological trains, but ones that order particular memories according to the importance that they seem to have at the time of recollection.[20] In other words, the mind reconstructs reality—a fundamental principle of Wundt's *Völkerpsychologie*.

It is significant, then, that what Wundt emphasizes first in his autobiography is neither his personal history nor the scientific and philosophical ideas that influenced him, but rather *politics,* especially the liberal politics of Baden in his youth and his own part in them.[21] Was this because Wundt, like Virchow, remained an active politician all his life? Not at all. In the 1850s and 1860s he had been a member of liberal political organizations and in the 1860s a deputy to the Baden legislature, but he had abandoned active politics in the late 1860s. He paid attention to political questions thereafter and was vaguely aligned with the liberal part of the political spectrum, but he tended later in life to look on the ideological liberalism of his early years as something that had been superseded both by the politics of imperial

Germany and by changes in his own interests.[22] Instead, Wundt saw politics as the key to understanding an important part of consciousness. A person's consciousness, according to Wundt, is formed through the complex interactions the person has with other people and, at its higher levels, belongs to the community rather than uniquely to the individual. The most significant manifestation of this community consciousness, and at the same time its most important shaper, is politics—the most formal and purposive aspect of the community's life. Politics ties together the other aspects of social existence (and of individual consciousness of social existence).[23]

Wundt saw his own political experiences as matters of great importance: not because of his deep involvement in them, but because, by focusing and ordering the experiences of the community in which he lived, politics shaped his thought and work even though, as a scientist, he recognized the need to be as objective as possible. In fact Wundt's intellectual development corresponds fairly closely to the pattern that we have observed in other members of his generation: that of a liberal social scientist confronting the problems of liberalism and in consequence looking for new theoretical patterns in cultural science. His response, his version of *Völkerpsychologie,* although originally conceived within a neoliberal framework, eventually overstepped the boundaries of neoliberalism.

As a teenager, Wundt witnessed the 1848 revolution in Baden and its bloody suppression. He entered adulthood in the 1850s as a moderately left-leaning liberal. Like many of his generation, he was highly critical of the liberals' previous performance and became particularly concerned lest the reactivated liberals of the late 1850s and 1860s, in their eagerness to associate themselves with expanding business interests, ignore the working classes and the social question. Wundt was not a democrat.[24] He thought democracy a recipe for mediocrity, a threat to higher culture and to the ideal of liberal government by the educated. But social order and eventual liberal success depended on building a bridge between progressive elements among the educated and the masses. This could be accomplished through a liberal alliance with the "better" and more responsible segments of the artisanry. The alliance should be based on real liberal commitment to improve the condition of the working class, on a limited degree of political participation by the respectable part of the working class, and especially on a program of worker education.

The last was Wundt's major political concern. In the 1860s, he helped to found an educational association in Heidelberg that aimed to provide courses to interested workers, partly in order to shape the thought and behavior of artisans along liberal lines and partly to increase sympathy for workers among bourgeois liberals teaching in the program.[25] The movement of which Wundt's association was a part briefly acquired considerable political importance in Baden and elsewhere during the 1860s. Through the worker education movement he was elected to the Baden *Landtag.* But with the rise of organized working-class political organizations in the 1860s and the spread of socialist ideologies, the prospects for Wundt's kind of social liberalism faded and with them faded Wundt's interest in direct participation in liberal partisan politics.

Wundt (who also, after initial doubts, shared the general excitement about the formation of the *Reich*) thus experienced the crisis of liberalism in the 1860s in a particular form, but in much the same general way as other people. Unlike Virchow, however, but like a great many other academics, his response was to withdraw somewhat from active politics and to subscribe—increasingly as time went on—to the notion that a nonpartisan politics based on liberal foundations but transcending the ideological and practical limits of traditional liberalism was needed. He also displayed the distaste for industrialization and big business fashionable among academics, although he never became a radical antimodernist or a conservative.[26]

In his autobiography, Wundt implies that his experience of politics was closely linked to the formation of his scientific outlook and to his professional career, but he is not very specific about how the linkage occurred (apart from his general statements about the role of politics in structuring consciousness).[27] There were probably some personal factors involved: Wundt's tendency to follow the political and intellectual fashions of the philosophical faculties in order to be accepted by them and wounded pride at the failure of his worker education efforts. But more fundamental connections can be discerned in the changing ways in which Wundt's psychology confronted perceived inadequacies in the liberal theoretical pattern in social science as well as inadequacies in the ways others had attempted to correct the pattern. This appears to be the kind of relationship between science and politics Wundt had in mind—at the level at which a shared political consciousness helps to structure specific social ideas.

First, of course, there was the problem of the individual. Wundt's interest in psychology led him to pay special attention to the problematic character of notions of the individual built into classical liberal social thought. Like Waitz and Bastian, Wundt believed that the model of the rational individual was inadequate, and like Waitz he believed that one of the problems that liberalism—or, indeed, any other ideology encompassing the idea of human progress—faced was relating a rational social vision to people who were not naturally entirely rational. Wundt's involvement with worker education as a means of encouraging rational political behavior had been based in large part this belief, and his commitment to psychological research was at least reinforced by the less-than-satisfactory results (from Wundt's point of view) of the venture.[28]

Wundt started in the 1850s with a view of individual psychology similar to Waitz's: one heavily influenced by physiological materialism but also by the neo-idealism of J. F. Herbart. He found that he could not explain real human behavior either through a utilitarian calculus of reasoning from pleasure and pain (he was in fact highly critical of Jeremy Bentham), nor could he do so through associationism (the theory that mental phenomena consist of natural associations of ideas or images, the patterns of which are governed by universal laws). Like Waitz, Wundt was driven—in part by his perception that political thinking did not take place in a cultural, historical, or social vacuum—to investigate the relationship between the individual mind and its cultural environment.[29]

To psychologists who remember Wundt mainly for experimental work on perception and cognition, his interest in cultural matters, in *Völkerpsychologie,* may seem an aberration of his later years, entirely peripheral to his main activities. This view is reinforced by the late date (1900–1920) at which Wundt's ten-volume opus in the subject was published.[30] In fact, however, Wundt began to lecture occasionally at Heidelberg on *Völkerpsychologie* as early as 1859, and he was one of the earliest contributors to the *Zeitschrift für Völkerpsychologie,* which was founded in 1860. Even in his earliest general statements of his psychological views in the 1860s, he made it clear that cultural factors were at the very heart of his psychology and that in the greater scheme of things, the experimental work for which he was already becoming known was quite secondary in importance.[31]

Wundt, again like Waitz, divided the phenomena of the individual mind roughly into two groups.[32] One group included such elements as relationships between sensations (forms of energy arising from contact between the nervous system and the external world) and feelings, which were seated in the mind itself. These relationships were grounded in physiology. They were best studied in individuals and could, to a large extent, be tested and measured like any other physical phenomena. The most basic psychological characteristics of individuals fell into this category, the boundary of which lay roughly at the point at which language and memory entered the picture. Some elements of the category could be studied by measuring reactions to external stimuli. Other, more complicated ones could be examined by training subjects to describe their own mental experiences in a rigorous way—Wundt's famous (and highly questionable) method of "introspection." Basic human mental activity was therefore quite complex. It included various sets of psychic relationships that constituted the foundations of rationality, although not necessarily every manifestation of it.

Wundt argued that these basic patterns of relationship among sensations, feelings, and the other more complex forms of psychic energy were essentially the same in everybody. Through empirical research on individuals (not through searching for a residue from a comparison of different cultures, as Bastian tried to do), the basic patterns could be accurately delineated, and that was the purpose of Wundt's psychological laboratory. In other words, like other neoliberals, Wundt—at least in the early and middle stages of his career—hoped among other things to be able to replace the inadequate model of the rational individual at the center of the liberal theoretical pattern with a more sophisticated, accurate, and useful picture of the individual mind derived from empirical research, without giving up the basic structure of the liberal pattern and the beliefs to which the pattern was attached. The result of his research in this area would be a set of psychological laws, arrived at by systematically testing hypotheses until accurate statements of regularities could be formulated.

But according to Wundt, laboratory work and introspection could only reveal the constituents of *one* of the two major categories of mental phenomena—the more basic and, to Wundt, less interesting. The higher mental processes, those involving language, that allow people to function in groups, to create technologies, to establish societies and civilizations, could not be studied in the same way as the basic mental patterns—although unlike Helmholtz and unlike the proponents of hermeneutics, Wundt did think that the same general principles of inductive, empirical science could be applied to them. The study that resulted from such an application was *Völkerpsychologie.*[33]

According to Wundt, the key to understanding the higher mental processes was to understand their genesis, their development from the more basic and universal psychic phenomena.[34] The processes themselves appear in many different forms among different people. The most significant forms are embodied in the different cultures of nations and peoples; therefore, general laws could not be reliably discovered by focusing solely on individuals. Even synchronic cross-cultural comparison could reveal little more than the ways in which cultures and the mentalities associated with them differ from one another. But cultural study on a worldwide basis that aimed at uncovering the manner in which actual cultures develop and how differences between them appear could produce statements to explain how the higher category of human mental activity evolved from the lower one. Cultural study would also show that, with respect to higher, more important things, cognition is not an individual activity at all, but rather a collective one. Thinking on the higher plane means that individuals are participating in culture.

Wundt's position on this point underwent some change during his career. In his early years of work in *Völkerpsycholgie,* Wundt seems to have seen culture in the standard neoliberal way, as a concept that could be used to explain variations in human behavior, resistance to progress, and so forth.[35] Like Bastian, however, Wundt was not so much interested in the process of socialization and education that caused the mental patterns of individuals to vary and that could be deliberately altered to change the patterns as he was interested in the mental patterns themselves. More or less at the same time that he distanced himself from traditional notions of political liberalism, Wundt moved even farther away from neoliberal concerns in human science. By the time his major books on *Völkerpsychologie* appeared after the turn of the century, Wundt had taken leave of the neoliberal theoretical pattern in a fairly radical way. Culture was no longer a consensus among individuals, an aggregation of ideas, words, and so on, that were passed on by persons of one generation to those of another. Instead, the mental structures of individuals were literally *part* of the larger culture.[36]

A culture, to the later Wundt, was an active psychic force that had coherence in itself and that to a large extent defined the very individuals who participated in it. This force followed laws of development that could be understood but that could not be easily manipulated by altering the educations of individuals. In other words, Wundt was no longer employing a study of culture to supplement the study of the individual. He had (like others we shall examine shortly) shifted the focus of his theoretical pattern largely away from the individual and onto culture as the prime object of scientific study. It is perhaps not surprising that Wundt's students, attracted to his laboratory because of its success in displaying the uniform features of individual mental activity, should often have found his larger theories perplexing— increasingly so, as time went on. Especially those who made their careers in America—people such as Edward Titchener and Hugo Münsterberg—brought hardly a hint of Wundt's *Völkerpsychologie* with them.[37] As we saw in the case of Boas, the prevalence of the liberal theoretical pattern in America in the absence of effective checks to political liberalism created a favorable intellectual climate for certain approaches to cultural and social science and not to others. In the case of

Wundt's psychology, this meant that only part of his work was allowed through the filter of the liberal theoretical pattern, where as the rest was quite literally ignored.

Wundt's *Völkerpsychologie* was a "psychological developmental history of mankind."[38] As such, it reflected both Wundt's theory that the laws of higher mental activity were developmental laws and the prevailing tendency in German social and human science to emphasize historical approaches. Although Wundt borrowed some things from the diffusionist school of ethnology, his notion of development remained largely rooted in the idea of developmental stages (each stage producing the next) that had been popular at midcentury and that was largely consistent with the liberal idea of progress. He was not a Darwinist in that he did not employ a Darwinian model to account for the dynamic of stage change, but in some respects his thinking paralleled that of the British social evolutionists.[39]

According to Wundt, the structure of the human mind and its limited capabilities largely shape the stages of social development—evidence for the existence of which mainly comes from observations of contemporary cultures stuck in early stages. Wundt's *Völkerpsychologie* attempted to identify the mental pattern or disposition (*Volksseele*) characteristic of each stage. Each people's *Volksseele* differs from others of the same stage in terms of specifics, but all are generically similar. The full range of human activities that make up a culture must be studied—not as objects in themselves, but as clues to the *Volksseele*. Certain elements of culture are crucial: language, myth, and custom. These are the major manifestations of the dynamic relationship between the social and physical environment and the structure of the mind. Studying the language, myth, and customs of peoples in each developmental stage reveals the underlying mental patterns and the causes of changes in the patterns.[40]

Wundt presents four stages in cultural development. In the earliest—"primitive man"—language and myth reflect in their concreteness a direct confrontation with the physical environment.[41] Myth takes the form of a demonology to aid in explaining immediate surroundings. Social order is limited and informal. But at some point, language and myth become constituents of custom, which is passed on from generation to generation, and a crucial transformation occurs. The minds of a people, which have retained ideas (linguistic elements and myths) developed by the community, no longer merely respond to sense stimuli. With their ideas, they can mentally *construct* the world around them and as a result, physically confront it more successfully. Natural phenomena that need to be explained are no longer the sole generators of myth. Rather, myth interacts with the environment and partly generates *itself*. Language follows the same pattern. As custom develops, the concrete origins of many words and myths are forgotten and they become, in themselves, autonomous parts of the *Volksseele*. Society becomes more complex, not primarily as a response to environment, but because culture becomes more complex and finds expression in the social order. Once social order becomes embedded in custom, it, too, enters into the process of interaction. At some point, the next stage of human development—called "totemism," after the form of myth characteristic of this stage—is reached.[42] Totemism begets the "age of gods and heros," which, in turn, produces the fourth and present stage: the "development toward humanity."[43]

Wundt's developmental theory provides a framework for explaining progress that is, in many ways, an improvement over similar structures in early nineteenth-century liberal thought. It contains a dynamic model of cultural change that is not wholly dependent on arguing from the situation of the rational individual confronted with environmental factors, an approach that had caused difficulties for liberal thinkers in the past and would continue to do so for advocates of cultural diffusionism in the future. It links social and cultural change to one another, and both to a highly sophisticated individual psychology without making society and culture mere reflections of a uniform individual mind. At the same time, however, Wundt's theory goes considerably farther than most neoliberal thinking in subsuming the individual under the group, in the end making the individual mainly a manifestation of culture. In this respect, Wundt resembles other cultural scientists, such as Ratzel, who moved in the same direction toward the end of the nineteenth century.

Many of Wundt's ideas about *Völkerpsychologie* sound surprisingly modern—sound, indeed, as though Wundt might have found a place in some of the intellectual traditions that rejected positivist human science. In fact, Wundt's influence on fields other than experimental psychology was quite limited. When his theories were employed by a cultural historian, Karl Lamprecht, they were violently opposed by establishment historians who featured an antipositivist, essentially hermeneutic approach to social analysis.[44] In large part, this was due to Wundt's insistence that he was practicing science strictly defined, that by the means he proposed, the actual laws of human mental development could be understood in the same way that he thought his laboratory experiments showed the laws of psychophysics. His interesting insights into the cultural construction of reality, which to another person might suggest that an alternative model of understanding human phenomena was needed, were thus essentially lost within a framework of nomothetic science that showed the effects of the intellectual tradition from which it arose.

Even as nomothetic science, Wundt's *Völkerpsychologie* was seen by other psychologists—including those who accepted his approach to experimental psychology—to have severe defects. The most prominent of these was that it was not really empirical science according to the standards Wundt himself accepted and which he attempted to apply in his laboratory work.[45] That is, rather than regarding the elements of his *Völkerpsychologie* as hypothetical statements to be tested, he presented them as a complete theory, a framework into which the data supplied by ethnography could be fitted. The ten volumes of his major book on *Völkerpsychologie* are filled with data, but the data are not used as an empirical test of the central propositions he advances.

Wundt's work was really the last gasp of *Völkerpsychologie*. By the time his magnum opus on the subject was published in the early twentieth century, the discipline had already begun to disintegrate. By adhering to the notion that it was a nomothetic science, *Völkerpsychologie* had held aloof from several new directions in cultural interpretation. By not demonstrating its validity as an empirical science, it cut itself off from "scientific" psychology. Not only did the experimentalists simply ignore the cultural part of Wundt's work, but also some of the younger practitioners of *Völkerpsychologie*—people such as Alfred Vierkandt—essentially turned it into an early form of social psychology. They dropped the historical and developmental aspects and instead used comparative ethnological studies as a way of establishing the categories of human social behavior.[46]

Völkerpsychologie was also shut out of the later history of anthropology in Germany. Much of the reason for this was the discipline's peculiar relationship to prevailing theoretical patterns in cultural science, especially after Wundt became its leading proponent in the late nineteenth century. As *Völkerpsychologie* increasingly separated from the neoliberal theoretical pattern, it could no longer fit comfortably with approaches to human phenomena that retained close links to the traditions of liberal social science. As we saw, that was probably one of the reasons that *Völkerpsychologie* found little resonance among Wundt's disciples in America. At the same time, in several significant ways, especially in its continued focus on individual psychology (however much Wundt may have subordinated the individual to culture), *Völkerpsychologie* remained closer to the traditional liberal pattern than did other theoretical patterns that emerged in the later nineteenth century and that, in part because of their close connections to prevailing political ideologies, came to be much more fashionable than neoliberalism.[47] *Völkerpsychologie* lost out in competition with these new patterns, to which we shall turn next.

7

Bauer, Volk, and *Kultur:*
The Peasant as the
Foundation of Culture

Some of the most important challenges to the neoliberal theoretical pattern in German cultural science arose from the work of people who originally shared with the neoliberals a foundation in liberalism and traditional liberal social science but who built differently on it. One of the things that many of these people did *not* share with the neoliberals, one of the things that made their cultural science distinctive, was a working definition of culture that revolved around the notion that the peasant farmer is the main bearer and transmitter of a "real" *Volk*'s culture. One implication of this view was that social changes and social policies could be judged according to the criterion of whether they benefitted or injured the peasantry.

This was only partly a matter of formal definition. In formal terms, what agreement there was among cultural scientists about the meaning of *Kultur* cut across lines of theoretical pattern and discipline. So did definitional disputes, such as arguments over the distinction between *Naturvölker* and *Kulturvölker* and the relationship between culture in its anthropological and culture in its elitist senses.[1] It was much more a question of connotations, mental images, assumed implications, and an informal hierarchy of values assigned to certain cultural phenomena. To neoliberals, there was no privileged link between "culture" as a concept to be employed in human study and "agriculture" as a human practice. People like Riehl and Ratzel, on the other hand, although accepting largely the same formal definitions of culture as the neoliberals, believed that such a link did exist. Some went so far as to argue that the etymological connection between "culture" and "agriculture" (*Kultur* can mean both in German) demonstrated a necessary linkage between their referents.[2]

This peculiarly agrarian view of culture arose from various sources. Obviously, one was the literary Romanticism of the early part of the century, with its favored image of a happy and virtuous peasantry that derived its felicity from direct contact with Nature. More recently, consciousness of the results of early industrialization—the squalor of modern cities, the threat to the livelihoods and self-respect of the traditional lower and lower-middle classes—had created a fashion for romanticizing the rural alternative.[3] But to see how peasant agrarianism in cultural science derived from these sources, to see how intelligent observers like Riehl and Ratzel could view country life through deeply rose-tinted spectacles, it is necessary to understand how the politics and ideology of liberalism intertwined with these and other factors.

Liberalism, Social Science,
and the Image of the Peasant

The enthusiasm of the early nineteenth-century Romantics for the culture of the countryside was closely connected to a contemporaneous movement for liberal agrarian reform.[4] Far from being antagonistic to each other (as they would be widely portrayed later in the century), early peasant agrarianism and *Vormärz* liberalism were generally regarded as wholly compatible.

The late eighteenth-century administrators and academics who laid the groundwork for the liberal movement to modernize German society naturally turned their attention to the state of the peasantry. Peasants (using the term broadly) made up the majority of the German population, and the whole economy depended on their labor. Any thoroughgoing economic reform and any political change that encompassed improvements for the "people" would necessarily have to put considerable emphasis on the lower and middle farming classes. The sons of peasants in Napoleon's armies, who swept all before them across Europe, also engendered in reformers a desire to harness and control such power. Clearly, the concepts of "people" and "nation," which the French Revolution had made matters of urgent concern in Germany, could have no meaning without reference to the peasantry— although how such a group, previously denigrated in political thought, could be effectively incorporated into the political nation was difficult to imagine.[5] There was also a tendency to look (theoretically, at least) to the rural population as a source of genuine "national" character traits to replace the French ones that German aristocrats and *Bürger* had previously adopted.

These concerns led to a change in the public image of the peasant among the educated in the early nineteenth century. The free, landowning farmer became the ideal-typical German citizen who made the economy work, whose military service was the basis of national strength, and whose acquiescence, if not participation, in politics was essential to the effective functioning of the *Volk*.[6]

But, of course, image and reality were quite different from each other. Because the educated knew very little about real peasants and their culture, it was necessary to do research. The Grimm brothers and the followers of Herder set out to do just that—taking, however, their idealized picture of the peasant as their given framework and attempting to fit what they actually saw into it.[7] Even so, the reality of a poor, heterogeneous, and highly dependent peasantry obtruded itself into their imaginary world of sturdy yeomen and led to demands that the "real" peasant be created if he could not be found in sufficient numbers. Liberal hopes for the economic advancement of the German states and for the creation of a proper German *Volk* in any event depended on modernizing German agriculture, and that, in turn, required the conversion of the varied mass of serfs, sharecroppers, and free but dues-burdened *Bauer* into autonomous free farmers. During the post-1806 upheaval in Prussia, Baron Heinrich vom Stein and other reformers set about trying to free peasants from the bondage of feudalism and from dues and controls that discouraged individual initiative.[8] The fate of Stein's reforms (modified by *Junker* landowners in order to maintain the economic dependency, and often the poverty, of their former serfs) did not accord with liberal expectations. But because, by the end of the Napoleonic Wars, the image of the free, economically autonomous peasant as the foundation of the *Volk* in a liberal state had become well established in the minds of progressive people, the gap between image and reality led liberals to continue to press for reforms aimed *both* at increasing agricultural productivity *and* at freeing the peasantry economically.

By the 1830s and 1840s, it became clear that there was a more practical political factor as well. Because liberal reform was obviously not going to be implemented by the authorities without pressure, widespread popular support for change would have to be mustered—and that meant peasant support. In Baden, where representative institutions existed, an appeal to at least the wealthier peasantry was a regular political necessity for the liberals.[9] But all of this created a problem. It was difficult for liberals to reconcile the liberal aims of fostering economic modernization through capitalism with the actual wishes of most small farmers. The desire of the latter for secure tenure of land they already possessed outright could be accommodated, but security against creditors, increases in the sizes of holdings (which required expropriation from the nobility), and state protection of farmers against market forces, these went against the liberal grain.[10] Because of such problems, most *Vormärz* liberals were rather vague about the details of the agrarian reforms they favored. All the more reason for romanticizing and idealizing the peasantry: to display sympathy and respect for the rural population without having to be too specific about what was to be done for it. The need became even greater in 1848 when many peasants clearly resisted liberal political aims.

That these problems remained in the 1850s can be shown by comparing two articles in the *Staatslexikon*: one by the journalist and politician Karl Mathy on "*Ackerbau, Landwirtschaft*" and the other by Welcker on "*Bauer, Bauernstand.*"

Mathy's article displays its author's belief in the necessity and inevitability of economic modernization and the need of the farmer to contribute to the process.[11] The farmer's main contribution was to make agriculture so efficient that a surplus of capital and people could be sent into an expanding industrial sector. Agriculture is not the foundation of culture; it is merely one part of an integrated, increasingly industrial economy. "A nation that neglects agriculture never becomes great or remains great for long; a nation that remains agricultural will not maintain itself in balance with others that, at the right time, augment their powers through industry, trade, and shipping."[12] Mathy, although highly complimentary about peasants, calls for their transformation into modern, market-oriented farmers through state programs to guarantee land tenure and afford investment capital. Peasants should be regarded as members of an integrated, progressive *Volk* or nation, not as the bearers of a cultural tradition with a value in itself.

Welcker's basic policy recommendations are quite similar to those of Mathy: because the general progress of German society depends on the peasants, they should be independent, free farmers with protected tenure, encouraged to save and invest in their farms.[13] (In fact Welcker *defines* the *Bauer* as a free, landowning farmer and bases the rest of his analysis on reasoning from this ideal type. This allows him to skirt the issue of what to do about the millions of peasants who do not really fit the type.) But in other respects, Welcker's presentation differs greatly from Mathy's. He emphasizes the *Bauer*'s natural conservatism—which is due, he says, to the habit of patience that dependence on weather and other uncontrollable factors instills. Mathy views such conservatism as an obstacle to progress that must be overcome; Welcker sees value in it. Conservatism in outlook together with independence afforded by land ownership "gives the bearing of peasants something strong, straightforward, manly."[14] It is true that the peasant is "unenlightened" and "raw," but this is not his "natural" condition. Rather, peasant backwardness is a specific historical result of the Middle Ages, which relegated the previously free *Bauer* to servile status. In recent times, increasing freedom, economic independence, and education have allowed the peasant to regain much of his natural state of homely enlightenment. This kind of progress must be encouraged. It is good for the peasant and for the nation because *Bauer* contribute more to the *Volk* than food. The *Bauernstand*, "through its healthy natural circumstances, appears to protect the nation more than do other classes against the dangers and corruptions of our modern civilization."[15] (Welcker uses *civilization* in the Romantic sense, standing for urban, commercial, implicitly foreign, behavior patterns.) This protection extends to encouraging responsible politics and discouraging revolution. Of all occupations, agriculture is "the most important, in that it is one of the healthiest and happiest and, in terms of its natural moral effect, also one of the noblest."[16] The peasant gives stability to the body politic, presents an example of true freedom, maintains virtue, and so forth. In other words, the peasantry is an inherently valuable class and must be protected.

Welcker foreshadows much of the later agrarian ideology: the value of small, independent farmers to the rest of society, the superior virtue embodied in peasant culture (itself largely a product of environment), and the centrality of the peasant to the *Volk*. Welcker was clearly a liberal, although a rather moderate one. And yet these ideas were to become staple features of certain forms of agrarian *conservatism* later on.[17] They were taken by people such as Friedrich Ratzel and Adolf Wagner out of their original liberal political framework and placed in new ones after Welcker's time—frameworks in many ways much more conservative than the originals. They were also placed in a correspondingly new theoretical framework through the use of the idea of culture as a social scientific concept. On the other hand, Mathy's approach, to some extent, foreshadows neoliberal social science. There is sympathy for the peasant, but Mathy sees the cultural content of peasant life as something that must be modified in the interests of modernity. There is ambiguity in Mathy's attitude toward peasants, but it is minor compared to that in Welcker's. Like some later agrarians, Welcker seems to be unable to decide whether he wants peasants to evolve into rational participants in a modern market economy or to protect them from such an economy.[18]

The revolution of 1848 and the difficulties subsequently experienced by liberals in maintaining rural support led to even more widespread attention to agricultural reform. The political crises of liberalism in the 1850s and 1860s and the concomitant fragmentation of the liberal theoretical pattern in social science were reflected in approaches toward rural problems. Mainstream liberals continued to take positions similar to Mathy's. Serious empirical research into agricultural economics emerged.[19] In the 1870s and 1880s, some economists (such as Adolf Wagner) who worked in this tradition moved toward a kind of agrarianism that ostensibly aimed at defending peasant farming even at the cost of economic efficiency and that rejected much of the traditional liberal approach to socioeconomic change.[20] Similar tendencies appeared throughout academia—not least among cultural scientists.[21] The evolution of agrarianism and its contribution to constructing alternatives to neoliberalism in cultural science theory can be seen in the work of W. H. Riehl and Friedrich Ratzel.

Agrarianism and Cultural Science

We have already discussed Riehl as a forerunner of the cultural scientists of the 1870s and 1880s who, discontented with both liberal ideology and liberal social science, constructed variant ideologies and built variant theoretical patterns around the concept of culture. Riehl's influence on these people was probably substantial, although it was often unacknowledged—perhaps because in the 1860s, when people like Ratzel first came into contact with Riehl's ideas, Riehl (by then a conservative) was in the opposite political camp to what was then their own.[22]

The basis of Riehl's agrarianism is laid out in his writings of the 1850s. According to Riehl, there are in Germany two social forces: the force of persistence and the force of movement. The first of these is manifested in two *Stände* or classes: the peasantry and the aristocracy.[23] The second is present in the bourgeoisie and the "fourth *Stand*" (the proletariat). The proletariat is not a full-fledged estate because it does not yet possess a true consciousness of itself and its place in society. A stable, progressive society depends on the balanced interaction of all the *Stände*. Competition among them, and among their components, is perfectly natural.[24] The characteristic culture of each *Stand* is only an amalgamation of regional and occupational varieties, and the common national culture rests atop all the component cultures. Trying to impose civil peace through uniformity—whether political or cultural—is pointless. So is the pursuit of stability through idealizing a supposed medieval order in which everyone knew his place because that would be incompatible with the modern economy. Rather, a stable society is one in which the forces of the various *Stände* regularly counteract, without destroying, one another. Persistence restrains movement. Counteractivity helps to prevent the "degeneration" of *Stände* and is itself threatened if *Stände* do degenerate into more vicious social forms. Proper relations among *Stände* depend on general recognition of the culture of each *Stand* and its components.

Society, according to Riehl, is mainly defined by the constituent cultures of the *Stände*. These cultures, partly autonomous and partly shared with others, largely determine political perception and action. Unlike most liberal nationalists, Riehl says that the the unique, not the common, features of a group's culture give the group its value in relation to others in society.[25] In particular, he argues that an independent peasantry, because of the nature of its peculiar culture, is vital to the existence of the German *Volk* in a way that none of the other *Stände* are.

"The peasant is the preserving power in the German people: therefore this power should also be preserved."[26] Riehl thus states the central proposition of agrarianism. The other *Stände* have their roles. The aristocracy (in which Riehl includes the nobility and other traditional elites, such as professors and guild masters) kept order in the medieval world. It remains a force for persistence, but it has also produced from within itself the bourgeoisie, the major source of movement. The aristocracy has moreover weakened itself by adopting (until recently) foreign (French) cultural patterns and by contributing to the growth of bureaucracy—a thoroughly degenerate social form.[27] Its role in maintaining continuity has been taken over in large part by the more numerous and less degenerate peasantry— hence the great importance of the *Bauernstand*. The bourgeoisie performs important services as well, not least of which is affording progress: useful, needed change, both material and spiritual.[28] It is only degenerate *Bürger* who become revolutionaries and philistines and try to tear the *Volk* apart. "Good" bourgeois realize that to prevent their own culture's tendencies toward degeneracy, they must cooperate as well as compete with the other *Stände*. Their culture forces them to push for change; they cannot themselves embody persistence. But they *can* work to preserve the peasantry, which by *its* nature will maintain the force of persistence. The proletariat cannot help in this work because it is not yet fully formed and in any case must manifest the force of movement.[29]

After allowance is made for regional differences, peasants come in two cultural varieties: the "good sort" and the "degenerates."[30] Like Welcker, Riehl argues that peasant degeneration is due mainly to economic dependency. Like the serfs of former days, modern peasants burdened with debt or having little land of their own cannot readily develop the characters of fully formed *Bauer* and cannot perform their social roles. "Good" peasants require long-term, independent tenure of adequate land. But Riehl pays less attention to the economic underpinnings of peasant independence than he does to the nature and sources of peasant culture. These vary from place to place and so can only be revealed in detail by firsthand research, but Riehl advances some general notions.

The key to peasant culture is the peasant's environment and daily life. Independent farmers must respond effectively to more variable environmental circumstances than any other social group. Their behavior, daily schedules, even their oral tradition reflect the resulting commonsense flexibility. Because of their constant direct contact with the realities of nature, peasants are better than others at distinguishing the actual from the illusory. Their folk literature represents neither some disembodied national spirit nor a logical framework of ideas, but rather shrewd observations of the ways real people behave. Their response to the revolution in 1848 was to see it as an opportunity to achieve limited, personal, practical goals— but to dismiss the revolutionary rhetoric of the educated. It is the skeptical outlook inculcated by the peasants' culture that makes them so valuable a conservative force in society.[31] It is not, as Welcker implies, that peasants are patient and perhaps a little dense that makes them conservative; it is rather their culturally based ability to see that most demands for radical change are not sufficiently grounded in reality. Peasants have other virtues (courage, honesty, etc.), which are also outward manifestations of a culture derived from interacting with their environment.

Riehl, despite his claim to having founded his analysis on empirical investigation only, did in fact romanticize the peasantry and construct his description around images derived from traditional liberal agrarian thought. But his empirical work made him considerably more convincing than most social scientists who had pre- viously studied rural society. He modified the pattern of thinking he had inherited. He was not, however, an antimodernist. His approach allowed him to criticize modern society without wholly rejecting it. Riehl maintained the liberal equilibrium concept, but he altered it by using collectivities (*Stände*) as units of analysis rather than individuals. As ideology, Riehl's agrarianism took change (and the need for policy to deal with it) into account without either worshipping or rejecting it. The key idea was the protection of the independent peasantry for the benefit of all society. Riehl was quite clear about the link between science and politics in what he was doing: "It is a true, heartfelt desire of the author that people may recognize in the following contributions to 'the science of the *Volk*' evidence which shows that a thorough investigation of modern social conditions, undertaken with loving devotion to the manners and customs of the people, must lead in the last instance to the justification of a conservative social policy."[32]

Riehl was a forerunner of German agrarianism, both in politics and in social science. The people who actually constructed agrarian ideologies and theoretical patterns in social science based on agrarian assumptions, however, were mostly academics who had started as liberals and who belonged to the generation of the 1860s. One of the most important of these people was Friedrich Ratzel (1844– 1904).

In later life, Ratzel drew a glowing, nostalgic literary picture of his childhood in a rural village in Baden, implying that his peasant origins lay at the root of his agrarian orientation and his special knowledge of the *Bauernstand*.[33] Actually, Ratzel's background was very similar to that of Riehl: he was the son of a senior domestic servant of the grand duke of Baden. He grew up in a house in the ducal park, an idyllic setting that grew no less idyllic in his memory later but had little to do with real rural life. His direct experience of peasant agriculture was at best very limited—most of it derived from the period in his late teens and early twenties when he worked as an apothecary in small Swiss and German villages. Ratzel was in fact a bourgeois: *Kleinburger* (member of the lower middle class) by birth, *Bildungsburger* (member of the educated upper middle class) by education. But he tended, like many other *Bürger*, to romanticize everything about rural life and to a considerable extent to identify himself with it.[34]

Ratzel's actual career, although it did not quite fit the peasant-to-professor model, was still very impressive. Like Waitz, Andree, and Virchow, he was rec- ognized early as a clever boy. But although Ratzel would have liked to study at a *Gymnasium* and offers of support were forthcoming, his father refused.[35] The father, who possessed a court-butler's view of the proper order of things, apparently believed that young men of Ratzel's status should not receive the educations and assume the lifestyles of their betters—not just because this would threaten the social hierarchy, but also because a classical education would unfit them for doing society's real work. Some of these attitudes reveal themselves in Ratzel's later writing, just as Ratzel's early political radicalism may have represented a form of rebellion against his father. In any event, Ratzel became an apothecary's apprentice and then a journeyman—all the while studying by night for examinations in science that would allow him to follow the new alternative path to the university through the polytechnic in Karlsruhe. He got through with flying colors, entered first the polytechnic and then Heidelberg University, where he took his doctorate in zoology in 1868.[36]

At twenty-four, Ratzel had much to congratulate himself about. He had worked hard, overcome handicaps, and achieved an honorific status in an accepted social hierarchy. There were problems, however. His original social standing, his lack of polish and a classical education, his technical and scientific training all ensured that he would not fit easily into the culture of the *Bildungsbürgertum*.[37] Moreover, he had no job and no independent means of support while enduring the next stages of academic apprenticeship.

Before we pursue Ratzel's later career, we must take note of one clue to his agrarianism that Ratzel himself suggests in an autobiographical piece written just before his death.[38] Like millions of other middle-class children, Ratzel spent much of his childhood reading romantic adventure fiction; his favorite was *The Swiss Family Robinson*. The habit persisted into his adulthood. Ratzel says that this reading was as important in shaping his world-view as was his early formal education—by which he apparently means that it influenced his tendency to romanticize such things as rural and frontier life.[39] Even the title he gave to the collection of his early reminiscences, *Glückinseln und Träume* (*Happy Islands and Dreams*), seems to imply that they are themselves a kind of romantic semifiction.

In his middle twenties, though, Ratzel had to confront reality. His inability to support himself in an academic career led him, almost inevitably, to journalism. His first endeavor was a book for laymen on Darwinism.[40] After serving briefly but enthusiastically in the Franco-German War, he was hired as a travel correspondent by the *Kölnische Zeitung*. In this capacity he visited several parts of the world in the early 1870s, including, for a lengthy period, the western United States. Ratzel's journalistic experience was crucial for two reasons: it gave him an interest in geography and a reputation as a geographical commentator that won him his first academic job in Munich in 1875, and it helped shape his connections with politics.[41]

In the late 1860s, Ratzel had been a radical liberal. In chapter 4, we saw that his enthusiastic acceptance of Darwinism was bound up with a vaguely defined but passionate desire to remake society, spread freedom, and build a German nation— a desire shared by thousands of other young people.[42] Darwinism was one of the banners behind which many of his generation of scientists rallied to assert themselves not only against the leaders of their fields, but also against both the forces of political conservatism (aristocracy, church, etc.) and the increasingly discredited leadership of standard liberalism. (Adopting a radical liberal stance in the 1860s also meant taking a favorable view of peasants, but nothing more specific than that.) But then came the final stages of German unification and Ratzel's participation in the war against France. Ratzel felt himself swept up in a current of enthusiastic nationalism.[43] He also found that he had to admire the successes of Bismarck as against the failures of liberal politics. By the early 1870s, Ratzel was on the verge of a break with liberalism in its traditional forms.

Ratzel's journalistic work reinforced and gave shape to these tendencies in his political attitudes. Even though he specialized in geography and travel, he was expected to include political commentary in his articles. The political positions taken by the newspapers for which he worked created a general framework around which Ratzel constructed his own outlook. Up to the mid–1870s, Ratzel wrote mainly for the *Kölnische Zeitung,* the leading middle-of-the-road liberal paper. Thereafter, as he gained academic standing, he wrote primarily for *Die Grenzbo-ten*—traditionally the preferred vehicle of intellectual liberalism and a journal that, under the editorship of Gustav Freytag up to 1870, had devoted much space to discussions of German culture. Both of these journals exhibited a strong tendency to accommodate themselves to the Bismarckian state.[44] On the whole, they favored the National Liberals and maintained a sentimental connection to the liberal tradition, but they also adopted stances that allowed them to support measures pushed by the conservative parties. They emphasized elements in the liberal tradition that could be reconciled with moderate political conservatism. They tended to present political reform as a slow, evolutionary adjustment to real socioeconomic circumstances and stressed the need to cooperate with Bismarck, accept the growth of big industrial interests as a consequence of economic growth, and rethink some of the basic points of liberal theory as a result of these and other developments. Ratzel both accepted and, in a small way, contributed to these tendencies. His links to the National Liberal party came largely through his journalism.

In such journals as the *Grenzboten* and in the writings of former 1860s' radicals, such as Ratzel, Treitschke, and Haeckel, agrarian themes took on increasing importance in the 1870s and 1880s.[45] In Ratzel's case, the agrarian theme mingles with others (social policy, immigration, imperialism), but it is clearly present. Why? Apart from the reasons that may lie in Ratzel's personal background, there were some that he shared with other contemporaries.

In the first place, rightward-moving National Liberals needed some way of convincing themselves and other people that they were not completely knuckling under to the landed aristocracy or the new industrialist interests while they readjusted their political outlooks.[46] Peasant agrarianism helped them to do this. The small farmer, traditionally exploited by the landed nobility, now seemed to be threatened also by industrialization. Defending him was not only in keeping with the liberal oppositional tradition, but it could also in a sense be regarded as a modernization of the tradition because it responded to a real social problem and to the latest version of the liberal political bogey: the concentration of power in the hands of narrow elites. At the same time, speaking up for peasants and idealizing their culture was not the same as supporting the industrial working class. Peasants, not workers, had long been identified with the *Volk* of the liberal nation-state, whereas workers, not peasants, were being organized by the socialists into an overtly antiliberal, anti-bourgeois movement that aimed at overturning the social order. By defending peasants, one could claim political independence, even a hint of radicalism, without being called a Red or running other risks.

There were other practical political considerations. In the 1870s, Ratzel became, largely through his journalistic connections, a National Liberal. In the 1880s, he was one of the heterogeneous group that provided the increasingly rudderless party with ideas and debated questions of direction.[47] As we saw in chapter 4, the National Liberals were in serious trouble by the early 1880s. They had split over the 1879 tariff issue and they had lost their position as the most important party in the Reichstag. Their popular support was slipping. National Liberal leaders concluded that something drastic had to be done, but they could not agree about what it should be.[48] Their strong support for colonialism in 1884–1885 (at the urging of Ratzel, among many others) was partly an attempt to reestablish a close alliance with Bismarck, to injure their liberal rivals in the Progressive party, and to see how imperialism played with the voters.[49]

But colonialism was not enough. The question was, what combination of ideas and issues would appeal to the disparate groups whose support the National Liberals sought? The segment of the party with which Ratzel associated himself wanted the party to adopt a comprehensive program calling for national self-assertion in foreign affairs, imperialism, economic development, and (partly to avoid the image of toadying to big business, which the third point conjured up) protection for important social sectors threatened by economic modernization—particularly skilled artisans and peasants—and for the rural environment.[50] Such a program was intended partly to maintain the National Liberals' traditional appeal to artisans, peasants, and shopkeepers, but it was also supposed to appeal to anyone, regardless of social background, who was disturbed by the apparent consequences of modernization but not opposed to economic progress—a category that included millions of bourgeois Germans.[51] Agrarianism fitted quite well into this ideological pattern, a pattern Ratzel continued to employ in the 1890s as he lost interest in the National Liberals and involved himself increasingly with extraparty political organizations.

Ratzel's ideological emphasis on the peasant began to display itself in his scientific writings in the late 1870s, just after he moved out of full-time journalism and into academic geography at the Technische Hochschule in Munich.[52] We shall follow Ratzel's academic career and discuss his relationship with various intellectual influences in chapter 8. Here, we shall outline his peasant agrarian position as it is found in both his political and his professional work.

Like Riehl, Ratzel claimed that independent farmers possessed traits essential to the whole *Volk* that other groups did not possess, at least not to the same extent. "The activity of the farmer is many-sided; it is not the monotonous, repetitive turn of a cogwheel, requiring all a man's strength of being, as the labor of a worker is. On this account, the true farmer is a better-rounded person, and even more, a more creative one."[53] Peasant creativity was rather a novel idea, and as we shall see, it was extremely important to Ratzel's theories of cultural diffusion. Ratzel agreed with Riehl that peasants were a conservative social force not because they were dullards, but because they were realists. Their native perceptiveness allowed them to penetrate the sham of most schemes for radical reform—indeed, of most party politics. The peasant, in other words, was a kind of natural model for the ideal of *Unparteilichkeit* (nonpartisanship).

The peasants' community attitudes were also to be prized and emulated. "In a community whose members all more or less practice agriculture, a reciprocal giving and receiving of help is possible as in no other—but it is also necessary."[54] Not, perhaps, a wholly original observation, but an important one in defining Ratzel's relationship to the traditional liberal theoretical pattern. Ratzel rejected the classical economists' image of the selfish individual as the basic unit of social dynamics, and he emphasized groups. He did not, however, want to eliminate the individual from consideration altogether. Like other agrarians (for example, Thomas Jefferson), he argued that the culture of the independent farmer integrated individual self-reliance with a cooperative attitude toward other members of the community. These traits were not just the results of a rational cost-benefit analysis performed by each individual, but also a product of a cultural pattern developed in the rural environment—a pattern that could, to some extent, be transferred to people outside that environment. What was needed was some means of transfer (such as the exemplary effects of settlement colonies abroad.)[55] In any event, it was essential to maintain the class that bore most of the cultural traits required by a *Volk* that wanted to combine individual self-awareness with community spirit.

The specific ways in which Ratzel worked these and other ideas into two of his major theoretical constructs—his cultural diffusionism and his concept of *Lebensraum*—will be discussed in later chapters. One general characteristic of Ratzel's use of peasant agrarianism in comparison with Riehl's is, however, important to note. Whereas Riehl merely implied the greater importance of the peasantry within a model of separate interacting estates that were formally equal in value, Ratzel was very explicit about the primacy of peasants and their culture. One of Ratzel's standard methods was to construct hierarchies of social phenomena, identifying some of them as more basic, more determinative, and thus more valuable in an evolutionarily successful society than others. Almost always, it was the culture, economic organization, and social structure centering around the independent peasant farmer that Ratzel identified as the most basic and most valuable of all.[56]

Ratzel was not alone, either among rightward-moving liberals or among cultural scientists, in emphasizing peasant agriculture from the 1870s onward. Treitschke, for one, included in his ideological framework an agrarianism akin to Ratzel's.[57] In cultural science, although not everyone was as explicit about the primacy of peasant agriculture as Ratzel, the *connotation* that such agriculture gave meaning to culture in general was widely accepted, especially among cultural scientists attempting to break with the neoliberal theoretical pattern.[58] Various combinations of factors—some of them personal and individual, some implicit in academic and political debates during the last quarter of the nineteenth century—lay behind the adoption of forms of agrarianism by many cultural scientists. The notion of the *Bauer* as the foundation of the *Volk* and its culture provided a significant basis for revising the concepts of the individual, of the empirical foundation of social science, and of social change and equilibrium that had been part of the traditional liberal theoretical pattern. We shall see in more detail how this happened in chapter 8 when we examine the emergence of cultural diffusionism in ethnology.

8

The Diffusionist Revolt

Before Ratzel made his switch to full-time academic employment in the mid–1870s, he had spent brief periods studying under some of the leading figures in geography and *Völkerkunde*, including Bastian in Berlin.[1] But he had not stayed at Berlin. Because of his irregular entry into academic life and the fact that his first appointment was at a technical institute in Munich, Ratzel was more or less destined to operate outside the Berlin establishment. This, combined with the antagonism toward the previous generation of social scientists, partly manifested in Ratzel's politics and his Darwinism, led Ratzel to see himself as a potential leader of a revolt against the neoliberal theoretical pattern identified with the Berlin establishment.[2]

Ratzel led this revolt mainly in his capacity as a geographer. But Ratzel's interest in human geography involved him in cultural anthropology from an early stage. Indeed Ratzel, in the tradition of Alexander von Humboldt, set himself the task of fitting humankind into its place in the whole of nature and thus could not avoid cultural concerns. Although his direct contribution to ethnology in terms of research was rather limited compared to some of his other work and although his approach was not entirely original, Ratzel's anthropology was taken by many as the origin of a theoretical pattern in cultural science that offered a direct alternative to the neoliberal one. This alternative pattern, cultural diffusionism, became fashionable in the 1890s among Ratzel's contemporaries and among younger cultural scientists.[3] After the turn of the century, it effectively unseated neoliberalism from its place of dominance in German ethnology and led to Germany's separation from the main currents of international anthropology.

Ratzel's Diffusionism

Ratzel's development of diffusionist concepts actually began even before his Munich years while he was under Bastian's influence in the early 1870s. Although Bastian's anthropology eventually became the prime target of the diffusionists, Bastian (like Waitz) had in fact included a diffusionist element in his discussion of culture.[4] He argued that, to considerable extent, the actual culture of a *Volk*—the system of folk-ideas developed from universal elementary ideas—was a result of adaptation to particular geographical areas with distinctive environmental conditions. The study of cultural differences among *Völker* presupposed the prehistoric movement of peoples into the areas they occupied. Cultural traits brought from elsewhere or found in the new location that were useful in coping with the new environ-

ment were presumably adopted into the *Volk*'s culture. Thus, part of Bastian's
"comparative-genetic" approach to cultural study was supposed to involve some
tracing of paths of trait transfer. More important, it also involved laying out the
boundaries of "cultural provinces"—regions that, because of their particular array
of geographical features, displayed a high level of similarity in their inhabitants'
cultures. This was not the central part of Bastian's theoretical work, and it rested
on some rather confused concepts, but it was taken very seriously by many of his
followers, including Richard Andree and Franz Boas.[5]

In terms of intellectual genealogy, Ratzel's diffusionism could be regarded as
a direct development from Bastian's and from other similar theories of the 1870s.
But in fact it was not so regarded at the time, and in the folk-history of German
anthropology, Bastian and Ratzel are seen as clashing opposites.[6] The reason for
this is that Ratzel placed individual ideas, many of which he shared with Bastian,
into a theoretical framework that was constructed very differently and that had
radically different political connections, including links to agrarianism.

Ratzel took his first major steps in a new ethnological direction at Munich in
the late 1870s and early 1880s while he was in the process of making himself
Germany's most renowned theoretical geographer (and as he was moving away
from traditional liberalism, in part through his involvement with imperialism). In
his first really major work, his *Anthropo-Geographie,* published in 1882, he tried
to establish the kind of general human geography that Alexander von Humboldt
and Ritter had called for but had not produced.[7] Ratzel recognized what had made
the work of his great predecessors incomplete: the lack of a theory around which
the descriptive detail of a holistic geography could be organized. Like Ritter, Ratzel
acknowledged that a full theory could only be developed out of a lengthy examination of the data. But unlike Ritter, Ratzel believed that he had the key to such
a theory, an outline that could be used to organize observed data and suggest more
refined theories. The basis of his theory was a modified Darwinism. Ratzel later
dropped his formal adherence to natural selection, but in 1882 he was still waving
the Darwinian flag in the faces of people like Virchow and Bastian.

Ratzel's anthropogeography focused on migration. In this, Ratzel was heavily
influenced by the "law" of migration propounded by the zoologist Moritz Wagner,
Ratzel's first mentor at Munich.[8] Wagner had developed his theory independently
in the 1850s and 1860s, partly as a result of his interest in the political question of
German emigration, but he presented it to the world as a correction to Darwin's
theory of natural selection. As another outsider in academia, he had recognized a
kindred spirit in Ratzel, helped to draw him into an academic career, and provided
him with his first theoretical framework (and possibly some of Wagner's own
resentments against scientific establishments).[9] According to Wagner, Darwin's
description of species change was essentially correct, except that Darwin had taken
insufficient account of a fundamental characteristic of living organisms: their unavoidable tendency to spread across the earth's surface. Wagner believed that he
had discovered a law in this tendency. He claimed that the rate and degree of change
of a species over time is proportional to the physical separation of its members.[10]
Thus a widely distributed species would show more variation than a less diffused
one and would produce new species more readily; change would occur more often

among the members of a species the more distant they were from the areas of greatest concentration.

By the 1880s, Ratzel realized that Wagner's "law" was incorrect, but it suggested to him a way to build an integrated approach to explaining human life. Ratzel had been interested in the emigration question for years—first as a journalist, then as a geographer, and finally in the early 1880s as a leading advocate of German colonies as receptacles for emigrants.[11] He now claimed that the natural propensity of humans to move over the earth's surface, which they share with all other species, was the key to a holistic human geography that could, among other things, justify migrationist colonialism. "Restless movement is the signature of mankind."[12] Thus the interactions of human groups with the various features of terrain, climate, and vegetation essentially structure society and history. The inevitable Darwinian competition between human groups takes place in a spatial dimension; the most fundamental struggle is for space itself.

We shall discuss Ratzel's human geography in a later chapter. What is important here are its implications for ethnology. In the decade following the publication of *Anthropo-Geographie,* Ratzel undertook comparative museum studies of types of primitive material artifact in support of his theories. In his 1887 and 1893 articles on the geographical distribution of the bow and the spear, Ratzel laid the foundations of the particular form of diffusionism that later captured German ethnology.[13]

The object of ethnological study was, according to Ratzel, primarily historical: to trace the movements of people and cultural traits across the earth's surface in ages gone by and to link the pattern of those movements to similar phenomena in the present so as to be able to predict the future.[14] Ratzel assumed that he already knew the general framework of history—the existence of constant migration and adaptation to environment—as a result of contemplating the data. Detailed research (e.g., on the bow and the spear) was needed to fill in the details. To Ratzel, a scientific law, at least one applying to the living part of nature, was a very complex thing. The general notions of population movements that he advanced were only the underpinnings of laws; the laws themselves had to be constructed through detailed empirical research.[15] Such research would also confirm the general correctness of the overall theory. Although this is an oversimplification of Ratzel's approach, the problem of circularity it reveals was in fact a very real one, to which we shall return later.

According to Ratzel, physical similarities between useful material artifacts were evidence of cultural movement.[16] Following the model established by historical philology, Ratzel assumed that if different peoples, physically separated from one another, made material objects in much the same way, it was probably evidence of previous cultural contacts between them. Combining both the philological model and Wagner's migration theory, Ratzel also argued that high levels of similarity between individual cultural traits (e.g., in shaping bows) and large numbers of similar traits shared by peoples of different regions were firm evidence of the paths of cultural diffusion.[17] Moreover, the colocation within a geographical area of a great many similar traits essentially defined the physical boundaries of a cultural area—an idea originally of Bastian, which would later be denoted as the concept of the "*Kulturkreis.*" Ratzel identified specific areas in Africa in which the bow predominated in hunting and warfare and areas where the spear was used. In each area, the different varieties of bows and spears that were found could be grouped into patterns according to their relative closeness and distance in appearance, and the patterns could be transferred to a map that showed the probable routes by which patterns of bowmaking or spearmaking had diffused within each of the regions.[18]

The importance of all this lay in the inferences that could be drawn from the distribution patterns thus revealed. Ratzel was somewhat reticent to draw the widest possible conclusions without considerably greater research, although he did make suggestions that were readily taken up by followers such as Leo Frobenius in the 1890s. The general inference was that, if the material traits were directly related to mental traits and all were part of the distinctive cultural patterns of *Völker,* then the framework within which the formation of whole cultures took place had been revealed together with the historical relationships among cultures. In the case of Africa, Ratzel concluded that the distribution of artifacts showed a series of conquests in which spearmen had taken over territories from earlier bow-using inhabitants.[19]

To understand the significance of Ratzel's diffusionism for cultural and social science, we can consider some of its implications (as Ratzel and his followers saw them) for major elements of the traditional liberal and the neoliberal theoretical patterns. We can use our now-familiar triad of individualism, nomothetic scientific aim, and notions of change and equilibrium.

Ratzel actually accepted significant parts of the traditional liberal model of the rational individual, modified, of course, to take cultural conditioning into account. Ratzel retained both the idea of fundamental human unity and the belief that rationality made up a substantial proportion of people's mental properties.[20] His theory of human adaptation to environment depended on being able to predict the rational responses of different groups of people to similar environments, at least within a range of possibilities. Group rationality had of necessity to derive, to a certain extent, from individual rationality. But Ratzel was not particularly interested in the subject of individual rationality. Rather than treat the common factors in the human psyche(including rationality) as a hidden mystery and the central object of cultural inquiry (as Bastian and other neoliberals did), Ratzel regarded these things as fairly obvious. Human rationality was only an extension of the general mental capabilities of higher vertebrates (which allowed Ratzel to apply "laws" of animal life and movement to humans—if only by implication).[21] He did pay attention to some aspects of psychology, especially late in his career when he came under the posthumous influence of Gustav Fechner, and he acknowledged that cultural science revolved broadly around psychological phenomena, but he effectively moved traditional psychological concerns to the periphery of cultural study.[22]

Ratzel was really interested in *groups*—not just for the neoliberal reason that group culture influenced individual thought, but also because the important actions in history were performed by groups, not separate persons. In fact, Ratzel essentially reversed the traditional liberal practice of reasoning about the nature of society by inference from the individual; he inferred the nature of the individual's mind from the individual's customary behavior in groups.[23] The most important point about the relationship between the individual and the group was that, far from reflecting the manifold capabilities of the individual, the group (or society as a whole), through the division of labor, made up for the very real deficiencies of the average person.

One of the best-known assumptions of Ratzel's diffusionism was that humans are naturally uncreative. They have an inherent tendency toward inertia, from which they must be forced in order for any significant change to occur. Only occasionally does a people produce an innovator—essentially through natural variation, which to Ratzel required no further explanation. In some senses, these creative individuals were like the geniuses of *Sturm und Drang* or the *Übermenschen* of Nietzsche, except that Ratzel was not terribly interested in them as persons or in the reasons for their creativity. What was important to Ratzel was the process by which inventions, once conceived, are adopted by a people and transmitted spatially.[24]

Ratzel held that the process of innovation occurs in both the material and the nonmaterial spheres of life. But the crucial innovations are those that arise in the activities through which people directly confront their physical environments.[25] Inventions are more likely to be adopted by the uncreative members of a society if they provide some utilitarian advantage. Other innovations, material and nonmaterial, more or less group themselves around these crucial ones. Ratzel usually saw them as tools or weapons, but sometimes he also perceived them as forms of political organization. Because material innovations are so important, it was legitimate to use them as the main evidence in tracing patterns of cultural diffusion and change.

An innovation, once adopted, becomes a characteristic trait of a particular people. Ratzel tended to present cultures as aggregations of traits. This bothered him because he was sure that there was some deeper essence, some life force beneath the trait aggregations that gave them meaning.[26] He was never able, however, to work out a coherent theory that expressed the nature of this force. Some of his followers, especially Leo Frobenius, attempted to fill the gap—with questionable success. In the main line of German diffusionist theory, from Ratzel to Fritz Graebner and Wilhelm Schmidt, culture remained for practical purposes a collection of traits.[27] In essence, what Ratzel had done was to replace the abstract individual as the unit of social and cultural analysis with another abstraction: the trait. Supposedly, traits could be apprehended directly through empirical observation; their various arrangements defined different cultures. Ethnology became, in the diffusionist view, the systematic comparison and tracing of traits. It all seemed simple enough. Trait analysis appeared to reduce the excessive abstraction of traditional liberal social science and to eliminate many of the difficulties in explaining the relationship between humans and their societies. In fact, the definition of what a trait was and the identification of actual traits turned out to be considerably more problematical than Ratzel could tell from his few exercises in trait comparison.

Ratzel's approach to ethnology, therefore, although it borrowed many ideas from liberal social science and neoliberal ethnology, represents a substantial break with both in terms of its treatment of the individual. It moved the individual mentality out of its position as a prime object of study and replaced it with cultural traits.

Like the neoliberal cultural scientists, Ratzel accepted the second element of the traditional liberal pattern (a nomothetic view of social science), but he added his own characteristic twists. Ratzel was a convinced empiricist, but he was by training a zoologist and geographer, not an experimenter. To him, as to Alexander von Humboldt, Ritter, and Darwin, empiricism meant *observation* and *comparison* rather than the experimental testing of hypotheses.[28] He looked by preference for the "hardest" available data for cultural analysis: material artifacts, especially utilitarian ones. Once the patterns of relationship among material artifacts had been established in a time dimension, it was possible to fit intellectual, political, religious, and social traits into the pattern. Ratzel insisted that the laws derived from studying such patterns were not simple propositions reducible to mathematical formulas, but complicated statements concerning complex realities.[29] Today, we might say that Ratzel was looking for central statistical tendencies in sets of phenomena, but he did not see it that way. He had some notion that ethnological "truth" depended on the perspective of the observer, but he did not develop the idea. In other words, although in some ways he foreshadowed the relativistic anthropology of the twentieth century and although he displayed awareness that the sciences of culture might be methodologically different from the physical sciences, he strongly resisted following these tendencies very far. He remained, like most of the neoliberals, firmly in the positivist (or more accurately, nomothetic) camp.[30]

But Ratzel's positivism was of an increasingly old-fashioned sort, mainly because he did not rigorously apply the procedure of hypothesis testing in his work. His articles and books are filled with examples that are meant, by sheer weight of the data, to convince the reader of the truth of whatever proposition Ratzel was advancing. Darwin's works have some of the same character. But this methodology involves dangers, especially that of circular argument. Ratzel usually commenced his analyses already knowing the pattern of explanation to be applied, and the data he cited were fitted into the pattern, fleshing it out. At the end, Ratzel would assume that he had proved his point, but often he had done nothing of the sort. What he had shown was that certain observations could be interpreted in such a way as to be consistent with his theory, but he had not advanced much beyond the formulation of a hypothesis. To demonstrate a law, according to the standards that had come to be accepted in the exact sciences, he would have had to treat his initial explanatory schemes as hypotheses and systematically attempted to falsify them, and that he did not do. Ratzel's theories are notoriously difficult to prove or disprove.[31] If Ratzel had taken a different view of the purpose and methodology of cultural science, if he had, for instance, adopted something like the hermeneutic approach of Dilthey or the interpretive stance taken by Max Weber, this difficulty would have been less serious. But there is little evidence that Ratzel even considered entering the methodological dialogue between the proponents of nomothetic social and cultural science and the advocates of hermeneutic approaches, much less that he considered dropping the nomothetic aim. The latter was too much a part of what science was all about as far as Ratzel was concerned. In this respect, Ratzel retained an allegiance to the traditions of liberal social science. Ratzel insisted that he was discovering real scientific laws, however complex they might be.[32]

This was exactly the sort of thing that worried Rudolf Virchow, and obviously not because Virchow favored hermeneutics. The dangers were more significant than simply the assertion of incorrect statements about human culture. As we shall see in a later chapter, Ratzel's most famous and comprehensive theoretical formulation—*Lebensraum*—had a very significant (and deleterious) effect on German politics at least in part because it could be represented as the unquestionable product of science in its nomothetic sense. Ratzel's theory of cultural diffusion did not have that kind of political effect and Ratzel's claims for it were much more modest. But the same general pattern was present, and Ratzel's successors were not so hesitant.

The whole thrust of diffusionism broke strongly with traditional liberal approaches to the questions of social change and equilibrium. Although Ratzel's conception of cultural diffusion owed a great deal to the diffusionist theories of neoliberals, such as Bastian, Richard Andree, and Waitz's pupil (and Ratzel's severe critic) Georg Gerland, it substantially shifted the weight of theory toward a complex historical view in which universal stages of cultural development were subordinated to unique patterns of cultural diffusion.[33]

According to Ratzel, once an innovation has been adopted by a particular people, it becomes part of the aggregation that constitutes their culture. What determines whether an innovation is retained or dropped in a culture is mainly its effectiveness in helping a *Volk* confront the environment in which its members live.[34] Ratzel was not a full-fledged environmental determinist like Carl Andree. Human ingenuity and randomness of invention play their roles, and humans are quite capable of altering their environments. But the physical environment, to Ratzel, constitutes the overall framework for innovation and culture building and determines the general tendencies in the change of cultural forms over time.

Ratzel paid less attention to innovations themselves than to their transmission, and the most important key to transmission was the movement of peoples. In Ratzel's view of nature, living species that survive and thrive are those that move into new areas and either adapt successfully to the environment or adapt the environment to themselves. This is true of human *Völker* as well. Human adaptation is a group activity, and what determines whether or not a group can adapt are the cultural traits it brings with it.[35] Although Ratzel had a greater belief in human physical adaptability than, for example, Vorchow had, he thought human social adaptability was much more impressive. A migrant people moving en masse into a new land must confront not just physical features, but usually also the people already there. A limited range of outcomes is possible. The would-be conquerors might be kept out, or they might coexist with the older population, or they might take over completely. In the latter two cases, there can be a great deal of cultural mixing as traits already appropriate to the environment are picked up by the newcomers and new traits are passed on to the natives. Many conquering peoples, including the various "barbarian" conquerors of China, have been culturally absorbed by the conquered—which simply means that the exchange of traits went essentially one way. The conquering culture disappeared in the process. Conquest in such cases does not imply superiority; it means the death of the *Volk* as a result of inevitable migration.[36]

But the most successful *Völker* of all are the ones who move into a new region and take over, impressing themselves and their culture on the area because the array of traits they bring with them allows them to adapt readily to new circumstances. They may pick up some useful things from the previous inhabitants in the process of adaptation, but the pattern of overall change is that of a transplantation of a culture into new soil.

Significantly, Ratzel referred to the successful migrant peoples of history as "colonizers" and claimed that most of them display certain common traits, of which the most important is a basis in peasant agriculture.[37] He cited other significant factors: effective political organization, appropriate military and agricultural technology, and a strong sense of cultural identity. The last factor to some extent contradicted Ratzel's acknowledgment that the colonizers adapt in part by taking over cultural traits from their predecessors, but he argued that only a coherent culture can absorb traits without itself disintegrating. The key, though, to everything else was the peasant foundation—the taking over of the land by the newcomers, who then farm it themselves. Peasant farmers are the bearers of cultural continuity and coherence. They are also the basis of effective political organization.

Cultural traits can also, according to Ratzel, be transferred by other forms of contact between peoples, especially trade.[38] He did not think, however, that diffusion through trade is nearly as important as diffusion through the migration of peoples—for one thing, because a trait brought by commerce is not always accompanied by the social and cultural framework that gives it meaning. Trade is more important as a shaper of the characters of the people who conduct it than as a means of transmitting individual traits. Many of Ratzel's followers thought otherwise.[39]

Migration and adaptation, supplemented by occasional innovation and diffusion by trade, are therefore the wellsprings of history. Progress does occur, but not inevitably or in universal stages. It occurs through the aggregation of superior traits by certain peoples, who spread themselves and their cultures over wide areas, absorbing other traits and innovations into their cultural being without losing its essence. Segments of a *Volk* that separate from each other in the course of migration will (according to Ratzel's version of Moritz Wagner's "law") develop different cultural characteristics, but they will continue to possess a sufficient number of common traits that the ethnologist will be able to link them.[40]

Ratzel also noted that practically every type of contact between peoples involves biological mixing, so that there are now no pure races on earth—if there ever have been.[41] On this issue, Ratzel and most of the anthropologists he influenced were in general agreement with the neoliberals. Indeed, Ratzel (in theory, at any rate) was less of a racist than Virchow. Although allowing that racial features had some bearing on the adaptability of a migrating people to a new physical environment, Ratzel also (like Boas) emphasized the adaptability of human physical features to the environment through natural selection. A *Volk* was a cultural, not a racial entity. Ratzel shared his era's prejudices against some *existing* races (Africans, for instance). On the other hand, he had enormous respect for the peoples of East Asia.[42] And in the long run, he argued, racial factors did not matter very much. It was culture that counted.

One of the most obvious characteristics of Ratzel's ethnology was its emphasis on history—or more especially, the early histories of peoples. To study the processes of change in society and culture, one must study the histories of specific peoples and infer from them historical laws.[43] We have seen that a historical orientation was characteristic of German social science (including neoliberal ethnology), and we shall see in chapter 10 that this orientation was intensified in such disciplines as economics in response to dissatisfaction with the concept of equilibrium. Ratzel also displaced equilibrium from the focus of his theoretical approach. What was left of equilibrium in his theories was a kind of ecological stability that some cultures (usually peasant-based ones) achieved if they possessed the appropriate array of traits, but that stability was continually threatened by the imperatives of population movement.[44]

The specific factors that led Ratzel to adopt a historical orientation were probably quite varied. In the first place, such orientations were fashionable in academia by the 1870s and 1880s, for reasons that we shall discuss later. Intellectual fashion was always important to Ratzel because of his social and educational insecurities.[45] Second, a historical approach seemed to many people interested in understanding contemporary social and political change to explain much more than the approaches associated with liberalism in the past. Ratzel, like others, took the fact of irreversible change as a given and tried to explore it rather than arguing about it on moral or political grounds. This was consistent with Ratzel's need to combine an acceptance of change (partly a ghost of his early radicalism) with a growing conservatism in social outlook as he became older. By joining elements of continuity and change in one "scientifically" legitimated pattern, Ratzel's historical orientation could fill this need at the level of theory—and at the level of politics as well, because, for him, theory and politics were never far apart. But Ratzel's use of history was *not* the same as that of the historicists who followed Ranke and Droysen and who had come to dominate professional historiography. Ratzel hoped to find natural laws in historical patterns, whereas Ranke did not think that such natural laws were there to be found—although patterns, reflecting the will of God, did exist. The historicists who adopted Droysen's approach focused on politics because they thought that was the area in which human freedom most clearly operated and in which other factors of human existence were ultimately shaped. Ratzel, although deeply interested in politics, considered it to be an aspect of culture like any other, formed by human interaction with a complex environment.[46]

Ratzel's diffusionism, then, shows both the impact of his acceptance of peasant agrarianism and the extent of his divergence from the traditional theoretical pattern of liberal social science (and from neoliberal cultural science.) The agrarianism is obvious in his description of successful migrating cultures. The divergence from the traditional liberal pattern can be seen in Ratzel's restructuring of the object of culture study so as to emphasize the broad histories of peoples and to deemphasize the understanding of the individual's relationship to society. It is present (as a change in emphasis) in his representation of social laws as complex inferences from the historical interactions of peoples and environments. And it manifests itself in Ratzel's view of the process of social change as a product of population movements affected by a multiplicity of variables. At the same time, on a number of significant points—the retention of the nomothetic aim of social science, for example, and the rejection of racialist interpretations of culture and society—Ratzel showed that the roots of his theoretical pattern lay in liberal social science. Although he differed in many respects from his neoliberal opponents, he also shared a great deal with them because of their common intellectual ancestry.

There are serious problems with Ratzel's anthropological theories, some of which are inherent in the whole theoretical pattern he helped to establish. For one thing, it turns out that the trait—like other, more recent anthropological abstractions, such as "function" and "structure"—is not as easily and unambiguously identifiable as Ratzel thought. Tools and weapons are more readily observable than other traits, but the attempt to trace a trait such as "divine kingship" led diffusionist historians of Africa into a number of blind alleys.[47] And even weapons cannot be understood as traits in Ratzel's sense without being placed in their peculiar social contexts. The bow, for instance, had an entirely different social significance (and, indeed, a different military function) in ancient Persia than it did in medieval England or than it does among Central African pygmies. The same thing could be said about the different roles the chariot played over time in ancient societies. The evidence of diffusion tells us something, but not always a great deal—especially with respect to the *meanings* of traits in different societies. And if the meanings of traits vary among different cultures, then the concept of "trait" itself loses its status as the fixed unit of cultural analysis—that is, the factor that permits the ethnologist to construct laws explaining the continuities and divergences among peoples. The trait, unfortunately, is not much of an analytical improvement over the individual—indeed, from some standpoints, it is less useful because it implies a spurious claim to objectivity on the part of the observer of culture.

There are many other specific difficulties with Ratzel's version of diffusionism: uncertainties about the implications of trait analysis for explaining contemporary social phenomena; problems with Ratzel's tendency to infer connections between observed material traits and unobserved historical events (the prevalence of spears in a region, for instance, as evidence of early conquest by a warrior aristocracy); questions about whether or not Ratzel's very broad, metahistorical context was really the best one for the empirical study of peoples; and the very fundamental issue of whether or not Ratzel's theories, with their picture of an uncreative humanity adapting to environment, really could explain change at all—as opposed to the maintenance of constant level of cultural sophistication among migrating peoples.[48] To some of Ratzel's own followers, his singleminded concentration on traits meant that the cultures he portrayed were, in the course of analysis, atomized to such an extent that it was difficult to get at the essence of what a particular culture or people was. This was one of the reasons that successors, such as Graebner and Ankermann, developed the idea of the *Kulturkreis*: an area dominated by an integrated array of cultural traits.[49] As he grew older, Ratzel sought the solution to the problem elsewhere. He looked for the meaning of human culture in the principles governing all nature, not just humankind—the essence of his idea of *Lebensraum*.

Many of the anthropologists who followed Ratzel in developing diffusionist ethnology rejected his overwhelming emphasis on mass migration as the key to cultural history. Most agreed that although large-scale migrations obviously occurred, the ethnographical evidence indicated there that there were a great many equally important ways in which cultural traits could be passed: trade, the movements of small groups of people, fashionable imitation of the outward characteristics of prestigious peoples, missionary work, and so forth. It was, therefore, not acceptable to conclude because a group of traits in one place was very similar to traits in another that a large-scale migration must necessarily have occurred between them.[50]

This last point brings us back to the context in which Ratzel developed his diffusionist theories. His emphasis on migration reflected, of course, a number of elements in his own and his age's intellectual background. Historical philology, the model for the study of early and "primitive" cultures, similarly assumed that languages are spread by the migrations of their speakers. Well before Ratzel, European prehistory had come to be envisioned as a succession of invasions by whole peoples coming out of the Russian steppes. The revelation of how small some of the migrations were (especially those that destroyed the Western Roman Empire) had not yet arisen from historical scholarship. Darwinian theory also, of course, paid great attention to the migration of species. But these factors cannot explain the overriding importance that Ratzel ascribed to migration—an emphasis that is even more obvious in his human geography.[51] They might explain the presence of the migration concept, but not its centrality.

In fact, the idea of migration was important to Ratzel not only as a scientist, but also as a journalist, ideologist, political activist, and private individual. Its centrality in his theoretical work was closely connected with its centrality in other aspects of his life.

Ratzel's first interest in migration apparently arose in childhood. He came from an area and social environment that produced large numbers of emigrants to America throughout the nineteenth century. During his stay in the Western United States in the early 1870s, he had seriously considered remaining there.[52] As a journalist, he was something of a specialist in contemporary migration. Some of his earliest serious geographical writings concerned Chinese emigration.[53] But two other factors had a more direct effect: the influence of Moritz Wagner, and Ratzel's own involvement—before and during the period in which he developed his cultural diffusionism—in the German colonial movement.

Moritz Wagner had made a reputation before Ratzel knew him not as a scientist, but as a proponent of a colonial solution to Germany's emigration problem.[54] He was a contributor to what can be called migrationist colonialism, the best-known German conception of what colonies were all about. This view held that emigration was an unavoidable phenomenon of German economic and social life. The proper policy of German governments faced with overpopulation and the loss of subjects through emigration was neither to restrict emigration nor just to let it happen, but rather to direct it toward German colonies in temperate regions overseas where the emigrants could better themselves economically, retain their connections to German culture, and continue to contribute, through trade, to the common good of their home states. The typical colonist was envisioned as a peasant farmer. In the migrationist vision, settlement colonies became places where the independent farmer-citizen of liberal agrarian ideology could be developed. Migrationism and agrarianism were thus quite closely linked.[55] Wagner was involved in several schemes to set up colonies in Central America in the 1840s and 1850s. He owed his academic position in Munich at least in part to King Maximilian II's brief interest in colonialism as a solution to Bavaria's social problems.[56]

Wagner subsequently broadened his ideological conception of migration and colonialism into a framework for comprehending all living things: his migration theory, which, as we have seen, strongly influenced Ratzel. In other words, Ratzel absorbed into his scientific thinking a heavy dose of migrationist ideology overtly linked to agrarianism and to the other offshoots of political liberalism that developed as liberal academics began to move away from the classical patterns of liberal thought. And he did it ostensibly (although presumably not unconsciously) by taking a scientific theory as a model.

But Ratzel's direct link to migrationist colonialism was also important. In the 1870s, his involvement as journalist and geographical expert in the politics of migration and colonialism led him to draw connections among migrationism, imperialism, and agrarianism and to put those connections at the center of his cultural science.

Ratzel was one of the early academic recruits to the growing colonial movement of the late 1870s. He first became involved as an academic geographer in the activities of export-interest groups who were pushing the national government to give stronger support to German overseas businesses, including the declaration of colonies where appropriate. Not surprisingly, his first pronouncements on the subject dealt with colonies as possible adjuncts to trade.[57] But by the early 1880s, it had become clear that most Germans thought of future colonies as settlement areas, as solutions to the problem of emigration, and as symbols of German power, not as commercial establishments. The increasingly active colonialist organizations—the *Kolonialverein* of 1882 and its successor, the German Colonial Society—took up the more popular migrationist line, although they did not drop the commercial one. The National Liberal party, anxious to regain the initiative against the Progressives and to augment its dwindling support base, did likewise. It became, together with the smaller Free Conservative party, the main force for colonialism in the Reichstag.[58]

Many young and early middle-aged intellectuals saw in the migrationist version of colonialism an ideological pattern within which some of their criticisms of the existing order could be organized and transformed into a political program. Like migrationism colonialism itself, the ideological outlooks of these people were largely founded on traditional liberalism, but they reflected a growing belief that liberalism in its present forms was inapplicable to contemporary German society because it was based on faulty premises, and yet that the other traditional approaches to politics and society were even more irrelevant. Many different political positions were consistent with such attitudes (including various forms of socialism), but most of the academics drawn to migrationist colonialism in the 1880s had little sympathy with the radical left or with the industrial working class. Many were moving toward the loosely defined ideological stance that can be called radical nationalism or radical conservatism.[59] Their hero (for a while) was Carl Peters, the "founder" of German East Africa. One of Peters's most fervent admirers was Friedrich Ratzel.[60]

By 1885, Ratzel, under criticism from other budding radical nationalist colonialists, such as Ernst Hasse (the later Pan-German leader), had committed himself fully to the migrationist line, although he also argued that migrationism was consistent with commercial colonialism.[61] This was a significant point, for people like Hasse were arguing that the idea of commercial colonies by itself was merely a reflection of the big industrial interests that were ruining German life and culture.[62] Ratzel believed that the act of establishing settlement colonies overseas, the national spirit that colonialism would engender in the German *Volk,* and the model Germans who would be produced in settlement colonies would create the means by which the new forces of industrial society could be tamed and integrated into German culture. Ratzel warmly applauded the seizure of German colonies in Africa and the Pacific in 1884–1885 and shared in the colonial movement's disappointment that Bismarck was thereafter unwilling to go beyond these essentially commercial territories to establish viable settlement colonies in temperate areas.[63]

Ratzel's complex involvement with migrationist colonialism helps to explain some of the crucial features of his diffusionist theories: his characterization of successful cultural diffusion as a result of the "colonization" of a new area through the occupation of the land for peasant farming; his insistence on the relationship between success in the struggle between *Völker* and the ability of a culture to adapt to new environmental circumstances; and the underlying imperative of human life that a people must spread (migrate) and colonize or die. The first could be seen as a generalized anthropological rendering of the argument of the migrationists as against the advocates of trading colonies.[64] The second was a way of insisting that Germany's future depended on her displaying the kind of adaptablity that other imperial peoples had. And the third was "scientific" backing for the most fundamental of all political arguments: that there was no acceptable alternative to the policies Ratzel favored. Although in his *Anthropo-Geographie* and his ethnological articles Ratzel did not make these points specifically in reference to the German colonial movement, he certainly mustered the scientific evidence for them in his political and journalistic writings on imperialism.[65] The timing of Ratzel's development of diffusionism—during and immediately following his heavy involvement in the colonial enthusiasm of the 1880s—strongly suggests that the main direction of influence was from his politics to his scientific theorizing. It appears that what he took from the political sphere was part of a theoretical pattern that could be used to array his scientific observations of human culture.

Ratzel's colonialism also engaged him once again in the dialogue between the neoliberal Berlin anthropological establishment and the establishment's rivals. The latter were originally heterogeneous and disorganized. Ratzel presented to them a theoretical pattern around which many of them, at least in ethnology, could rally. That is a large part of Ratzel's significance in the history of German cultural science, which far outweighs the immediate contribution to knowledge of his few rather superficial articles about spears and bows. In Kuhnian terms, the larger framework of political, generational, and regional rivalry that informed the origins of diffusionism made diffusionism revolutionary, in contrast to the neoliberals' desperate attempts to retain the integrity of normal cultural science. As in any such revolution, it was not that all the individual elements of the previous paradigm were rejected (we have seen that many of them were in fact carried over) as it was that the pattern of relationships among them and the ostensible goal of the whole endeavor (the definition of what needed to be explained) were altered—not primarily because the new paradigm displayed superior explanatory power, but because the new arrangements met a variety of needs (many of them political) of the group in question.

Whereas Ratzel and many of the other leading ethnologists of his generation were aggressive colonialists, the leaders of neoliberal cultural science on the whole opposed colonial acquisition for Germany. Virchow and Bastian had seen nothing wrong with government support for German commercial expansion (especially in the form of geographical research) in the 1870s, but they saw a great deal wrong with the hysterical colonialism of the 1880s.[66] One of the things to which they particularly objected was the migrationist turn of the colonial movement in the 1880s. Virchow presented his objection in scientific terms: it could be shown from the evidence of physical geography and population distributions that peoples could not readily adjust to radical changes in climate.[67] Among Europeans moving to tropical areas, death rates were high, although some survived. More important, reproduction rates fell so drastically that a migrant population could not sustain itself. Migrationist colonialism was therefore absurd.

Ratzel responded in two ways.[68] He pointed out that the colonial movement sought colonies in temperate regions, not the tropical colonies that were most of the booty of Bismarck's colonial forays of 1884–1885. He also argued that Virchow had read the data incorrectly. Europeans *could* acclimate themselves to different environments—through technology and superior social organization as well as through biological adaptation along the lines of natural selection. A new environment selects among an emigrant population for appropriate features, and these are passed on. Ratzel, basing his opinion on studying Chinese emigration, was of course correct. The debate was important to him in suggesting the importance of examining acclimatization and developing theories of migration. His thinking on the matter influenced his later work on human geography, as we shall see in chapter 12. Virchow continued to disagree.[69]

But the scientific dispute—although a perfectly valid and legitimate one—was not all there was to it. Virchow was led to make his argument about acclimatization (a subject in which he had taken little interest previously) because he disapproved of aggressive colonialism. Ratzel attacked Virchow's argument not only because it touched on his scientific interests and his current political ones, but also because it fitted into a general pattern of ideas and attitudes that he had come to oppose. The negative position of Virchow and Bastian on aggressive colonialism was based on certain beliefs that had, by the mid-nineteenth century, come to be considered by many liberals throughout Europe to be part of the essence of liberalism itself: colonies were an unwarranted, distortive interference with free trade, at best jus-tifiable only as means of introducing international commerce into a backward area. Under any other circumstances, they were a waste of blood and taxes. Virchow's Progressive party took this line—as had Bismarck until political considerations caused him to abandon it temporarily in the early 1880s.[70]

But as the colonial movement expanded and began to emphasize migrationism, Virchow and Bastian saw in it something more sinister: a threat to their hopes for a liberal Germany. By adopting, in migrationist colonialism, an ideology that had well-known roots in one particular area of German liberal thought, the colonial movement might assist Bismarck, some of the nonliberal parties, and the right wing of the National Liberals in attracting away many of the supporters of the Progressive party—of which Virchow was a leader and the party that he believed to be the bastion of true liberalism. If the Progressives did not themselves adopt a colonialist position, they risked a loss of support; if they did turn toward colonialism, they risked losing their identity as liberals—as Virchow defined liberalism. Either way, it was Bismarck and the forces of reaction who stood to gain—a view that was confirmed when Bismarck suddenly revealed himself as a colonialist.[71]

Especially disturbing was the proclivity of younger academics and intellectuals, including Ratzel, to jump on the colonialist bandwagon and to advertise it as the means of creating a new Germany. These were the very people on whom the future of progressive politics in Germany most depended. Their tendency to recast their adherence to liberal ideology in hypernationalist terms was already worrying. Virchow was himself a strong nationalist, but one who saw the realization of liberal principles in institutional form as the only means of revealing the nation itself.[72] Ratzel, on the other hand, belonged to a group that increasingly viewed parliamentary institutions and other forms of liberal apparatus as obstructions to the self-realization of the *Volk* and nation.[73] And just as bad, many of these same younger people had earlier rallied behind Darwinism and Ernst Haeckel and had violently challenged the scientific approach of the ethnological establishment. All of these things appeared to be connected.[74]

Ratzel's enthusiastic adoption of colonialism, therefore, and his tendency to allow colonialist ideology to inspire his cultural theories fit into an already-developing pattern of antagonism between the neoliberal elite of cultural science and a new generation of academics, many of them located outside Berlin. The latter were groping for what they saw as an ideology beyond liberalism and toward a theoretical pattern beyond neoliberalism. We shall discuss the first later as a major constituent of turn-of-the-century radical nationalism. The second was an impetus toward the foundation of new theoretical patterns in cultural science, of which Ratzel's diffusionism and his human geography became archetypes.

Ratzel's Successors

When Ratzel's ideas of diffusionism appeared, they were taken by many perceptive younger neoliberals, such as Franz Boas, as useful hypotheses that broadened theoretical understanding without directly threatening their own fundamental approach to culture.[75] Boas, of course, fell to some extent out of the broader context of political and generational conflict in Germany by his emigration to America. Others, such as Boas's brilliant contemporary, Heinrich Schurtz (1863–1903), remained within the context and were much more profoundly affected. During his brief career, Schurtz developed the outlines of a comprehensive ethnology that in some ways foretold the structuralism of a later era. He retained a neoliberal concern for psychology and for understanding the workings of social structure, but he placed his analysis in a historical and in part a diffusionist framework strongly influenced by Ratzel.[76]

But the development of diffusionism into a full-fledged theoretical pattern was mainly the work of people who were much more clearly disciples of Ratzel. Chronologically, the first of these was Leo Frobenius (1873–1938), but we shall save a discussion of him for later because his diffusionism eventually became extremely radical and because he was not, for many years, fully accepted into the academic ethnological community.[77]

As we saw in chapter 5, the main line of diffusionist ethnology received a firm theoretical grounding and revealed itself as the dominant force in German anthropology at the 1904 meeting of the *Berliner Gesellschaft* when Fritz Graebner and Bernhard Ankermann presented papers on "Kulturkreise und Kulturschichten" (cultural areas and cultural layers) in Oceania and Africa, respectively. Not only were the papers delivered in the center of the Berlin establishment, but they were published the next year in the establishment's organ, the *Zeitschrift für Ethnologie*.[78] The papers were immediately accepted throughout Germany as classic statements of the essence of ideas that had been gaining currency since Ratzel's articles some years before and that had been spread by other young ethnologists, such as Frobenius and Schurtz. Within a few years, Graebner in particular had emerged as the leader of what had become the dominant fashion in German anthropology. The diffusionist revolution was complete.[79]

The ethnology of Graebner and Ankermann was very complex and not wholly uniform.[80] Following suggestions by Frobenius but rejecting his specific conclusions because of his poor treatment of evidence, Graebner and Ankermann proposed that the key to recreating the cultural history of peoples was identifying and delimiting the boundaries of *Kulturkreise*.[81] *Kulturkreise* were held to be the proper framework for analysis in ethnology and prehistory. The immediate object of ethnological research was to isolate traits of all sorts that made up the culture of a particular people in a particular place and then to compare them in a comprehensive, systematic way with arrays of traits of other peoples elsewhere. Most of Graebner's career was spent trying to establish a detailed methodology for performing this sort of comparison.[82] When the points of comparison were established, the next step was to identify the relationships among isolated traits that affected the dynamics of a people's culture and also to note the amount and degree of cultural similarity between peoples on the basis of the number and forms of traits they had in common. From there, a geographical area could be determined within which certain cultural forms, taken in the context of a people's whole culture, were clearly dominant. This area was the *Kulturkreis*. The pattern of traits that allowed the boundaries of the *Kulturkreis* to be laid out was the unique general culture of which the specific cultures of the individual peoples in the region were in some sense manifestations.

Diffusionism was a theoretical pattern rather than a coherent theory. Even the classic formulators, Graebner and Ankermann, differed on some issues, and the detailed theoretical approaches of the other leading diffusionists of their generation (Frobenius, Wilhelm Schmidt, and William Foy) varied substantially.[83] But all of these people and their acolytes acknowledged a shared theoretical pattern: a common set of classics, a similar view of the proper behavior of members of their discipline, and a common set of assumptions, aims, and modes of discourse that clearly set them off from other anthropologists. Although they differed to some extent as individuals about politics, they and their theories shared a similar relationship to the larger context of German political ideology in the first half of the twentieth century. Their theories also shared certain distinctive weaknesses, of which they were generally quite aware.

The common classics we have already seen: Ratzel, Bastian to a lesser extent, and, of course, Alexander von Humboldt and Herder among the distant ancestors.[84] As to behavior, they were for the most part socialized into the pattern of professional scholarship that had become fairly rigid in the generation before theirs. Frobenius and Schmidt were a little outside the pattern. Frobenius, without his degree, had to subsist on journalism and through the sponsors of his expeditions. Even he, however, had as his goal the attainment of academic standing, which he eventually achieved.[85] Schmidt was a Catholic priest resident in Austria, an official of a missionary society who specialized in the training of missionaries. But he took part in all the standard activities of an academic scholar and eventually was awarded a professorship at the University of Vienna.[86] These backgrounds may help to explain Schmidt and Frobenius's deviations from the Graebner–Ankermann norms. But in general consensus among diffusionists about academic behavior and values was very high. One of the hallmarks of German diffusionism—its "bookish, museum-oriented" appearance—was due in part to the absence of field experience in the backgrounds of some of its leaders (such as Schmidt and Graebner) and in part to the diffusionists' efforts to make their published work conform to the patterns of conventional scholarship.[87] On the whole, diffusionists subscribed to most of the prevailing fashions in German academia, including the tendency to sigh with despair for the future of humane education in an increasingly materialistic (i.e., industrial) world.

Much of the theoretical content of diffusionism can be discussed in terms of similarities and differences with respect to the earlier liberal theoretical pattern, which was to a large degree its ancestor. The removal of the individual from the focus of attention that was evident in Ratzel was also characteristic of his diffusionist successors. It was most extreme in Frobenius, who eventually came close to denying the existence of any unique individual consciousness.[88] The others followed Ratzel's lead by accepting much of the traditional liberal view of the individual, including the essential uniformity of human mental apparatus and the physiological unity of humankind—and by not being very interested in these matters.[89] The real concerns of ethnology were not the understanding of individual psychology, but rather explaining how people came to act collectively in the ways that they did—which was a function of the cultural patterns they shared with the other members of their communities. Cultural patterns could best be understood by tracing their origins through the process of systematic trait comparison.[90] Father Schmidt, it is true, proclaimed his concern with the individual as possessor of a soul (entirely appropriate for a priest, although he denied—not very convincingly—that his Catholicism had anything to do with it). But in practice, Schmidt's concern did not mean very much. Schmidt concentrated on the comparison of traits (especially linguistic ones) just like everybody else.[91]

In their various treatments of traits and *Kulturkreise*, the later diffusionists displayed considerably more sophistication than Ratzel had. They fully recognized the problematic character of the trait and the varying social contexts within which seemingly identical cultural entities might have quite different meanings.[92] They attempted to deal with these problems by placing relationships among traits in patterns characteristic of certain cultures, so that individual traits ceased in practice to be discrete atoms of culture. Although Graebner, Schmidt, and Ankermann retained the relatively low opinion of human inventiveness displayed by Ratzel, they modified it somewhat in order to avoid one of the contradictions in Ratzel's views. Innovation occurred mainly through contact with other peoples. But the most successful peoples (presumably the ones with the most superior cultures) were those who colonized (i.e., displaced other peoples and took over their land) while they migrated—the circumstance seemingly least likely to promote a high level of trait acquisition by the peoples who mattered. This implied that successful migrating peoples were inherently inventive—something that Ratzel thought unlikely. His successors allowed humankind a little more creativity than Ratzel had. Some also emphasized an aspect of human initiative that Ratzel had to some extent neglected: the human propensity to *borrow* traits from others.[93] Peoples in one area, becoming aware of traits in another area, deliberately seek them out and add them to their own cultures—often without necessity or imposition—as when an exotic fashion is adopted. "Borrowing" conjured up for ethnologists images of familiar social processes rather than the rather unreal one of the solitary, eccentric inventor in the midst of doltish neighbors that Ratzel's approach conveyed. And borrowed traits could pass through any medium: trade, tourism, word of mouth. They did not require migration and colonization, which Ratzel had emphasized much more than the other forms of trait transfer.[94]

The later diffusionists disagreed about the importance of borrowing, but they all made use of it because of its flexibility. It allowed them to paint a picture of premodern peoples involved in a complex series of cultural interchanges out of which novelty could frequently arise. They paid a price for this flexibility, however. It became more difficult to infer from the distribution of traits the paths and manner of their diffusion and thus to recreate the histories of peoples. The *Kulturkreis* was supposed to help with this. By identifying certain characteristic sets of important traits common to peoples within a particular area, the ethnologist could establish a broad spatial unit of historical analysis. The existence of a *Kulturkreis* permitted inferences about the relationships of people within the area, even if the paths of individual traits could not be traced.[95] It also supposedly had practical contemporary value. Missionaries could use it as a convenient basis on which to develop a strategy of conversion suitable to a whole area, and colonial governments could also employ it for political analysis.

Identifying *Kulturkreise* was an essential step in studying the relationship between culture and environment. In turn, this provided a clue to the inner workings of the cultures of particular *Kreise*. A *Kulturkreis* defined by trait similarities was a useful way of acknowledging the importance of the physical environment in shaping culture and simultaneously explaining why it did not always prevail. The expansion, for example, of the Indonesian *Kulturkreis* into Central Africa explained why extremely different cultures could exist side-by-side within the same environment and also why similar (Indonesian) traits could be found on both sides of the Indian Ocean.[96]

This last point suggests that the *Kulturkreis* was a little *too* useful as a theoretical structure. It could be used to disguise blatantly circular reasoning. The *Kulturkreis*— defined as an aggregation of observed traits—came to be employed as the criterion for determining which traits in a people's culture were significant for analysis.[97] Thus, having defined *Kulturkreise* in Sudanic Africa on the basis of various peoples' common possession of a divine kingship, later diffusionists tended to select only traits consistent with their images of divine kingship as significant in Sudanic cultures, thus confirming their original assessments and ignoring data that displayed inconvenient differences among peoples of the same supposed cultural set.[98] This sort of thing was most notable in the work of Frobenius. He conducted his field expeditions across Africa as hunting trips in search of signs of the *Weltanschauungen* of the *Kulturkreise* he was investigating and paid relatively little attention to the ways in which the people he visited actually lived.[99]

The trait and the *Kulturkreis* in combination, then, took the place of the liberal model of the individual in the diffusionist theoretical pattern. Although most diffusionists continued to share Ratzel's tendency toward agrarianism in establishing hierarchies of significance among traits, they did not follow him in concentrating on material objects, such as tools and weapons. They focused more on mental phenomena: religious beliefs, images of social structure, political institutions.[100] Implements were interesting to the extent that they were outward signs of characteristic mental patterns, not in themselves.[101] And in focusing on the mental patterns of particular peoples, they tended to create what amounted to models of abstract individuals who represented those peoples—the "typical" Polynesian or Australian, for instance. Even Frobenius, who had little regard for individuals as objects of study, failed to resist this tendency.[102] Despite everything, a form of the abstract individual remained part of diffusionist ethnology.

Most of the twentieth-century diffusionists continued to think of themselves as scientists; as such, they tried to function within the nomothetic tradition of cultural science. They sought to establish the rules that governed the development, transmission, and operation of cultural phenomena.[103] They did not visualize their work as purely descriptive, nor did they develop a notion of interpretation rather than objective scientific understanding as their goal. The diffusionists argued violently among themselves about the existence, nature, and boundaries of particular *Kulturkreise* under the common assumption that *Kulturkreise* were objectively real things, not heuristic devices or reflections of variable interpretive postures.[104] And despite the more or less *pro forma* statements they made about not differentiating among cultures according to judgments of value, they did not really subscribe to modern ideas of cultural relativity. Most still accepted a theoretical distinction between *Naturvölker* and *Kulturvölker* as well as subdistinctions within those categories.[105]

And yet, diffusionism did not fit fully into the category of traditional nomothetic social science. So completely had they adopted the belief that their main function was to discover the patterns of particular peoples' cultural development over time that the diffusionists paid comparatively little attention to formulating clear statements of the *general* principles of cultural diffusion. Contemporary application received even less attention; the diffusionists simply assumed that the patterns of cultural history they established would, if connected continuously to the present, reveal something important. This is one reason, as we shall see in chapter 9, that a tradition of official colonial anthropology did not develop in Germany to anything like the extent that it did in Britain. The main theoretical line of German anthropology could offer little of use to colonial authorities apart from a certain amount of intellectual legitimation.

By the 1920s and 1930s, the idea that ethnology was a useful, nomothetic science had clearly declined. Diffusionists, although committed to conducting themselves as practitioners of *Wissenschaft* broadly conceived, increasingly saw themselves as investigators of the early histories of preliterate peoples rather than as formulators of general statements about humanity and culture.[106] To some extent, this was a consequence of the tension that formed throughout anthropology in the twentieth century between the model of a generalizing science that anthropology retained from the nineteenth century and the particularistic, relativistic implications of studying culture as an object. But the form in which the tension manifested itself in Germany, especially the tendency toward historicizing, was a product in large part of the intellectual and political environment in which diffusionism had emerged.

Much of what has been said thus far about the diffusionist theoretical pattern bears also on the question of change. More than anything else, diffusionism is defined by the distinctive way in which it approaches the dynamics of cultural change: ostensibly historically and emphasizing the overriding significance of intercultural contact and the transmission of cultural traits. Once diffusionism rid itself of Ratzel's heavy emphasis on mass migration, it showed itself to be a highly flexible theoretical framework, the broad popular appeal of which was in large part due to its ability to tie up large segments of human history into neat, if complex, patterns of cultural and demographic movement. It seemed as though the diffusionists had replaced the speculative, universalist evolutionary view of human development with one that took the evidence of human cultural diversity into account. At the same time, the notion of stages of human development was not lost. It was simply worked into the diffusionist framework.

According to Graebner and Ankermann, most of the important *Kulturkreise* in Africa and Oceania were made up of layers or levels.[107] In each layer, groups of people subscribed to distinctive cultural forms that were to some extent (often a considerable one) different from those of the other layers. The layers were usually formed by migration, conquest, and colonization as people from one *Kulturkreis* moved into a new area and imposed themselves on or alongside others of different culture already there. A clear example of this was the two-layer society of Rwanda and Burundi in Africa, where the warrior class of the Tutsi (presumed to be pastoral conquerors from the north) lorded it over the agricultural Hutu, the earlier inhabitants. Each layer, or class, belonged to a different *Kulturkreis,* although they lived in the same place and although there was considerable exchanging of traits.[108] From the interaction of these layers, new cultural forms had arisen.

This interpretive pattern could have innumerable variations, but its general form was fairly simple. Complicated class societies and new cultures arose from cultural mixing, which formed the context of human progress. Progress did not occur according to a sequence of uniform stages through which peoples went at different rates, but in a wide variety of ways, depending on the mixture of cultural ingredients and the nature of the environment in each case. There *were* regularities. To Frobenius, for instance, most real "civilizations" (the most advanced *Kulturvölker*) arose from the conquest of culturally developed but politically disorganized peasant peoples by groups of nomadic warriors with less advanced cultures but with the ability to organize the society politically.[109] But this was a general observation of a common phenomenon, not a rigid schema like the evolutionists' stages of cultural development.

Frobenius, however, eventually went beyond this sort of argument. He came to conceive of the essence of a culture as a spiritual (or more properly, demonic) force that existed of itself and that manifested itself, within the area of a *Kulturkreis,* in the various traits of particular cultures.[110] Culture was not simply an aggregation of traits, nor was it just the inner patterns and logic of a people's existence as Schmidt and Graebner claimed. It was an overwhelming and fundamentally irrational force, something Frobenius eventually called the *Paideuma*. Individuals, cultural traits, cultures themselves were merely external parts of the *Paideuma*. The history of humankind was the history of the manifestations, expansions, and contractions of *Paideuma*s. Each *Volk* represented a *Paideuma* at work. There was no universal human *Paideuma*.

With Frobenius, the diffusionist pattern clearly left behind most traces of the liberal theoretical tradition, as Frobenius certainly intended it to do. Frobenius was a radical nationalist who did not hesitate to mix his scholarship and his politics quite openly.[111] Other diffusionists were reluctant to go so far into meta-anthropology. Most of them were also, in the early twentieth century, much less political. Several of them actively supported colonialism, but no more so than the interests of their discipline seemed to demand.[112] They were as patriotic and anti-socialist as most academics. Graebner was a National Liberal—but he was the only leading diffusionist after Ratzel to give himself a party label in biographical publications (before the Nazi era). The growth of *Unparteilichkeit* was quite pronounced among diffusionists as opposed to ethnologists like Diedrich Westermann who retained connections with their neoliberal roots.

Yet, the *theoretical pattern* of diffusionism remained highly political because of its close connections in structure and content to political ideologies. Diffusionist ideas were widely used in radical nationalist and conservative propaganda after 1900—mostly, except for Frobenius, by nonanthropologists.[113] To some degree, it really did not matter that most diffusionists themselves avoided party politics. The framework of ideas they accepted for their professional work bound them as surely to particular ideologies as if they were practicing politicians. And they received considerable benefit from the connection. The success of diffusionism in displacing rival theoretical patterns from dominance in the German-speaking anthropological world was probably due in some measure to its compatibility with the ideological patterns of radical nationalism. As these patterns became more prominent in Germany in the twentieth century, the stock of diffusionism rose also.[114] Forms of anthropology more closely linked to traditional liberal ideas were increasingly incompatible with the larger political context; diffusionism, like some other patterns in cultural science, fit right in regardless of the apolitical attitudes of many of its academic advocates. To see how this happened, we shall have to look at wider developments in cultural science and politics in the late nineteenth and early twentieth centuries.

9

Exploration, Imperialism, and Anthropology

Thus far, we have focused primarily on the development of the cultural sciences in Germany in the context of German intellectual life, politics, and society. It would, perhaps, have been more traditional, at least with respect to anthropology, to have concentrated also on the experience of Europeans who were in contact with the rest of the world's cultures as another source of interest in the systematic study of culture. According to one standard interpretation of the history of anthropology, the impetus to scientific ethnology arose mainly out of an eighteenth-and early-nineteenth-century enthusiasm for exotic peoples that accompanied a flood of information into Europe about them at that time.[1] Explorers were led to go out and procure even more information, and intellectuals began to see the need to classify and analyze the data thus acquired more systematically than the dilettantes of the past had done. The scientific ethnology that grew from these roots received, in the last third of the nineteenth century, a sudden and decisive boost from the "New Imperialism": the rapid establishment of bureaucratic colonial administrations in European countries' vast and newly acquired overseas possessions. The requirements of colonial administration are held to have been the main influences on the development of anthropological theory and organization at the end of the nineteenth century and during the first three decades or so of the twentieth.[2]

Even in the case of Germany (a country that came to colonialism late), this interpretation has a certain amount of validity. The attractiveness of many of the cultural-science disciplines was clearly due in part to their exotic subject matter and to the opportunities that foreign fieldwork might bring to an aspiring academic. And yet, as we have seen, essentially the same theoretical concerns, essentially the same dynamic of intellectual change, can be found in areas of cultural science that did not focus particularly on the overseas world and the clash of cultures. This will become even clearer when we examine historical economics in chapter 10. Although many of the *uses* of cultural science (real or imagined) were presented by its practitioners in terms of understanding and governing colonial societies, such concerns rarely had much to do with the actual *structures* of the cultural sciences. This is particularly apparent in Germany, where, for instance, a strong tradition of functionalist anthropology never developed before the mid-twentieth century and

Segments of this material were originally published as chapter 3 of *Germans in the Tropics: Essays in German Colonial History*, Arthur J. Knoll and Lewis H. Gann, eds. (Greenwood Press, Westport, CT, 1987). Copyright by Arthur J. Knoll. Used with permission of Greenwood Press, Inc.

where the dominant varieties of the discipline (e.g., diffusionism) had little practical value in colonial administration. The really significant developments in German cultural science occurred with reference to the *domestic* context in which cultural scientists lived—something that has been remarked of their brethren in other countries as well. The overseas context—the activities of explorers, fieldworkers, colonial officials, and so on—played its part and we shall examine this in the present chapter. But even so, that part was mainly a function of the ways in which Germans at home mentally constructed the non-European world in reference to their own. Marshall Sahlins has remarked that the early anthropologists went abroad to look for "primitive man" and ended up finding themselves.[3] It can be argued that they found themselves because that was what they were really looking for in the first place.

Anthropology and Exploration

Although official German colonies did not exist before the 1880s, this does not mean that the activities of the many important German travellers and explorers before that time were not connected to European colonialism. Many of the most important of them—from Georg Forster to Heinrich Barth to Johann Ludwig Krapf and Johannes Rebmann in East Africa—operated in the employ of British organizations, some of whose aims were clearly imperialistic. Alexander von Humboldt worked largely within the administrative as well as the geographical confines of the Spanish overseas empire. The advent of a German colonial empire did not substantially change the relationship between anthropological travel and colonialism outside Germany. What it did was to change the meaning of travel and exploration as these were interpreted politically at home—and even here, the groundwork for the new meanings had been prepared before Germany had a single colony.[4]

As we have seen, part of the functional infrastructure of geography and anthropology in Germany developed in close connection with the business enterprise of geographical publishing. This was especially true of exploration. Cartographical publishing depended heavily on the systematic acquisition of new data by fieldworkers throughout the world, mostly British in the first half of the nineteenth century. The formation of the *Reich* in 1871 and the establishment during the previous decade of national organizations of professional and amateur geographers, ethnologists, and the like, created a structure within which the geographical publishers could seek direct government support for information-gathering enterprises that could be advertised as conducive to the prestige and economic advantage of Germany. They could also hope to increase sales of the more popular geographical publications by emphasizing the accomplishments of German travellers as *Germans*.[5]

German business interests, especially those concerned with trade with the underdeveloped part of the world, also became more interested in sponsoring the activities of German travellers in the 1870s. Some businesspeople genuinely believed that if the enterprise of exploration remained largely British, in the then-current depressed, competitive economic climate, exploration would lead to British colonization, which might lead, in turn, to an exclusion of German interests from newly developed marketing and investment areas. Others wanted to use association with state-sponsored exploration as a means of prying support for their overseas business activities from the government. The intersecting interests of export-import businesses and geographical publishers created in the 1870s a limited but important structure of support for exploration, one capable of eliciting a certain amount of assistance from government and one that had good reason to interpret exploration in nationalist, and ultimately imperialist, terms.[6]

The leaders of the main centers of the ethnological and geographical establishment—Bastian, Virchow, and their associates in Berlin and the network of publishers, academics, businesspeople, and officials interested in such things in Saxony and Thuringia—naturally did their best to encourage the emergence of a support base for exploration. They made as much use of it as they could, up to the early 1880s.[7] But something happened at that time that made them—especially the Berlin establishment—ambivalent about the whole process. We have already seen what that was: the advent of the colonial movement as a significant force in German politics. In part the colonial movement arose out of the practical interests of the very business groups we have just discussed, to whom various organizations of heavy industry added their weight (mainly in order to appear firmly patriotic) as the movement's public impact widened after 1882. In part the movement expanded because of support by politicians in the National Liberal and Free Conservative parties seeking various short-term domestic ends—and ultimately, of course, because of Bismarck's short-lived desire to use the colonial movement to achieve even more complex political and diplomatic goals.[8] But at the core of the colonial movement was a relatively small number of propagandists—mostly youngish men with academic credentials and journalistic experience—who saw in the creation of a colonial movement and a German colonial empire not only the solution to many of Germany's political problems, but also the advancement of their own careers. Among these, several of the people who had made names for themselves as travellers and explorers, and others who intended to do so, began to figure substantially.

Cornelia Essner, in her detailed study of German travellers in Africa in the nineteenth century, has shown that a large proportion of the people who followed in the footsteps of Heinrich Barth to fame owing to their explorations (and often to early graves because of sicknesses acquired while engaging in them) were university graduates who temporarily became ''professional'' explorers in the hope of achieving full-time academic positions at home.[9] Few of them were in the business for sheer love of adventure. They turned to travel for much the same reasons that many of their contemporaries turned to journalism; indeed, the two activities were closely linked. In order to achieve the desired career results, they had not only to undertake spectacular journeys, but also to publish accounts of them in newspapers, journals, and books and to capture the public fancy. They also required sponsorship from organizations willing to supply sufficient money to allow them to achieve significant results. In the 1860s and 1870s, that meant either working for British societies (something that did not sit well with a German public) or becoming dependents of the geographical-ethnological establishments. Gustav August

Schweinfurth, Gustav Nachtigal, and Gerhard Rohlfs, the most famous German travellers in Africa in the 1870s, all to some extent followed these patterns.

These people, like Barth before them, became popular heroes through a combination of publicity and spectacular exploratory exploits.[10] Only a few of them, however, achieved their basic ambition of finding secure academic employment—at least in the short run. (Barth had in fact been appointed to a university faculty, but only to an honorary chair, and he died shortly thereafter.)[11] They ran afoul essentially of two things. The first was, in many cases, their own intellectual inadequacy compared to the competition. Although Nachtigal, Schweinfurth, and Rohlfs were all intelligent, none had achieved the kind of academic record that could give them much of a chance in the contest for the tiny number of teaching positions available in geography or related fields. A few eventually occupied positions as museum directors (Max Buchner, for instance—a more minor figure, best known for his role in the seizure of the West African colonies in the 1880s).[12] None was really a theorist. Their contributions to geography and ethnography were largely descriptive, and as useful as, for example, Nachtigal's work on the Sahara was from that standpoint, it could have no lasting effect on geography and anthropology as sciences.

The second obstacle was related to the first. The increasingly formal structure of the cultural sciences in the 1870s involved, as we have seen, a tendency toward a division of labor between the academic elite of ethnology and geography (with their immediate disciples) and the people who delivered the raw data. The former could be fieldworkers (as Bastian for example was), but their main impact, their main scientific activity, was supposed to be theoretical.[13] Travellers were welcome in the *Berliner Gesellschaft* and the participation of anyone who could be useful in providing data was encouraged, but such people were not expected to cross the boundary that marked off the territory of the academic theorist. A few people managed the transition—most notably Friedrich Ratzel, whose abilities were, however, quite extraordinary and who acquired a theoretical reputation while building a journalistic one. Even Ratzel did not get over the feeling of being an outsider—at least not until quite late.[14] For most, the transition could not be made.

It was, therefore, not surprising that leading explorers should have joined the colonial movement with great alacrity in the early 1880s. Nachtigal, a person of considerable presence, offered himself as a pathbreaker of colonialism; made a consul by Bismarck, he was in charge of establishing protectorates in Togo and Cameroon in 1884. Even Rohlfs, temperamentally unsuited to politics and previously uninterested in them, found himself lionized on the colonialist speaking circuit in the 1880s. Much more minor travellers, such as Wilhelm Hübbe-Schleiden, became publicists of colonial expansion; others, such as Max Buchner, temporarily found positions in the jury-rigged colonial administration that Bismarck put together during his brief flirtation with colonialism.[15]

The explosion of interest in colonialism in the 1880s and the possibility that imperialism would become an active force in German politics attracted the attention of several young men who wanted to make careers for themselves and thought that presenting themselves as explorer/empire builders would be the best way to do it.

The most spectacular case was that of Carl Peters, who as the representative of an organization he founded in 1883, "explored" the already well-known coast of East Africa for a few weeks in 1885 and signed with local chiefs the treaties on which Germany's claim to imperial rule there was based. Thereafter, kept out of direct control of East African affairs by Bismarck (who recognized Peters's political ambitions and his personal instability), Peters undertook various highly publicized expeditions—the best-known of which was the German expedition to "rescue" Emin Pasha in the southern Sudan from the Mahdists. (Peters was hoping to claim Uganda for Germany in the process.)[16]

The pattern established by Peters and his somewhat less overtly political predecessors remained a model for many individuals throughout the existence of the German colonial empire. Germany produced its share of well-known explorers before the First World War, although the prestige and the publicity attached to exploration declined throughout that time. In Germany as elsewhere, the decline of publicity and the establishment of regular colonial administrations meant that the political scope available to travellers seeking to enhance their careers was greatly restricted. Neither Peters nor anyone else was ever able to become a leading figure in national politics on that basis.

But what about cultural science? What effect did the brief elevation of exploration to a matter of national importance have on the disciplines of geography and anthropology? Some, but not a great deal. As we have seen, the anthropological and geographical establishments were happy enough to make use of the heightened interest in exploration and the expansion of overseas economic interests in the 1870s in order to acquire government and private support for their enterprises. But the rapid blossoming of the colonial movement in the early 1880s took some elements of the establishment aback. On the whole, the Saxon-Thuringian network accepted the colonial movement for practical reasons: geographical publishers could develop new markets among people with a nationalist interest in prospective colonial areas, and the leaders of light industry in the region hoped for cheaper raw materials and increased export sales. But even these people were becoming increasingly worried about the tendency of the colonialists to emphasize the importance of future colonies as areas for the settlement of German emigrants rather than as trading centers.[17] As we saw when we considered Ratzel's migrationism in chapter 8, migrationist colonialism was (with political agrarianism) one of the first forms of radical nationalism to arise within the ranks of younger liberals, and its domestic political implications were disquieting, even in Saxony.

They were even more disquieting in Berlin, the center of the neoliberal cultural-science establishment. We have seen why Virchow, Bastian, and their associates took essentially an anticolonialist line during the period of colonial enthusiasm: ideological opposition to large-scale imperialism; fear of the use that Bismarck might make of a program of colonial expansion in drawing support from the left liberals; fear of the possibilities of migrationist colonialism as the core of a nationalist ideology in opposition to the more traditional forms of liberalism; resentment against people like Ratzel who used colonialism as they had used Darwinism in the past as a rallying point for younger cultural scientists trying to shake off control by those of Virchow and Bastian's generations.[18] The adherence of their former dependents among the travellers and explorers to the colonialist cause—indeed, the explorers' transformation into heroes of imperialism—was seen by the members of the Berlin establishment as an especially serious threat of the same sort. Not only did it strengthen the procolonial forces, but it also threatened the vision of an organized division of labor within the expanding disciplines of geography and ethnology. With figures like Peters dominating the exploration business and with fieldworkers like Rohlfs and Nachtigal now able to obtain support on their own because of their new-found political prominence, the establishment's goal of creating a manageable system of data flow from overseas into the academic centers of cultural science in Germany seemed to be in jeopardy.[19] How could the leaders, the theoreticians of cultural science, enforce their demands for certain kinds of data collected in certain ways by withholding publicity and support from incompetent fieldworkers? The thought of having to rely for ethnographical data on people like Peters, whose idea of intercultural research was to shoot first and ask questions later, must have made Virchow's flesh crawl.

In the event, however, the cultural-science establishment managed to protect itself—at least with respect to its relationship to the process of data collection. Although Bastian campaigned against colonial acquisition when the issue was a hot one in politics and although Virchow vigorously opposed, at the podium of the Reichstag, the measures of colonial acquisition taken by Bismarck in 1884–1885, the depth of their anticolonialism was not so great as to prevent their trying to accommodate themselves to the colonial empire when it was formed.[20] When it became clear that Bismarck intended only a very limited commercial empire, not a massive one encompassing large areas for settlement that the colonial enthusiasts were calling for, left liberals like Virchow and Bastian had little trouble in accepting it, although they grumbled at the waste of money involved. Their main objections had been to the migrationist interpretation of colonialism and the ways in which colonialism could be used for promoting ideological defections from among the ranks of liberals. With the decline of colonialism as a political force in the late 1880s, the Berlin establishment's broader political fears were temporarily allayed. Virchow was able to exercise his enormous skill at influencing government agencies to promote a place (admittedly a small one) for establishment cultural science within the improvised structure of the overseas empire as it was erected. And whatever was lost by the new autonomy that explorers could assume with respect to the establishment (which in the long run was not much) could be compensated for in the growing availability of data collectors among the officials and missionaries who established themselves in the colonies.[21]

Therefore, even the new political construction of exploration that arose from the appearance of imperialism as a political force in Germany did not fundamentally affect either the disciplinary structure or the theoretical content of German cultural science. As we saw in the previous chapter, however, the colonial enthusiasm of the 1880s *did* play a role in defining the differences between the establishment, or neoliberal, theoretical pattern in cultural science and its challengers from among the ranks of younger cultural scientists, such as Friedrich Ratzel. Moreover, the colonialist fad of the early and mid-1880s also contributed to the formation of radical nationalism in German politics, and that also, in conjunction with the new theoretical patterns, eventually worked to unseat neoliberal patterns from their dominance of German cultural science. But this process had very little to do with what went on outside Germany, and only a few travellers (e.g., Leo Frobenius) had a role in it.

Cultural Science and Colonial Administration

Although Germany acquired an overseas empire in 1884–1885, it cannot be said to have had a regular colonial administration until after Bismarck's fall in 1890. Bismarck had never intended that the *Reich* government make a substantial investment in either the governance or the development of the newly acquired colonies. He had been assured by his advisors that the business enterprises operating in the colonies would provide most of what was needed for them. Naturally enough, they did not. Bismarck's disenchantment with the politics of colonialism made him disinclined to change his attitude toward administrative expenditure, and so it was only after the appointment of Leo von Caprivi as chancellor in 1890 that steps toward erecting a structure of colonial governance were taken.[22]

The Colonial Department that was then organized within the Foreign Office was supposed to coordinate the affairs of the widely separated (and at the time, unprofitable) colonies. (A separate Colonial Office was only established in 1907.) Colonial administrations were organized on a rather piecemeal basis in each of the colonies during the 1890s. The Colonial Department and the individual colonial governments faced serious problems: severe underfinancing and the absence of adequate sources of revenue in most colonies; the lack of trained, experienced personnel—a difficulty compounded by the low level of prestige accorded to colonial service in bureaucratic circles; and vague, contradictory policy guidelines with which to work (under close Reichstag scrutiny). They were supposed to foster economic development, encourage (in some colonies) European settlement, and protect and control indigenous peoples. They needed help from whatever sources they could get it. One source—a minor one, but they could not be too choosy— was academic anthropology.

The leaders of academic anthropology in Berlin and elsewhere had aims that complemented those of the colonial authorities. In order to promote the expansion of ethnology as a discipline, they needed ways of justifying the new university chairs, museums, and research assistantships they demanded from the state governments and the support they sought from private sources for anthropological expeditions. They also wanted to extend the informal system of collection by amateurs on which the flow of much of their data depended. One of the ways in which these aims could be achieved was by promoting an anthropological element in the training of prospective colonial officials.

In the 1890s, the Colonial Department began to try to solve some of its personnel problems by reforming the infant colonial service and making it conform to the standard German civil service model. It dismissed some (not all) of the sadists, alcoholics, and drug addicts among the "pioneers of empire" in the administration (Carl Peters figuring prominently in the first category). Attempts were made to fill administrative openings with career bureaucrats at the level of *assessor,* a salaried junior grade that required previous university study, the passing of the state examination (in mostly legal subjects), and an administrative apprenticeship.[23] The new policy tapped an impressive source of able, educated people, but little in the standard training of a German bureaucrat prepared him specifically for the problems to be faced on overseas duty. Ethnology and comparative linguistics were ideally suited, as organized disciplines, to filling some of the gaps in bureaucratic preparation. The Berlin cultural science establishment had in fact already anticipated the need when it encouraged the foundation of the Oriental Languages Seminar at the University of Berlin in 1887. In the 1890s, this seminar developed as the focal point of instruction in colonial subjects, both for students interested in future colonial employment and for postgraduate training of serving colonial officials.[24] The seminar concentrated on teaching Swahili to those bound for East Africa. The need to render Swahili and other colonial languages into teachable form stimulated much research in linguistic anthropology. In addition, expansions of the Royal Ethnological Museum and the anthropological faculty at the university were justified by the need for colonial instruction. Other universities followed Berlin's example, although Berlin's leadership in colonial training was not effectively challenged until the foundation of the Colonial Institute in Hamburg in 1908.[25]

A close connection between anthropological research and colonial training afforded other advantages. The academic anthropologists could attempt to improve the quality of amateur data collection by recruiting and training some of the abler prospective colonial officials as part-time ethnographers. The effort succeeded, on the whole. Officials, like missionaries, remained on location for extended periods and could be induced to look for what the academic ethnologists wanted. The colonial authorities, both individually and collectively, also benefitted. A few junior civil servants who might have gone to other departments may have been attracted to the colonial service by the opportunity to participate in research. Ethnographical publications by colonial officials helped the Colonial Department to enhance its obscure public image; such publications could also improve the career prospects of individual officials, whose educations usually fitted them better for anthropological and linguistic work than for the economic or technological research that might really have been more appropriate.[26]

Although the development of an ethnographical research network of officials improved the quality of information available to academic anthropologists, it did not fundamentally alter either the organizational or the theoretical structures of the cultural sciences. Even the most able of the officials who regularly published ethnographical or linguistic research were not encouraged to violate the division of labor implicit in anthropology and to engage in theorizing—especially before the public at large. A few did not conform, but they tended to be people like Richard Kandt, an explorer and the German Resident in Rwanda, who was a holdover from the early prebureaucratic days.[27] More typical was Heinrich Schnee, the governor of German East Africa from 1911 to 1918, who is best known as the despised, slightly ridicuous civilian governor who had perforce to tag along with Paul von Lettow-Vorbeck during the latter's East African campaign in the First World War.[28] Actually, Schnee was one of the most active intellectuals among the first cohort of

Germany's professional colonial officials. Before 1910 Schnee published several articles on his extensive research in Polynesian language and ethnography. He received little encouragement, however, to proceed to synthesis (for which he was intellectually well equipped), and his small efforts in that direction were largely ignored. From the standpoint of the academic elite, perhaps the ideal reporting official was Julius Count Zech, governor of Togo from 1903 to 1910. Zech's reports of his ethnographical surveys of northern Togo conducted as a junior official were concise, accurate, painfully objective, and devoid of any evidence of interpretive thought.[29]

Some officials—those with complete academic credentials who occupied scientific positions—were partly exempted from the prohibition against higher-level theoretical discussion. Franz Stuhlmann, the director of the research institute at Amani in German East Africa, presented his extensive ethnographical observations within a framework borrowed from the most fashionable trends in cultural-science theory.[30] But Stuhlmann was not, strictly speaking, a government functionary, and his basic interest was in applied science and agricultural technology.

Apart from what amounted to hobbies followed by civil servants, officially sponsored ethnological research was quite limited in the German colonial empire, especially before the administration of Bernhard Dernburg as colonial director and colonial secretary (1906–1910). Two reasons for this present themselves: the colonial authorities' lack of financial resources and the absence of a body of anthropological theory in Germany that would have been really useful to colonial administrators. By his successful dealings with the Reichstag, Dernburg overcame some of the financial difficulties, but this increased official sponsorship of anthropological research only marginally.[31] With such limited resources, the colonial authorities were in no position to hold out incentives to the anthropological community to develop approaches that would give them direct assistance—apart from contributions to legitimation and training. It is possible, of course, that had Germany kept her colonial empire past the First World War, a strong tradition of anthropology directly applicable to colonial administration (like British functionalism) would have emerged along with a career pattern of official anthropological work parallel to an academic career. But up to 1914, the signs were against it. Most important, without really extensive pressure from a grant-giving colonial administration, the issue of what kinds of ethnological research were useful for colonial government could not have much impact on the theoretical directions taken in academia. As we saw in the previous chapter, a combination of intellectual and ideological factors led to the dominance of diffusionism—a historically oriented theoretical pattern with small relevance to colonial administration—in German ethnology in the early twentieth century. Diffusionists claimed, for example, to be able to tell one the geographical paths by which Tutsi feudalism had come to Rwanda and Burundi, but that was of little help in understanding the contemporary political system in those areas. Not only did the colonial authorities have no effect on the process that led to diffusionism's triumph, but the fact that a pattern of such little utility from their standpoint was dominant presumably discouraged them from emphasizing anthropological research in their requests for appropriations.[32]

Nevertheless, there was *some* official and semiofficial cultural research done in the German colonial empire. The Colonial Economic Committee (*Kolonial-Wirt-schaftliche Komitee*—KWK) of the German Colonial Society sponsored a fair amount of research, although mostly on economic and agricultural topics. Some of its personnel, such as Stuhlmann, did ethnographical work on the side—for which they were seldom specifically trained. After 1908, the Colonial Institute also supported similar research.[33] And the Colonial Office and the individual colonial administrations undertook a limited amount of ethnological research, especially after the beginning of the Dernburg era in 1906 when anthropology was regarded as a minor part of Dernburg's "scientific colonialism." In response to directives from the Colonial Office in 1907, several of the governments undertook surveys of the customary laws of their subject peoples. The results were centrally collated and eventually served as the basis for Erich Schulz-Ewerth and Leonhard Adam's *Das Eingeborenenrecht*, a classic of legal anthropology. But the project was never fully completed, and it was not matched by anything else German officialdom undertook.[34]

On the other hand, the Colonial Office did nothing about commissioning impartial, professional anthropological research into the causes of the major revolts that convulsed the overseas empire between 1904 and 1907; the Herero and Nama revolts in Southwest Africa (now Namibia) and the Maji Maji rebellion in East Africa. Instead, the major analyses of these events were self-exculpatory books by the men who had been governors of the two colonies when the conflicts began. Both were intelligent observers, but they were not professional ethnologists and their perspectives could hardly be called unbiased.[35] Yet, even if the Colonial Office *had* been interested in professional anthropological research on the rebellions (and there is no evidence that it was), it is not clear where, among German anthropologists then flocking to enlist under the diffusionist banner, it could have found the people with the theoretical perspective for the job. Again, diffusionism's orientation toward a past regarded largely as a process of trait and population movement made it unsuitable for explaining political violence except in terms of historical patterns of ethnic displacement.

It is difficult to avoid the conclusion that although German anthropology and the official apparatus of Germany's colonial empire affected one another, they did not affect one another very much. This was certainly true of the theoretical foundations of anthropology. The theoretical patterns of cultural science were intimately connected to the political and ideological currents that shaped imperialism *within Germany*, but only tangentially to the actual administration of Germany's real colonies.

Missionary Anthropology

There is a further wrinkle, however. Overseas missions played an important role in the affairs of most of Germany's colonies. They also supported and conducted a great deal of anthropological research, the nature of which was often affected by the missions' political positions both in the colonies and in Germany.

Catholic missionary organizations had long traditions of ethnographical investigation. However, because of fallout from the *Kulturkampf,* the entrance of German

Catholic missionary societies into the German colonies was slow.[36] The main centers of missionary training appeared in Austria-Hungary rather than the *Reich*. Around them formed a community of anthropological educators and researchers the locus of which, by the first decade of the twentieth century, was the *Anthropos-Institut* of Saint Gabriel (near Vienna) under its director, Father Wilhelm Schmidt.[37] Schmidt turned out a succession of first-rate ethnographical fieldworkers and became one of the leading anthropological theorists in the German-speaking world. Although Schmidt's ethnological approach had a distinctly religious, Catholic slant, his organization and his theoretical work conformed in general to the prevailing patterns in German anthropology. Schmidt was a leading diffusionist. He maintained the structural distinction between data collection and central theorizing—a distinction reinforced when Schmidt accepted an appointment at the University of Vienna. Schmidt was involved in German colonial politics, but only to a minor extent.[38]

The relationship of the German Protestant missions to the colonial empire was very complex.[39] The colonial authorities depended heavily on them, especially for providing education in the colonies, but the missions in several colonies sometimes intervened in politics, often to protect indigenous people against government policies. This ambivalence was reflected in Protestant missionary ethnological work. Missionaries, many of them professionally trained for the task, did much of the linguistic research in Africa and the Pacific that was used for official language training and for academic theorizing. The best known of these was Diedrich Westermann, who began his career as a missionary in Togo, made his reputation by studying the language and culture of the Ewe, and eventually became both an academic anthropologist and a critic of German colonial policy.[40]

As a missionary in Togo at the turn of the century, Westermann took part in the missions' efforts to protect the Ewe and other coastal peoples from land expropriation and "proletarianization" by development companies. This involvement strongly influenced his research. Although Westermann was in general terms a diffusionist, his work, like that of other Protestant missionaries, was more directly informed by the missionary aim of finding ways to accommodate indigenous colonial cultures to socioeconomic modernization without excessive exploitation and dislocation. In German politics before 1914, this aim was associated with reformist groups in the left wing of the liberal parties—groups to which Westermann himself belonged.[41]

Like colonial officialdom, then, the missionary enterprise had an effect on German anthropology. But despite particular thrusts of some missionary research—Schmidt's accommodation of diffusionism to Catholic theology, Westermann's connection of anthropology to the political movement for "native protection" before the First World War—it remained the case that, on the whole, missionary anthropology followed the same patterns as the rest of the anthropological community. Fieldworkers contributed data, not theoretical insights. (Even Westermann, who made the transition from fieldworker to academic, was not really a theorist of great repute except to some extent in linguistics.) The missionaries did not alter, or even challenge, the prevailing fashions in German anthropological theory, especially the dominance of diffusionism in the early twentieth century. They had less reason to do so than the officials. Although the diffusionist pattern was useless for most practical purposes in their work, it did at least focus on the process in which they were engaged—the spreading of cultural patterns from one people to another—and placed it in a legitimating historical context.

10

Historical Economics
and Cultural History

The disciplines on which this book primarily concentrates—anthropology, *Völk-erpsychologie,* and human geography—are all clearly *cultural sciences* as that term has been used here. That is, in all three disciplines, the dominant theoretical patterns throughout the nineteenth century focused mainly on the culture concept and featured the traditional nomothetic aim of liberal social science extended by a heightened emphasis on empirical research. Two other disciplines closely linked in origin and theoretical orientation with these cultural sciences were historical economics and cultural history. In some senses, they can be regarded as cultural sciences themselves in that the culture concept had a central place in both. Both encompassed nomothetic approaches to understanding, although the nomothetic aim came to be seriously questioned in each—more so than in anthropology or human geography. Both disciplines became involved in the methodological disputes that were central to the revolution in German social science at the turn of the century. The cultural sciences on which we have concentrated thus far remained at the periphery of those debates.

This chapter will briefly examine historical economics and cultural history as cultural sciences. It will focus on their connections to the other cultural sciences and the extent to which their most important theoretical patterns developed in response to common factors that influenced all of the cultural disciplines. Because of the methodological struggles in which historical economists and cultural historians engaged, the chapter also presents an opportunity to consider links between nomothetic cultural science and other major tendencies in social studies.

Historical Economics

Historical economics, a distinctively German approach to social science, arose in the 1840s and 1850s in the work of Wilhelm Roscher (1817–1894), Bruno Hildebrand (1812–1886), and Karl Knies (1821–1898). Roscher was the first to announce the existence of the field and was usually considered its father.[1]

The intellectual influences on Roscher and the others were quite varied: Hegel's historical philosophy, Savigny's historical approach to legal studies, the philological analysis of history professed by Roscher's teacher Barthold Georg Niebuhr, and the method of treating materials advocated by Ranke–some of the same sources from which the other cultural sciences drew. Roscher in particular was influenced by his deep Lutheran religiosity, which led him to emphasize order and due sub-ordination in society, and by the moderate liberal historiography of F. C. Dahlmann. Throughout his life, Roscher remained a liberal of Dahlmann's stamp—one who abjured revolution and disorder but favored progress and reform within the context of constitutional monarchy.[2] He intended his social science to support his political aims. Like Welcker, he believed that his liberalism was superior to the politics of other groups precisely because it was supported by science. This kind of attitude, essentially consistent with the *Vormärz* liberal theoretical pattern in social science, was inherited by Roscher's successors.

Roscher was trained in history and *Staatswissenschaft* at Göttingen and Berlin, where he absorbed the conviction that historical study was necessary for under-standing current governmental problems.[3] But unlike his contemporary Droysen, Roscher believed that concentrating on politics alone as the prime focus of historical investigation was incorrect. The economy also had to be comprehended in order for history to be applied successfully to the making of political decisions. This led Roscher to pay close attention to the classical economists Smith, Malthus, and Karl Heinrich Rau. Roscher accepted the validity of classical economics as an accurate description of what happens in markets in the short run. But in the early 1840s, he concluded that no specific political or economic act could be understood unless it was placed in its appropriate historical, institutional, and cultural context. This classical economics did not do.[4] This was the fundamental principle of the historical school of economics, which was, at least as Roscher conceived it, as much a cultural as a historical discipline.

The outlook of the early historical economists was also affected by their per-ceptions of political and social conflict in mid-nineteenth century Germany, per-ceptions informed by their standing as liberals. Like many other liberals, Roscher, Hildebrand, and Knies were attracted in the 1840s by the social question—the issue of what, if anything, should be done about the social consequences of rapid economic modernization.[5] They believed that modernization was desirable, but worried about what would happen to the classes exploited or occupationally displaced by new industries. We have already seen the effects on liberal theory and ideology of concern for the peasant farmer: the origins of political agrarianism and certain varieties of colonialism—in the development of which Roscher played a significant part.[6] But liberal concern also extended to the artisan, the cottage worker, the small manufacturer facing incipient industrialization, and eventually to the employees of large enterprises organized along English lines.

The social question elicited a variety of responses among liberal intellectuals in the years before 1848, including the form of social liberalism that envisioned state intervention to help the working class adjust to modernization.[7] The 1848 revolution, which demonstrated the power of classes threatened by change, made the social question more significant politically. Liberals interested in economics went in various directions on the subject. Some, led by Karl Rodbertus, began to cast doubt on the desirability of economic progress, although not usually on its inevitability. These "social conservatives" argued for state action to soften the effects of economic change on the laboring classes and to protect preindustrial occupations.[8] Others, such as Ludwig Rochau, emphasized rapid, state-encouraged industrialization as the best solution to outstanding socioeconomic problems.[9] Still others, including John Prince Smith and his fellow German "Manchestrians," argued for the largest degree of free enterprise. This last kind of thinking helped to stimulate the German-Austrian schools of neoclassical and marginalist economics later in the nineteenth century. It temporarily prevailed among the organizers of economics as a discipline in Germany in the 1860s and early 1870s.[10] They tended to treat the social question as a nonissue, something that, because its definition did not fit within the narrow limits of classical theory, could not be dealt with by policy based on such theory.

To Roscher even before 1848 and to Knies and Hildebrand afterward, none of these approaches seemed to be adequate, either as politics or as social science. None put the central fact that created the social question—the phenomenon of economic change—into the historical and cultural perspectives that gave it meaning. To be able to understand what happened to economic life in the course of change and thus in order to be able to make policy, it was necessary to comprehend the processes of change itself, which could only be done by systematically consulting the historical record and by comparing change in different cultures through time and around the world. Historical economics thus began as a means of adjusting liberal thinking and political practice to the realities of the social question—much as the neoliberal theoretical pattern in other cultural sciences emerged in the aftermath of liberalism's problems of the 1840s and 1850s. What made historical economics distinctive was its focus on economic factors and its concentration on the importance of the social question within the range of problems facing liberals.[11]

This was especially apparent in the work of Hildebrand, who started out in the 1840s as a radical liberal, served as a delegate to the National Assembly in 1848 (with a special interest in social and economic issues), and became frightened by the socialist tendencies of working-class organizations. Thereafter, he used historical economics to argue that a socialist or revolutionary rearrangement of society was inconsistent with the laws of social, economic, and cultural development. A liberal approach to socioeconomic change, emphasizing political and economic freedom and the need to accept the inevitability of economic progress, was the one most in keeping with the stage of historical development that Germany had reached.[12]

To explore the connections among historical economics, liberal ideology, and cultural science, we can refer once again to the elements of the traditional liberal theoretical pattern in social science. The abstract model of the rational individual had been taken to its extreme form in British classical economics. The historical economists pointed out that not only was it difficult to construct an explanation of long-term, irreversible change on the basis of the classical system, but the reliance of the classicists on the rational individual placed the collective cultural, social, and institutional factors that strongly influenced real human behavior on the periphery of economists' concerns. Actual changes in, for example, manufacturing did not occur in a vacuum; instead, they were embedded in the culture of the country and the historical period in which they took place. The economic decisions of real individuals were not made entirely on the basis of an abstract, logical calculus of self-interest. They reflected also the values that individuals derived from their cultures.[13]

With respect to the nomothetic element in social science, the historical econ-omists wanted (like most cultural scientists) to put their discipline on a firmer empirical foundation. Roscher, with his strong religious orientation, also sought to include a specific examination of values in economics as a means of maintaining the moral freedom of the individual as against the supposedly inexorable laws of economics. In this, he resembled Droysen and the Prussian school of history, except that Roscher also wanted to maintain the nomothetic character of social science, whereas Droysen believed that the concept of moral freedom was ultimately in-compatible with the existence of universal social laws. Roscher thought that such laws could be found—as laws of cultural change that explained alterations in the general pattern within which individual moral freedom was exercised. Both Hil-debrand and Knies recognized the difficulties inherent in postulating the freedom of the moral individual in a nomological world, but they agreed with Roscher that an economic science that placed the individual in a historical and cultural perspective offered the best way to resolve the problem.[14]

Roscher, nevertheless, retained a fairly traditional notion of the nomothetic aims of social science.[15] The "laws" of classical economics were not so much incorrect as they were applicable only to particular aspects of human life under particular historical and cultural circumstances. Truly general economic laws had to be ones that took cultural variation into account and focused on the phenomenon of *change*.[16] This view had political implications in terms of the social question. Liberal ad-herence to the "iron law of wages" and other classical theories that forbade state intervention to improve the plight of the working class was not only politically foolish in the face of working-class radicalism, but also incorrect on theoretical grounds. As the industrial economy developed beyond the conditions that gave rise to classical economics, a liberal social policy had to be developed to fit that economy without threatening the essence of either liberalism or capitalism.

But what form did such laws of culture and change take? They should be empirical laws derived by examination and comparative analysis of the histories of various nations. Roscher thought that historical investigation would reveal a pattern of change that manifested God's will but could be represented in statements es-sentially like the laws of natural science. Knies and Hildebrand were less certain about God's will and the exact similarity between social and physical law, but they both held that natural laws could be approximated through the use of statistical analysis and (in the case of Knies) something like Max Weber's ideal types.[17] As to methodology, Roscher wrote vaguely of a method of constructing analogies between modern European social conditions and those of other peoples and times. Knies attempted to formalize the analogical method, arguing that analogical rea-soning was the appropriate approach of the social sciences. Social science could employ neither the positivist methods of physical science (because of the complexity of social data) nor a hermeneutic approach because the kind of understanding the latter produced from close textual analysis was not useful for the purpose of rec-ommending policy.[18]

Despite these efforts, the historical economists still faced the basic problem of nomothetic comparative cultural studies: in order to infer a lawful statement from analogies between things observed in different cultures (or times), it is necessary to have some kind of fixed framework for comparison, some set of categories that will allow the cultural scientist to say that particular data are in fact comparable. This was the problem that the diffusionists experienced in ethnology and never satisfactorily solved. The alternative was a radical relativism that made every state-ment applicable only to the cultural and historical circumstances that produced the evidence on which it was based. By implication, such an approach would make nonsense of the nomological claims of social science—as Dilthey and other ad-vocates of hermeneutics believed. In fact Knies, like Gustav Schmoller of the "younger" historical school, came close to relativism. Schmoller sometimes sought refuge from the methodological dilemma by attacking excessive theorizing in eco-nomics.[19] But like most German ethnologists, the historical economists continued to believe that, somehow, their approach was ultimately compatible with what they thought to be the nomothetic aim of social science. Many of them thought that they could conduct effective comparative historical analysis of change by making use of a device that had been part of the traditional liberal theoretical pattern: the stage approach to history.

Roscher and Hildebrand both claimed that it was possible to classify data con-cerning economic systems and general culture from peoples around the world into temporal categories that usually followed the same sequence. These categories, or stages, could serve as a fixed framework for comparison, a basis for inference about future developments, and a set of criteria for determining what was universal and what was peculiarly national in the cultural experience of a people. There were differences between their stage schemes. Roscher's stages were based on an analogy to human growth: peoples went through stages of infancy, growth, and maturity corresponding to economies built, respectively, around "Nature," labor, and cap-ital.[20] Hildebrand focused on changing structures of exchange and identified the sequence of the natural economy, the money economy, and the credit economy. This allowed him to advocate his favorite answer to the social question: control of the credit system in the industrial economy.[21] But the general idea of stages was the same in both cases.

One problem with stage theories is that they must include some mechanism of change from one stage to another. Both Roscher and Hildebrand were influenced by Hegel in this respect, but Hegel's exact approach—focusing on changes in the intellectual structures of particular stages—seemed (as it did to Marx) to be too remote from the actual, observed patterns of cultural life. Instead, the historical economists usually portrayed the characteristic modes of economic exchange in one stage as the source of transformation into the next.[22] But in any case, they postulated the stages abstractly and then applied them to the empirical data. To characterize a whole economy in any period, together with its cultural linkages, according to such simple typologies did violence to the complexity of human existence and worked against the historical economist's own aim of giving due weight to the cultural embeddedness of economic phenomena. In some ways, it was not a great deal different from postulating the characteristics of the abstract rational individual and inferring from them the laws of market behavior. The main difference was the assumption of historical perspective, but even that was, in practice, essentially theoretical. Furthermore, if it were true, as many economists claimed, that industrialization had driven European economies into a stage of development for which there was no exact precedent in the past, then the applicability to the present of an analysis based on stages was doubtful. It is not surprising that the younger historical economists of the last third of the nineteenth century tended to avoid the stage approach in explaining change and to search for other approaches.[23]

Despite such deficiencies, historical economics became the dominant theoretical pattern in German academic economics from the 1870s onward. The first associations of German economists, founded in the 1860s and early 1870s, had been oriented toward classical economics and Manchestrianism. This was consistent with the circumstances of Germany at unification and during the great economic boom that immediately followed it, a time when the new national government was committed to industrial expansion through free trade and free enterprise. But historical economics was already established in major universities and was becoming fashionable, especially among liberal academics interested in the social question and those who believed that classical economics was showing too great a tendency to separate itself from other intellectual currents. In the later 1870s, a dramatic shift toward historical economics occurred.[24]

There are several reasons that this happened. For one thing, historical economics was closely connected to some of the most fashionable tendencies in contemporary German intellectual life: to the well-established emphasis on history and historical interpretation, to philology, and to the new currents of cultural science that we have examined here.[25] The parallels between historical economics and the other nomothetic cultural sciences are very striking, especially in the employment of historical developmental perspectives and in the relationship between the development of theoretical patterns and perceptions of inadequacy in earlier liberal social science. In addition, there was something distinctly appealing about the holistic approach of historical economics (another characteristic it shared with other cultural sciences), despite the problems of methodology that arose in consequence. The holistic approach was constructed on a foundation of humanistic intellectual concerns: on the study of the classics, on the belief in the connectedness of philosophical inquiries, on the whole tradition of *Bildung* within which most German academics were educated and within which classical economics appeared to be intellectually shallow.[26]

The economic context of the period of depression after 1873 also helps to account for the triumph of historical economics. The confident expectations of the Manchestrians and the proponents of industrialization as the main solution to the social problem were called into question. The organization of a socialist working-class political movement worried bourgeois academics. Furthermore, the increasing size of industrial enterprises brought into doubt the applicability of classical economics—with its presumption that markets consisted of large numbers of competing small producers and consumers—to the realities of the time. A turn to historical economics, as one of the few coherent theoretical alternatives to classical economic theory that was not revolutionary and that directly confronted the issues of social conflict and structural change, seemed a reasonable response to these circumstances.[27] The change of economic climate in the 1870s was accompanied, as we have seen, by changes in the political climate—especially that of German liberalism—that affected all of the social sciences. All of these factors (particularly the last) can be seen in the history of the *Verein für Sozialpolitik* and the centering of its activities around historical economics.

The *Verein* was started in 1872 by a group of academics and officials concerned about the lack of interest in the social question in existing organizations of economists.[28] Although its founders included economists of differing theoretical orientation, the *Verein* soon became the preserve mainly of the historical economists (after the first of the great *Methodenstreiten*, between the historical economists, on one hand, and the classicists and marginalists, on the other). Until after the turn of the century, the dominant figures in the *Verein* were the historical economists Adolf Wagner (1835–1917), Lujo Brentano (1844–1931), and especially the long-time president of the *Verein*, Gustav Schmoller (1838–1917).

The intent behind the formation of the *Verein für Sozialpolitik* was overtly political. The majority of its early leaders were self-acknowledged liberals, although they differed greatly on specific issues, in their attitudes toward state intervention in the economy, and in their party affiliations. They shared an outlook derived from the traditions of liberal social science: they believed in the possibility of a social science linked to basic political propositions of liberalism that could be used to validate those propositions, but that could also stand by itself as an objective science providing nonpartisan recommendations for policymakers.[29] Schmoller in particular hoped that the *Verein*'s combination of engagement and objectivity could have an effect on policy more profound than the activities of any political party in the Reichstag. As it was originally conceived, the *Verein* was supposed to identify pressing social issues in need of careful academic research, organize a research project among its members, debate the results of the research, and finally arrive at a consensus that would be passed to the state, the politicians, and the public in the form of recommendations for government action.[30] To Schmoller and many others, this represented an effective updating of both liberalism and social science, one that accepted the structure of the Bismarckian state but pushed for social reforms within it—in part to ward off the specter of social democracy.[31] Historical economics seemed to be particularly well suited for these tasks.

The later history of the *Verein für Sozialpolitik* displays both the difficulties inherent in the attempt to build a new liberal politics around social science and the impetus to creativity that such an attempt produced. The *Verein*'s leaders had by the 1880s to give up any thought that the *Verein* could speak with one voice on policy.[32] It could identify research topics—as it did, for example, with the project of investigating the agrarian economy of eastern Prussia in the early 1890s on which Max Weber first made a name for himself. The theoretical pattern that the *Verein* adopted was adequate for that purpose, and current political issues indicated what questions were important. But when it came to debating the results of research, the *Verein*'s consensus almost invariably fell apart. Factions appeared, often paralleling lines of ideological differentiation in politics in general. Because many of the topics of research were identified by their political prominence, it was natural that research results would be interpreted along political lines. Rather than science producing objective truth and thus consensus on political questions, politics produced dissensus in science. The theoretical pattern of historical economics did not of itself impose

consensus on those who adopted it. The *Verein* had to give up the idea of rec-
ommending policy. It concentrated instead on encouraging research and its discussion before a public audience.

Historical economics did, however, provide a pattern which informed much of
the research done by the *Verein* under the leadership of Schmoller and the other
founders, and it strongly influenced the work of such *Verein* members as Max
Weber, Ferdinand Tönnies, and Werner Sombart who revolutionized social science
at the turn of the century. The pattern continued to incorporate concerns of the
cultural sciences.

Schmoller had, by the end of the 1870s, insinuated himself into a pivotal position
in the Berlin academic establishment, dominating the economics section of the
philosophical faculty at Berlin University and serving as advisor to several *Reich*
and Prussian ministries. For many years, he had a major voice in the selection of
social science professors at Prussian universities. He was, in other words, the
equivalent of Virchow in terms of bureaucratic and academic politics—although he
did not share Virchow's commitment to democracy and parliamentarism and was
much more willing to accommodate himself to the power structure of imperial
Germany. Schmoller saw reform as a gradual process administered by a bureaucratic
state, involving the education in social responsibility of officials, members of economic elites, and ultimately the masses.[33]

Schmoller's treatment of cultural topics within the pattern of historical economics reflected some of his general social and political views.[34] He had less use for
the principles of classical economics than Roscher and Hildebrand did and believed
that the main focus of economic research should be the institutional context of
human life. It was within the framework of institutions that humans publicly expressed their cultural values and conducted their economic activities. Markets, for
example, were not immediate expressions of universal human economic rationality,
but rather institutions with particular structures that were defined culturally and
historically and that changed through time. Schmoller wanted, in essence, to build
a holistic approach to social reality by using institutions as the objects of attention.
He held that historical research was research into the development of institutions,
that current research should focus on the functioning of current institutions, and
that policy recommendations should mainly be suggestions about ways in which
existing institutions could shape their actions to suit new realities in the course of
social change. Schmoller's institutional focus was extremely well suited to his
politics of building social consciousness and introducing new policies within the
context of a German national state, the structure of which he believed to be generally
consistent with the traditional aims of moderate German liberalism and therefore
in no need of drastic change.

Schmoller was, like many other cultural scientists, extremely skeptical of abstraction in economic theory—whether the classicist and marginalist forms of
abstraction or the various stage theories of development within his own theoretical
pattern. He advocated, instead, a rigorous empiricism based on statistical and
institutional analyses focusing on current issues but putting them in historical perspective. Had Schmoller been willing to pursue the matter further, he might have
come to the conclusion on these grounds that assumption of a nomothetic aim for

social and cultural science was inappropriate, but he did not do so. As with Virchow, Schmoller was content to rule out excessive or hasty generalization. He could not part either with the security of a theoretical grounding in nomothetic science or with the political utility of the belief that the economist spoke with the authority of one who understood the laws of nature.

Other major figures of Schmoller's generation in the *Verein für Sozialpolitik* pursued quite different political and scholarly lines within the theoretical pattern of historical economics, but most shared the tendency to downplay theory and (in practice) the search for social laws without eliminating the nomothetic aspect entirely from their conceptions of what social science was. Lujo Brentano, as a self-acknowledged left liberal, retained an allegiance to representative democracy, free markets, free trade, and material progress.[35] His approach to social reform was to insist that the maintenance of the free-market system required that the interests of workers as participants in the system be protected through the recognition of unions and through collective bargaining. Brentano's economics mirrored his social vision. Like Roscher, he accepted classical economic theory up to a point. He devoted most of his early career, however, to studying historical examples of collective producers' associations (especially guilds) and more contemporary institutions with implications for social relations. Although he agreed that economic behavior was embedded in broader cultural phenomena, he did relatively little research on the latter.

Adolf Wagner, Schmoller's colleague at the University of Berlin, was simul-taneously more radical and more conservative than either Schmoller or Brentano.[36] On the one hand, he readily accepted the epithet "socialist of the chair" and advocated state intervention to protect social classes exploited by large capitalist enterprises or threatened with displacement by economic change. On the other hand, Wagner was not sympathetic to Marxian socialism, to the labor movement, or to the Social Democratic party. He was in fact much less concerned about the industrial working class in general than about traditional occupational groups threatened by industrialization: peasants, artisans, the *Mittelstand*. Wagner criticized heavy in-dustry, big capital, and *Junker* agriculture for destroying the cultural basis of *Deutschtum* by proletarianizing such groups. His advocacy of state intervention constituted "socialism" only in a rather peculiar sense. His economics was heavily tinged with an agrarianism based on a cultural analysis very similar to Ratzel's. Wagner was essentially a social conservative, although one who, like Schmoller, believed that he was operating in the political and theoretical tradition of moderate, socially conscious liberalism.

Despite the wide range of viewpoints among the leaders of the *Verein*'s historical economists, before the mid–1890s most of the organization's members continued to think that they could work together. They believed that they possessed, in the general theoretical pattern they had adopted, a basis for consensus among intellec-tuals about social policy and an objective guide to social reform without revolution. In the 1890s, however, these beliefs were increasingly viewed by critics, some of them younger members of the *Verein* itself, as being problematic. We shall examine later some of the grounds for the skepticism of people such as Max Weber about the validity of the nomothetic view of social science and about the claims of

Schmoller that scientific objectivity and political engagement could be effectively combined. Weber and others also criticized the assumptions that underlay historical economics as a theoretical pattern, especially the ways in which historical economists treated the relationship of the rational individual to the sociocultural context and the problems that had arisen in historical economists' treatments of change.[37] But before we can consider these matters, which lay at the heart of the creative revolution in social science at the turn of the century, we must turn to an examination of cultural history.

Cultural History

Most studies of German historiography in the nineteenth century focus on the theoretical patterns established by Ranke and Droysen that informed the "Prussian" school and became the dominant approach of the historical establishment in the late nineteenth century.[38] Establishment historiography concentrated on politics, especially on the emergence of the German national state. Although many of its practitioners, especially at midcentury, considered themselves to be liberals, their theoretical pattern had little contact, even in its origins, with that of liberal social science. They were not much affected by the development of cultural science before the 1890s.

But alongside establishment history had grown up a heterogeneous discipline of cultural history—practiced sometimes by professional historians, sometimes by journalists, art critics, and philosophers. Cultural history found its place in various corners of German universities, but it also found a large public audience. Unlike standard Prussian-school political history, which was the product of a limited academic elite that regarded its methods as a science for the adept, cultural history was connected to a growing network of amateur interest groups, semiacademic professionals, and schoolteachers similar to the networks that supported the other cultural-science disciplines.

Some cultural historians contributed heavily to the formation of the hermeneutic approach to understanding society. Dilthey himself was a theorist of cultural history.[39] Cultural history produced the kinds of epistemological and methodological questions that encouraged the development of hermeneutics. We shall concentrate here, however, on cultural historians who did not consciously adopt a hermeneutic approach—who either saw cultural history as a discipline with a method of its own or thought that cultural history was one of the nomothetic social sciences. Jacob Burckhardt is an example of the former case, Karl Lamprecht of the latter.

Jacob Burckhardt (1818–1897) was a Swiss whose political and historical thought was strongly influenced by his outlook as a member of the traditional republican oligarchy of Basel, where he taught at the university.[40] He was also, however, an active participant in German intellectual life and a commentator on German politics. Burckhardt began his university education in Germany as a largely nonpolitical person interested in classical subjects and art history; but in the mid-1840s, he was briefly attracted to the kind of moderate liberalism that prevailed in the *Staatslexikon*—although as a Swiss, he was largely immune to the enthusiastic nationalism that was concomitant to most varieties of midcentury German liberal thought.[41] To Burckhardt, the orderly city-state (such as Basel) was the most desirable context for politics. Part of his later conservatism was present even when he was a self-conceived liberal: his belief that the modern national state, the national economy, and the development of mass national public opinion threatened the viability of this most admirable of all political structures. He realized, however, that the historical tide was moving decidedly away from his ideal.

Burckhardt, both in the 1840s and later, had little quarrel with moderate liberal conceptions of political order and institutions, which he thought to be largely compatible with the traditional model of the city-state ruled by officials chosen by, and from, a limited electorate. On the broader stage of a nation, the kind of stable, monarchical constitutionalism advocated by Welcker and Dahlmann—a *Rechtsstaat* with a legislature acting as a check on the government—seemed to be the closest possible analogue to Burckhardt's ideal. Moderate *Vormärz* liberals almost all abhorred the notion of violent revolution, and so did Burckhardt. Moderate *Vormärz* liberals mostly believed that a state organized along liberal lines could manifest the morality inherent in human nature and work to restrict immoral human propensities by adopting laws with a strong ethical content,and so did Burckhardt. Burckhardt never deviated from these basic views; thus whatever he called himself later in political terms, he retained an alignment with moderate liberalism of the *Vormärz* variety.[42]

Burckhardt was offended by the 1848 revolution and its consequences. He disliked political violence, and he disliked the democratic tendencies of the radical liberal politicians who most openly condoned revolutionary violence in 1848–1849. He thought that the latter were following age-old patterns of pandering to the demands of the masses for a share of political power, which could only lead to illegitimate rule by popular tyrants. Like Dahlmann, Burckhardt believed that change had to be rooted in the history and traditions of a people and could not be suddenly imposed—one of the major sources of his interest in broadening the scope of his studies beyond the elite aspects of culture on which he had concentrated when starting his work in art history.

After 1848, Burckhardt's dislike of political violence crystallized into a view both of history and of politics he described as conservative. Social change occurred inevitably, but did not necessarily improve things. People were basically always the same in terms of their moral potential. Sudden or violent change upset the systems of order (both the external political ones and the internalized cultural ones) that encouraged the good and repressed the evil in people. Rapid change for its own sake or in pursuit of some theoretical good was therefore not desirable. Change would occur in its own way and time, and the cultural supports for morality would adjust to it. By almost any generic definition, this really *was* conservatism—but a conservatism with obvious links to moderate midcentury liberalism.[43]

In some ways, Burckhardt resembled both Riehl and Roscher. Like Riehl, Burckhardt was a moderate liberal who was driven by his experiences of 1848 to proclaim himself a conservative, and his conservatism, like Riehl's, had little to do with a favorable attitude toward the autocratic-bureaucratic state or the interests of hereditary landed nobilities. Like Riehl, Burckhardt was not impressed by forms of nationalism that offered to replace local singularities with national uniformities. But unlike Riehl, Burckhardt was not particularly interested in the social question. Burckhardt's tendency to expand his notions of culture in the 1850s to include popular culture—a tendency reflected in the later chapters of his *The Civilization of the Renaissance in Italy*—did not arise from a desire to put the social question into an appropriate political context. He appears to have regarded the social question largely as a means by which politicians manipulated the lower classes.[44]

Burckhardt differed from Roscher in a great many ways—in rejecting the label of *liberal* after 1848 and in refusing to try to find laws of social change in history, to apply social scientific theory to present phenomena, to see a providential pattern immanent in history, or to accept the notion of continuous human progress. But he resembled Roscher in viewing politics as ultimately grounded in morality and subject to moral valuation, and partly for that reason, in emphasizing the connection between politics and the general culture of a people or period—for culture defined a people's morality.[45]

Because Burckhardt never conceived of himself as a social scientist, his creation of a distinctive approach to cultural history cannot be explained as a result of a reevaluation of the liberal theoretical pattern in social science. Nevertheless, Burckhardt's cultural history was closely linked to his ideological outlook. His attempt to explain particular aspects of the life of a people or nation (their politics, art, literature, etc.) at a certain period in terms of their general "cultural horizon" was partly an effort to counter the idea of uniform, inevitable progress. His desire to show the importance of the moral element in political life and the consequences of believing that politics could be divorced from morality may have been a direct response to such tendencies in liberal thought in the 1850s as Rochau's *Realpolitik* and Droysen's identification of power as the central moral aim of the state.[46] Part of the point of the first chapters of *The Civilization of the Renaissance in Italy* is to locate in the Renaissance the origins of these mistaken tendencies.[47] One of the reasons for Burckhardt's insistence on taking a worldwide view of history was to deflate the claim of many radicals that modern social and political changes were, in terms of what really mattered, something new that was going to alter the nature of human life. And one of the reasons for his treatment of politics and high culture as phenomena embedded in the general culture of an era was Burckhardt's goal of indicating the complex and morally problematic nature of conscious attempts to create novelty. All of these elements of Burckhardt's thought can be seen as rejections of particular tendencies in liberal ideology and social science after 1848, but they also reflect continuity with some of the values of moderate *Vormärz* liberalism.

Burckhardt was, of course, only one of a number of cultural historians who became prominent in the second half of the nineteenth century, and he was far from the most typical. The novelty of his approach and the ways in which he used evidence made him appear something of a dilettante to the dominant Prussian school of historiography—or at best, a respectable outsider.[48] Social and cultural scientists employing the theoretical patterns we have examined in earlier chapters regarded Burckhardt as unrigorous in methodology. Of all the schools of historical and cultural thought that were prominent in the second half of the century, Burckhardt comes closest to those of hermeneutics and *Geisteswissenschaft*. But he was not sufficiently interested in questions of epistemology—in the basic issues of how historical knowledge of society is possible—to be classified in that category, either.[49] Burckhardt was, however, extremely popular with the educated public.

Other historians concerned with cultural questions were more closely aligned with the dominant theoretical pattern of political history. One of the most prominent of these was the eminent classical historian Theodor Mommsen (1817–1903), whose view of what was important in history was always much broader than those of most his colleagues at the University of Berlin.[50] Trained in the Rankean approach to primary sources and raised in a liberal political tradition, Mommsen refused to subscribe either to the idolatry of the Bismarckian state or to the extreme nationalist focus common in the Prussian school. Although Mommsen encouraged a movement toward cultural history that became apparent among younger followers of the Prussian school (and also influenced Max Weber), he created no theoretical pattern of his own.

Despite its peripheral place among professional historians before the end of the nineteenth century, cultural history found a wide public audience. In part this was due to the efforts of people who straddled the gap between journalism and scholarship and who interested themselves in cultural history to a large extent because of what they perceived as its political relevance. W. H. Riehl was one of these people, but the best known was Gustav Freytag (1816–1895).

Freytag was a self-proclaimed liberal all his life. He was best known as editor of *Die Grenzboten* in 1848–1861 and 1867–1870 and as the author of the best-selling novel *Soll und Haben*.[51] *Die Grenzboten* became, under Freytag's leadership, the preferred journal of intellectual liberalism in Germany. From the 1860s, it displayed, as Freytag himself did, a National Liberal tendency to accommodate itself to the structure of the Bismarckian state—without ceasing to advertise itself as liberal.[52] *Soll und Haben* (1855) is a ringing defense of the bougeoisie, of the labor of independent artisans, of the virtues of work, private ownership, and Victorian morality in general. It was written as a contribution to the debate over the social question in the 1850s and as the outline of a social policy that would adjust moderate liberalism to the intellectual and political demands of post–1848 industrial society.[53] In both his journalism and his fiction, particularly after the 1850s, Freytag made heavy use of the concept of culture, attempting to put the wide range of political and social issues he discussed into a broader framework of national culture. Toward the end of his life, he devoted himself to a cultural history of the German people, focusing on the history of the family as the shaper of individual behavior and the main force for continuity in society. Freytag turned increasingly to cultural history as his political outlook became more conservative; unlike Riehl, he did not abandon his general association with liberalism as the ideological context for social, economic, and political progress.

Although Freytag remained a liberal and an advocate of the ethic of progress, the kind of cultural history that he and others popularized found one of its strongest audiences among educated people outside the academic elite who were, in large part because of dissatisfaction with the course of socioeconomic modernization, looking for a replacement for standard liberal ideology. These included both straightforward conservatives and people attracted to the radical right—essentially the same people who made Riehl a well-known figure again in the 1890s and who composed the rank and file of organizations such as the Pan-German League. One of the most impressive products of this sort of interest in cultural history was a series of monographs on aspects of early modern German culture put out between 1899 and 1905 by the Leipzig publisher Eugen Diederichs.

Diederichs was a major figure on the radical right, an active member of many radical nationalist organizations and an advocate of *völkisch* ideologies.[54] He was also the publisher of many books by social scientists and historians meant for a popular audience as well as a significant participant in the networks of scholars, businesspeople, officials, and publishers that constituted the informal structure of the Saxon-Thuringian intellectual establishment. The Diederichs series, edited by Georg Steinhausen, consisted of twelve volumes, each written by an amateur or nonacademic historian.[55] Each volume was concerned with the culture of a particular occupational or ethnic type in the early modern period: peasants, soldiers, Jews, and so forth. Without being outright nostalgic for ways of life that had changed, the series managed to convey a sense that Germany's future depended on maintaining the heritage of her past. The volumes themselves were deliberately archaized (a specialty of the Diederichs press): they were printed in *Fraktur* of an old-fashioned type, and they were replete with illustrations derived from old woodcuts.

In some ways, the general attitudes displayed by the Diederichs series were consistent with the kind of moderate, historically and culturally conscious liberalism that Freytag exemplified. But another element was also present. The Diederichs series was connected, as was Diederichs, to the emergence of conservative forms of radical nationalism at the boundary between scholarship and popular culture. These forms had little to do with traditional aristocratic conservatism. Their character is suggested rather than overtly stated. The monographs on the German soldier and peasant treat their subjects with great sympathy, whereas the one devoted to the Jews, although supposedly neutral with respect to the then-current "Jewish question," nevertheless portays Jews as an unassimilated, alien presence among the German people.[56] Cultural history could readily be employed to express the kind of anti-Semitic sentiment that associated Jews as a group with the threat of modernization to traditional German culture. And yet Diederichs's venture—and his general interest in cultural history—cannot simply be dismissed as propaganda from the radical right. Freytag was sympathetic to many of Diederichs's views, and Karl Lamprecht, who did not share Diederichs's politics, was willing to cooperate with Diederichs as a legitimate sponsor of scholarly endeavor.[57]

Karl Lamprecht (1856–1915) was the best-known cultural historian of the turn of the century, the center of a major methodological controversy, and the creator of a theoretical pattern in cultural science consciously derived from the earlier liberal one. The son of Lutheran pastor (a background that he shared with many historians and philosophers but few cultural scientists), Lamprecht studied history at Germany's major universities at a time when the approach of the Prussian school was becoming dominant in the German historical establishment. The Prussian school, as we have seen, emphasized the hermeneutic intellectual tradition and focused on politics as the significant factor in any historical period and as the field within which humans exercised their freedom of decision, their ability to impose on events a moral meaning. The moral meaning might reflect a spirit immanent in an age, but because political events arise from free moral choices, the notion of underlying, determinative social laws had to be rejected. There was, in other words, a great methodological gulf between the nomothetic cultural sciences and the kind of history to which Lamprecht was exposed.[58]

Lamprecht quickly became dissatisfied with the Prussian school. On the level of historical theory, his earliest objection was that the dominant approach was too narrow in scope. His own university education was very broad, encompassing art history and philosophy, and when he attended Leipzig University beginning in 1877, he came under the influence of Roscher in economics, Wundt in psychology, and Georg Voigt (a follower of Burckhardt) in history. Lamprecht's exposure to the intellectual environment of Leipzig (which, as we shall see in chapter 11, was self-consciously different from Berlin's and tended to favor interdisciplinary endeavors) appears to have been a turning point in his life. The intellectual direction he took then, which was reinforced when he obtained a professorship at Leipzig in 1891, set him on a course that brought him fully into the fold of nomothetic cultural science—and into conflict with the historical establishment.

Lamprecht was always primarily a scholar, although one with a good eye for publicity and a popular audience. There is every reason to think that he was attracted to the idea of a broad-ranging nomothetic cultural history primarily by his intellectual interests, perhaps compounded by certain factors in his personal background.[59] But from an early period, he also viewed his work in cultural science as having political implications. Lamprecht's political position was never very exactly defined, but he was certainly a democrat and a left liberal in favor of reforms in the *Reich* that would eliminate some of its autocratic elements, increase the level of popular participation in politics, and (perhaps contradictorily) increase the impact of the academic elite on policy. He was also, in a vague way, interested in the social question and its implications for liberalism.[60] He tended, with some justice, to equate the narrow political focus of the Prussian school of historiography with its adulation of the Bismarckian state, which he saw as an obstacle to meaningful reform—an obstacle doubly significant because the founders of the Prussian school were themselves moderate liberals.

Lamprecht's main aim in the last two decades of the nineteenth century was to produce a general history of the German people that incorporated all aspects of their cultural and social development over time within a framework that afforded comparison with other peoples throughout the world and that also permitted the uncovering of the laws of historical change.[61] To Lamprecht, the concept of culture was the key; it encompassed all elements of history, including politics, social structure, art, literature, and economic life. His was therefore a holistic, Burckhardtian notion of culture compatible with the outlook of the historical economists but at variance with the political focus of the Prussian historical school. Unlike Burckhardt, however, Lamprecht emphasized the need to find and apply the "laws" of history. He thereby aligned his approach with those of his Leipzig colleagues Roscher, Wundt, and Ratzel—and also took over many of the theoretical difficulties that they faced.

Lamprecht's approach to cultural history can be discussed in terms of the elements of the liberal theoretical pattern that served as the starting point for his attempt to construct his own theoretical pattern. First, the rational individual. Lamprecht (like Ratzel) concluded that the important aspects of human history and human life were not to be understood in terms of individuals, but rather in terms of larger collective entities. He accepted the notion that humans shared basic mental capacities and modes of perception (without which it would be difficult to postulate universal social laws), but he agreed with Wundt that these were much less important in understanding history than culturally derived forms of thought and behavior, which were different for different peoples. Thus, like many other cultural scientists, Lamprecht wanted to replace the classic model of the rational individual with collective units defined in terms of culture.[62]

Lamprecht did more than that, however. Following to some extent in the footsteps of Roscher and the other historical economists, he also identified the idea of the rational individual and the individualist behavior patterns associated with it as objects of study for cultural historians. He argued that the notion of the autonomous individual standing apart from the rest of society and serving as the criterion for judging social phenomena was itself a historical product, arising in the West during the Middle Ages and surviving into the modern era.[63] But, whereas in the late Middle Ages in the politically independent city, individualism as a cultural and behavioral form reached its highest point of creative achievement precisely because it was balanced by a continuing traditional collective ethic, in the modern world individuals came to be assumed to be in fact distinct from society, and their particular form of selfish rationality came to be the model for rationality in general. Classic theories of social science thus made the mistake of universalizing what was actually a particular (and in terms of world history, a highly unusual) cultural artifact. To the extent that social scientists accepted the rational individual model as the basis for their theorizing, they were doomed to failure. And more than that, they were legitimating social and economic policies built around the idea of the rational, selfish individual—policies that were creating needless social unrest in industrial society.

The collective entities within which the behavior of the individual was circumscribed and around which history was written were both institutional and intellectual. All were given meaning by an idea that Lamprecht took mainly from Wundt: that of *Seelenleben* (psychological disposition).[64] According to Lamprecht, the history of every *Volk* develops through a series of epochs, each of which is characterized by a particular psychological disposition that informs its culture and therefore informs the thinking and actions of people at that time. Lamprecht, in other words, adopted Wundt's solution to the problem of explaining the relationship between the individual and the environment—whether social or physical. The *Seelenleben* of a people develops according to a particular temporal sequence: from an emphasis on symbolism characteristic of primitive cultures to individualism and subjectivism in more modern ones. All peoples have shown the same general pattern of development, but particular peoples, such as the Germans, display their own peculiarities because of their environment and the internal logic of the psychological dispositions they possessed in earlier eras. The *Seelenleben* is manifest not only in the conscious artistic products of a people and era, but also in their politics and economic arrangements.[65]

Although Lamprecht's downgrading of the importance of the individual in history was objectionable to many mainstream historians, what caused the most controversy was his decision to assert loudly the validity of the nomothetic aim of social science. Lamprecht claimed that a comparative examination of the histories of all the peoples of the world revealed laws of cultural development that ought to be regarded as the proper bases not only of historical and social interpretation, but also of state policy. Germany's foreign policy should be built around the realization that the laws of cultural change identified Germany as the current leader and innovator in modern civilization and that this could be presented in a positive, peaceful light to other countries. Domestic policy should recognize the laws of cultural change, which indicated that an end to the extreme individualism and fragmentation characteristic of modern society was at hand and ought to be encouraged.[66]

Lamprecht's vigorous assertion of a nomothetic approach to social understanding set off violent opposition to Lamprecht from his colleagues in the historical profession. It made him appear to be a traitor to the consensus that had developed around the hermeneutic theoretical pattern of the Prussian school. Cultural scientists in other fields had not aroused such reaction from the historians, partly because the prestige of historical scholarship made historians feel secure when confronting outsiders and partly because German ethnologists and geographers tended to hedge and qualify their statements about social laws. Lamprecht, on the other hand, preached apostasy within the historical profession itself, and he did so in a radical manner. He claimed that there was no essential difference between the cultural or human sciences and the natural sciences and that (sources of data permitting) the procedures in both areas should be the same. Lamprecht, in other words, consciously aligned himself with the positivists in France and with Herbert Spencer and Henry Thomas Buckle in Britain—all of whom were anathema to establishment German historians.[67] There was in fact nothing inherently foreign in Lamprecht's approach, and although Lamprecht had read Comte, his "positivism" came not from Comte but from the nomothetic element of the main German social scientific tradition. It was rather Lamprecht's brashness, the disciplinary location from which he asserted his position, and the lack of qualification in his presentation that waved a red flag in the faces of his colleagues.

Lamprecht also dealt with the third element of the traditional liberal theoretical pattern: the attempt to account for change. His approach was similar to those of Wundt, Bastian, Ratzel, and Roscher. His discussion of change focused on discrete "civilizations" occupying distinct geographical areas in the world. Lamprecht's concept of civilization had, of course, deep and complex origins in Western thought, but it was especially influenced by the historical economists and by Ratzel's ideas about cultural areas (the *Kulturkreise* of the later diffusionists). According to Lamprecht, each civilization goes through a series of stages of development as the particular *Seelenleben* of its *Volk* changes. In a basic (not always consistently described) way, changes in *Seelenleben* are linked to changes in the social and economic structures of society—in modes of exchange, division of labor, class organization, and so forth.[68]

The process of change within the context of civilization is complicated by the fact that although individual civilizations experience stages of development that are both unique in detail and yet conformable to a general pattern, civilization as a whole also goes through its own pattern of development, which must be taken into account as well. Lamprecht's difficulties in coordinating these various processes of change provided much ammunition to his critics.[69] In general Lamprecht adopted the approach that was to be taken over later by Oswald Spengler. The stages of general human cultural history are dominated, for large areas of the world, at least, by particular peoples with particular civilizations. These peoples, through their political and economic power and their prestige, act as media of cultural diffusion as they go through their own individual processes of rise and fall. In recent centuries, the West has produced one of these significant civilizations. Western civilization is unique in that it is not dominated by a single people, but rather by several, each taking its turn in acting as cultural leader. It is also unique in having acquired the capacity to impress its culture, and thus the impetus to cultural growth and advancement, on the entire world.

This aspect of Lamprecht's analysis of cultural change was the basis of his concept of cultural imperialism, an idea that had considerable resonance in Germany in the decade before the First World War. Just as the English had succeeded the French as the political and cultural pacemakers of Western civilization and had used their empire to impress their version of that civilization on the rest of the world, so now it was Germany's turn to perform this important historical mission. As long as educated people of all the major powers and the educated elites in the countries (including the United States) that were to be the beneficiaries of Germany's cultural expansion understood what was going on, there was no need for war to occur as a result. Similarly, if Germans of all classes would realize that they had a part to play in this historical process, the level of class antagonism would be reduced within German society.[70]

Lamprecht became very popular with the educated public in the 1890s and retained his popularity down to the First World War. He became a major figure in the academic establishment of Leipzig University and a participant in the attempt to formulate an interdisciplinary study of culture at Leipzig, which we shall examine in chapter 11. He did not, however, establish a school of thought or a discipline of his own, nor did he formulate a permanent theoretical pattern in cultural history. He tried to do so through his Institute for Universal History in Leipzig, but the institute's importance died with him.[71] The main reason for Lamprecht's lack of ultimate success was that his academic reputation never recovered from the attacks of the historical establishment (and some social scientists) on him at the turn of the century.[72] His affirmation of nomothetic cultural science within the historical field singled him out as a target, and the many theoretical inconsistencies and factual errors in his work made Lamprecht's case a weak one.

One of the main functions Lamprecht performed in the history of German social science was that, by acting as an object of attack for people like Max Weber who were dissatisfied with the nomothetic approach but who were also uneasy with neo-idealist *Geisteswissenschaft*, he stimulated attempts to create alternatives to both.[73] And notwithstanding their attacks on Lamprecht's methodology, many of his severest critics among the establishment historians—people such as Otto Hintze and Erich Brandenburg—were challenged by Lamprecht and the cultural scientists with whom he was associated to undertake their own investigations of cultural history and to secure thereby the position of the field within German academia.[74] Part of the new popularity of cultural history after the turn of the century was due to the political attractiveness of the idea of *Kulturpolitik* among academics, an idea Lamprecht helped to formulate. We shall turn to that subject and to other connections between academic politics and cultural science in the next chapter.

11

Intellectual Politics and Cultural Science in the Wilhelmian Era

Many German academics specializing in the social and cultural sciences experienced a quickening of their interest in politics in the early 1890s and perceived an opportunity to exert an influence on the nation's future that they had not had in many years.[1] The opportunity arose in part from obvious sources, including the fall of Bismarck in 1890, the adoption of the "New Course" by the Caprivi government, and the appearance of highly divisive issues (such as those surrounding the Caprivi policy of lowering tariffs) that encouraged the disputants to seek academic buttressing for their positions. In addition, the colonial movement had recently demonstrated the ability of imperialism to mobilize educated Germans for political action. This demonstration was taken to heart by alert politicians—who increasingly tried to tie domestic issues to those of foreign and imperial policy in order to garner the support of the educated—and by politically oriented academics, who did the same thing.[2] The latter recognized that they had a chance of affecting politics by focusing their fields of study on major issues (such as the social question and its political cognate, the growing power of the Social Democrats) within some sort of nationalist ideological context.

That academics (together with a large portion of the *Bildungsbürgertum* in general) should have been anxious to participate in Wilhelmian politics in new and more extensive ways has been explained variously by historians. Some have seen it as a result of growing fear on the part of humanistically trained people of the threat of modernity to their own status—hence the antimodern bias in much of turn-of-the-century intellectual politics.[3] Some have presented it as a generational phenomenon, the attempt by younger intellectuals to assert themselves against the generation that founded the *Reich*.[4] Still others, more recently, have seen the politicization of intellectuals in the 1890s as a reversion to the liberal tradition of political engagement (admittedly under vastly altered circumstances that included the fragmentation of the liberal tradition itself) instigated in large part by bourgeois resentment against the monopoly of power by elites and the threat to stability from the working class.[5] Each of these interpretations contains a strong element of truth, but we shall approach the phenomenon in a somewhat different way: as a complex set of reactions by academics to their perception of a society with serious problems, problems that fortuitous political circumstances in the 1890s gave them the opportunity to solve through the application of their expertise. According to Rüdiger vom

Bruch, the belief that such an opportunity existed lasted only from the early 1890s to about 1907, but the academics' enthusiasm for politics and their later reflections on it were important ingredients in the upheaval in German social science that took place around the turn of the century.[6]

Cultural science was involved both with the political background of the upheaval and in the upheaval itself. The present chapter will examine this involvement in very general terms before focusing on one important instance: the attempt to create a unified cultural science at the University of Leipzig.

Varieties of Intellectual Politics

One of the most frequently remarked characteristics of Wilhelmian Germany was its fragmentation. To many educated Germans, it appeared not only that society itself was as divided as ever among antagonistic social classes, religious and ethnic segments, and regions, but also that the structure of government and politics, instead of working against this fragmentation, contributed to it. The *Reich* government was seen as divided and indecisive, especially after the fall of Bismarck—traits inappropriate for a nation that was militarily so powerful and economically so successful. The party system that operated in the Reichstag and the state assemblies was fragmentary and responsive to a multitude of seemingly irreconcilable organized interest groups. No single ideology or set of ideologies was accepted as the core of political thinking. Given such perceptions by intellectuals, it is not surprising that so much of their political thought should focus on unity, nationalism, and means of promoting national coherence—all of which involved considerations of national culture.[7]

Liberalism, the ideology and movement that had once (before and just after unification) served as the foundation of national politics, was itself particularly fragmented and apparently weak in the early 1890s. Since midcentury, liberals had branched out in a variety of ideological directions, some of them radically rejecting ideas that had once been considered fundamental to liberalism. Just what liberalism stood for in the 1890s, apart from a distinct historical tradition, was a question that the liberal parties had been asking themselves for some time. The left liberals split in 1893 into two parties, the *Freisinnige Volkspartei* and the more innovative *Freisinnige Vereinigung,* over (among other things) how far the liberal movement could accommodate an active social welfare policy to attract working-class voters and promote social peace without ceasing to be liberal. All the liberal parties, including the National Liberals, experienced serious erosions of voting strength in the 1890s.[8]

Yet, at the same time, it was clear that the political and intellectual traditions of liberalism had penetrated into the basic fiber of the *Reich.* Liberal patterns of thought largely defined notions of progress and industrialization, which were seen as the engines of change in politics and society. Institutions derived from the liberal tradition, especially the Reichstag, were increasingly, if ambiguously, significant in the pseudoparliamentary politics of the *Reich.* All parties, including antiliberal ones, had adopted approaches to politics pioneered by the liberals and identified, in the past, with liberalism, including the designation of public opinion as a decisive factor in politics.[9] The embedding of liberalism in the politics of the Reich paralleled the embedding of liberal ideas in the political culture of intellectuals, in much the same way that theoretical patterns with roots in *Vormärz* liberal social science became embedded in the cultural sciences—even among academics who had dropped their formal allegiance to liberal parties.

This embedding is one of the many reasons that it is difficult to classify the manifestations of Wilhelmian intellectual politics into clear ideological categories, at least before about 1910. Not only was the political thought of academics and other intellectuals enormously varied and changing, but attempts to categorize them according to whether or not they were liberal or antiliberal, progressive or conservative are all problematic because of the extent to which liberal ideas, liberal traditions, and liberal modes of discourse were built into their outlooks and backgrounds.[10]

There is, therefore, no point in trying to put social and cultural scientists of the early and middle Wilhelmian periods into ideological categories defined (as such categories usually are) in terms of their acceptance or rejection of liberalism. It is more useful to think in terms of loose communities of political discourse among social and cultural scientists as the primary units of their political thinking.[11]

Communities of political discourse among intellectuals arose in the 1890s as a result of the newly perceived opportunities for political involvement that the period afforded. Many of these communities (including all three that will be discussed here) had strong connections to liberal political traditions. For the most part, they did not produce structured ideologies or political parties. Instead, the people who participated in them tried to assemble already-existing ideological tendencies (nationalism, various forms of liberalism, newly evolved ideologies such as agrarianism and the major types of imperialism, etc.) together in ways that were suggested by the general aims, attitudes, and vocabularies that defined their communities. Academics also tried to bring into the same connections the major theoretical patterns of their disciplines. These aggregations of ideology and theory fell apart rapidly. The communities of discourse, although flexible and overlapping, proved to be incapable of incorporating each other and therefore failed to overcome the fragmentation of politics. Instead, it was combinations of ideological tendencies that arose partly outside the scope of intellectual politics—the newly refurbished, broad-based democratic liberalism that dominated the nonsocialist left by the time of the First World War, and the radical nationalism that operated in uneasy alliance with older forms of conservatism by the same period—that came to define the political landscape. By about 1910, the communities of political discourse that had earlier characterized intellectual politics had largely dissolved and their elements had been absorbed into the prevailing ideological trends and (to a large extent) parties. The fluidity of intellectual politics had disappeared, and it became easier to classify academics' political positions in terms of recognized ideologies and organizations.[12]

Communities of discourse were defined in part by particular arrays of words and ideas used by their participants to discuss political and social issues. The arrays overlapped to a substantial degree, but their central structures can be generally identified. Communities were defined also by the intentions of the individuals who participated in them. It is difficult, however, to identify communities in terms of consistent membership by particular people. It was quite possible for individuals to participate in two or more communities, and very common for important academics to move from one to another in the course of time. Such movements were closely connected to the turn-of-the-century burst of creativity in German social science. In the cases of people like Max Weber and Werner Sombart, the process of joining a community of discourse, criticizing received opinion from the standpoint of that community, and then recognizing the intellectual and political limitations of the community and moving elsewhere underlay (in part at least) their innovative contributions to social theory.[13] Here we shall be concerned with the implications for nomothetic cultural science (not *all* of social science) of three of these communities: apoliticism, neoliberalism, and radicalism.

Apoliticism

The terms *apolitical* or *nonpartisan* can be applied to a wide variety of political postures. Among Wilhelmian academics, the terms referred not only to the large number of academics who were simply uninterested in politics, but also (and what is more important) to those who, although deeply concerned with political issues, affected to be above the competition of parties and interest groups and to regard such competition as a major source of Germany's problems. The *truly* apolitical were not an important factor in Wilhelmian politics except to the extent that their attitudes, widely publicized, gave passive support to the public image of scientific objectivity on which much of the prestige (and therefore the potential political strength) of German scholarship rested. The community of discourse that is here called apolitical corresponds more closely to the other end of the range of meanings of the term.[14]

In chapter 10, we discussed certain precursors and examples of this kind of apoliticism: some of the founders of historical economics and the leadership of the *Verein für Sozialpolitik*. Among the former, Wilhelm Roscher associated a moderate liberal ideological stance with rigid nonpartisanship with respect to liberal parties. Roscher regarded liberalism in politics and the liberal theoretical pattern in social science as intellectual frameworks of modernity in general, which could best be advanced by people like himself if they did not concern themselves with the day-to-day affairs of specific parties and interest organizations.[15] We have seen how this general attitude was adopted by the leaders of the *Verein für Sozialpolitik*—most notably by Gustav Schmoller. The *Verein*'s original plan of adopting a program of social reform based on the findings of objective, empirical social research was a model of the apolitical approach in action. The fact that it proved to be impossible to find consensus on interpretations of such research and thus impossible to develop a comprehensive reform program did not prevent Schmoller's conception of apoliticism from becoming a major focus of intellectual politics in the 1890s.[16]

We have already seen how Schmoller used his notion of apoliticism and his role as leader of establishment social science to advocate a gradualist, elitist approach to social change. Liberal reform should come about through a slow process of persuasion and education rather than through class conflict that fragmented the nation or through the operation of parties that became entangled with the limited interests of particular groups. Social scientists, through their research and through their engagement in politics from a nonpartisan standpoint, should do the persuading and educating. The basic institutions and the basic power structure of imperial Germany had to be accepted as the framework for reform and for political action—in much the same way that modern capitalism had to be accepted as the basis of the economy—however much they might be reshaped in detail to take broad social concerns into account.[17] Schmoller's apoliticism and that of many of his disciples in the *Verein* therefore revealed an intention to continue the process of accommodating liberalism to the new realities of power in Germany. Historical economics, with its institutional and cultural analysis of the process of change, was brought into the apoliticist community of discourse to support this intention.

Many social scientists, even ones attracted for intellectual and political reasons to the notion of scientific objectivity as a basis for political action, could not accept Schmoller's intentions and began, originally within the framework of the same community of discourse, to criticize Schmoller's whole approach.[18] Many of these people eventually found themselves drifting into other communities. The most important was Max Weber.

One of the aspects of apoliticism as practiced by Schmoller on which such critics as Weber fixed was its connection to the claim that social science was nomothetic. The assertion that social scientists could pronounce on political issues with the authority of objective social law behind them was essential to the apolitical community of discourse, but it was objectionable on several grounds. Both Weber, who operated within the community in the early 1890s, and Dilthey, who was always outside, believed that the nomothetic assertion was the basis of Schmoller's excessive accommodation of liberal reformism to the existing structure of power. The laws of social change had decreed that things should be as they are; so, they must be accepted as the context within which further change would occur. This reasoning, which made sense within the apolitical community of discourse, seemed to Weber and Dilthey to permit its employers to avoid the necessity of real social reform.[19] Equally important, the emphasis on the nomothetic assertion within the apolitical community of discourse obscured the need to reevaluate the assertion itself. Many trends in social and cultural science—particularly in historical economics and cultural history—suggested that social science could not really be a nomothetic or nomological enterprise like physics. If the social and cultural sciences were to make a reasonable claim to validity and significance, they would have to develop a theoretical basis that recognized the fundamental difference between themselves and physical science. But the utility of the nomothetic assumption within the apolitical community of discourse stood in the way of this needed reassessment. Social science clung stubbornly to its claim to be being a law-finding and law-applying enterprise.

Max Weber moved out of the apolitical community in the mid–1890s as he became a radical, although he always maintained some connections with it. The tension between his criticism of the nomothetic assumption and his continued attraction to ideas of apoliticism are revealed in his effort to define the boundaries and the behavioral attributes of "value-free" social science later in his career.[20]

Weber's assertion of the possibility of value-free social science reflected his belief that the academic social observer should try to separate his political convictions and activities from his professional research, as Schmoller (and Weber himself, in his early days) had not. Weber did not agree with Dilthey that scientific objectivity was impossible, but he did think that it was threatened by too close contact between the social scientist's politics and scholarship. But the kind of objective scholarship practiced by the conscientious social scientist could not be nomothetic in the traditional sense. This was another reason for separating it from politics with its overwhelming temptation to adopt a law-giving posture. Rather, fundamental considerations of epistemology required that the social scientist's representation of reality be regarded as partial and hypothetical, inevitably affected by the context within which the scholar operated.

Apoliticism as a community of political discourse affected the *cultural* sciences in two major ways. In the first place, it reinforced the tendency (which we shall examine more closely in the case of Friedrich Ratzel in chapter 12) to retain the nomothetic aim within prevailing theoretical patterns. In addition, it supported the notion that academic social science could, and ought to, approach politics from a standpoint that stood apart from the interplay of parties and ideologies. In the years immediately after 1900, this kind of thinking contributed to a tendency (that we shall examine later) to look to concepts of culture and to the cultural sciences as the basis of a new approach to politics: *Kulturpolitik.*[21]

Neoliberalism

The term *neoliberalism* is applied here to a Wilhelmian community of discourse in intellectual politics, but with many misgivings, because the word has already been used for an earlier phenomenon of liberal politics and cultural science. The neoliberals of the period 1890 to 1910 were not, for the most part, the same people who had developed the neoliberal theoretical pattern in cultural science in the 1860s and 1870s. Earlier reformers like Virchow and Bastian were considered by their successors to be somewhat old-fashioned, particularly with respect to certain issues around which many of the Wilhelmian neoliberals oriented their political activities: Should the liberal parties adopt a thoroughgoing social welfare platform that recognized the special needs of the industrial working class? And should the liberals accept overseas imperialism as a main thrust of German foreign policy? The older neoliberals generally answered "No" to both questions, whereas their Wilhelmian descendants usually answered "Yes."[22]

On the other hand, both old and new neoliberals continued to share a commitment to democratic political reform in Germany. Both criticized the National Liberals (and the adherents of apoliticism) for compromising with illiberal aspects of the Bismarckian state. Both acknowledged that in order to maintain the viability of liberalism in the modern world it was necessary to foster the integration of all classes into a participatory political system through the agency of the democratic franchise. Both usually accepted the need to operate through the medium of parliamentary liberal parties. And more deeply, all neoliberals shared one basic belief or attitude: that it was essential to modify specific elements of traditional liberalism in order to preserve the general thrust of the movement under new historical conditions. Older neoliberals had focused on the adoption of democratic interpretations of liberalism. Wilhelmian ones wanted to alter at least part of the individualist economic thinking that had often been used within the liberal camp to question the legitimacy of extensive social welfare policies and yet to preserve in some way the intellectual basis of rational individualism.[23]

The Wilhelmian neoliberal community of discourse, like the other communities of intellectual politics, intersected with theoretical patterns in the social and cultural sciences, with substantial effects on the latter. Max Weber, after operating within the apolitical and radical communities before 1900, eventually settled into the neoliberal one as neoliberalism was partly absorbed into the main liberal parties just before the First World War.[24] His brother Alfred associated himself even more thoroughly with neoliberalism.[25] The eventual success of the Weberian theoretical pattern in becoming a dominant force in sociology and related disciplines later in the twentieth century may well be linked to its founder's eventual connection with a community of discourse that, although it did not itself become a sustainable ideology, insinuated itself strongly into the general liberalism of Western Europe after the First World War.

One of the best examples of a cultural scientist who participated actively in the neoliberal community of discourse and whose academic work was affected by it was the economist Karl Bücher (1847–1930). Bücher was a leading figure at Leipzig University and was heavily influenced by his teacher, Wilhelm Roscher. The main thrust of Bücher's approach to cultural and social science was the idea of updating the traditional theoretical pattern of liberal social science to make it more directly applicable to modern industrial society.[26]

Bücher attempted to explain the nature of modern socioeconomic structure and behavior, and particularly of contemporary class conflict and alienation, in the context of cultural evolution. According to Bücher, alienation—primarily a psychological condition—arose when the modes of production characteristic of a society at a particular time were out of harmony with the culture that predominated among the people.[27] Reduction of alienation, and thus the reduction of social and political conflict, occurred when production and culture were adjusted to each other. This adjustment was not one-sided, as Marx had implied. The impetus to historical change may arise more often than not from production, but this is not inevitably the case, and in a stable society production adjusts itself to the prevailing culture as much as the elements of culture adjust themselves to production.[28] By *culture*, Bücher meant not just the ethical norms that concerned the more sociologically inclined social scientists at the turn of the century, but also such things as the rhythm and timing of work and leisure, the learned psychological frameworks within which people view the significance of their labor, their family roles, their play, and so forth—essentially anthropological factors.

Bücher's approach reflects many elements of his intellectual background: historical economics, his involvement with empirical survey research, his acquaintance with the literature of ethnology, and his involvement with the Leipzig Circle of cultural scientists that we shall examine shortly. But it also reflects his politics. According to Bücher, the adjustment of production to culture—indeed, the adjustment of any discordant element to culture in general—occurs most readily in a regime of freedom and openness in which public opinion (in some senses the formal, conscious manifestation of culture) can be readily established and can have political effect. Political action to end the alienation of the workers in modern society is needed, but it must be action that takes place within a context of consensus building in which workers and employers, state officials and citizens, interact readily with each other.[29] All of this was consistent with the outlook that defined the neoliberal community of political discourse. Bücher believed that his version of cultural and social theory could provide a scientific basis for political understanding between progressive liberals and the nondoctrinaire followers of Eduard Bernstein among the socialists.

Radicalism

The phenomenon of nonsocialist radicalism is one of the most difficult interpretive problems in the study of Wilhelmian Germany. It is a significant problem, however, first because many important intellectuals—including people as politically different as Max Weber, Karl Lamprecht, and Friedrich Ratzel—belonged to radical organizations such as the Pan-German League, and second, because of the influence that Wilhelmian radicalism had on the later formation of Nazism.

   Until recently, historians usually interpreted the kind of radicalism represented by the Pan-Germans as a conservative reaction on the part of members of Germany's social and intellectual elites to the processes of modernization and democratization.[30] Conservative outlooks were certainly well represented among participants in radical organizations, but recent studies have shown that in terms both of leadership and of membership, groups such as the Pan-German League and the Navy League were ideologically very broad and heterogeneous. They included people who welcomed and people who feared most aspects of modernization, people who believed that the traditional and monied elites needed to be curbed as well as people who favored close cooperation with them. Typically, members of the radical organizations belonged to the educated middle class—the kind of people who had in the past supported the liberal parties. Many, although not all, Pan-Germans still did—especially the National Liberals.[31]

   We are not directly concerned here with the radical organizations, but rather with a fairly short-lived community of discourse that appeared among academics and other intellectuals in the 1890s more or less simultaneously with their entry into such organizations. Identifying a radical community of discourse has major interpretive advantages. It allows us to avoid having to classify early and mid-Wilhelmian radicalism as being either conservative or progressive. Many, probably most, of the important radical intellectuals were, or had been, liberals of one sort or another and acknowledged an attachment to liberal nationalist traditions.[32] But their particular ideological allegiances in the early 1890s ran a substantial gamut, reflecting the fragmentation of liberalism as a political movement and ideology and the appearance of elements of what would eventually become radical conservatism. Also, focusing on the radical community of discourse permits us to explain how tendencies in intellectual politics that appear quite different to us now could be seen by intelligent social and cultural scientists at the time as assimilable to each other.

In the 1890s and just after 1900, many social and cultural scientists, including Ratzel, Weber, and Lamprecht, joined the Pan-German League and consciously engaged themselves in a political discourse centering around certain concepts and verbal formulas that were much employed within the league.[33] Many of these concepts and formulas arose from the political tradition of liberalism, although they were expressed in such a way as to criticize (often violently) current manifestations of liberalism in national politics. Indeed, one of the central assumptions of the radical community of intellectuals was that there was something seriously wrong with Germany's current political and social structure and that the models of traditional liberal political thought in Germany were inadequate sources of guidance for dealing with the situation. At the same time, the patchwork structure of the Bismarckian *Reich,* with its combination of liberal, autocratic, and bureaucratic elements, could not generate alternative models out of itself, and the socialist approach was, to most bourgeois radicals, out of the question.[34] The task, then, was to create a new basis of politics. In this, the radicals differed greatly from the adherents both of apoliticism, with their tendency to accept the status quo as a foundation for reform, and the neoliberals, who looked to democratic liberalism for that purpose.

In explaining what was wrong with Germany, radicals focused on the fragmentation of society and what they perceived as the consequent indecisiveness of the political system. Many of them tended to blame fragmentation and indecisiveness in part on liberal notions of party politics and on parliamentarism in general— thereby (quite consciously) reflecting the earlier moderate liberal distrust of parties (although not of parliaments), a distrust that can also be seen in Wilhelmian apoliticism.[35] (Weber was in a minority, although not alone, among the radicals in viewing parliaments as means of overcoming the political effects of social fragmentation, but even so, he fully developed this position only after leaving the Pan-German League and the radical community of discourse in the late 1890s.)[36]

More broadly, fragmentation was seen to be due to the existence of unresolved antagonisms among segments of the German population, of which the antagonism between the working classes and the bourgeoisie was probably the most important. Although some the radical intellectuals, including Weber and Lamprecht, were sympathetic to the working classes and willing to accept their organized participation as a class (through workers' parties and unions) in national politics, their view was not widely shared within the radical community of discourse. Specific positions on the social question varied, but the overall opinion was that Marxian socialism and the Social Democratic party had to be fought.[37] But it was not specific positions that made for community among radicals. Instead, it was an overall agreement that the most significant problem facing Germany was social fragmentation and its political consequences, not the points specifically at issue in the social question. Class conflict was unacceptable because it led to fragmentation, and the causes of class conflict (including the exploitation of the working class) could be eliminated if Germans thought of themselves as one people and if the political system could act decisively on the basis of national consensus.[38] Just *how* it should act on social issues was something about which radicals disagreed, but *that* it should act was not in dispute. This tendency to perceive social issues in the context of a politics of national consensus was, of course, another legacy of the liberal tradition to Wilhelmian radicalism, to which a new concern for decisive action was added.

The elite classes of Germany and the post-Bismarckian governments also came under considerable criticism from radical intellectuals. The tendency to attack governments for weakness in foreign policy and vacillation on domestic issues was partly a result of the structure of the Wilhelmian political system, in which the most effective means of attracting public attention and affecting policy was by taking strong oppositional stances. But it was also symptomatic of a general dissatisfaction among intellectuals with the way Germany was run and a consciousness of dissonance between the great respect accorded to people of education and the lack of real political power that the *Reich* afforded them.[39] This outlook, although not specifically liberal, certainly had roots in moderate liberal attitudes, especially among academics, earlier in the century.

The radical community also shared general notions of how fragmentation was to be overcome: through the enunciation of ideologies that were overtly nationalist and imperialist; through campaigns to force the government to adopt an aggressive, imperialist line in foreign policy (this would, in turn, encourage decisiveness in policy-making and popular identification with the aims of the nation as a whole); and through the development of an approach to politics and policy that centered around the concept of German culture.[40] Although radical cultural scientists involved themselves with the first two items (witness Lamprecht's attempt to formulate a kind of cultural imperialism as a basis for foreign policy and his advocacy of German support of the Afrikaner republics during the Boer War),[41] it was naturally the third that most often led to connections between their politics and their professional activities. The Pan-German League was particularly interested in enunciating an ideology based on German culture—indeed, its name arose from its aim of uniting all people of German language and culture into the *Reich*. The Pan-Germans and the equally radical *Ostmarkverein* focused heavily on the perceived need to Germanize eastern Prussia, eliminate elements of Polish culture there, and strength *Deutschtum* (a cultural concept) in the region through the settlement of German farmers on "unused" land.[42]

Rather than attempt a general analysis of the relationship between the radical community of discourse and cultural science, we shall examine particular instances in the latter part of the present chapter and in the discussion of *Lebensraum* in chapter 12. This is appropriate because the radical community among social and cultural scientists was never very homogeneous in composition or in specific thinking. Two examples can be cited briefly here, however. Leo Frobenius, a political radical of increasingly conservative leanings, provided "scientific" support for aggressive, bellicose imperialism as a basis of national political life by tracing societal aggressiveness back through the ethnological past and comparing organized violence in various cultures.[43] Frobenius insisted that humans are naturally warlike and that society is largely built around an underlying structure of aggression. Eduard Hahn, a renowned student of prehistoric culture and one of the few major ethnologists who avoided being co-opted by the diffusionists, used his studies of the origins of agriculture and the division of labor in primitive societies to argue quite explicitly in favor of authoritarian government and against democratic political reform, equality for women, and pacifism.[44]

The radical community of discourse among intellectuals and academics proved to be extremely unstable. Its adherents in the 1890s recognized the differences in political outlook among themselves, but they believed that in the fluid circumstances of the time, it would be possible to convert the shared elements that defined their community into an effective ideology and perhaps an effective political movement.[45] Among the reasons that the social and cultural scientists among them thought this might be possible was their apparent belief in the underlying unity of their professional disciplines and the capacity of the theoretical patterns of those disciplines to create part of the basis for a new approach to politics. They were aware also, of course, of the differences among themselves over questions of theory and methodology, but they thought that these, too, were symptomatic of an intellectual fragmentation that was undesirable and could be overcome by emphasizing commonalities. One of these commonalities was a vision of cultural science as a foundation for the social science of the future.[46]

The Wilhelmian radical intellectual politicians were wrong on almost all counts. Their differences over such political issues as the desirability of democratic political reform and the value of parliamentary institutions turned out to be stronger than their belief in their own underlying unity. The theoretical patterns to which the social scientists among them subscribed turned out to be more firmly established, and the differences between patterns more deeply etched, than they had thought. Members of the radical community of discourse fell away almost continuously from the late 1890s onward; by about 1907, it becomes difficult to identify a radical community at all. Instead, some radicals drifted into one form or another of apoliticism. Others aligned themselves with a newly revived reformist liberalism that was arising among a broad cross-section of the liberal parties and the Center party and that also absorbed much of the neoliberal community of discourse into itself.[47] Still others followed tendencies that could be seen in the Pan-German League as, under its new leader Heinrich Class, it made connections with conservative interest groups and, eventually, the conservative parties and adopted an ideology that can reasonably be called radical conservatism. It emphasized authoritarian notions already present in the earlier radical community of discourse, became more violently antisocialist and imperialist, and tended toward anti-Semitism.[48]

Thus the radical community of discourse and the other communities disappeared in the first decade of the twentieth century, to be replaced by more coherently structured ideologies associated with increasingly broad-ranging political coalitions. And with the communities of discourse, the idea of intellectual politics as an autonomous part of Germany's political structure, as a means of overcoming perceived deficiencies in political practice, also essentially disappeared.

But while it lasted, the era of intellectual politics strongly influenced theoretical directions taken by many cultural scientists. In chapter 12, we shall examine the connection between Friedrich Ratzel's concept of *Lebensraum* and intellectual politics and see how propagation of the idea was connected to the drawing of part of the Wilhelmian radical community of discourse into the general phenomenon of radical conservatism after Ratzel's death in 1904. In the remainder of the present chapter, we shall examine an attempt to create a unified cultural science that could be used as the basis of a broad-ranging intellectual politics transcending the turn-of-the-century communities of discourse. We shall also look at the reasons that the attempt failed.

The Leipzig Circle and the Politics of Unified Cultural Science

One of the most remarkable developments in German cultural science around the turn of the century was the appearance at Leipzig University of a group of outstanding academics—some of them cultural or social scientists by disciplinary calling, some professors of other subjects—who believed that a unified, nomothetic cultural science could be created. The establishment of such a science would work to reintegrate the increasingly fragmented philosophical disciplines in academia and assist in the process of creating political consensus among intellectuals. These beliefs led to very little of a permanent nature, but the attempt to create a unified cultural science had substantial effects on the professional lives of many members of the group. Following previous example, we shall call this group the *Leipzig Circle,* although the term may imply a degree of coherence and organization that is not really justified.[49]

The Leipzig Circle centered around a loose array of personal and intellectual relationships among important members of the Leipzig faculty between about 1890 and the First World War, augmented by extra-academic connections to the networks of publishers, businesspeople, and officials that had for decades been a significant feature of intellectual life in Saxony and Thuringia. The specific projects on which the Leipzig Circle (or some significant subset of them) can be said to have worked collectively was quite small. We shall focus shortly on one of them: a classic collection of essays on the nature of the modern metropolis called *Die Grossstadt.* For a time just after the turn of the century, however, their expectations about what they might accomplish together appear to have been high. In some senses, the Leipzig Circle represented a particular phase of the enthusiasm for intellectual politics among German academics—a Leipzig phase, coming at the end of a period of domination by Berlin.[50] The Leipzig phase was particularly notable for the extent to which it emphasized *Kulturpolitik*: the idea of orienting politics and policy-making around the culture concept.

The leading figures of the Leipzig Circle were, according to their own reports in their various memoirs, Wilhelm Wundt, Karl Lamprecht, Karl Bücher, and Friedrich Ratzel, to whom must be added Wilhelm Ostwald (1853–1932), one of the founders of physical chemistry, an early Nobel Prize winner, and, as Ernst Haeckel's successor as president of the German Monist League, one of the leaders of radical intellectual politics in the Wilhelmian era. There were also a number of lesser luminaries.[51]

The leading members were some of the most famous scholars in Germany. Most of them had made their careers as outsiders with rivalries of varying intensity going on with the orthodox establishments of their disciplines—establishments usually headquartered in Berlin. They shared other characteristics as well: usually, a background in liberal politics at some stage in their careers; a tendency to take their membership in the university's philosophical faculty very seriously and to regret philosophy's fragmentation into separate disciplines; and a belief that academics, as Germany's intellectual leaders, could and should play a leading role in the nation's politics.

What brought the members of the Leipzig Circle together, apart from these shared characteristics, was a deep interest in the subject of culture and in the possibilities of nomothetic cultural science as a means of approaching the study of modern society. What separated them were essentially two things: the fact that they belonged to different communities of discourse in intellectual politics and subscribed to different ideological tendencies within those communities and the fact that the theoretical patterns of cultural science they had adopted were different as well. The first fact they appear to have recognized, but they also seem to have believed that it did not matter very much because within the context of a unified cultural science that rose above mere politics, ideological differences could be contained or overcome.[52] They also believed that they shared a fundamental core of political ideas that arose from the liberal tradition and from national patriotism. The second point seems not to have been as clear to them, obscured as it was by the fact that they were all in the same camp in the competition with antinomothetic approaches to scholarship.

One of the most significant factors in the emergence of the Leipzig Circle was its setting: in the University of Leipzig and in Saxony. Certain features of this setting strongly influenced the kind of cultural science that emerged there.[53] One such feature was the runner-up attitude of the Saxon upper classes. Although Saxony had retained its political identity in the new *Reich* and although the Saxon economy had industrialized successfully, the country had been vastly overshadowed by its huge neighbor Prussia in almost every respect. The elites of Saxon politics, business, and intellectual life were therefore usually ready to support anything that would show Saxony to advantage in comparison with Prussia. This was part of the reason that they were so interested in supporting Leipzig University.

In the eighteenth century, Leipzig University had been widely regarded as Germany's leading university, but it had lost its predominance to the University of Berlin early in the nineteenth century. Lavishly supported by the Prussian state, Berlin University emerged as the source of innovations in curriculum and academic ideology that were rapidly adopted by the rest of the German universities. Leipzig University withdrew grumpily into Berlin's shadow until about the 1840s when the Saxon government and the leaders of Saxon society and business decided that it was time for Saxony to reassert itself and saw the university as one of the ways of accomplishing that end. They forced the university to adopt a modified version of the Berlin reforms and to seek out leading faculty in new and rapidly developing fields—especially fields directly relevant to Saxony's new policy of orderly economic development.[54] Leipzig's appointment of Wilhelm Roscher to its faculty in 1848 was a first deliberate step in turning Leipzig into a leading center of social studies.

Leipzig did in fact take the lead in several new fields—linguistics, for example, at midcentury, and historical economics shortly thereafter—only to have Berlin move in later. By the end of the century, Leipzig had assumed undisputed possession of second place among German universities. Leipzig still encouraged innovation. The more distinguished of its faculty had close and cordial links to the social and political elite of Saxony.[55] Most important, Leipzig tended to harbor theoretical patterns that deliberately challenged the ascendancy of those that were dominant in Berlin. We have already seen this in the case of Ratzel, who accepted an appointment at Leipzig in 1886 because he thought that the Leipzig atmosphere would be more congenial to new approaches to cultural science.[56]

Saxony also displayed certain peculiarities in socioeconomic development that affected the kind of social and cultural science professed there. Although Saxony had industrialized successfully and relatively rapidly, it had done so on the basis of an agricultural economy in which small farmers, not large estates as in Prussia, predominated and of a manufacturing sector in which skilled artisanal labor and cottage industry continued to play an unusually important role. Questions about cultural change in consequence of economic change—especially about whether or not the process of modernization had to be uniform—were in a sense more significant in Saxony than in many other places. Saxony also had one of the largest and most active branches of the Social Democratic party in the nation, which made the social question an issue of great importance for the Saxon elite and their close associates in local academia. In other words, the climate was particularly appropriate in Saxony for applying cultural science to problems of socioeconomic change.[57]

Finally, there was at Leipzig an intellectual tradition that arose from the influence and longevity on the faculty of two individuals: Wilhelm Roscher and Gustav Fechner—both of whom exerted an enormous (although posthumous) influence on the members of the turn-of-the-century Leipzig Circle. Although Roscher and Fechner differed from each other in many ways, they shared, and bequeathed to their successors, the idea that science was essentially uniform and that tendencies toward fragmentation in *Wissenschaft* had to be resisted.

As we have already seen, one of the keys to Roscher's approach was his deliberate attempt to connect economics to the rest of scholarship: in part by trying to replace abstract inference with empirical research based on historical analysis and cultural comparison and in part by putting economic theory in a larger context of cultural study. Much of Roscher's intellectual legacy to Leipzig University after his death in 1894 (apart from the fact that he had had a major say in the selection of three generations of professors in the philosophical faculty) lay in the assumptions about the connectedness of all social knowledge that were implicit in his work.[58] These assumptions were extremely attractive to academics because they permitted a vigorous defense of the philosophical faculty's traditional belief in the coherence of the liberal arts and the value of a general humanistic education. If a discipline, such as economics, that was supposed to deal directly with the most important contemporary issues of practical politics could best be conducted in an intellectual framework that stressed the historical and cultural embeddedness of social phenomena, then the other fields that investigated aspects of the historical and cultural context or that (like the classics) made the scholar sensitive to the values that permeated the context were just as significant in terms of immediate social and political utility. This accorded well with the general outlook of the Saxon elite, who favored adjustment to social change within an intellectual framework that was comfortably traditional.[59] It was necessary, however, to construct such a framework, one that would permit the integration of the various disciplines for purposes of contemporary social analysis. Apart from proposing a broadly defined conception of historical economics, Roscher did not move very far in that direction. The Leipzig Circle, which was composed to a large extent of people who had been Roscher's students or junior colleagues, consciously tried to finish the job.

Gustav Fechner (1801–1887) was for most of his life an intellectual fixture of Leipzig University, influential among students, professors, and the local intellectual community at large.[60] He was recognized in his own time as a man of genius in many fields, although he is best known today as one of the pioneers of modern psychology—specifically as the formulator of Fechner's law, which relates the intensity of stimuli to the intensity of attendant sensations according to a mathematical equation. In Leipzig in the late nineteenth century, however, his influence across the disciplines was due mainly to his connected beliefs in the unity of science and the vitality of the universe. Friedrich Ratzel, who had been at Leipzig only a very short time when Fechner died in 1887 and may never have met him, claimed that Fechner's ideas about these things fundamentally affected his own thinking at the height of his career.[61]

Fechner postulated the existence of an underlying unity of physical and psychic existence and held that it was the prime goal of science to establish, preferably in the form of mathematical laws, the nature of this unity. Living forces animated the physical world; physics and psychology thus studied aspects of the same thing, and linkages of a similar sort should also be established among the other disciplines. Fechner thus combined elements of the vitalism that had been popular in Romantic scientific thought early in the century with a commitment to a severely nomothetic approach to science that would appeal to the most extreme positivist. This made Fechner especially popular among intellectuals who wanted to be able to account themselves scientists of the type now dominant in the exact physical sciences without having to subscribe to the radical philosophical materialism with which the type had been commonly identified. To many, radical materialism was intellectually unsatisfactory, politically suspect, and inconsistent with the philosophical idealism that held pride of place at German universities in the later nineteenth century. Fechner's approach legitimated attempts to understand thought and consciousness (central features of the idealist tradition) from an empirical and nomothetic standpoint without adopting the hermeneutic approach of *Geisteswissenschaft*. By implication, however, these attempts had to be coordinated with one another because no particular discipline could reveal the totality of connections among life forces, physical existence, sensation, and consciousness. To Fechner all science, all scholarship must be part of the same transcendental endeavor. Fechner was not, however, very clear about how the unity of science was to be manifested. This may perhaps explain why a methodological debate did not arise in response to his writings in the way that one did over, for example, Lamprecht's assertions. There was little methodology to debate.

The spirit of Fechnerian vitalism and Fechnerian scientific unity spread very widely at Leipzig and intersected with other intellectual currents moving in the same general direction—especially the popular scientific philosophy of Ernst Hae-ckel and his disciples. At Leipzig, the juncture of these currents was represented by the participation of Wilhelm Ostwald (a scientist influenced by Fechner and Haeckel's successor as head of the German Monist League) in the activities of the Leipzig Circle and other interdisciplinary groups.[62] Leipzig scientific thought was also influenced by international movements, such as Comtean positivism, but the outlook of the Leipzig Circle seems primarily to have been shaped by home-grown tendencies.

A combination of these and other factors—some present in the social and political context of late nineteenth-century Saxony, some in the peculiar intellectual circumstances of Leipzig University—combined to create an environment in which the idea of an interdisciplinary, nomothetic science focusing on culture (one that could be applied to issues of current politics) was particularly attractive. Added to these factors was another: the presence at Leipzig at the turn of the century of a number of first-rate academics who happened to be interested in much the same thing from different perspectives. Of course, their presence was only partly for-tuitous because people such as Roscher and Fechner had tended to favor the ap-pointments of new professors who thought along the same lines as they did.

The activities of the Leipzig Circle took many forms. There were regular (and usually informal) meetings among like-thinking scholars from various disciplines—especially Ratzel, Bücher, Wundt, Ostwald, and Lamprecht.[63] The central core of members of the Leipzig Circle was supplemented by other Leipzig faculty of less distinction or less regular attendance at exchanges of ideas and, apparently, also by important people from the publishing, business, and government worlds. The informal interactions of the members of the Leipzig Circle led to a loosely defined agenda that manifested itself in a number of formal interdisciplinary efforts just after the turn of the century. These were organized through the university and through the network of intellectual societies for which Saxony was noted. In the decade before the First World War, certain new, permanent institutions at Leipzig University—especially Lamprecht's Institute for Universal History and, to some extent, Bücher's Institute for the Study of Journalism—also embodied the spirit of the Leipzig Circle.[64]

The Leipzig Circle's agenda can be described in very broad terms, although much of it has to be inferred from members' individual statements and from the parallel theoretical directions they took after becoming associated with each other rather than from any formal program.[65] They all believed that it was possible to create a general, nomothetic human science applicable to understanding modern society and current social problems. They agreed that such a science was, in some senses, immanent in the humanistic approach to knowledge central to traditional education in Germany and that the full assertion of its existence would reestablish the connections between disciplines that had recently diverged. The universal sci-ence would also provide one means of establishing coherence among the various communities of discourse in intellectual politics and of recommending decisive policies for the *Reich*. The science would be historical in structure, embodying among other things the insights of historical economics, but the central concept around which it would be constructed was *culture*. The universal human science would be, in effect, the culmination of the development of nomothetic cultural science through the turn of the century. It would be constructed within the general tradition of intellectual liberalism and in a thoroughly liberal manner: through the reasoned intercourse of educated, thoughtful people conducted openly before an educated public.[66]

The Leipzig Circle's activities resulted in a disappointingly small array of joint productions, and the circle itself had largely dissolved by the First World War. Its greatest impact can be seen in the work of individual members: Lamprecht's plans for universal history, Ratzel's *Lebensraum,* and Wundt's final, broad version of *Völkerpsychologie*. All of these were built on foundations laid down before the turn of the century, but as we shall see in the case of Ratzel in chapter 12, they marked substantial movements away from earlier work. In the remainder of the present chapter, however, we shall focus on one of the relatively few collective works embodying the outlook of the Leipzig Circle.

Die Grossstadt, published in Dresden in 1903, was a collection of essays on the modern metropolis from different disciplinary perspectives. It was the product of a conference organized by the editor of the collection, the publisher and scholar Theodor Petermann (a fixture of the Saxon business and intellectual elite) through one of the foundations that made up the Saxon-Thuringian cultural science network.[67] The contributors to the collection included some of the most famous Leipzig academics (including leaders of the Leipzig Circle, such as Ratzel and Bücher) together with a leavening of scholars from Berlin. It was one of the major works in the development of urban studies in Germany, and some of the pieces, especially the papers contributed by Ratzel and Georg Simmel, became classics.[68] Like the Leipzig Circle itself, the contributors to *Die Grossstadt* represented many different communities of political discourse. Their participation in the project indicates a common acceptance of the idea that interdisciplinary cultural science could be successfully applied to current social problems and that it could transcend differences in political viewpoint.

The problem with which they were dealing was a very current one. In the previous decade and a half, the rapid growth of large industrial cities had revealed even more vividly than previously the need for new ways of looking at urban phenomena, new modes of administrative organization, new approaches to economic and social policy in urban agglomerations. The policy and social welfare problems of big-city life had become a topic of discussion and research in the *Verein für Sozialpolitik* in their own right. But the question of the big city had emerged as a major issue in the 1890s even more because of its political significance in the context of the furious dispute over economic development that had arisen from the Caprivi government's policy of reducing agricultural tariffs in order to expand industrial markets abroad.[69]

The question of tariff policy mobilized agricultural interests (including, but not limited to, the *Junker* elite of Prussia) and gave them a common cause in opposing both Caprivi's policies and the kind of thinking that lay behind it: the idea that Germany's future lay in further industrialization, the expansion of which should be the main aim of national policy.[70] The organized manifestation of opposition to industrialization, the *Bund der Landwirte,* put together all existing ideological elements of political life that could be bent to its purpose in order to bolster the argument that agricultural tariffs, by protecting the culture and social structure of rural Germany, were performing a service for all of the nation. Most of the agrarian ideology (the origins and effects of which we have already examined) was arrayed for the purpose. Social and cultural scientists, such as Adolf Wagner, whose scholarly perspectives were partly established by their agrarianism were brought by that means into the tariff debate.

The tariff issue was a particularly attractive and yet difficult one for academics interested in intellectual politics. It was attractive because its generalization into a debate on national economic policy gave huge scope for their expertise and an opportunity to show what a disciplined, social scientific approach to issues could achieve.[71] Cultural scientists were especially attracted because the central questions had to do with the relationship between culture and socioeconomic change. The issue was difficult because it tended to divide existing communities of political discourse. Although probably most neoliberals favored low tariffs and industrialization, the fact that it was fashionable among intellectuals to decry the defects of modernity put such people on the defensive and made them apologetic. The radical and apolitical communities were sharply split, particularly the former. Many radical nationalists were committed to Germany's industrial expansion as a source of strength in international politics, but at the same time they had subscribed to part, at least, of the critique of modernity that was implicit in the agrarian ideology. The Pan-German League put off a decision about whether or not to oppose the tariff reduction and support the *Bund* as long as possible. When it did support the agricultural interest, it predictably lost members, such as Max Weber, who believed that the *Bund* and, indeed, the whole tariff issue were merely covers for an attempt by the *Junkers* to hold onto power.[72]

The issue of the big city and its place in modern society and culture—the subject of *Die Grossstadt*—became fashionable in large part because of the tariff and development debate. Not only was the modern metropolis the location of many of the problems of modern society that the agrarians decried, but the image of the metropolis itself was composed of images of modernity against which the opponents of industrialization could effectively focus their attacks. People not opposed to the low-tariff policy or those who saw compensating virtues in modernity found in the metropolis a set of vivid, concrete representations of the conceptual problems with which they had to deal if they wanted to make their position intellectually respectable.[73] We see both of these uses of the big city in *Die Grossstadt.*

Theodor Petermann was probably a little disappointed in the results of his effort at interdisciplinary engineering. A consensus did not in fact emerge at the conference, and Petermann, as editor, made no serious attempt to construct one in the published proceedings. It may have been that he had expected, in traditional liberal fashion, that a general sense would appear as the participants worked on their assigned topics and discussed them with each other; when none did (despite the apparently serious efforts of at least Ratzel and Bücher), he made the best of a bad job. It is difficult to see how, considering the range of viewpoints and quality of the contributions, he could have done otherwise. Yet the collection is truly a classic of German urban studies by virtue of the strength of some of the individual contributions—many of which manifest the Leipzig Circle's notion of what a universal cultural science should be like.

The first essay in the book was by Karl Bücher, whose theoretical and political viewpoints we have already discussed.[74] His version of social science focused on the cultural and psychological aspects of the stages of human history. It was therefore appropriate that the task that Petermann assigned him was to write about "the metropolis past and present."

As a prominent member of the neoliberal community of political discourse and as a supporter of the low-tariff policy, Bücher, on the whole, has good things to say about the modern city. In the tradition of historical economics, he presents the *Grossstadt* as a product of irreversible social evolution that must be accepted. The cities of classical times were, he claims, largely continuous with the surrounding countryside, whereas medieval and modern cities are economically and culturally differentiated from their environs.[75] The cultural separation of the city from the country in the Middle Ages permitted a division of labor between them, followed by specialization among cities. Within the cities developed a distinctive way of life (connected with craft production) around which a feeling of community grew. The medieval city set the stage for the next development: the modern city.

The modern metropolis, Bücher continues, is a product not so much of industrialization as of the earlier urban exchange economy and the modern nation-state. The latter destroyed the city's political autonomy, widened its markets, and fostered an increase in its size through immigration.[76] Industrial production evolved in this context, and around the factory (a sociocultural form) rather than around the machine. Because the development of the present cultural stage is not yet complete, there are disharmonies between characteristics of modern production and older economic and cultural forms. Nowhere are these disharmonies more obvious than in the city, which therefore lacks a sense of community. But a metropolitan culture will appear and with it a new sort of community sense—clues to which are already present. The *Grossstadt,* according to Bücher, is the "pathbreaker on the road to an upward-striving, truly social cultural environment."[77]

Bücher's piece is a good example of neoliberal cultural science in a framework of historical economics. It also illustrates some of the weaknesses of the approach. Bücher has accepted the urban–rural dichotomy as fundamental—a dichotomy derived as much from the agrarian ideology as from observation, and one that did not completely fit, for example, the realities of the situation in Saxony. Although he asserts the future value of urban culture, he acknowledges the deficiencies of the present version in many of the same terms used in anti-industrial propaganda. In essence, Bücher adopts a politically defensive posture as a consequence of the theoretical pattern and the vocabulary he employs. The political implication of his analysis is quite traditional among moderate liberals: the problems created by industrialization and urbanization will sort themselves out in time. This was not an implication that appealed to radicals of any ideological tendency.

Friedrich Ratzel's contribution to *Die Grossstadt,* an essay on the geographical situation of big cities, is a Ratzelian classic that influenced two generations of academic geographers.[78] Ratzel begins (typically, for him) by differentiating between aspects of the urban environment, assigning them places in an implied hierarchy of value. He claims that humans bear four sorts of relationship to the *Boden,* or soil: relationships to the specific place where they live, to their *Heimat* (the place where they feel at home), to the land from which they derive their sustenance, and to the land that protects them from their enemies.[79] The degree of emotional attachment to the *Boden* decreases as one goes down the list. These types are then used as a framework within which to define the nature of a city, which is characterized by a high level of coincidence between the places where people live and the places from which they obtain their livings—as well as by other factors, such as a dynamic, changing relationship between inhabitants and their physical environments and by the conjuncture of transport facilities in one place.[80] The historical character of a city is determined to a large extent by the ways in which people move commodities through the neighboring land and sea. Cities usually appear at transport bottlenecks; their cultures are partly formed out of their relationships, through transport, with their hinterlands.

It quickly becomes clear that Ratzel is trying to develop general laws of urban development from these insights. His aim is nomothetic, but he forms his generalizations in terms of central tendencies in complex sets of data over time and accepts a great deal of variation. To present his laws of urban growth he sets up another system of classes, this time of relationships between a city and its hinterland. A city has a "natural" hinterland (the part of its environs that affects individuals' sensibilities) as well as political, productive, marketing, and trading ones. (Hamburg and Danzig [now Gdańsk] are both seaports, but their characters are different because the latter, as a result of tariffs, has a more restricted marketing hinterland.) In principle, a city's future can be predicted through the use of laws revealed by Ratzel's scheme.

The point about Danzig is a reference to the dropping of Caprivi's policy and the raising of agricultural duties in 1902 which, by prevoking Russian retaliation, boded ill for the city's economic future. Even when he is at his most "scientific," Ratzel is seldom far from politics; political implications are typically unstated, but obvious. Ratzel was generally committed to agrarian primacy, although he was not irreconcilably opposed to modernity or industrial society. Although modernization (in the form of the big city, among other things) threatened the rural environment and rural culture, the threat could be avoided by state policy.

Ratzel's essay sounds some of his other favorite themes. Cities, like other social phenomena that reflect the interaction between humans and their environments, have a natural tendency to grow.[81] Their growth patterns are influenced by their specific locations and the nature of the land around them. A city on a hill will expand to encompass other hills, and so forth. Urban expansion is natural, patterned, and predictable—and the modern metropolis is no exception simply because it is big. If national urban policy were built around the laws of growth that Ratzel expounds, cities could continue to expand by incorporating other places like themselves without threatening the places where small agricultural towns predominate. Truly huge cities, Ratzel says, usually appear in areas where there are few other cities and a low rural population density. Other areas have multiple middle-sized cities. If state policy accorded with natural laws, there would be ample room for the geographical bases of traditional culture in an industrial society. Cultural despair? Not here. Ratzel is certainly a radical in politics, but he gives no hint that he thinks that industrialization and urbanization are incompatible with maintaining the agrarian roots of German culture. He ends by describing cities as monuments to human permanence and the modern city as the probable site of a coming high point in the continuous cultural development of humankind.[82]

The other essays in *Die Grossstadt* display a variety of theoretical and political postures. Georg von Mayr, later to be the dean of the German geographical establishment, discusses the sizes of cities and the volume of migration into them in the nineteenth century.[83] Mayr represents the tradition of descriptive statistics so strong in German social science. Only at the end of the essay does he attempt generalizations. The most important of these—that in order to function, big cities must continue to grow by taking in immigrants—does not appear to be supported by his statistics. It is rather a product of the organic metaphors that Mayr, like Ratzel, uses—metaphors that have, as we shall see in chapter 12, important political implications. There is also an essay by a Dr. H. Waentig on the economic significance of the city that devotes nearly forty pages to restating a political theme treated more interestingly by Ratzel and Bücher: cities, Waentig writes, are essential to commerce and industry, but at present the social contrast between them and the countryside (especially the intensity of urban class conflicts) threatens the stability of politics.[84] But hopefully the further evolution of the metropolis will see the overcoming of these problems. Waentig and especially Mayr appear to represent the apolitical community of discourse in claiming that an impartial examination of statistics will yield the appropriate basis of policy-making.

Dietrich Schäfer, newly appointed professor of history at the University of Berlin, was, like Ratzel, a radical nationalist with a National Liberal political background, but his politics were much more violent and militaristic.[85] His essay on the military significance of the metropolis displays his politics quite openly, following the example of his mentor Treitschke.[86] Schäfer shares with Ratzel the same framework for urban analysis, but their differing concerns about political implications shows the range of outlooks that existed within the radical community.

According to Schäfer, cities have become important because they are the decision-making political centers of modern states and therefore the places around which military operations revolve. For this reason, and because of their industrial capacities, they are essential to modern warfare. They are also dangerous. The excessive concentration of French political and military control in Paris contributed to the German victory in 1870–1871. To prevail in the struggle among nations, a country ought to lessen its dependency on big cities.

From this relatively limited strategic analysis, Schäfer turns to a much broader critique. The urbanization of culture (which Paris again illustrates) is a fundamental threat to the well-being and strength of a *Volk*.[87] Big cities, by shoving all sorts of people together, promote a dangerous degree of ''democracy'' in all aspects of life and an eventual tyranny of urbanism over the more stable and ordered countryside. The culture of the countryside is the real basis of a nation's strength because the virtues instilled in farmers by rural culture are those that make good soldiers. The modern metropolis erodes these virtues, warps the education of the young, and thus weakens the nation. Cities breed socialism and class conflict. To prevent this, all of society must work to protect the bases of rural culture, to reinstate its dominance, and to integrate urban culture into it.[88] Schäfer, in other words, restates the standard agrarian cultural line in his specific context, using it to support his radical nationalism, his opposition to working-class socialism (Schäfer was one of the few leading scholars of his time who came from a working-class family), and his tendency toward anti-industrialism.

Most of the contributions to *Die Grossstadt* noted thus far display similarities in general approach, despite differences over specific interpretations and political implications. Most of the major contributors address the subject of the metropolis from the standpoint of nomothetic cultural science as it was generally understood by the Leipzig Circle. That is, in terms of the traditional model of liberal social science, they downplay the significance of the rational individual in their analysis and emphasize collective cultural factors, they attempt to derive or apply social and cultural laws, and they place modern urban phenomena in a developmental historical context. Schäfer, as a historian, would probably not claim that he is deriving laws, but he certainly draws conclusions from recent history that are meant to be applied as prescriptive rules to other situations. The contributors show a substantial range of political attitudes, from Bücher's neoliberalism to Schäfer's radical antiurbanism. However, most of them share the belief that, although there is a great deal wrong with the present culture of the city, in time urban problems will be corrected. (Schäfer is an exception to this.) Approaching urban phenomena from the standpoint of nomothetic cultural science does, then, seem to have created the basis for a fair amount of apparent consensus—although what could be done with the consensus is somewhat difficult to say.

The most remarkable of the contributions to *Die Grossstadt*, however, does not fit into the same pattern as the others. It is Georg Simmel's essay on "The Metropolis and Spiritual Life," which was one of the first works with which Simmel established his place as a major innovator in social thought and which is still considered a classic of Simmel's sociology.[89]

Simmel was an outsider both at his own institution (Berlin University) and in German academia at large. Born to wealthy Jewish parents, his background made him highly objectionable to anti-Semites like Dietrich Schäfer. (Later Schäfer advised the Baden educational authorities not to appoint Simmel to a professorship at Heidelberg—despite Max Weber's warm support—on the grounds that Simmel's work displayed his Jewishness and his lack of grounding in the intellectual framework of German culture. He cited as evidence Simmel's essay in *Die Grossstadt*, which had evidently been the subject of considerable dispute at the conference that preceded publication. Simmel did not get the job.)[90] Simmel was also a democratic, progressive liberal—clearly a member of the neoliberal community of political discourse. Like Dilthey and Max Weber (in their different ways), Simmel believed that the existing theoretical frameworks of social and cultural science were a hindrance to liberalizing German society. Like Dilthey but unlike Weber, he refused to flirt with radicalism as a response to the weakness of political liberalism, and unlike Bücher, he refused to attempt to modify nomothetic, historical cultural science from within in order to make it more effective as a means of understanding the modern world. Instead, influenced by Dilthey, the neo-idealist advocates of *Geisteswissenschaft,* and to some extent Weber, Simmel struck out on his own. His essay in *Die Grossstadt* was one of the first clear evidences of his new approach, and it did not sit well with the other contributors.[91]

In his essay, Simmel reveals one of the main thrusts of his general approach, which is to put the individual back at the center of social and cultural analysis. Simmel shared the general consensus that the abstract model of the rational individual was inadequate, but he did not accept the ways in which most nomothetic cultural scientists had set about replacing it. Instead of looking at collective cultural entities as objects about which lawful generalizations could be made that would explain individual behavior, Simmel questioned the need to make lawful statements at all if it meant losing the focus on the individual and the individual's perceptions and attitudes.[92] The essence of social science to him was the observer's impressions of the mental life and behavior of people, not the production of scientific laws. His generalizations tended to be catalogues of the multiple ways in which individuals associated with each other and the ways in which they gave meaning to their associations. Although Simmel by no means rejected all of the aims of nomothetic cultural science, his essay in *Die Grossstadt,* in which his approach was clearly manifest, was regarded by other contributors as an unexpected challenge from the "antipositivist" schools of social thought.

Simmel's essay is really an exercise in social psychology rather than in cultural science as the latter had been defined in Germany. He describes the modern city as a unique environment impinging uniquely on the senses of the people who live there. Extremely varied sensory impressions follow one another quickly and compete for attention. The urban dweller must process impressions and fit them mentally into a coherent pattern at a very fast rate. This, together with structural factors such as the concentration of the apparatus of commercial capitalism in the metropolis, means that the rhythm of life (both external and internal to the individual) is literally accelerated in the big city. To people new to the city or to those mentally tied to a slower-paced agricultural society, the impact of the metropolis is disorienting and frightening. But to those accustomed to the pace of urban existence, a whole new (and for the most part attractive) way of life is opened up. Urban life is exciting, and it offers opportunities for the development of individual mental capabilities at all social levels. On this basis, a new form of culture is emerging that will be the foundation for the spiritual life of the future. The main task of urban culture—one that it is already beginning to perform—is to transcend the apparent contradiction between individualism and imposed sociocultural conformity, *both* of which are pushed to their extremes in the modern city.

There is a great deal more in Simmel's essay, but from this summary can be seen the extent of Simmel's deviation from the thinking of the Leipzig Circle. In terms of cultural theory, he focuses on individual impressions and makes culture dependent on them rather than the other way around. He does not try to find or apply laws. And although there are suggestions about developments in culture over time, he employs neither a stage schema nor a historical perspective to locate his subject and make predictions. His position corresponds to his progressive liberal political orientation: he gives the modern metropolis a ringing defense rather than apologizing for its problems, and he presents the values of progress and individualism in a new and assertive form. Although his political orientation was in fact similar to Bücher's, its manifestation in his contribution to *Die Grossstadt* took a notably different form because he broke with the theoretical patterns to which Bücher, like the other contributors, subscribed.

All this was too much for Theodor Petermann, the editor. Although he recognized the contribution of big cities to cultural life, he also shared the fashionable attitude of many intellectuals who saw the metropolis as a concentration of what was dangerous in modernity. Petermann claimed that a more balanced account was needed than Simmel had provided, one closer to Petermann's conception of the assigned subject and to the pattern of Leipzig cultural science. So Petermann exercised his editorial prerogative of including Simmel's piece but supplementing it with an essay of his own on the same subject, concentrating on his own field: publishing.[93] He emphasizes the ambivalent effect of the big city on this essential element of modern culture. The metropolis has quickened intellectual life by concentrating it and creating opportunities for writers from all over the country, but it has also led to increasing dominance over publishing—and thus over intellectual life itself—by the daily newspapers. This lowers the level of intellectual discourse. On the whole, the metropolis ends up with a clear deficit on the spiritual account of Petermann's balance sheet.

Die Grossstadt was one of the major products of the fashion for urban studies in Germany before the First World War, and Ratzel and Simmel's contributions became classics in their authors' own fields. But otherwise the collection, like the Leipzig Circle's whole attempt to create an integrated cultural science and direct it toward current problems, led to very little. Few new policy ideas arose from the project, and little progress was made toward political accommodation even among the participants. In fact, if the case of Schäfer and Simmel is any indication, antagonisms may have been sharpened by confrontations over theory, methodology, and political implications in the course of the project. Certainly, no new consensus, either about policy or theoretical approaches, was produced. Why was this?

A great many reasons could be given for the overall failure of the Leipzig Circle: the early death of Ratzel in 1904, the unwillingness of Leipzig professors to give up the considerable autonomy they possessed, the increasing tendency of disciplines to be organized independently of one another, and so forth. But the factors that stand out in the example of *Die Grossstadt* are the incompatibilities among the different theoretical patterns to which members of the Leipzig Circle subscribed as well as among the communities of political discourse to which they belonged. Apart from the substantial theoretical differences evident in *Die Grossstadt* between Simmel and the others, there were also major distinctions between Bücher's stage approach to cultural change and Ratzel's environmentalism, between Petermann's notion of the relationship of economic change to intellectual structure and Bücher's, and so forth. The political differences between Bücher and Ratzel are obvious as are, indeed, the differences between two radicals like Ratzel and Schäfer. Moreover, particular theoretical patterns and particular communities of political discourse did not necessarily coincide as pairs. In the decade that followed the publication of *Die*

Grossstadt, as communities of political discourse dissolved and ideological polarization increased, connections between theoretical patterns and ideological tendencies became stronger, as we shall see in chapter 12. But this made it even more difficult to promote common approaches to social questions among cultural scientists.

Nevertheless, although the Leipzig Circle's own efforts to create a unified, practical cultural science (as exemplified in *Die Grossstadt*) were failures and although the circle itself dissolved before 1914, there was some fallout. One of the effects of its activities was to publicize the idea (designated as *Kulturpolitik*) that the study, identification, and propagation of German culture should underlie German policy and politics in general. This idea became very popular among academics in the decade or so before the First World War. Its most persistent advocate was Lamprecht, who was supported not only by many of his colleagues at Leipzig who joined the various organizations devoted to *Kulturpolitik,* but also, after 1909, by Lamprecht's old schoolmate Bethmann Hollweg, the imperial chancellor. Bethmann, himself an intellectual who believed in the traditional ideal of rule by a humanistically educated civil service elite, agreed with Lamprecht that an emphasis in politics and mass education on cultural identity and cultural expansion would be a significant response to Germany's domestic social problems. He also agreed with Lamprecht's enthusiastic belief that a self-assertive German foreign policy could be presented (especially to other countries) as a result of Germany's desire to share her cultural (i.e., intellectual, artistic, and scientific) accomplishments with the rest of the world.[94]

The fashion for *Kulturpolitik* has been investigated in depth by Rüdiger vom Bruch. It attracted academics and other intellectuals from all disciplines, and within the social and cultural sciences, from among adherents of all theoretical patterns and almost all ideological dispositions (with the exception of some of the most bellicose radical nationalists.)[95] Not surprisingly, the same thing occurred that happened to the Leipzig Circle. Instead of the culture concept imposing coherence and unity among theoretical approaches and encouraging political cooperation among intellectuals, the *Kulturpolitik* movement fragmented along the lines of divisions among theoretical patterns and ideologies. Neoliberals like Lamprecht interpreted the political significance of *Kulturpolitik* differently from Schmoller and the defenders of of accommodation with the existing order (and thus probably differently from Lamprecht's backer, Bethmann). Scholars operating from different theoretical bases interpreted the meaning of culture and cultural study in quite divergent ways. Even Lamprecht's enemies in the historians' *Methodenstreit* of the 1890s—members of the Prussian and Rankean schools and people influenced by neo-Kantian idealism—became interested in culture as an object of study.[96] This had important intellectual effects, in that it encouraged the development of an approach to cultural history outside the nomothetic and Burckhardtian traditions among some of the leaders of the Prussian historical establishment. But because such people did not in the process seriously alter their assumptions about the nature and purpose of historical study, the new interest in cultural history did not work, as Lamprecht and others hoped, to reintegrate the philosophical disciplines any more than the efforts of the Leipzig Circle had done.

There were many other ways in which the major theoretical trends in cultural science were connected with politics before, during, and after the turn of the century in Germany, but only one of them will be pursued here. In the next chapter, we shall examine the relationship between theoretical developments in human geography and the ideology of radical nationalism, focusing on the concept of *Lebensraum*.

12

Lebensraum—Theory and Politics in Human Geography

Thus far we have been concerned with the interaction between politics and cultural science mainly from the standpoint of how the the former affected the latter. The relationship can, of course, go the other way. The fact that ideologies or current political issues can influence the structure of theory in the social sciences is often due to the previous absorption into ideology of concepts and vocabulary from the world of theory. And ideas from social science, even those adopted in politics mainly as a form of legitimation, can become important guidelines for policy in their own right. Darwinism, for example, was used throughout Europe in the later nineteenth century to legitimate preexisting ideologies (*laissez-faire* liberalism, imperialism, etc.). But the Darwinian conception of the dynamics of life also strongly affected the ways in which social Darwinists constructed the political world around them.[1] Theoretical structures with strong affinities to ideologies can, by influencing political thinking, also influence the outcome of politics.

In the present chapter, we shall consider an example of this: *Lebensraum,* a concept developed by Friedrich Ratzel ostensibly as a contribution to cultural and biological science.[2] *Lebensraum* had its roots in the interaction between radical nationalist politics and one of the theoretical patterns that emerged from liberal social science. Its immediate context was the radical community of political discourse at the turn of the century. Although Ratzel's classic presentation of *Lebensraum* displayed it as a purely scientific idea, its connections to then-current political debates over economic policy and imperialism were obvious and immediately publicized. *Lebensraum* ultimately found its way into the vocabulary of the German right in the 1920s and into Hitler's foreign policy.

Ratzel was, as we have seen, primarily a geographer. He regarded his excursions into ethnology as subsidiary endeavors in his quest to establish an all-inclusive human geography in the tradition of Karl Ritter, the founding father of theoretical academic geography. Ritter's aim, to uncover the laws governing the interaction between humankind and its physical environment, had been taken up from the 1850s by his students at Berlin and his followers elsewhere. Some concentrated on specific fields that had immediate economic or political significance.[3] Others continued the Humboldt–Ritter tradition of geography as the study of the whole, as the framework for all science.

Ratzel was one of the leading generalists. Ratzel never studied under Ritter and was not a member of the clique of Ritter's successors in the 1870s—people such as Oscar Peschel and Ferdinand von Richthofen who had close links with the Prussian government.[4] But with the publication of *Anthropo-Geographie* in the early 1880s, it was Ratzel who became the leading figure in constructing a human geography. He did so within the general disciplinary framework established by Ritter and his followers, but he imposed his own perspective.

Some of the factors that informed the ethnological aspect of Ratzel's anthropogeography were discussed in earlier chapters—especially the various antagonisms between generational groups with respect to Darwinian theory, colonialism, politics, and the dominance of the Berlin anthropological establishment. Many of these contextual factors applied also to the larger framework of Ratzel's geography and were joined by others as time went on to influence Ratzel's ultimate development of the *Lebensraum* concept. But before we consider such factors, we must look at the theoretical problems of human geography as Ratzel perceived them during the 1880s and 1890s—using as a guide, once again, the structure of the traditional liberal theoretical pattern in social science and Ratzel's response to it.

As we have seen, Ratzel's cultural science tended to displace the rational individual—indeed, the individual however defined—from the center of attention.[5] What was important to Ratzel was the group, the nation, the *Volk,* the state—the collectivities within which humans lived, established their identities, and confronted their environments. Collectivities possessed cultures made up of thousands of traits. Cultures, by structuring individual consciousness, largely shaped most of the historically significant part of human behavior. A culture was not a mere response to the physical environment in which a group lived. *Völker* could interpret and alter their environments on the basis of capabilities implicit in their cultures—for example, when a colony of peasant farmers took over the land of a pastoral people and reordered it according to their own agricultural customs. But cultures did, over time, form themselves through dealing with the limits imposed by particular environments. Although he was not a radical environmental determinist, Ratzel believed that environment was the most important influence on cultural and social forms, and therefore on the content of individual minds.

The implications of Ratzel's thinking about individuals, groups, and environments for the traditional liberal theoretical pattern have already been examined. The important question for Ratzel as geographer was what to do with the explanatory framework he had developed in his *Anthropo-Geographie.* He could, of course, have focused on the ways in which culture mediates between the environment and the minds of individuals—a kind of environmental psychology. He had some interest in this possibility, but he was usually drawn toward quite different matters. Significance in human studies meant, to Ratzel, the big picture. What larger framework existed within which the phenomena he had treated in *Anthropo-Geographie* could be understood in their full meaning? It was necessary to link human environmental interactions to the processes of historical change that Ratzel believed to be the source of political life.[6] Thus, even at the most abstract theoretical level, the subject of politics arose. Like any other form of social science, human geography should promote good policy-making by identifying the laws that appeared to govern society.

Ratzel, of course, continued to accept the nomothetic element of the liberal theoretical pattern, although he believed that the laws obtained in cultural science were very complex and had to be placed in a historical context. Ratzel's cultural science thus differed decisively from the hermeneutic *Kulturwissenschaft* of the neo-idealists and from the approach of Max Weber. But what sort of laws did the relationships over time among humans and culture and environment follow? In his *Anthropo-Geographie*, Ratzel had made heavy use of the concept of migration, and he would continue to do so in the future.[7] But migration was a characteristic not only of humans, but also of other living species. Ratzel's view of migration assumed a continuity between the factors influencing the migration of both human and nonhuman organisms. A framework relating the physical environment to all living species was therefore needed for the laws of human geography. Moreover, although migration was a matter of crucial importance, it was not the only central phenomenon in humankind's relationship to the physical environment. Trade, transportation, politics, agriculture, and so forth, all had to be incorporated within a comprehensive set of laws. And according to the consensus among German academics, these laws had to be laws of change.

Ratzel, like many other German cultural scientists, rejected rigidly unilinear, evolutionary theories of progress and had little use for traditional concepts of equilibrium to which they had been so awkwardly connected in the old liberal theoretical pattern.[8] But he was deeply concerned about understanding irreversible change over time and the factors that make for stability within the overall process of change. Ratzel's training as a biologist led him to see environmental balance as a paradigm for a social equilibrium frequently upset by intruding forces. His tendency to put phenomena in historical perspective caused him to represent continuity in the midst of change as cyclical recurrences of balance and disorder. Ratzel had tried to frame laws of human geography that incorporated these features in his *Anthropo-Geographie,* but he knew from the heavy criticism of his approach by establishment geographers and ethnographers, such as Hermann Wagner, that he would have to make them more convincing.[9]

The problematic of human geography confronted by Ratzel from the mid–1880s can therefore be interpreted as an intellectual interaction with the liberal theoretical pattern. But, of course, other factors than purely intellectual ones were also involved.

One of these factors was Ratzel's presence in Leipzig from the mid–1880s until his death in 1904.[10] His already-broad perspective became even broader when he came into contact with the interdisciplinary tendencies of the Leipzig academic establishment, and his orientation toward history was reinforced. At Leipzig, Ratzel operated for the first time in a prestigious environment in which his intellectual position was secure and respected and in which he could interact with some of the world's leading scholars. As one of the central members of the Leipzig Circle at the turn of the century, Ratzel helped to establish its informal aim of a comprehensive cultural science that could serve as a basis of intellectual consensus for social action.

Ratzel's association with radical nationalism was also important. As we have seen, Ratzel had taken part in the colonial movement of the 1880s—one of the sources of radical nationalist politics. After 1885, Ratzel remained an active member of the German Colonial Society and a frequent commentator on colonial affairs as a journalist. His tendency to use concepts and vocabulary from colonial politics (especially migrationist ones) became even stronger.[11] Like many other intellectuals, Ratzel was disappointed at Bismarck's refusal to maintain the momentum of overseas colonial acquisition. He took part in the colonialists' campaign of criticism of the *Reich*'s policy in the late 1880s, in part through promoting Carl Peters as the hero of Germany's new imperialism. At Bismarck's fall in 1890, he was one of the journalists and academics who decided that the time was ripe for a new political force–an organized nationalist and imperialist movement outside the existing parties that would overcome the fragmentation of German society. Ratzel involved himself heavily in the organizations out of which the Pan-German League grew. Although he was never a national leader of the league, he participated actively in it and later in the Navy League.[12] Ratzel was also one of the major figures in the radical community of political discourse in the 1890s—partly through his work in radical nationalist organizations and partly through his frequent contributions to political journals.

Ratzel's scholarly work in the last decade of his life shows a high degree of intersection between his scientific and his political concerns, although he was usually careful to identify the context in which he was writing at any particular time. His support for Admiral Alfred von Tirpitz's naval construction program led him to write a pamphlet about the relationship of world power to naval strength.[13] He published reviews of a wide range of political literature and became one of the best-known academic imperialists of the turn of the century.[14]

Some of Ratzel's importance was probably due to the fact that he seldom let his political enthusiasms outrun his intelligence. For example, in opposition both to the Pan-Germans and to his Leipzig associate Karl Lamprecht, Ratzel argued that any form of German intervention against Britain in the Boer War would be silly.[15] Although Ratzel was a radical nationalist and an imperialist, he was neither a fool nor a hypocrite. He clearly did not believe that the fact that what he studied had political significance lessened its value as science as long as he maintained an adequate critical posture. In this respect, Ratzel had the weight of the liberal social scientific tradition behind him.

These, then, were some of the contextual factors that influenced Ratzel as he addressed himself to the problems of human geography at Leipzig in the 1880s and 1890s. His main formal concern was with the intellectual questions noted earlier, but because the larger issues of politics were (according to Ratzel) legitimately within the scope of cultural science, his current political interests also affected his thinking—a fact of which he was clearly conscious.

The Concept of Lebensraum

Ratzel produced several quite similar theoretical formulations in his Leipzig years— his theory of urban places, for example, which bore a considerable resemblance to his ideas about biological distribution. But Ratzel is best remembered for his concept of *Lebensraum* (living space), which he presented in several formats but most notably in a lengthy contribution to a *Festschrift* for Albert Schäffle published in 1901.[16]

In this classic essay, Ratzel describes a conceptual structure within which he claims the movements and development of all living beings can be understood. The scale is so cosmic that humankind is hardly mentioned. The central element of the structure is *Lebensraum,* which is defined as the geographical surface area required to support a species at its current population size. The exact bounds of a species' living space are relative to its members' metabolic requirements, their characteristic mode of obtaining sustenance, and the nature of the land on which they live. As the population inevitably grows, the amount of *Lebensraum* required grows also. If nothing impeded, the search for additional living space would lead to an even covering of the earth's surface by the species.

In reality, however, all sorts of obstacles have to be confronted. Topography, climate, and therefore the sources of sustenance vary from place to place, so that the physical characteristics of the species and its modes of behavior may be unsuited to new areas into which it moves. And some of the other species it meets will be competitors for the means of existence, or else predators. This is the spatial dimension in which the Darwinian struggle for existence takes place: at the frontiers of an expanding *Lebensraum.* A species' evolutionary success is determined by its ability to adapt or otherwise to overcome obstacles in its pursuit of expanded living space. If it cannot expand, if it cannot adapt or overcome, it must die. The key, then, to explaining the natural history of living organisms, to predicting their future, and to drawing inferences from nature in general to specific cases is the identification of *Lebensraum.*

It is not difficult to see in Ratzel's presentation of *Lebensraum* an outgrowth of the emphasis on migration in his earlier *Anthropo-Geographie.* In *Lebensraum,* however, the idea is much more cogently stated as a universal process of living nature. As a part of nature, humankind must also (by implication) search for living space. The groups in which humans conduct the search are not, however, species like other organisms, but rather the *Völker* into which humankind is divided. The means that allows a people to acquire new *Lebensraum* is its culture. The significance of *Lebensraum* for humans is not drawn out in Ratzel's *Festschrift* essay, although it is implied. It becomes clearer in other places in Ratzel's later writings.[17]

Not only is Ratzel's earlier emphasis on migration further developed in his concept of *Lebensraum,* but his use of the idea of colonialism is also retained. Ratzel continues to refer to the process by which a successful species takes over a new territory as "colonization," which seems to imply a form of adaptation that does not require the species to transform itself into something new and different. The language of Ratzel's references to colonization clearly suggests an analogy between the expansion of species and the process by which human colonists "root" themselves as farmers in new lands.[18]

These fundamental elements of Ratzel's framework of geographical thought had had ideological connections to his agrarianism and colonialism since the early 1880s.[19] But *Lebensraum*'s linkages to both theoretical and ideological structures were broader still. From the standpoint of theory, *Lebensraum* responded to many of the problems that had confronted Ratzel in designing a broad-ranging human geography. It gave him the largest of possible frameworks within which to fit the patterns of interaction between humans and their environments and to present the workings of culture. The framework purported to be derived from observation of a large sample of living things and therefore to be empirically sound. At the same time, because it centered around a particular pattern of repeated environmental interaction, it avoided the theoretical diffuseness of Humboldt's equally broad notion of *Kosmos*.

Lebensraum also provided a way of extending general biological theories, including Darwinian ones, to humans. If humans could be shown to follow the same overall behavior patterns as other species with respect to the necessary search for living space, then a *meaning* for human activity could be identified scientifically rather than as a matter of faith. Human institutions could be explained not only as responses to the static characteristics of the environment, but also as products of a dynamic, changing interaction between peoples and their biological environments in the search for additional living space. The natural selection of institutions resulted from their relative effectiveness in the search. Culture—technology, intellectual traits, social organization—was not simply the medium between the individual consciousness and the environment; it was also the means by which humans fitted themselves for colonizing new environments.[20]

Living space was also the key to the nomothetic possibilities of human geography. Valid laws governing human behavior on the earth's surface over time could be constructed around *Lebensraum*. According to Ratzel, the imperative of expanding living space was a universal, empirically observable, and fundamentally important property of life.[21] The human pursuit of *Lebensraum* was undoubtedly more complex than that of other species, but it followed the same overall patterns. Ratzel did not claim that he had revealed the laws of living space in their entirety, but he did claim that he had identified their form. Even as an incomplete theoretical structure, *Lebensraum,* according to Ratzel, was vital for conducting politics. The imperative of living space had to be understood by leaders of states if they wanted to know the limits of the options available to them and if they wanted to shape their actions to the historical circumstances in which their nations found themselves. A nation that neglected the findings of empirical cultural science was a nation at risk. A nation that did not seek to expand its living space was a nation condemned to decline by the laws of natural existence.[22]

All of the major ways in which humans interacted with their environments would eventually be encompassed within the "laws" of *Lebensraum,* including migration and colonization (in Ratzel's sense of the word) as well as other peculiarly human activities that had proved to be more difficult to fit into Ratzel's anthropogeography and his diffusionist ethnology: trade, transport, and the diffusion of spiritual influences. According to Ratzel, human groups simultaneously possessed several *kinds* of living space. Using the same approach that he employed when writing of the hinterlands of big cities, Ratzel argued that the *Lebensraum* of any particular *Volk* consisted of the place where its people lived, the land out of which they drew their means of nourishment, the area within which they regularly travelled and conducted exchanges, the region (defined by natural defenses) around which their plans for security against competitors were centered, and so forth. Of these, it was the land from which the agricultural population raised a people's sustenance that was most significant (agrarian primacy, once again), but the other aspects of

Lebensraum were important as well. Therefore, the principles of *Lebensraum*, although universal in overall form, had to be applied differently in detail depending on whether one was considering the alimentary, commercial, or strategic requirements of a people and depending on the people's geographical situation and characteristic culture.[23]

The concept *"Lebensraum"* was also useful with regard to the third part of the liberal theoretical pattern: the consideration of change and equilibrium. The search for living space was the engine of change in human history, influencing the development of cultures, creating and destroying institutions, impelling the movements of peoples. The physical environment and the presence of competing peoples did not so much determine the nature of a *Volk*'s culture as they defined the range of options and obstacles presented to it. Sociocultural change, including the invention or borrowing of new technologies and new forms of political organization, was a partly voluntary, partly random response to the options available. The particular historical result of a people's pursuit of living space was unique.[24]

In a fluid, constantly changing world like Ratzel's, it might seem that the concept of equilibrium would have no place. But no, *Lebensraum* provides for that as well in a variation of the balance-of-nature idea. At any moment, the relationship between a species or a people and its living space will usually be in equilibrium. Its members will obtain the food they need, they will have adequate defense against enemies, they will conduct their relations among themselves according to an established order, and, if they are human, they will obtain a sense of psychic balance from aesthetic contemplation of their environment. But the equilibrium is unstable. External forces may upset it, and reproduction will create additional demand for resources. Moreover, prolonged stability will produce the seeds of its own destruction by encouraging character traits in the population—"softness" in some, rebelliousness in others—that will upset the order. More living space must therefore be acquired, both to sustain a growing population and to prevent the degeneration of the species or people. Thus the imperative to expand *Lebensraum* arises to a considerable extent from the need to maintain a form of equilibrium. If that equilibrium is not maintained, the species or people is likely to fall apart and to be annihilated.[25]

The links between Ratzel's scientific formulation of *Lebensraum* and the political ideologies to which he subscribed can be viewed in various ways. Certainly, *Lebensraum* can be regarded as an elaborate device for legitimating elements of Ratzel's radical nationalism and imperialism through science. We have already seen that the notion of agrarian primacy could be used to justify the agrarian position in the tariff and industrialization controversy. Ratzel's views on migration and colonization were to a large extent a scientific formulation of his migrationist colonialism. All of these ideas were worked into the fabric of *Lebensraum* as part of a truly cosmic vision of the regularities underlying life (and tied also to Ratzel's increasing acceptance toward the end of his career of Gustav Fechner's notion that the universe itself is alive).[26]

Lebensraum, however, had greater implications for the legitimation of political ideas than these, especially in the context of the radical community of political discourse in the 1890s. The doctrine that expanding living space was essential for the growth of a *Volk* and that growth was the only alternative to a people's death provided a "scientific" basis for the limitless imperialism that had become the hallmark of radical nationalism and the means by which organizations like the Pan-German League tried to dissolve contradictions in their programs. *Lebensraum* provided a defense against the claims of critics that the radical nationalists' aims were so vast as to defy practical reason and to exceed Germany's needs. It was possible to respond by saying that because Germany's *Lebensraum* could never remain static without threatening the future of the German people, a continuous expansionary impetus and a continuous pressure against the peoples hemming Germany in were needed.[27] Ratzel's analysis of living space requirements could also be used to support the fleet-expansion program. Because the need for *Lebensraum* was something that changed over time (sometimes quite rapidly), the flexibility of naval power as a means of carving out and defending new living space was a clear advantage to a *Volk*. That the actual fleet Tirpitz was building was not very flexible (because it was useful only in European waters against other battle fleets) was something that in the sheer breadth of Ratzel's metastrategic vision was easily ignored.[28]

Ratzel himself developed only some of these political uses of *Lebensraum*. He used it in politics most effectively when he presented it, not as a direct response to a specific issue, but rather as a general frame of reference within which the issue could be discussed—a frame the validity of which had been established apart from politics (or even human affairs) by science. Such employment of theory was particularly important as a means of maintaining links among radicals who might disagree on specific issues of politics and also as part of the efforts of the Leipzig Circle to create a general framework of cultural thought that linked the various political communities among intellectuals. This usage can be seen in Ratzel's advocacy of a Central European economic union after 1900.

The idea of an economic *Mitteleuropa* consisting of Germany, Austria-Hungary, and their smaller neighbors was much discussed at the turn of the century.[29] An old idea dating back to Friedrich List, it appeared in the *Kaiserreich* at first as a support for further industrialization. An industrial Germany would exchange manufactured goods for foodstuffs and raw materials with the agrarian economies of the rest of Central Europe in a system in which the markets of all the partners would be protected against excessive external competition and the vagaries of the business cycle. This version of *Mitteleuropa* was associated with the aims of the Caprivi tariff policy and with *Weltpolitik* as economic imperialism. Several members of the Pan-German and Navy leagues accepted it, although it was rather difficult to square with other aspects of radical nationalist ideology. Its focus on the expansion of German industry ran afoul of the populist element in radical nationalism and the implication that Germany, in order to create the structure of industrial-agrarian exchange, would give up much of its agriculture to the rest of Central Europe went against the agrarianism of many of the more conservative nationalists. These difficulties became especially pronounced after the Pan-Germans came out against the Caprivi tariff policy and after the Bülow government, responding to agrarian pressure, started raising agricultural tariffs in 1902.

Under these circumstances, several academic social scientists began to develop versions of the *Mitteleuropa* idea that were consistent with radical nationalism and some forms of conservatism. One of these was the economist Julius Wolf—a fixture on the right wing of the *Verein für Sozialpolitik*—and another was Ratzel.[30] Ratzel did not live to articulate his position fully, but the outlines of his approach can be found in his commentaries on Wolf's proposals.[31] According to Ratzel's analysis, *Mitteleuropa* contained most of Germany's *Lebensraum*. Germany's national security depended on the expansion of the manufacturing sector; so, the aim of expanding markets, sources of raw materials, and investment areas within a controllable Central European economic union was justified according to the strategic definition of *Lebensraum*. Thus, despite the incompatibility of the general aim of *Mitteleuropa* and the distrust of industrialization fashionable on the radical right, this aim could be adopted as a goal of policy because of its overriding importance for the future of the *Volk*.

But what about German agriculture? If the agricultural sector were driven out of Germany, where would the *Volk* find its foundation, its cultural continuity? The answer could be formulated in terms of *Lebensraum*, although Ratzel only suggested it, leaving its full expression to others.[32] *Lebensraum*, to Ratzel, also consisted of the land that the peasants farm. Therefore, something had to be done to protect the peasant-agricultural part of the economy. That something was already familiar to radicals: "inner colonization" of underused land in eastern Germany by German farmers (a direct extension of the idea of migrationist colonialism). Schemes for sending people out of the cities to the country, combined with an extension of the existing system of subsidies to German small farmers to allow them to buy and keep farms in areas of heavy Polish immigration, would not necessarily lead to German self-sufficiency in agricultural production. They might not even pay for themselves, but they would prevent the loss of the basis of German culture and a diminution of an essential aspect of living space. Thus, the multiple dimensions of *Lebensraum* served as a framework within which a contradiction in radical thought could be at least theoretically resolved.[33]

Lebensraum was also consistent with an idea widely discussed in radical nationalist circles at the turn of the century: the establishment of German peasant colonies in eastern Europe beyond Germany's borders. If "inner colonies" were insufficient to maintain the basis of German culture, then external ones in Europe could do so, without endangering Germany's industrial sector. Although Ratzel himself was not an advocate of Eastern European settlement, he had come by the early twentieth century to see the European continent, not colonies overseas, as the most appropriate venue for German imperialism, and his idea of *Lebensraum* would be used extensively after his death as a support for demands for annexation in the east.[34]

Ratzel's conception of *Mitteleuropa* is only one example of the ways in which *Lebensraum* fitted into the structure of radical imperialist ideology and of its uses in overcoming contradictions in the programs of the radical right. There were drawbacks from other standpoints, however. In the first place, *Lebensraum* offered no limits to the widest possible expansion of imperialist goals. It could justify *any* form of expansion as a natural consequence of the need for living space. It was therefore, if taken seriously, a poor basis for policy because it could not be used to identify a consistent and distinct set of goals. It was also a bad source of policy guidelines for many of the same reasons that it was an inadequate foundation for social scientific theory.

Ratzel clearly believed that he could separate research and theory building from the political uses to which his theories were going to be put. In this, he deceived himself. He was, indeed, able to apply his independent critical judgment to scientific questions with political implications and to reject ideas popular among his political associates—most notably the use of biological race as a valid category in social analysis and a major factor in politics.[35] But because *Lebensraum* was in fact drawn from a theoretical pattern intimately involved with politics throughout its evolution, the political element was present from the start. Therefore, *Lebensraum* was not, as Ratzel claimed, simply a scientific theory derived from objective empirical observation and then applied to politics.

This was not necessarily damning, but in fact *Lebensraum* had vast weaknesses as theory, many of them traceable to the political element in its origins. One of the main problems was that *Lebensraum*, like most political ideologies but unlike most scientific theories, was not structured to permit testing or even effective evaluation of its principal elements. This deficiency was disguised by Ratzel's mode of presentation. He would describe a huge number of natural phenomena or processes as examples of the regularities he claimed to display. He would then use the broad range of the examples to imply the universality of the underlying regularities, whereas really all the examples validly proved was Ratzel's ability to employ the same language to describe many different things. What Ratzel did *not* do was to suggest a test of his hypotheses, either by experiment or by observation of ongoing phenomena. But it all *looked* authoritative because of the sheer weight of evidence.[36]

Darwin, of course, has been accused of much the same thing. The difference was that Darwin's natural selection, although admittedly elastic as a concept, was not infinitely so.[37] Its starting point, natural variation, was a universally recognized phenomenon, and competition among individuals for sustenance and mates, the keys to the central process of selection, were relatively simple, clearly identifiable behaviors. Thus, although experimental testing was difficult, it was possible to search for natural phenomena that would falsify Darwinian predictions. Ratzel's *Lebensraum*, on the other hand, was so flexible that it precluded any empirical test. Almost any form of group behavior could be described as part of a search for *Lebensraum* or as a consequence of the failure to obtain it. If a species flourished, expanded, and evolved, that showed that it had successfully obtained the necessary living space. If a species declined, it was evidence of the contrary. A mode of description that has the vocabulary to cover all cases can appear to be an all-encompassing theory without necessarily saying much of importance or serving as a basis for predictions, the outcomes of which will test the theory. Despite the suggestiveness of many of Ratzel's insights, *Lebensraum* was not really a theory at all.

Another difference between natural selection and *Lebensraum* lay in what had to be done to fit them for political use. In order to turn Darwin's theory into a suitable basis for ideology, it was necessary to play fast and loose with certain important Darwinian concepts—most especially, to equate Darwin's species with such human groupings as *Volk,* nation, and state and to ignore his focus on the individual organism. With Ratzel's *Lebensraum,* this was not necessary. Ratzel himself claimed that the imperatives of living space applied to species, subspecies, local varieties, and so on, of animals—however defined—even though he allowed that human groups were more complex and unpredictable.[38] He readily shifted (although with some modifications in argument) between animal and plant species, *Völker* and states—categories that are not sufficiently similar to justify their being treated in the same way. This difference reflected the fact that Darwin did not conceive of his work as political in implication, whereas Ratzel was constructing theories to be applied directly to questions of politics and policy. In politics, it is very useful to be able to claim that one's recommendations are based on general laws of nature.[39]

Even the most appealing part of the *Lebensraum* concept from the standpoint of social science—its attempt to establish a framework for understanding the total process of environmental adaptation—is deficient. To the question that naturally arises in seeking such understanding—"Adaptation to what?"—Ratzel essentially answered "everything." Because this is not very helpful for purposes of comprehending specific cases and even less helpful in making predictions, Ratzel took the approach that we have already remarked several times: he postulated a universal hierarchy, or order, in forms of adaptation that corresponded roughly to an implied hierarchy of importance in the ways in which nature impinged on living things. But like most other results of Ratzel's theorizing, the hierarchy was very flexible (apart from Ratzel's insistence that adaptations that affected a species or group's means of sustenance took priority over others), and even the existence of such a hierarchy was asserted rather than demonstrated.

Lebensraum, therefore, did not really offer a means of systematically predicting what would happen to a human group. At best, it could provide a vocabulary for explaining what had happened to it in the past. It was useless as a guide for responsible policy-making. But for some of the very reasons that made it so, it had enormous appeal as an element of a radical nationalist ideology aimed at creating an imperialist consensus. One could support almost any kind of expansionary initiative as necessary to the future of the *Volk* on the basis of *Lebensraum.* Both the theoretical deficiency and the political utility of *Lebensraum* were compounded by Ratzel's use of the organic analogy (i.e. human social forms are like individual living organisms). This led to the dictum that a *Volk* or state had to expand its living space or decline.[40] We have already seen some of the theoretical difficulties of the organic analogy as it was used by early liberal social scientists and by some historical economists. The difficulties did not abate under circumstances in which the analogy had significant political utility.

The Diffusion of *Lebensraum*

It did not take long after Ratzel's death in 1904 for *Lebensraum,* both as an idea and as a word, to become broadly diffused in public discourse in Germany. *Lebensraum,* together with several other parts of Ratzel's theoretical corpus, exerted considerable influence on the Swedish political scientist Rudolf Kjellén, who constructed an applied science he called *geopolitics*. Kjellén's work, and parallel ideas from Ratzel's own students in Germany, had a wide following among officers, academics, and the educated public before 1914.[41] They seemed to offer a new, needed global framework for visualizing international politics in a world that had outgrown older conceptions. Kjellén's assertion that, building on Ratzel, he had developed a science through which the national interest could be correctly identified in a world context had the effect of intensifying *Lebensraum*'s claims to being an extension of scientific truth to policy-making. It suggested to responsible policymakers that the pursuit of living space was a valid aim of the modern state.

The arguments of people like Kjellén did not, however, operate purely in an academic or policy context. It was not an accident that they were accepted most readily by people breaking out of the radical community and moving toward the political Right: toward accommodation with conservative elements in the German social and political establishment and toward an acceptance of imperialist war as a practical aim of policy. *Lebensraum* worked in the ways we have seen to frame and legitimate concepts of imperialism that acted as a medium of integration on the Right. This became especially significant in the few years just before the outbreak of the First World War. In response to the electoral victories of the SPD in 1912 and a movement toward integration among the liberal parties and liberal business interests, a countermovement appeared among the conservative parties, organizations of big business and big agriculture, and radical nationalist groups (including the Pan-German League).[42] This powerful alliance was in constant danger of falling apart; its public voice needed to stress factors that held the factions together. This was one of the reasons for the heavy emphasis on imperial expansion in the propaganda of the Right in those years, and also one of the reasons that the alliance concentrated so much of its effort on attacking the government for every sign of weakness in foreign policy, calling for its replacement by a more nationalist and imperialist one. The attempt to integrate the Right along these lines was one of the major factors leading Germany into the First World War. And the *Lebensraum* idea played its part in it.

Resonances of *Lebensraum* (together with a kind of warmed-over, hyperbolic Darwinism) can be seen in the prewar pamphlets of Friedrich von Bernhardi—one of the leading publicists of the radical nationalists and of the right-wing coalition. Bernhardi argued in 1912 that war among the European powers was inevitable because underlying all international relations was the competition among *Völker* for survival.[43] Because the relative strength and security of a *Volk* were determined in part by its continued growth in numbers, each *Volk* needed an expanding base of subsistence that could only be obtained, ultimately, by fighting other peoples. Struggle of this sort was not bad; it was the means by which a people developed and tested the strength of its collective character. The losers deserved to go to the wall. Germany, therefore, had to prepare for war, and soon. A government (such as Bethmann Hollweg's current one) that did not do so, that avoided the conflict and refused to understand the imperative to expand, had to be removed. Parties that opposed an expansionary foreign policy or weakened the unity of the German *Volk* in their struggle had to be defeated.

That *Lebensraum* was generally consistent with this kind of thinking is obvious, but the concept itself had a more specific role as well. The crux of Bernhardi's argument when it came to the particular objectives of an expansionary policy, to the goals that were to be achieved by a successful war, was that these objectives must be conceived quite broadly. Not only did Germany require more defensible boundaries, but also German industry, which was essential to the nation's military strength, needed markets and secure sources of raw materials—ideally, within an autarkic German-dominated European economy augmented by adequate overseas colonies. In addition, the German *Volk* itself needed an area in Europe where its surplus population could settle as peasant farmers, thus maintaining the agricultural self-sufficiency of the Reich and the peasant foundations of German culture.[44]

The broadness of Bernhardi's expansionary goals reflects the broadness of the right-wing coalition, the desire to include something for every major interest group that supported it and to avoid the disputes that had previously split the elements of the Right. The industrial and agrarian interests had traditionally fought over development policy. Expansion would allow both industrial expansion and agrarian protection. Many radical nationalists had been to some degree anticapitalist and anti-*Junker*. Expansion, by acquiring living space for peasants in eastern Europe and establishing opportunities for other elements of the *Mittelstand*, would create a counterweight to both segments of the elite without threatening either and would protect the bearers of an idealized preindustrial culture from extinction.[45] And so forth. The framework within which Bernhardi chose to integrate these aims (and thus to create an ideological basis for integrating the Right) was *Lebensraum*. Even though he did not use the term as a slogan, the concept was clearly there. Each of the general objectives of expansionary policy was dictated by the universal biological and cultural requirements of any people, and the specific objectives—especially the acquisition of peasant land, which he, like Ratzel, claimed to be the most fundamental aim of all—were determined by the particular cultural qualities of the German people. Science, according to Bernhardi, made it clear that this was what Germany must do to survive. Anyone who argued otherwise was a muddlehead with his mind in the comforting illusions of the past—or a traitor.[46]

Bernhardi was only one of many publicists and politicians using arguments built around *Lebensraum* in the period just before and during the First World War.[47] During the war itself, in the course of the politicking that surrounded the making of war-aims policy, a whole range of ideas that had come to be the property of the political Right—including *Lebensraum*—were put together to fashion the so-called annexationist position on the goals of the war. The annexationist position was intimately connected to the attempt to maintain an antireformist coalition in domestic politics and to use the demand for the maximum possible gains from the war as a means of preventing democratization in Germany by discrediting the liberals and Bethmann Hollweg's government. The concept of *Lebensraum*, together with related arguments, was used to give "scientific" justification to the Right's demand for essentially unlimited war aims to be achieved through the total defeat of Germany's enemies: complete economic control of Central and Eastern Europe, a huge colonial empire, expansion of Germany's strategic boundaries in the west and the east, and sufficient direct control of eastern Europe to permit an agricultural resettlement policy in many regions.

But these were not just means of achieving particular political ends in Germany.

Their advocates actually believed in them as well—to the extent that after the right-wing coalition gained the ascendancy in Germany with the "silent" dictatorship of Paul von Hindenburg and Erich Ludendorff in 1917 and after the defeat of Russia in 1918, responsible authorities began to try to implement parts of the coalition's war-aims policy: settlement schemes for war veterans, an autarkic economic system in Central Europe dominated by Germany, and so forth. The intellectual and political background to these policies was extremely complex and the policies themselves derived from many sources, but the *Lebensraum* concept helped to frame and legitimate them.[48]

The transformation of *Lebensraum* into a highly significant element of German politics after the First World War has been described elsewhere.[49] As a basis for policy-oriented social scientific theory, it became a central part of the geopolitics of Karl Haushofer, a retired general and a professor at the University of Munich who attracted a great many students—including Rudolf Hess. Haushofer acknowledged his obligation to Ratzel, using both Ratzel's notion of living space and his technique of identifying different levels of a people's requirements for *Lebensraum*.[50] Haushofer was particularly important in making *Lebensraum* a major, conscious part of the ideological composition of the Right because of his use of the concept to demonstrate "scientifically" the deficiencies of the Treaty of Versailles. The *Lebensraum* idea was popularized among the mass of conservative and radical nationalist rank and file by Hans Grimm's famous novel *Volk ohne Raum*. Even though Grimm did not make much use of the word itself, he was closely acquainted with the Ratzelian corpus and, in essence, used the concept as the framework of his novel.[51]

The most important fact about *Lebensraum* between the wars, however, was its adoption as an aim of policy by Adolf Hitler and the Nazi party.[52] In the early 1920s, ideas akin to *Lebensraum* were part of the loosely defined Nazi program, but played a fairly minor role compared to anti-Semitism, anti-Bolshevism, and anticapitalism. From the mid–1920s onward, however, when expansionism in general became more important to Hitler as a basis for framing his conceptions of foreign policy and as a means of seeking integrated support on the political Right, the idea of *Lebensraum* became more and more significant to him. Probably introduced to the idea by Hess and through the writings of the geopoliticians, Hitler saw in the concept a scientifically validated means simultaneously of establishing a political consensus through an updated imperialism and of reconciling the various discordant aspects of his own thinking about foreign policy. The framework of *Lebensraum* permitted him to identify a set of national aims that included both industrial expansion through German control of an autarkic Central European economy and the more basic goal of protecting German culture against the threat of industrialization by settling peasant farmers outside Germany's boundaries. And although after coming to power, Hitler was forced by circumstances to tailor his short-term policies to more immediate needs, there is little question that *Lebensraum* loomed ever larger in his mind as part of the formula for long-term planning. And so it was that in 1941, while engaged in a war to secure Germany's economic and political hegemony in central and western Europe, Hitler launched an invasion of Russia in pursuit of living space in the east—an aim that in fact contradicted many of his other goals and in any event led to a predictable disaster for Germany. By giving a "scientific" justification for imperialism, by disguising contradictions in radical nationalist thinking, by adjusting itself—mainly because of the political nature of its origins—to the needs of radical nationalist and conservative politicians, *Lebensraum* had had a real and terrible effect on the course of European history.

13

Cultural Science and Politics

At the beginning of this book, several questions were raised about the history of the cultural sciences in Germany. The answers that have been given are necessarily only partial—sometimes amounting merely to suggestions. The factors involved in the creation of an intellectual phenomenon such as cultural science are very numerous, and the emphasis that has been placed here on the political side of the process is admittedly somewhat arbitrary. Even if the development of German cultural science could be wholly understood, it is not certain that such an understanding could be automatically applied to parallel events in other countries. Nevertheless, it may be useful to try to summarize the answers to the questions posed at the start.

Why did cultural science arise when and in the forms in which it did in nineteenth-century Germany? A great many factors were involved—some of them residing in the general intellectual life of Europe, some in the particular features of German philosophy and humanistic education, and some deriving from the processes of social and economic modernization. This study has, however, emphasized politics—and more specifically, the vicissitudes of liberalism as a political movement and ideological tendency in Germany—as the decisive factor. Politics was of crucial importance in this regard because it created much of the motivation to try to understand social change and much of the intellectual framework around which such understanding could be constructed. The idea of social science itself—the idea from which the notion of nomothetic cultural science arose—was closely connected in origin and evolution to the ideology of liberalism in the first half of the nineteenth century. Most (although not all) of the important German theorists of social science in that century considered themselves liberals for some substantial parts of their lives and believed that their academic and political activities were highly relevant to one another. A common core of words, concepts, and images reinforced the linkage between liberal ideology and the theoretical pattern of early social science. For these reasons, changes in the structure and political fortunes of liberalism (especially its fragmentation after midcentury) strongly affected the social sciences and the emergence within the latter of the cultural sciences.

Unlike Britain, the United States, and eventually France, Germany did not witness the unqualified political triumph of liberalism in the nineteenth century. Liberal concepts and vocabulary, indeed, the whole liberal apparatus for conducting politics diffused throughout German political culture from the 1840s onward. Liberal ideology and the social scientific theoretical patterns associated with it produced the most widely accepted framework for understanding the process of moderniza-

234

tion. But in 1848–1849 and again in the 1860s, the liberals failed to make themselves dominant in German politics and failed to unite Germany according to their own model. In the last third of the century, they watched as Bismarck created a nonliberal *Reich* and his successors tried to make it work. To the extent that liberalism strongly informed the thinking of the bourgeoisie in a society in which that class was increasingly the cultural and economic referent and to the extent that it helped to construct the consciousness of the new economic elite, imperial Germany could be called a liberal nation—if one accepts the wide range of the nineteenth-century ideological forms that could be called liberal. But in terms of the operation of the state and the aims and outlooks of many of the groups to whose interests the state responded, the *Kaiserreich* was not only unliberal, but distinctly hostile to liberalism. Liberal political parties experienced great difficulty even in maintaining public support after the first decade of the empire's existence.

Under such circumstances, successive generations of liberal intellectuals interested in social science were motivated to ask themselves why German liberalism's political performance was so unimpressive and to assess the grounds of their own commitment to liberalism. This led many of them to reconsider also the assumptions on which liberal social science was based. This kind of reconsideration, repeated generation after generation from the 1840s onward, was an important factor— perhaps *the* most important factor—in the appearance of new theoretical patterns in the social sciences in Germany. The specific points involved in reassessment varied, of course, with individual outlooks, with changing fashions in philosophical discourse, and with changes in the perceived nature of social and political problems. Liberal social scientists of the 1850s tended to be most concerned about the effects of the 1848 revolution, the liberal failure to attract the overwhelming support of the lower classes, and the incipient industrialization of Germany. Their successors in the 1860s and early 1870s focused on national unification and the ambiguous role of liberalism in the new *Reich*. The next generation concerned itself with the discordance between liberal orthodoxies and the new circumstances of an industrial, imperialist Germany. In the same way that German liberalism, as an organized political movement and as a set of ideologies, fragmented in response to searching reassessments as liberals adjusted themselves to a new political world, so too, the liberal-oriented theoretical pattern in social science fragmented and fragmented again—producing by the early twentieth century a body of academic social science unequalled at the time in variety and depth.

These were the circumstances in which the theoretical frameworks of cultural science appeared and developed. Many of the disciplines of cultural science were international in origin, but the particular theoretical approaches to culture that emerged in Germany—especially approaches that put culture into a historical perspective—were essentially German. One of the main reasons that German cultural science appeared and became such an important part of the national intellectual spectrum from the middle of the nineteenth century onward was that the culture concept had already developed in Germany, in large part as a corrective to some of the perceived deficiencies in liberal political and social thought. The idea of culture was therefore available and (partly because of its connection with Romanticism) highly attractive to academic social scientists who wanted to reevaluate their political and economic assumptions in the light of liberalism's mediocre political performance. It proved to be particularly useful to academics who questioned such elements of older liberal social science as the model of the rational individual and the progressivist-equilibrium approach to social change. But whether the questioning led to effective restatement of earlier assumptions, to their modification, or to their rejection, one thing that the cultural scientists whose work we have examined here had in common was a continued acceptance of the nomothetic aim of social studies—a feature that set them off from the dominant German historians of the late nineteenth century and from the advocates of *Geisteswissenschaft*. As we have seen, this adherence to the nomothetic aim was tied in many complex ways to a belief in the political efficacy of academic work—a belief that developed in large measure out of the original close connection between liberal ideology and social scientific theory.

There is no need to summarize here the processes by which the major theoretical patterns of cultural science developed within and between the disciplines of anthropology, human geography, psychology, historical economics, and cultural history in the second half of the nineteenth century. We have seen that many different factors affected these processes, including the increasingly diverse political involvements of cultural scientists as they pursued their careers and confronted a changing society. Still, discourses with liberal political thought as it continued to develop and with the traditional theoretical pattern of social science remained important sources of creativity in the cultural sciences.

Another question that was asked at the outset was why German cultural science tended, especially in the twentieth century, to diverge from the theoretical patterns of cultural science in countries such as Britain, France, and the United States. Again, a complete answer would involve far more phenomena than can be treated here. Differences between the German cultural sciences and those of other countries can easily be exaggerated. They were most pronounced in ethnology, culturally oriented psychology, and historical economics—and even in those fields there were important foreign resonances of German themes well into the twentieth century. In physical anthropology and archaeology and in some areas of geography, German peculiarities were minimal and German leadership remained strong at least up to the Nazi era.[1]

Nevertheless, there *were* divergences. In cultural anthropology, after the radical diffusionist pattern came to prevail in Germany around the turn of the century, the degree of German isolation became increasingly pronounced. Even though American anthropologists influenced by Boas continued at least to understand German diffusionism down to the 1930s, the overall tendency in the English- and French-speaking worlds was to move away from diffusionism (and from historical orientations in general) and toward functionalism and structuralism. By the post second World War period, German cultural anthropologists engaging in their dominant native mode of discourse were essentially speaking to themselves alone.[2]

Part of the reason for the international isolation of some German cultural sciences lay in their inability to compete with other, overlapping disciplines that could be more simply and strikingly formulated. *Völkerpsychologie*, for example, could not survive the expansion of experimental psychology and the appearance of sociology and social psychology. But politics also played a role, especially in the impetus to innovation provided by the fragmentation of liberalism in Germany. In other countries where the triumph of liberalism was more complete—Britain, for example, or the United States—and where major ideological competition to liberalism after the 1870s came only from Marxian socialism, there was less reason to explore the boundaries of social science, to question fundamental assumptions, and to probe fully the potential of the culture concept as a corrective to theoretical patterns inspired by liberalism. The comparative richness of German social and cultural science, a richness that had a profound effect on academic social thought in other countries, thus arose from the existence of important contextual differences, particularly in the realm of politics. The differences were not absolute, but they were sufficient to encourage a greater tendency in Germany than elsewhere to move away from theoretical patterns closely linked to traditional liberalism.

As we saw in the case of *Lebensraum,* certain areas of German cultural science in the twentieth century became closely connected to radical nationalist ideologies, which stimulated an emphasis on the differences between German cultural sciences and social sciences in other countries. The tendency became even more pronounced during the First World War, as the cultural sciences were mobilized for national propaganda and as the internal struggles over war-aims policy brought together the various segments of the political Right.[3] The results of such connections can be seen in the growing international isolation of the diffusionist theoretical pattern in cultural anthropology in the interwar years and afterward.

Although German academic anthropologists between the wars were on the whole no more politically active than any other group of social scientists, their way of approaching cultural science could be readily perceived as being closely linked to the ideologies of the radical Right—in large part because of the long-standing presence in diffusionist thinking of such elements as radical agrarianism and *Lebensraum.* Under the Nazis, the anthropological establishment allowed itself to be integrated into the new *Reich* with little, if any, resistance—although this was hardly unique.[4] More important was the way in which diffusionist ideas and other characteristic German academic notions about culture were brought together into Nazi ideological packages—as they were, for instance, by Walther Darré in his concept of *Blut und Boden,* which linked various ideas from the cultural sciences to forms of biological racism that people such as Ratzel had rejected.[5] Diffusionism, or at least some of the ideas associated with diffusionism, could thus be perceived abroad (and after 1945, by many younger German anthropologists) as being vaguely connected with Nazism. The relative isolation of German cultural anthropology and the low repute in which diffusionism as a body of theory has been held outside Germany since the 1930s are probably due in part to these developments.[6]

What was the relationship of the cultural sciences to the upheavals in German social science at the turn of the century? Again, the answer to this question is quite complex. Although cultural sciences such as anthropology and human geography were only tangentially connected to the developments that produced German sociology, this was not true of such disciplines as economics and history. Both of the latter disciplines included theoretical patterns closely linked to those of the cultural sciences. Historical economics in fact was considered by many of its practitioners to *be* a cultural science. Within these disciplines, controversies over methodology—controversies stimuated in part by political issues and the Wilhelmian fashion for intellectual politics—led to attempts to create not only new methodological bases for social science, but new social epistemologies. It was precisely the acceptance of culture as a category of social analysis (together with history as the conceptual context of social phenomena) that made it possible for people such as Max Weber and Werner Sombart to respond to the attack on "positivist," nomothetic social science, not by giving up on the idea of social science, but by seeking alternative approaches to social knowledge—approaches heavily influenced by visions of culture shaped by history. From the other direction, Karl Lamprecht mounted an attack on the hermeneutic assumptions of the historical establishment by focusing on laws of cultural change—a notion derived from the cultural sciences. In other words, even though some cultural science disciplines remained largely aloof from the methodological controversies that led to the revolutionary changes in German social science at the turn of the century, others did not, and concepts from the cultural sciences had a great deal to do with the ways in which the controversies were resolved in the establishment of new patterns of theory.

On the whole, however, the cultural sciences with which we have been primarily concerned—anthropology, human geography, and *Völkerpsychologie*—did not follow the new directions resulting from the turn-of-the-century controversies. In the case of *Völkerpsychologie*, the whole field was essentially torn apart on the one hand by psychologists who wanted to reinforce the positivist, experimental aspects of their discipline, and on the other by people like Georg Simmel and Alfred Weber who wanted to recast the study of group psychology in terms of non-nomothetic cultural comparison. In the cases of German anthropology and human geography, leading scholars resisted efforts to subsume their fields within sociology. Instead, in large part because it gave them a standpoint from which they could comment authoritatively on a wide variety of issues, they maintained the nomothetic orientation their fields had always had. There *were* modifications. German diffusionist ethnology became less and less concerned with enunciating universal laws of cultural movement and more involved with constructing elaborate cultural morphologies. German economic and political geographers, although they continued to talk about the laws of central places and the like, in fact moved toward the construction of geographical models.[7] But even in these cases, an estrangement between the traditional cultural sciences and other human studies has maintained itself in some respects down to the present.

Other questions, ones focusing on the relationship between politics and academic social thought, have implicitly arisen in the course of this study. Is there a difference, ultimately, between social scientific theory and political ideology? The answer suggested here is that, despite substantial overlap and despite the obvious impingement of ideology on theory (and vice versa), there is a difference. That academic social science is able to have political effects depends on the existence (or at least the popular perception) of such a difference, for in no other way could social scientists (or politicians consciously referring to the pronouncements of social scientists) be able to claim convincingly that what social science says is objectively true and should be embodied in policy. The structure of academic social science and the behavioral ethic associated with it work, although not perfectly, to maintain the distinction from ideology. Even in the present study, which has emphasized the decisive ways in which German liberal ideology and its offshoots shaped the nomothetic cultural sciences, we have still not come down to explaining away social science simply as an extension of politics.

Does this study have any relevance for current disputes in German historiography, especially the hotly debated question of the German *Sonderweg*? In the 1960s and 1970s, the dominant academic interpretation of modern German history was that its political peculiarities—especially the triumph of the Nazis—were results mainly of Germany's unusual pattern of socioeconomic modernization in the nineteenth and early twentieth centuries. Under the circumstances of very rapid industrialization, the "normal" pattern of social and political response to modernization as manifested in Britain and France—involving the dominance of the bourgeoisie and of political liberalism—was not followed in Germany. This resulted in a chaotic political system in which obsolescent, antimodernist elites exerted inordinate amounts of power and in which liberalism, as an element of political culture, was fatally weak.[8] In recent years, the assertion that Germany travelled a deviant path of modernization has been questioned on the grounds that "standard" modernization is something of a myth and that actual socioeconomic change in Germany was not inherently different from what happened in other countries. It has been suggested that the extent of the differences between German politics and those of other countries may have been exaggerated as well and that such circumstances of modernization as the expansion of the bourgeoisie and its culture, which took place everywhere in Europe, point to underlying similarities beneath the apparently different political experiences of Germany, on the one hand, and France and Britain, on the other.[9]

This study does not directly address itself to the *Sonderweg* issue, but because it deals with formal perceptions of social change and their relationships to political ideology, it does have some implications for the question. It is clear that as far as cultural science was concerned, Germany did follow a *Sonderweg*. Although German cultural science had enormous effects on the development of disciplines in other countries, the theoretical patterns of the German cultural sciences were in many ways particularly German. Moreover, in several cultural science fields, the very period in which the most obvious German political peculiarities manifested themselves (the Nazi era) was also the period in which the isolation of German cultural theory became most extreme. In addition, it has been shown that at least part of the reason for unusual developments in German cultural science was a certain set of political peculiarities in Germany: most obviously, the political performance of liberalism, which probably was in some degree connected to the process of German socioeconomic modernization.

On the other hand, we have also seen that the *Sonderweg* in cultural science was immensely complex, both in origin and in definition. The theoretical patterns of German cultural science tended to diverge from social scientific patterns in other countries as the former fragmented, which they did more or less consistently with the fragmentation of liberal political ideology in Germany. But both in ideology and in cultural science, the surviving fragments retained varying residues of their original liberal sources. This meant among other things that there was always, despite appearances, some similarity between German and foreign versions of cultural science because of shared connections to liberalism. Moreover, just as a constant dialogue continued to exist between the developing cultural sciences and the original liberal theoretical pattern in social science, so also a dialogue remained between many of the ideologies of German politics during and after the turn of the century and traditional liberal ideology. Theoretical constructs in the cultural sciences (such as *Lebensraum* and diffusionism) continued to display the influences of early nineteenth-century theoretical patterns closely linked to liberalism, despite the fact that the creators of such constructs had deliberately rejected significant elements of the liberal social science tradition. In the same way, ideological constructs, such as Wilhelmian radical nationalism, retained elements of liberal ideology, despite their advocates' rejection of much of contemporary liberal political thought. These continuities, both the ideological ones and the ones inherent in theoretical cultural science, presumably existed to some extent because of the bourgeois origins of so many political writers and academic cultural scientists and because of the existence of a limited range of standard bourgeois reactions to socioeconomic modernization. But the implication of this study is that they also existed in large part because educated Germans perceived, understood, and constructed the social world around them in terms of concepts and modes of discourse that they inherited from their predecessors and that they modified to suit new circumstances—circumstances that impinged on them primarily as new *political* phenomena. This study therefore suggests that the German *Sonderweg*, to the extent that the notion is meaningful at all, was founded at least as much on differences in social perception that arose out of politics as it was on concrete differences between the processes of socioeconomic modernization in Germany and those in other countries.

Notes

Introduction

1. See the assessment of the influence of German geographic scholarship in Harriet Wanklyn, *Friedrich Ratzel: A Biographical Memoir and Bibliography* (Cambridge, 1961), pp. 29–31, 43–44. Most English and American historians of anthropology tend to avoid dealing in depth with the influence of German thought on ethnology. See, for example, the best and most important recent study in the history of anthropology: George W. Stocking, Jr., *Victorian Anthropology* (New York, 1987), pp. 20–25 (where the German culture-history tradition is discussed as an aspect of Romanticism) and pp. 290–91. When German anthropology is discussed, it usually appears in the form of influences on Franz Boas: George W. Stocking, Jr., *Race, Culture, and Evolution: Essays in the History of Anthropology* (New York, 1968), pp. 195–233; and Clyde Kluckhorn and Olof Prufer, "Influences During the Formative Years," in Walter Goldschmidt, ed., *The Anthropology of Franz Boas* (*American Anthropologist* 61, 5, pt.2: Memoir No. 89 [1959]), pp. 4–28. Sometimes its influence is simply rejected out of hand: Marvin Harris, *The Rise of Anthropological Theory: A History of Theories of Culture* (New York, 1968), pp. 250–89.

2. The most important reason for the recent rapid expansion of the history of anthropology has been the work of George W. Stocking, Jr., and his associates. Besides Stocking's *Victorian Anthropology,* see George W. Stocking, Jr., ed., *Functionalism Historicized: Essays on British Social Anthropology* (Madison, WI, 1984). For older histories of anthropology that link developments within the discipline to broader intellectual tendencies, see Wilhelm E. Mühlmann, *Geschichte der Anthropologie,* 2nd ed. (Frankfurt am Main and Bonn, 1968); and Robert H. Lowie, *The History of Ethnological Theory* (New York, 1937). Rüdiger vom Bruch has attempted to relate developments in several *Kulturwissenschaften* in Germany to each other and to politics between 1890 and 1914, but he concentrates on the fields of economics and history, which are peripheral to this study (see chap. 10 herein) and are precisely the disciplines within which the nomothetic aim was most fully taken under attack. See Rüdiger vom Bruch, *Wissenschaft, Politik und öffentliche Meinung: Gelehrtenpolitik im Wilhelmischen Deutschland (1890–1914)* (Husum, 1980); and idem., *Weltpolitik als Kulturmission: Auswärtige Kulturpolitik und Bildungsbürgertum in Deutschland am Vorabend des Ersten Weltkrieges* (Paderborn, 1982).

3. Stocking, *Victorian Anthropology,* pp. 110–85; J. W. Burrow, *Evolution and Society: A Study in Victorian Social Theory* (Cambridge, 1966), pp. 113–16.

4. See, for instance, Klaus-Peter Koepping, *Adolf Bastian and the Psychic Unity of Mankind: The Foundations of Anthropology in Nineteenth Century Germany* (Saint Lucia, Queensland, Austral., 1983), pp. 77–94.

5. See Burrow, *Evolution and Society,* pp. 1–82.

6. Stocking, *Victorian Anthropology,* pp. 230–32, 251–52.

7. Woodruff D. Smith, "The Social and Political Origins of German Diffusionist

Ethnology," *Journal of the History of the Behavioral Sciences* 14 (1978), pp. 103–12; idem, "Friedrich Ratzel and the Origins of *Lebensraum*," *German Studies Review* 3 (1980), pp. 51–68; idem, *The Ideological Origins of Nazi Imperialism* (New York, 1986), pp. 141–52.

8. For an outstanding attempt to combine *both* class *and* generational analysis within a single study, see Dieter Lindenlaub, *Richtungskämpfe im Verein für Sozialpolitik,* supp. 52 and 53 of *Vierteljahrshefte für Sozial-und Wirtschaftsgeschichte* (Wiesbaden, 1967).

9. For a recent, searching critique of the meaning of *class* and its utility in historical interpretation, see William M. Reddy, *Money and Liberty in Europe: A Critique of Historical Understanding* (Cambridge, 1987), pp. 1–33.

10. A useful collection of summary discussions of new trends in interpretive theory is found in Quentin Skinner, ed., *The Return of Grand Theory in the Human Sciences* (Cambridge, 1985).

11. See two review articles in a recent issue of the *American Historical Review* that touch on these matters: John E. Toews, "Intellectual History After the Linguistic Turn: The Autonomy of Meaning and the Irreducibility of Experience," *American Historical Review* 92, 4 (1987), pp. 879–907; and Richard Harvey Brown, "Positivism, Relativism, and Narrative in the Logic of the Historical Sciences," *AHR* 92, 4 (1987), pp. 908–20. Michel Foucault's concept of the *episteme,* the "archaeological" layer of understanding on which formal and conscious theories are built, is somewhat similar to the notion of the *theoretical pattern* employed in this study. The major differences are that theoretical patterns are much more specific and limited than Foucault's *epistemes,* that theoretical patterns change more continuously in response to contextual factors, and that the people in whose minds they reside are (apparently) more conscious of the existence of theoretical patterns than they are of *epistemes.* See Michel Foucault, *The Order of Things: An Archaeology of the Human Sciences* (New York, 1970).

12. See the critique of psychohistory in David E. Stannard, *Shrinking History: On Freud and the Failure of Psychohistory* (New York, 1982).

13. Thomas S. Kuhn, *The Structure of Scientific Revolutions,* 2nd ed. (Chicago, 1970).

14. See Barry Barnes, "Thomas Kuhn," in Skinner, *Return of Grand Theory,* pp. 83–100.

15. Thomas S. Kuhn, *The Essential Tension: Selected Studies in Scientific Tradition and Change* (Chicago and London, 1977), pp. 221–22.

16. Ibid., pp. xix–xx; Kuhn, *Structure,* pp. 181–87. Thomas L. Haskell, *The Emergence of Professional Social Science: The American Social Science Association and the Nineteenth-Century Crisis of Authority* (Urbana, Il, 1977), pp. 1–23, also argues for the utility of Kuhn's earlier, looser concept of paradigm in understanding change in social science.

17. The approach to ideology employed here is discussed at greater length in W. D. Smith, *Ideological Origins,* pp. 2–20, 41–51. Ideology is treated as a structure of words and ideas, usually very eclectic in origin, that is developed for use in creating consensus in a political system. Ideologies have more or less coherent structures, but they tend to be tautological in terms of argumentation because the aim of creating consensus usually requires that they mask inconsistencies between constituent elements. This can create difficulties when ideologies come to be believed and used as bases for policy. Ideologies and social sciences can overlap and affect one another, but in terms of their fundamental structures and intentions, they cannot be the same thing.

18. To some extent, of course, the decision to feature politics and ideology as the keys to change in social and cultural theory is an arbitrary one. By focusing on politics, we shall turn important factors, such as economic modernization, new intellectual trends, and so forth, into matters of secondary consideration. The justifications for doing this will be explained in the chapters that follow, but the main reason is that politics affords an explanation

for the timing of change in social science and the appearance of autonomous cultural sciences that no other factor can provide. Rüdiger vom Bruch, in examining the bases of theoretical disputation among German economists and historians at the turn of the century, similarly emphasizes the role of politics. See Bruch, *Wissenschaft*.

19. In this study, *ethnology, cultural anthropology,* and *Völkerkunde* will be treated as essentially synonymous terms, except when their historical evolution is being specifically discussed.

20. *Radical nationalism* is, like *radical conservatism* (a term often used synonymously with it), a rather inadequate way of describing the wide variety of late nineteenth-century political tendencies that, having sprung to a large degree from liberal roots, questioned the correctness of standard liberal assumptions, opposed the fragmentation of German society that resulted from rapid economic change, and rejected accommodation with socialism. The interpretation of radical nationalism is presently a subject of historiographical controversy (see chap. 11 herein).

21. *Geisteswissenschaft* has no direct English equivalent. (''Spiritual science,'' the literal translation, hardly catches the meaning of the term.) In general, the term refers to academic approaches to understanding society and culture that were built on idealist (often neo-Kantian) philosophical assumptions and were self-consciously antipositivist. Such approaches rejected the argument that social and intellectual phenomena have a prior material or economic origin and asserted that natural laws that apply to the products of the human mind cannot be found. The term *Kulturwissenschaft* (''cultural science,'') is sometimes used in approximately the same way, especially with respect to late nineteenth- and early-twentieth-century advocates of *Geisteswissenschaft*. Needless to say, this is *not* the way *cultural science* is meant in the present study.

Chapter 1

1. The discussion of the *Staatslexikon* in the pages that follow is based mainly on the third edition of *Das Staats-Lexikon: Encyklopädie der sammtlichen Staatswissenschaften für alle Stände*, 14 vols., ed. by Karl von Rotteck and Karl Welcker (Leipzig, 1856ff.). Welcker's introduction in vol. 1 of the third edition incorporates verbatim (with acknowledgment) large segments of Rotteck's introduction to the first edition. Rotteck's contributions will be cited according to their page numbers in the third edition. Several important parts of the third edition were directly compared with the second. When differences are apparent and relevant, specific reference will be made to the second edition. Unless otherwise indicated, all notes will refer to the third, thus: *SL*, volume: pages.

2. Leonard Krieger, *The German Idea of Freedom: History of a Political Tradition* (Boston, 1957), p. . 315; James J. Sheehan, *German Liberalism in the Nineteenth Century* (Chicago and London, 1978), p. 84.

3. On Rotteck and Welcker; see Krieger, *German Idea of Freedom*, pp. 242–61, 314–22; Karl Wild, *Karl Theodor Welcker: ein Vorkämpfer des älteren Liberalismus* (Heidelberg, 1913); and Bernd Gall, *Die individuelle Anerkennungstheorie von Karl Theodor Welcker* (Bonn, 1972).

4. *SL*, 1:vii–viii.

5. Ibid., xxvii.

6. Ibid., vi.

7. On liberal ideology and political theory, see Krieger, *German Idea of Freedom*. On liberalism as a political movement, see Sheehan, *German Liberalism*.

8. For instance, by Krieger in *German Idea of Freedom*, pp. 139–74, 216–72.

9. On the prerevolutionary beginnings of German liberalism and the immediate impact of the French Revolution, see Fritz Valjavec, *Die Entstehung der politischen Strömungen*

in Deutschland, 1770–1815 (Munich, 1951). See also Krieger, *German Idea of Freedom*, pp. 139–215; and Sheehan, *German Liberalism*, pp. 35–36.

10. Sheehan, *German Liberalism*, pp. 36–48.

11. Krieger, *German Idea of Freedom*, pp. 296–329. Krieger's analysis of the liberalism of the second quarter of the nineteenth century divides liberal intellectuals into three categories: moderates, dualists, and radicals. He places Rotteck and Welcker in the second category on the grounds that they pursued a dual objective of a strong constitutional monarchy and a maximization of individual freedom, whereas more convinced monarchists, such as Friedrich Dahlmann, are placed in the first category. This makes sense in terms of Krieger's analysis of the history of the idea of freedom in German thought, but the distinction is of little help from the standpoint of this study. Krieger's moderates and dualists are all called moderate liberals here, as distinct (in some respects) from radicals.

12. On the situation of the professoriate in society after 1815, see Charles E. McClelland, *State, Society, and University in Germany 1700–1914* (Cambridge, 1980), pp. 101–89. On professors in liberal politics, see Sheehan, *German Liberalism*, pp. 19–22.

13. McClelland, *State, Society, and University*, pp. 106–11, 122–32, 141–45, 171–81.

14. Ibid. Of course, Baden, with the best-developed constitutional system in Germany, gave Rotteck and Welcker more scope for their political activities than other states afforded their professors, but in general the statements made here hold for most of the other states as well. See Krieger, *German Idea of Freedom*, pp. 233–37. See also the remarks of the psychologist Wilhelm Wundt (a Badener and, in the 1860s, a member of the Baden Chamber of Deputies) on the Baden constitution in Wilhelm Wundt, *Erlebtes und Erkanntes* (Stuttgart, 1920), pp. 9–13.

15. See *SL*, 1:v–ix.

16. Krieger, *German Idea of Freedom*, pp. 293–96; McClelland, *State, Society, and University*, pp. 111–22; Fritz K. Ringer, *The Decline of the German Mandarins: The German Academic Community, 1890–1933* (Cambridge, 1969), pp. 15–42, 81–127.

17. McClelland, *State, Society, and University*, pp. 156–61.

18. Ibid., pp. 217–32.

19. For the importance of journalism in academic careers, see chapter 3 herein. Among the most important contributors to the *Staatslexikon* were Friedrich List, Robert von Mohl, and Karl Mathy, all of whom were essentially journalists for much of their lives. See the discussion of the *Staatslexikon* in Donald G. Rohr, *The Origins of Social Liberalism in Germany* (Chicago, 1963), pp. 102–30.

20. Ringer, *German Mandarins*, pp. 81–127. As we shall see later, however, although the liberal social scientists benefitted from the climate of appreciation of scholarship that Wilhelm von Humboldt helped to create, Humboldt himself, although a liberal, had not accepted some of the most important assumptions of the liberal theoretical pattern in social science.

21. See, for example, the analysis of the ways in which the liberal business elite expressed its views on social policy in Rohr, *Social Liberalism*, pp. 91–101, 132–47.

22. Ibid., pp. 102–30. See, for example, Karl Mathy, *"Banken und Bankwesen," SL*, 2:265–318.

23. SL, 1:x–xviii.

24. On European liberal ideology, see Guido de Ruggiero, *The History of European Liberalism*, trans. R. G. Collingwood (Boston, 1959).

25. *SL*, 1:v–xi. See also Rotteck and Welcker's article on *"Abgeordenete"* in ibid., 31–38. Disagreements within German liberalism are discussed in Krieger, *German Idea of*

Freedom, pp. 296–329; and Theodore S. Hamerow, *Restoration, Revolution, Reaction: Economics and Politics in Germany, 1815–1871* (Princeton, NJ, 1958), pp. 56–67.

26. Hamerow, *Restoration, Revolution, Reaction*, pp. 64–67.

27. On pre-1848 discussions of social issues and economics, see Rohr, *Social Liberalism*.

28. See Georg G. Iggers, *The German Conception of History: The National Tradition of Historical Thought from Herder to the Present* (Middletown, CT, 1968), pp. 29–62; and Kurt Mueller-Vollmer, ed., *The Hermeneutics Reader: Texts of the German Tradition from the Enlightenment to the Present* (New York, 1985), pp. 105–18.

29. This is clear from the "Systematic Encyclopedia of the *Staatswissenschaften*" that Welcker appended to the introduction to the third edition of the *Staatslexikon*: *SL*, 1:xxix–lxiv.

30. The attempt to play down differences is displayed in SL, 1:x–xviii, xxvi–xxvii.

31. Ibid., x–xviii, xxxviii–xxxix, xl; 2:518–20; 4:228–30.

32. Peter Hans Reill, *The German Enlightenment and the Rise of Historicism* (Berkeley, CA, 1975), pp. 48–74, 127–89.

33. See Wilhelm Heinrich Riehl, *Die Volkskunde als Wissenschaft* (Berlin and Leipzig, 1935), pp. 7–22 (an 1858 address). The work of the late eighteenth-century historian Justus Möser, for instance, which was placed by conservative commentators from the 1850s onward firmly in a conservative, anti-Enlightenment framework, was before 1848 generally regarded as part of the Enlightenment legacy. On Möser, see Krieger, *German Idea of Freedom*, pp. 79–80; Klaus Epstein, *The Genesis of German Conservatism* (Princeton, NJ 1966), pp. 297–338, esp. pp. 298–99; and Jonathan B. Knudsen, *Justus Möser and the German Enlightenment* (Cambridge, 1986).

34. On Humboldt, Dahlmann, and Rotteck, see Iggers, *German Conception of History*, pp. 44–62, 96–103.

35. See, for example, Wundt, *Erlebtes und Erkanntes*, pp. 52, 57; and Koepping, *Bastian*, pp. 57–94.

36. Thus, for example, to refer to Max Weber—a thinker engaged in discourse with an immense variety of intellectual formulations—as a social thinker primarily influenced by neo-Kantian philosophy is simply inadequate, as is demonstrated in Wolfgang J. Mommsen and Jürgen Osterhammel, eds., *Max Weber and His Contemporaries* (London, 1987). See esp. Guy Oakes, "Weber and the Southwest German School: The Genesis of the Concept of the Historical Individual," in Mommsen and Osterhammel, *Max Weber*, pp. 434–46.

37. *SL*, 1:518–20 (H. Marquardson on "*Bentham'sche Schule*").

38. See the discussions of individualism in German liberal political theory in Krieger, *German Idea of Freedom*, pp. 179–85, 192–94, 259–61.

39. Burrow, *Evolution and Society*, pp. 101–8.

40. For a typical liberal treatment of irrationality, see Rotteck's article on "*Aberglaube*," SL, 1:16–20.

41. See Rotteck's article on "*Bildung*," *SL*, 2:725–35. For Humboldt, see Iggers, *German Conception of History*, pp. 44–62.

42. Gall, *Welcker*, pp. 23–26, 28–36.

43. *Ibid*.

44. *SL*, 1:xxxviii.

45. This is the point of Welcker's "Systematic Encyclopedia": *SL*, 1:xxix–lxiv.

46. As Welcker, for instance, was well aware: *SL*, 1:xxxviii.

47. This was, of course, a classic problem of liberal social thought. On the problem as seen in England by John Stuart Mill and others, see Burrow, *Evolution and Society*,

pp. 217–20. For a discussion of the problem as seen by a German liberal, see Gall, *Welcker*, pp. 39–49.

48. See Epstein, *Genesis of German Conservatism*, pp. 12–17, 297–338, 547–94; Iggers, *German Conception of History*, pp. 29–62; Mueller-Vollmer, *Hermeneutics Reader*, pp. 98–131.

49. Edwin G. Boring, *A History of Experimental Psychology*, 2nd ed. (New York, 1950), pp. 250–347; David Hothersall, *History of Psychology* (Philadelphia, 1984), pp. 57–100.

50. On the early development of statistics in Germany, see Anthony Oberschall, *Empirical Social Research in Germany 1848–1914* (Paris and The Hague, 1965), pp. 16–21, 36–42. On Engel, his work, his politics, and his students, see ibid., pp. 42–45; Lujo Brentano, *Mein Leben im Kampf um die soziale Entwicklung Deutschlands* (Jena, 1931), pp. 41–42; and James J. Sheehan, *The Career of Lujo Brentano: A Study of Liberalism and Social Reform in Imperial Germany* (Chicago and London, 1966), pp. 16–26.

51. Oberschall, *Empirical Social Research*, pp. 42–45.

52. See, for example, Montesquieu's treatment of the subject: Montesquieu, *Oeuvres complètes*, 2 vols. (Paris, 1951), 1: pp. 1419–21; 2: pp. 556–83.

53. See *SL*, 1:vi–viii, 16–20; 2:725–35.

54. Wilhelm Roessler, *Die Entstehung des modernen Erziehungswesens in Deutschland* (Stuttgart, 1961).

55. SL, 2:725–35 (Rotteck on *"Bildung"*).

56. Riehl, *Volkskunde als Wissenschaft* , pp. 7–22. For the empirical sources of Herder's thought, see Gerald Broce, "Herder and Ethnography," *Journal of the History of the Behavioral Sciences* 22 (1986), pp. 150–70.

57. On these issues in the eighteenth century, see Reill, *German Enlightenment*, pp. 127–89.

58. Broce, "Herder and Ethnography," p. 161.

59. Herder's major work is *Ideen zur Philosophie der Geschichte der Menschheit* (Berlin, 1879), which is conveniently summarized in Broce, "Herder and Ethnography." A general introduction to Herder's thought can be found in Wulf Koepke, *Johann Gottfried Herder* (Boston, 1987.)

60. Reill, *German Enlightenment*, pp. 161–89.

61. Broce, "Herder and Ethnography."

62. *SL*, 1:viii–ix, xix–xxviii.

63. Ibid., 38.

64. See Welcker's discussions of the elements of "healthy" social life (*SL*, 1:xxxix–li), and of *"Kultur"* (*SL* 1:liii), which is the same as in the second edition of SL. The third edition of *SL* compiled in the 1850s after cultural science had become fashionable contains for the first time a section in the introduction in which Welcker discusses the cultural development of Germany, although "culture" is not taken in a wholly anthropological sense (*SL*, 1:xix). The third edition also contains, for the first time, a regular entry under *"Kultur"* by Karl Biedermann (*SL* 4:227–39).

65. Epstein, *Genesis of German Conservatism*, pp. 674–75; Iggers, *German Conception of History*, pp. 29–43.

66. Reill, *German Enlightenment*, pp. 100–26.

67. Gall, *Welcker*, pp. 28–36; *SL*, 1:xxxviii–xxxix.

68. *SL*, 1:xxix–xxxi. This was what Welcker *said*. His practice, as we have already seen, was another matter. In fact Welcker relied very heavily on reasoning from basic assumptions about human nature. See Gall, *Welcker*, pp. 39–43.

69. *SL*, 1:xxx.

70. Ibid.

71. Ibid., xxi.

72. See Karl Mathy's article on *"Anthropologie"* in *SL*, 1:584–88.

73. Reill, *German Enlightenment*, pp. 127–89; *SL*, 1:xxix–xxxvii.

74. Gall, Welcker, pp. 26–39, 79–87.

75. *SL*, 1:xxxviii. On Gneist's politics and their relationship to his legal thought, see Krieger, *German Idea of Freedom*, pp. 356–58, 433–34. See also *Neue Deutsche Biographie* 60:487–89 and Rudolf Gneist, *The History of the English Constitution*, 2 vols., trans. P. Ashworth (New York, 1886), 1:iii–x.

76. See Welcker in *SL*, 1:xli.

77. See Adolph Lowe, "The Classical Theory of Economic Growth," repr. in *Social Research* 51, 1 and 2 (1984), pp. 111–42 (orig. published 1954).

78. Hiram Caton, "The Preindustrial Economics of Adam Smith," *Journal of Economic History* 45, 4 (1985), pp. 833–53.

79. For a classic treatment of Hegel's influence on social thought, see Herbert Marcuse, *Reason and Revolution: Hegel and the Rise of Social Theory*, 2nd ed. (Boston, 1960). There were decided limits to Hegel's influence, however. In developing the stage theory of cultural evolution that he added to the introduction to the third edition of the *Staatslexikon* (*SL*, 1:xix–xxvii), instead of working from Hegelian theory, Welcker went back to the eighteenth-century German culture-history tradition as described in Reill, *German Enlightenment*.

80. Burrow, *Evolution and Society*, pp. 24–64.

81. On the idea of the *Rechtsstaat*, see Krieger, *German Idea of Freedom*, pp. 252–61. For Welcker's general use of the concept of balance, see *SL*, 1:xxxvii. It should be noted that some versions of the *Rechtsstaat* idea emphasized it as the embodiment of its own ethical principles, not as a manifestation of equilibrium.

82. See Rudolf Virchow's essay "Atoms and Individuals" in his *Disease, Life, and Man: Selected Essays*, trans. L. J. Rather (Stanford, CA, 1958), pp. 120–41.

83. Lowe, "Classical Theory," pp. 111–42.

84. On List, see Rohr, *Social Liberalism*, pp. 104–9. For a compendium of List's thought, see List, *The National System of Political Economy*, trans. G. A. Matile (Philadelphia, 1856).

85. Peter T. Manicas, *A History and Philosophy of the Social Sciences* (Oxford, 1987), pp. 53–96; Burrow, *Evolution and Society*, pp. 42–64; Georg Wilhelm Friedrich Hegel, *The Philosophy of History* (New York, 1956), pp. 103–10.

86. See, for example, Welcker's idea of the stages of German social development in *SL*, 1:xix

87. Leopold von Ranke, *The Secret of World History*, trans. and ed. Roger Wines (New York, 1981), pp. 101–17; Mueller–Vollmer, *Hermeneutics Reader*, pp. 124–26.

88. Marx's critique of stage theories and an early presentation of his own are contained in *The German Ideology*. See Robert C. Tucker, ed., *The Marx–Engels Reader*, 2nd ed. (New York, 1978), pp. 146–200. Max Weber devoted attention to the weakness of stage explanations for the dynamics of historical change in his *Roscher and Knies: The Logical Problems of Historical Economics*, trans. Guy Oakes (New York, 1975), esp. pp. 81–83.

89. *SL*, 1:xix.

90. Lowe, "Classical Theory," pp. 111–42.

91. On the reception of Darwin's theory in Germany, see Alfred Kelly, *The Descent of Darwin: The Popularization of Darwin in Germany, 1860–1914* (Chapel Hill, NC, 1981), pp. 20–24. (Kelly does not, however, make the point outlined here.)

92. For a classic liberal discussion of associations, see Welcker's article on the subject in *SL*, 1:758–87, and also *SL*, 1:lxi–lxiv.

93. Wilhelm Heinrich Riehl criticized liberals for their lack of attention to practical empirical research in *Die bürgerliche Gesellschaft* (Stuttgart, 1861), pp. 36–47. Oberschall, *Empirical Social Research*, pp. 16–21, 36–37, also points to the relative paucity of empirical studies in early German social science. Welcker himself describes the "practical" nature of social science (*SL*, 1:xxx) in terms that would not impress a tough-minded pragmatist or a modern professor of public administration—which was, among other things, what Welcker was supposed to be.

94. On the continuity of the various forms of progress and their relationship to freedom, see Rotteck and Welcker in *SL*, 1:v–vi, xix, 1–9. See also *SL*, 2:716–24.

95. See Welcker's difficulties with the effects of economic change as experienced by peasants in his article "*Bauer, Bauernstand*" in *SL*, 2:371–80. See also Rohr, *Social Liberalism*, pp. 131–57.

96. *SL*, 1:vi–ix.

97. Ibid., li–lx.

98. For Humboldt's educational theories in practical form, see Wilhelm von Humboldt, *Schulpläne des Jahres 1809: "Über die innere und äussere Organisation der höheren wissenschaftlichen Anstalten in Berlin,"1810* (Hamburg, 1946).

99. *SL*, 1:lii.

100. Ibid. xxx–xxxvii.

Chapter 2

1. W. H. Riehl, *Religiöse Studien eines Weltkindes* (Stuttgart, 1894), p. 468.

2. *Ibid.*, pp. 391–472. The best study of the relationship between Riehl's politics and his social scientific orientations is Hannah Gädecke, *Wilhelm Heinrich Riehls Gedanken über Volk und Staat* (Heidelberg, 1935). Inaugural dissertation.

3. The best comprehensive discussion of the career of liberalism in Germany after 1848 is Sheehan, *German Liberalism*. The argument that the German liberals were more successful than was formerly thought is presented strongly in David Blackbourn and Geoff Eley, *The Peculiarities of German History: Bourgeois Society and Politics in Nineteenth-Century Germany* (New York, 1984).

4. Hamerow, *Restoration, Revolution, Reaction*, pp. 95–195.

5. Viktor von Geramb, *Wilhelm Heinrich Riehl: Leben und Wirken (1823–1897)* (Salzburg, 1954), pp. 183–85.

6. See, for example, the reactions of Rudolf Virchow, a radical of 1848, in Rudolf Virchow, *Briefe an seine Eltern 1839 bis 1864*, ed. Marie Rabl (Leipzig, 1907), pp. 139–41, 141–45, 161–64.

7. *SL*, 1:xix–xxviii.

8. Krieger, *German Idea of Freedom*, pp. 329–40.

9. See, for example, *SL*, 1:xix.

10. Riehl, *Bürgerliche Gesellschaft*, pp. 3–19; Virchow, *Briefe*, pp. 150–51.

11. The standard analysis of the liberal support problem, focusing on the incompatibility between liberal ideology and the perceived needs of groups threatened by modernization, is found in Hamerow, *Restoration, Revolution, Reaction*, pp. 137–72. Hamerow also (pp. 173–95) discusses the attempts by "social conservatives" in the 1850s to develop an appeal to traditional artisan and peasant interests. Recent research has emphasized that the liberals, nevertheless, managed to retain considerable lower-class support into the 1870s. See Sheehan, *German Liberalism*, pp. 79–94.

12. Krieger, *German Idea of Freedom*, pp. 388–97. Rohr, *Social Liberalism*, pp. 154–57, argues that social concerns lost their importance in the 1850s to many of the pre-1848 "social liberals," who became more interested in business and nationalism. This was true

in part, but it was balanced, as Krieger points out, by the increasing emphasis placed on social issues by other liberals. This can be seen most clearly in the work of Hermann Schulze-Delitzch and the liberal cooperative movement.

13. Rohr, *Social Liberalism*, pp. 158–66. See Carl Rodbertus-Jagetzow, *Zur Beleuchtung der socialen Frage*, ed. A. Wagner and T. Kozak (Berlin, 1875).

14. Iggers, *German Conception of History*, pp. 104–15; Günter Birtsch, *Die Nation als sittliche Idee* (Cologne, 1964).

15. *Neue Deutsche Biographie*, 2:223–24.

16. Krieger, *German Idea of Freedom*, pp. 353–56; August Ludwig von Rochau, *Grundsätze der Realpolitik angewendet auf die staatlichen Zustände Deutschlands* (Stuttgart, 1853).

17. See, for instance, Welcker's introduction to the third edition of the *Staatslexikon*: *SL*, 1:xix–xxviii.

18. Rodbertus, *Zur Beleuchtung*; Biedermann, "*Kultur*," *SL*, 4:227–39; Virchow, *Briefe*, pp. 177–79, 182–85.

19. See Eliot's review of Riehl's *Naturgeschichte des Volkes* in Thomas Pinney, ed., *Essays of George Eliot* (New York, 1963), pp. 266–99. For Riehl's career, see Geramb, *Riehl*, and the source on which much of Geramb's work is based, Riehl, *Religiöse Studien*.

20. See the discussion of Riehl in Klaus Bergmann, *Agrarromantik und Grossstadtfeindschaft* (Meisenheimam Glan, 1970), pp. 38–49; and George L. Mosse, *The Crisis of German Ideology: Intellectual Origins of the Third Reich* (New York, 1964), pp. 19–24. On the other hand, see the appreciation of Riehl as an empirical social scientist in Oberschall, *Empirical Social Research*, pp. 65–68.

21. Riehl, *Religiöse Studien*, pp. 396–415.

22. Gädecke, *Riehls Gedanken*, pp. 51–60, establishes Riehl's early liberalism definitively.

23. Ibid., pp. 1–10, 35–39, 51–60.

24. Geramb, *Riehl*, p. 185.

25. See Krieger, *German Idea of Freedom*, pp. 303–14.

26. Riehl, *Bürgerliche Gesellschaft*, pp. 3–19.

27. Hamerow, *Restoration, Revolution, Reaction*, pp. 199–237. King Maximilian II of Bavaria, who became Riehl's employer in 1854, fits nicely into this category.

28. Riehl, *Volkskunde als Wissenschaft*, pp. 7–22.

29. Oberschall, *Empirical Social Research*, pp. 65–68.

30. The first volume, *Die bürgerliche Gesellschaft*, was actually planned as the second volume in Riehl's series. He finished it first because it dealt with the social question and might (as it did) attract attention quickly. The supposed first volume was a general statement of Riehl's views on the relationship between culture and environment; the third focused on the family. A fourth volume of travel reports was later added. The full series was published as Wilhelm Heinrich Riehl, *Die Naturgeschichte des Volkes als Grundlage einer deutschen Social-Politik*, 4 vols, (Stuttgart, 1862–69).

31. Riehl, *Bürgerliche Gesellschaft*, p. 47.

32. Riehl, *Volkskunde als Wissenschaft*, p. 7.

33. Riehl, *Bürgerliche Gesellschaft*, pp. 36–47, 108–35.

34. Ibid., pp. 20–35. See also Pinney, *George Eliot*, pp. 266–99.

35. By using the term *Stand* for *class*, Riehl was, of course, identifying with the tradition of the corporate organization of society going back to the Middle Ages. Riehl was in fact one of the founders of conservative corporatism as a modern political ideology. It should, however, be kept in mind that the word *class* was not yet as widely used in German politics as it was in Britain and that the use of the word *Stand* for a major social grouping did not necessarily imply a break from liberalism. The subtitle of the third edition of the *Staatslexikon* indicates that it is an encyclopedia of useful knowledge "für alle Stände."

36. Riehl, *Bürgerliche Gesellschaft*, pp. 342–486.

37. Riehl, *Volkskunde als Wissenschaft*, pp. 19–22.

38. Ibid. pp. 18, 22, wherein Riehl discusses his predecessors.

39. Andree's biography is summarized in *Allgemeine Deutsche Biographie*, 46:12–15; and *Neue Deutsche Biographie*, 1:285.

40. On Rochau, see Krieger, *German Idea of Freedom*, pp. 354–56, and Rochau, *Realpolitik*.

41. Carl Theodor Andree, *Geographische Wanderungen*, 2 vols. (Dresden, 1859).

42. *Völkerkunde* eventually came to be the standard German term for cultural anthropology. Riehl's *Volkskunde* remained the title of the discipline practiced by Riehl and his followers—a very limited discipline, although it went through vogues at the turn of the century and during the Nazi period.

43. Biographical material on Waitz can be found in Otto Gebhardt, ed., *Theodor Waitz' Allgemeine Pädogogik und kleinere pädogogische Schriften* (Langensalza, Ger., 1910), pp. xix–cvlvii. Gebhardt's book includes most of Waitz's educational writings. See also the lengthy entry by Waitz's student and friend, the anthropologist Georg Gerland, in *Allgemeine Deutsche Biographie*, 56 vols, (Berlin 1967–1971; repr of 1871–1912 ed.), 40:629–33. The significance of the Lutheran *Pfarrhaus* in possibly influencing the thought of Waitz and other intellectuals of similar background will be discussed in chapter 3.

44. Waitz's ethnology is a compendium of anthropological knowledge as it existed at the end of the 1850s: in other words, just before the appearance of detailed ethnographical data from trained observers. Waitz's theory of evolution (Theodor Waitz, *Introduction to Anthropology*, ed. and trans J. Frederick Collingwood (London, 1863), pp. 80–89) was pushed aside by the much more comprehensive theory of Darwin. Much of Waitz's psychology was made obsolete by the development of experimental psychology.

45. Gebhardt, *Waitz' Allgemeine Pädogogik*, pp. xxviii–xxxii; Adolf Lemmer, *Der Begriff des Gemütes bei Waitz und Hildebrand* (Cologne, 1927), pp. 17–26. Inaugural dissertation.

46. Gebhardt, *Waitz' Allgemeine Pädogogik*, pp. xxiv–xxxvii.

47. Gerland, relying on personal contact with Waitz, makes this point strongly in *Allgemeine Deutsche Biographie* 40:629–33.

48. Gebhardt, *Waitz' Allgemeine Pädogogik*, pp. 345–71.

49. Gebhardt, *Waitz' Allgemeine Pädogogik*, pp. 15–25, 387–140.

50. Waitz's psychology is summarized in Gebhardt, *Waitz' Allgemeine Pädogogik*, pp. xxiv–xxxviii.

51. Ibid., pp. 38–78, 115–238.

52. Waitz, *Introduction to Anthropology*, pp. 259–68.

53. Lowie, *History of Ethnological Theory*, pp. 16–18; Waitz, *Introduction to Anthropology*, preface. With Jacob Grimm, Bastian, and Klemm, Waitz is one of the German authors most cited in Edward B. Tylor, *Primitive Culture*, 2 vols. (New York, 1977).

54. Stocking, *Victorian Anthropology*, pp. 48–53.

55. Waitz, *Introduction to Anthropology*, pp. 10–16, 90–143, 167–89.

56. Ibid., pp. 328–80.

57. Ibid., pp. 10–16; *Allgemeine Deutsche Biographie*, 46:12–15; *Neue Deutsche Biographie*, 1:285.

58. Erwin H. Ackerknecht, *Rudolf Virchow: Doctor Statesman Anthropologist* (Madison, WI, 1953), pp. 3–39; Virchow, *Briefe*, pp. 1–3.

59. Virchow described his position on social issues and on socialism in letters to his father in 1848 and 1849, included (although selectively edited to deradicalize them) in Virchow, *Briefe*, pp. 148–50, 177–79. His mature position is outlined in a party political address: Rudolf Virchow, *Sozialismus und Reaktion* (Berlin, 1878).

60. Virchow, *Briefe*, pp. 31–39. Virchow's two reports are bound together in a modern photoreproduced edition: Rudolf Virchow, *Die Not im Spessart. Mitteilungen über die in Oberschlesien herrschende Typhus-Epidemie* (Hildesheim, 1968).

61. Virchow, *Not im Spessart*, p. 217.

62. Ibid., pp. 224–29.

63. Ibid., pp. 13–14, 56, 59–81.

64. Ernst Werner Kohl, *Virchow in Würzburg* (Hanover, 1976), pp. 16–19, 24.

65. Ackerknecht, *Virchow*, pp. 29, 195–207.

66. Ibid., pp. 22–26.

67. Ibid., p. 45. See also Owsei Temkin, "Metaphors of Human Biology," in R. C. Stauffer, ed., *Science and Civilization* (Madison, WI, 1949), pp. 169–94.

68. For Helmholtz's position, see his lecture "On the Relation of Natural Science to General Science" in Hermann Helmholtz, *Popular Lectures on Scientific Subjects*, trans. E. Atkinson (New York, 1873), pp. 1–32.

69. Burrow, *Evolution and Society*, pp. 246–51. Lowie, *History of Ethnological Theory*, p. 83, quotes Tylor as stating that anthropology (including archaeology) is "essentially a reformer's science."

70. Ackerknecht, *Virchow*, pp. 27, 181–91; Virchow, *Not im Spessart,* pp. 59–81. These attitudes can be seen also in the thinking of the leading protagonists of materialism in Germany in the third quarter of the nineteenth century: Karl Vogt, Jacob Moleschott, Ludwig Büchner, and Heinrich Czolbe. See Frederick Gregory, *Scientific Materialism in Nineteenth Century Germany* (Dordrecht and Boston, 1977), pp. 1–10, 29–48.

71. Virchow, *Sozialismus und Reaktion*, pp. 3–4, 16–18.

Chapter 3

1. For treatments of the intellectual influences on cultural sciences, see Mühlmann, *Geschichte der Anthropologie,* 2nd ed., pp. 52–73; Wilhelm Roscher, *Geschichte der National-Oekonomik in Deutschland,* 2nd ed. (Munich and Berlin, 1924), pp. 480–699; Boring, *History of Experimental Psychology,* pp. 246–70; Preston E. James, *All Possible Worlds: A History of Geographical Ideas* (Indianapolis and New York, 1972).

2. An excellent, brief summary of the general history of German geography is Hanno Beck, "Geography and Travel in the Nineteenth Century: Prolegomena to a General History of Travel," in Gary S. Dunbar, ed., *The History of Geography: Translations of Some French and German Essays* (Malibu, CA, 1983), pp. 73–102. See also Hans-Dietrich Schultz, *Die deutschsprachige Geographie von 1800 bis 1970: Ein Beitrag zur Geschichte ihrer Methodologie* (Berlin, 1980).

3. The most detailed study of Humboldt is Hanno Beck, *Alexander von Humboldt,* 2 vols. (Wiesbaden, 1959).

4. Alexander von Humboldt, *Kosmos: Entwurf einer physischen Weltbeschreibung,* 4 vols. (Stuttgart, 1845–1858).

5. See the way Alexander von Humboldt's legacy is treated in Friedrich Ratzel, *Die Erde und das Leben: Eine vergleichende Erdkunde,* 2 vols. (Leipzig and Vienna, 1901), 1:51–55.

6. Ibid.; Beck, "Geography and Travel," pp. 85–86.

7. Beck, "Geography and Travel," pp. 77–85. See also *Allegemeine Deutsche Biographie,* 28:679–97.

8. Ritter's influence extended beyond academia. One of his students was the later Prussian war minister Albrecht von Roon, who was strongly affected by Ritter. See Waldemar Graf von Roon, *Denkwürdigkeiten aus dem Leben des Generalfeldmarschalls Kriegsministers Grafen von Roon,* 3 vols.; 5th ed. (Berlin, 1905), 3:55–59.

9. On Wilhelm Perthes, see *Allgemeine Deutsche Biographie,* 25:401–2.

10. Beck, "Geography and Travel," pp. 87–91.

11. On the British context, see Stocking, *Victorian Anthropology*, pp. 48–56.

12. Mühlmann, *Geschichte der Anthropologie*, 2nd ed., pp. 65–66, 87–93.

13. *SL*, 1:584–88; Waitz, *Introduction to Anthropology*, pp. 3–10.

14. Stocking, *Victorian Anthropology*, pp. 46–77.

15. The leading Berlin anthropologists named their journal, for example, the *Zeitschrift für Ethnologie* in 1870.

16. A summary of German anthropological nomenclature is included in Hans Fischer and Ludger Müller-Wille, *Ethnologen-Verzeichnis* (Bonn, 1977), p. 7.

17. Beck, *Humboldt*, 2:228–30; Cornelia Essner, *Deutsche Afrikareisende im neunzehnten Jahrhundert* (Stuttgart, 1985), pp. 76–81.

18. Mühlmann, *Geschichte der Anthropologie*, 2nd ed., pp. 59–61; Lowie, *History of Ethnological Theory*, pp. 10–11; Christoph Meiners, *Grundriss der Geschichte der Menschheit* (Lemgo, Ger. 1785).

19. Lowie, *History of Ethnological Theory*, pp. 11–16; Gustav Klemm, *Allgemeine Cultur-Geschichte der Menschheit*, vol. 1 (Leipzig, 1843).

20. See note 53 to Ch. 2.

21. See Stocking, *Victorian Anthropology*, pp. 110–43.

22. See Helmut Gipper and Peter Schmitter, *Sprachwissenschaft und Sprachphilosophie im Zeitalter der Romantik: Ein Beitrag zur Historiographie der Linguistik* (Tübingen, 1979).

23. H. P. Rickman, *Wilhelm Dilthey: Pioneer of the Human Studies* (Berkeley, CA, 1979), pp. 58–73.

24. Gipper and Schmitter, *Sprachwissenschaft*, pp. 77–116; Wilhelm von Humboldt, *Humanist Without Portfolio*, trans. Marianne Cowan (Detroit, 1963), pp. 125–44, 235–98. As we have seen, Humboldt did not accept some of the tenets of the liberal theoretical pattern in social science, although he was clearly a liberal. Humboldt helped to originate the process of intellectual development that produced the hermeneutic approach to social understanding. In the first half of the nineteenth century, however, the implications of the differences between the Humboldt legacy and mainstream liberal social science were not wholly apparent. In any event, the Humboldtian idea of humanistic education was generally accepted by most academics regardless of theoretical orientation.

25. Gipper and Schmitter, *Sprachwissenschaft*, pp. 49–59.

26. *Jacob und Wilhelm Grimm als Sprachwissenschaftler: Geschichtlichkeit und Aktualität ihres Wirkens* (Berlin, 1985). For a critical view of the Grimms's methods, see John M. Ellis, *One Fairy Story Too Many: The Brothers Grimm and Their Tales* (Chicago, 1983).

27. Gipper and Schmitter, *Sprachwissenschaft*, pp. 28–32, 37–40, 49–54.

28. George L. Mosse, *Toward the Final Solution: A History of European Racism* (New York, 1978), pp. 39–44.

29. James Whitman, "From Philology to Anthropology in Mid-Nineteenth-Century Germany," in George W. Stocking, Jr., ed., *Functionalism Historicized: Essays in British Social Anthropology* (Madison, WI, 1984), pp. 214–29.

30. Stocking, *Victorian Anthropology*, pp. 65–68.

31. The oldest major archaeological society in Germany, the Berlin Archaeological Society, was founded in 1841 (*Wer Ist's?* 10th ed. [Berlin, 1914], pp. lxix–lxxvi.) See also Kenneth R. Kennedy, *Neanderthal Man* (Minneapolis, 1975), pp. 1–4. One aspect of archaeology in which Germans played a major role, even in the eighteenth century, was the study of classical Greek and Roman buildings, but we shall not discuss classical archaeology here.

32. Ackerknecht, *Virchow*, pp. 219–29.

33. Stocking, *Victorian Anthropology*, pp. 69–74; Lowie, *History of Ethnological Theory*, p. 83.

34. Ackerknecht, *Virchow*, pp. 219–29, 230.

35. See Stocking, *Victorian Anthropology*, pp. 156–64.

36. Ackerknecht, *Virchow*, pp. 195–99; Waitz, *Introduction to Anthropology*, pp. 17–258.

37. Stocking, *Victorian Anthropology*, pp. 245–54; James Hunt, "On the Study of Anthropology," *Anthropological Review* 1 (1863), pp. 1–20.

38. See, for example, Oscar Peschel, *Völkerkunde*, 4th ed. (Leipzig, 1877), pp. 49–102; and Friedrich Müller, *Allgemeine Ethnographie* (Vienna, 1873). See also Leon Poliakov, *Le Mythe aryen* (Paris, 1971), pp. 262–345.

39. As, for example, in the work of Klemm. See Klemm, *Allgemeine Cultur-Geschichte*. See also Poliakov, *Mythe aryen*, pp. 244–62.

40. Waitz, *Introduction to Anthropology*, pp. 10–16; Poliakov, *Mythe aryen*, pp. 266–67.

41. Waitz, *Introduction to Anthropology*, pp. 259–380.

42. Franz Boas, *Anthropology and Modern Life* (New York, 1928), pp. 18–62.

43. Armand de Quatrefages, *La Race prussienne* (Paris, 1871); Poliakov, *Mythe aryen*, pp. 269–82. For a detailed treatment of one version of these arguments, see Heinz Gollwitzer, *Die gelbe Gefahr* (Göttingen, 1962).

44. Ackerknecht, *Virchow*, pp. 207–19.

45. Racism is covered comprehensively in Mosse, *Toward the Final Solution* and in Poliakov, *Mythe aryen*, pp. 282–88. See Virchow's attack on racist interpretations of physical anthropology in his "Rassenbildung und Erblichkeit," in *Festschrift für Adolf Bastian zu seinem 70. Geburtstage 26. Juni 1896* (Berlin, 1896), pp. 1–43.

46. Reill, *German Enlightenment*.

47. See Iggers, *German Conception of History*, esp. pp. 63–123. See also *SL*, 1:372–73. On Ranke, see Helmut Berding, "Leopold Ranke," in Hans-Ulrich Wehler, ed., *Deutsche Historiker I*, (Göttingen, 1971), pp. 7–24.

48. Iggers, *German Conception of History*, pp. 100–102; and *Allgemeine Deutsche Biographie* 4:693–99.

49. Iggers, *German Conception of History*, pp. 63–89.

50. Ibid., pp. 100–102.

51. *SL*, 1:xix–xxviii.

52. Iggers, *German Conception of History*, pp. 88–91.

53. Ibid., pp. 90–123, 134–44; Mueller-Vollmer, *Hermeneutics Reader*, pp. 118–31, 148–64.

54. On Savigny, see *International Encyclopedia of the Social Sciences*, 14:21–22.

55. On Gneist, see *Neue Deutsche Biographie*, 6:487–89.

56. On Roscher, see *Allgemeine Deutsche Biographie* 53:486–92. On Burckhardt, see Jörn Rüsen, "Jacob Burckhardt," in Hans-Ulrich Wehler, ed., *Deutsche Historiker III* (Göttingen, 1972), pp. 5–28; and Wolfgang Hardtwig, *Geschichtsschreibung zwischen Alteuropa und moderner Welt: Jacob Burckhardt in seiner Zeit*. Göttingen, 1974.

57. *SL*, 4:227–39.

58. Ibid., p. 227.

59. Ibid., p. 228.

60. Ibid.

61. Ibid.

62. Ibid., p. 230.

63. Ibid., pp. 234–35.

64. See the discussion of this point in the final section of this chapter, pp. 81–82.

65. The most general modern study of the history of nineteenth-century German academia is McClelland, *State, Society, and University*.

66. Ibid., pp. 101–61.

67. The pattern of a German professor's relationship to his faculty is best seen in academic biographies. See, for instance, Brentano, *Mein Leben,* esp. pp. 55, 85–90, 115–18, 141–65.

68. See Ringer, *German Mandarins,* pp. 253–69.

69. McClelland, *State, Society, and University,* pp. 151–89; Konrad H. Jarausch, *Students, Society, and Politics in Imperial Germany: The Rise of Academic Illiberalism* (Princeton, NJ, 1982), pp. 81–90.

70. Ringer, *German Mandarins,* pp. 81–127.

71. For Ratzel, see chapter 7 herein. For the humanistic inclinations of educated journalists, see the article by Theodor Petermann in Karl Bücher et al., *Die Grossstadt* (Dresden, 1903), pp. 207–30.

72. Ringer, *German Mandarins,* pp. 128–29; Fritz Stern, *The Politics of Cultural Despair: A Study in the Rise of the Germanic Ideology* (Garden City, NY, 1965), pp. 25–128.

73. *Allgemeine Deutsche Biographie,* 28:679–97.

74. See chapter 2 herein.

75. Wundt, *Erlebtes und Erkanntes,* pp. 53–57. Solomon Diamond, "Wundt Before Leipzig," in R. W. Rieber, ed., *Wilhelm Wundt and the Making of a Scientific Psychology* (New York and London, 1980), p. 75.

76. The academic career is described in Jarausch, *Students, Society, and Politics,* pp. 134–59.

77. Essner, *Deutsche Afrikareisende,* pp. 93–100. See also chapter 9 herein.

78. On the history of the German press in the nineteenth century, see Kurt Koszyk, *Die deutsche Presse im 19. Jahrhundert* (Berlin, 1966); and Anthony Smith, *The Newspaper: An International History* (London, 1979), pp. 118–20.

79. Wanklyn, *Ratzel,* pp. 11–16; Arthur Mitzman, *The Iron Cage: An Historical Interpretation of Max Weber* (New York, 1969), pp. 66–74.

80. For examples of successful academic journalists who operated in the way described, see Gädecke, *Riehls Gedanken,* esp. pp. 51–60; Wolfgang Mommsen, *Max Weber und die deutsche Politik,* 2nd ed. (Tübingen, 1974), esp. pp. 73–96; Wanklyn, *Ratzel;* Wundt, *Erlebtes und Erkanntes,* p. 40. See also Kelly, *Descent of Darwin,* pp. 10–35. On academics and journalism after 1890, see Bruch, *Wissenschaft,* pp. 32–56.

81. For an example of this kind of journalism, see the August issue of *Deutsche Monatshefte* 3, 11 (1903), esp. pp. 675–90, which contains an article on foreign policy by the anthropologist Heinrich Schurtz as well as other articles by Friedrich Ratzel, Heinrich von Treitschke, and Houston Stewart Chamberlain.

82. We shall see this particularly in the case of Ratzel's concept of *Lebensraum* in chapter 12.

83. See *Festschrift zur hundertjährige Bestehen der Berliner Gesellschaft für Anthropologie, Ethnologie und Urgeschichte 1869–1969,* pt.1 (Berlin, 1969), esp. pp. 157–83.

84. See chapter 11 herein.

85. On *Völkerpsychologie,* see Eno Beuchelt, *Ideengeschichte der Völkerpsychologie* (Meisenheim am Glan, 1974). On anthropology and archaeology, see *Festschrift . . . Berliner Gesellschaft.*

86. Jarausch, *Students, Society, and Politics,* pp. 165–74.

87. Ringer, *German Mandarins,* pp. 141–42.

88. Lindenlaub, *Richtungskämpfe,* 52:34–43, 141–53; Ackerknecht, *Virchow,* pp. 181–91; Bruch, *Wissenschaft,* pp. 63–66.

89. Ringer, *German Mandarins,* pp. 128–99. See also chapters 10 and 11 herein.

90. Ringer, *German Mandarins,* pp. 128–43.

91. See McClelland, *State, Society, and University,* pp. 217–32, 314–21; and Bruch, *Wissenschaft,* pp. 32–92.

92. For a general survey of socioeconomic change in nineteenth-century Germany, see Helmut Böhme, *An Introduction to the Social and Economic History of Germany: Politics and Economic Change in the Nineteenth and Twentieth Centuries.,* trans. W. R. Lee (New York, 1978).

93. The main sources of biographical information are the *Allgemeine Deutsche Biographie, Neue Deutsche Biographie,* and various editions of *Wer Ist's?* The subjects in the sample were:

Age Group One (born before 1820): C. Th. Andree, H. E. Beyrich, F. C. Biedermann, F. Dahlmann, A. v. Humboldt, G. Klemm, K. Mathy, K. Ritter, K. v. Rotteck, K. Th. Welcker.

Age Group Two (born from 1820 to 1832): H. Barth, A. Bastian, R. Hartmann, A. Lissauer, W. H. Riehl, F. G. Rohlfs, W. Roscher, R. Virchow, Th. Waitz, W. Wundt.

Age Group Three (born from 1833 to 1853): R. Andree, M. Bartels, M. Buchner, Th. Fischer, G. Fritsch, R. v. Kaufmann, M. Quedenfeldt, F. Ratzel, G. E. Seler, H. Virchow.

Age Group Four (born from 1854 to 1872): A. Baessler, F. Boas, K. Breysig, G. Buschan, P. Ehrenreich, E. Hahn, H. G. Kossinna, K. G. Lamprecht, F. v. Luschan, A. Vierkandt.

Age Group Five (born after 1872): H. Baumann, W. Foy, L. Frobenius, F. Graebner, W. Koppers, P. Schebesta, D. Westermann

94. This age group is essentially the one discussed in Peter Bergmann, *Nietzsche: "The Last Antipolitical German"* (Bloomington and Indianapolis, 1987), pp. 30–58. It is, of course, Nietzsche's generation.

95. Ringer, *German Mandarins,* pp. 25–61.

96. This was Marie Eysen, second wife of Richard Andree, the son of C. Th. Andree. Eysen is mentioned as a *Volkskundlerin* in *Neue Deutsche Biographie,* 1:285. Among the 591 "ordinary" members of the *Berliner Gesellschaft für Anthropologie, Ethnologie und Urgeschichte* (hereafter referred to as *Berliner Gesellschaft*) in 1887, only two were women, and neither appears to have been a practicing anthropologist. (*Verhandlungen der Berliner Gesellschaft für Anthropologie, Ethnologie und Urgeschichte,* 1887, pp. 6–14.) Women were at first not allowed to belong to the *Berliner Gesellschaft* at all for fear they would be offended by photographs displayed at lectures.

97. Stocking, *Victorian Anthropology,* pp. 49–109.

98. In 1871, sixty percent of all Germans in the Reich were Prussians; in 1900, seventy-one percent were Prussians. See B. R. Mitchell, *European Historical Statistics 1750–1975,* 2nd ed. (New York, 1981), pp. 30, 71.

99. See Wolfgang Weber, *Priester der Klio. Historisch-sozialwissenschaftliche Studien zur Herkunft und Karriere deutscher Historiker und zur Geschichte der Geschichtswissenschaft 1800–1970,* 2nd ed. (Frankfurt am Main, 1987), pp. 83–93, for the religious affiliations of historians. The ratio of Protestants to Catholics in the Reich was about two to one. See Hajo Holborn, *A History of Modern Germany 1840–1945* (New York, 1969), p. 259.

100. Roger Chickering, "Young Lamprecht: An Essay in Biography and Historiography," *History and Theory* 28, 2 (1989), pp. 198–214. Roger Chickering has pointed out to me the importance of looking closely at the religious backgrounds of cultural scientists, for which I am grateful.

101. W. Weber, *Priester der Klio.*

102. Stern, *Politics of Cultural Despair;* Ringer, *German Mandarins.*

103. Geoff Eley, *Reshaping the German Right: Radical Nationalism and Political Change After Bismarck* (New Haven, CT, London, 1980); Roger Chickering, *We Men Who Feel Most German: A Cultural Study of the Pan-German League, 1886–1914* (Boston, 1984). The tendency of this approach is to see the radical nationalism of the educated bourgeoisie of the end of the century not as a rejection of liberalism and the adoption of a form of conservatism, but as a continuation of certain tendencies in liberalism.

Chapter 4

1. For the traditional view of 1848 as the beginning of the decline of German liberalism, see Koppel S. Pinson, *Modern Germany: Its History and Civilization,* 2nd ed. (New York, 1966), pp. 106–7. Sheehan, *German Liberalism,* pp. 79–119, shows the strength (and the problems) of the restored liberalism of the 1850s and 1860s. For a more radical reinterpretation, which argues that the liberals were far more successful in the long run in shaping late nineteenth-century Germany than they have been given credit for, see Blackbourn and Eley, *Peculiarities of German History,* esp. pp. 127–55, 238–60.

2. On Rochau and Rodbertus, see Krieger, *German Idea of Freedom,* pp. 353–56, 384–88.

3. Ibid., pp. 363–70.

4. The best current analysis is Sheehan, *German Liberalism,* pp. 123–218, which the present discussion largely follows.

5. General discussions of German unification, especially significant because they emphasize the interrelationships among liberal politics, Bismarck's policy, and socioeconomic interests, are Helmut Böhme, *Deutschlands Weg zur Grossmacht: Studien zum Verhältnis von Wirtschaft und Staat während der Reichsgründungszeit 1848–1881* (Cologne, 1966); and Theodore S. Hamerow, *The Social Foundations of German Unification, 1858–71,* 2 vols. (Princeton, NJ, 1969, 1972).

6. See Hans-Ulrich Wehler, *The German Empire 1871–1918,* trans. Kim Traynor (Leamington Spa, Eng., 1985), pp. 52–99.

7. Sheehan, *German Liberalism,* pp. 123–40.

8. Dan White, *The Splintered Party: National Liberalism in Hessen and the Reich, 1867–1918* (Cambridge, MA, 1976).

9. Sheehan, *German Liberalism,* pp. 141–203.

10. Ibid., pp. 204–38.

11. For a broad (somewhat hypothetical) treatment of the effects of the great depression of 1873–1896 on German politics, see Hans Rosenberg, *Grosse Depression und Bismarckzeit: Wirtschaftsablauf, Gesellschaft und Politik in Mitteleuropa* (Berlin, 1967).

12. For an example of the effects of German unification and the Franco-Prussian War on one young liberal, see Friedrich Ratzel's autobiographical *Glückinseln und Träume: Gesammelte Aufsätze aus den Grenzboten* (Leipzig, 1905), pp. 115–260. See also Pinson, *Modern Germany,* pp. 148–55.

13. The phenomenon of *Unparteilichkeit* is registered quantitatively in the collective biography in chapter 3 herein. See P. Bergmann, *Nietzsche,* esp. pp. 48–49.

14. See Gordon Craig's introduction to Heinrich von Treitschke, *History of Germany in the Nineteenth Century,* ed. Gordon Graig (Chicago, 1975), pp. xi–xxix.

15. Woodruff D. Smith and Sharon A. Turner, "Legislative Behavior in the German Reichstag, 1898–1906," in *Central European History* 14 (1981), p. 11.

16. See, for example, Greta Jones, *Social Darwinism and English Thought: The Interaction Between Biological and Social Theory* (Brighton, Eng., 1980).

17. Philip Appleman, ed., *Darwin: A Norton Critical Edition*, 2nd ed. (New York, 1979), p. 37. (From the introduction to *The Origin of Species*.)

18. Kelly, *Descent of Darwin*, pp. 17–22; Gregory, *Scientific Materialism*, pp. 13–28.

19. Kelly, *Descent of Darwin*, pp. 22–25.

20. Fritz [Friedrich] Ratzel, *Sein und Werden der organischen Welt: Eine populäre Schöpfungsgeschichte* (Leipzig, 1869).

21. Ackerknecht, *Virchow*, pp. 199–207.

22. Kelly, *Descent of Darwin*, pp. 21, 23–24, 57–74.

23. See, for example, Wilhelm Hübbe-Schleiden, *Deutsche Colonisation* (Hamburg, 1881)—a radical imperialist pamphlet that also makes the generational aspect quite clear. See also Poliakov, *Mythe aryen*, pp. 269–88.

24. Ernst Haeckel, *Freie Wissenschaft und freie Lehre* (Stuttgart, 1878).

25. Rudolf Virchow, ''Die Freiheit der Wissenschaft im modernen Staat,'' *Amtlicher Bericht der Gesellschaft deutscher Naturforscher und Aerzte, 75. Versammlung . . .* (Munich, 1877), pp. 65–77; Kelly, *Descent of Darwin*, pp. 58–59.

26. Günther Buttmann, *Friedrich Ratzel: Leben und Werk eines deutschen Geographen* (Stuttgart, 1977), pp. 28–29.

27. Sheehan, *German Liberalism*, pp. 42–43; Krieger, *German Idea of Freedom*, pp. 313–14, 317–22, 327–29.

28. Frank Eyck, *The Frankfurt Parliament 1848–1849* (London, 1968), pp. 49–50, 135.

29. Hamerow, *Social Foundations* 1:359–99; Iggers, *German Conception of History*, pp. 104–21.

30. Sheehan, *German Liberalism*, pp. 121–77.

31. David Blackbourn, *Populists and Patricians: Essays in Modern German History* (London, 1987), pp. 143–67.

32. Hans-Ulrich Wehler, ''Bismarck's Imperialism, 1862–1890,'' in James J. Sheehan, ed., *Imperial Germany* (New York, 1976), pp. 62–92; W. D. Smith, *Ideological Origins*, pp. 129–40.

33. This interpretation of politics in the *Kaiserreich* follows the argument found in ibid., pp. 41–51.

34. The nature of the heavy industrial appeal to nationalism in support of protection in the 1870s can be seen in the layout of the campaign for tariffs by the metal-goods lobby: *Bundesarchiv* Koblenz, Bestand R13I, vol. 12, pp. 76–78 (in a manuscript on the history of the metals lobby by C. Klein).

35. Woodruff D. Smith, *The German Colonial Empire* (Chapel Hill, NC, 1978), p. 31.

36. This problem is analyzed in W. D. Smith, *Ideological Origins*, pp. 112–40.

37. On liberal (and postliberal) academics and nationalism, see Krieger, *German Idea of Freedom*, pp. 174–215, 313–14, 317–22, 362–70, 422–27, 446–47.

38. Mommsen, *Weber und die deutsche Politik*, pp. 36–72.

39. Ackerknecht, *Virchow*, pp. 207–19.

40. The disputes among cultural scientists over colonialism are discussed in chapter 9 herein.

41. Rosenberg, *Grosse Depression*, pp. 62–78; Shulamit Volkov, *The Rise of Popular Antimodernism in Germany: The Urban Master Artisans, 1873–1896* (Princeton, NJ, 1978).

42. Hans-Jürgen Puhle, *Agrarische Interessenpolitik und preussischer Konservatismus im Wilhelmischen Reich, 1893–1914* (Hanover, 1966); Wehler, *German Empire*. This interpretation is challenged by, among others, Blackbourn and Eley, *Peculiarities of German History*.

43. Ringer, *German Mandarins*, pp. 81–127.

44. Eley, *Reshaping the German Right*, pp. 8–10, 101–235; Chickering, *We Men Who Feel Most German*.

45. See chapter 7 herein.

Chapter 5

1. The following discussion of the founding and early history of the *Berliner Gesellschaft* is based on Christian Andree, "Geschichte der Berliner Gesellschaft für Anthropologie, Ethnologie und Urgeschichte, 1869–1969," in *Festschrift . . . Berliner Gesellschaft*, pp. 9–140.

2. Hermann Pohle, "Der Vorstand der Berliner Gesellschaft für Anthropologie, Ethnologie und Urgeschichte," in *Festschrift . . . Berliner Gesellschaft* pp. 141–42; Ackerknecht, *Virchow*, pp. 229–36.

3. Virchow and Bastian's style of leadership is revealed in the minutes of practically every annual meeting of the *Berliner Gesellschaft*. See *Verhandlungen der Berliner Gesellschaft für Anthropologie, Ethnologie und Urgeschichte*, 1871–1902.

4. Bastian's role as middleman with publications can be seen in his correspondence in the 1880s with Franz Boas, who was then doing research in America. *Microfilm Collection of the Professional Papers of Franz Boas* (American Philosophical Society, Philadelphia, 1972): letters of 10 October 1884; 7 August 1886; n.d. January, 1 March, 30 March, 25 April, 21 October, and n.d. December 1887; 3 February, 3 July, 13 November, and n.d. December 1888 (arranged in microfilm by date.)

5. *Festschrift . . . Berliner Gesellschaft*, pp. 33, 57; Virchow's obituary of Prussian Education Minister Falk in *Verhandlungen der Berliner Gesellschaft für Anthropologie, Ethnologie und Urgeschichte 1900*, p. 345. The museum was first established as a section of the Royal Museum in Berlin in 1874 and made an independent entity on the completion of its building in 1886.

6. See Sigrid Westphal-Hellbusch, "Hundert Jahre Ethnologie in Berlin, unter besonderer Berücksichtigung ihrer Entwicklung an der Universität," in *Festschrift . . . Berliner Gesellschaft*, pp. 157–83.

7. More irregular courses were, however, taught under various guises much earlier. Ritter taught ethnological subjects as geography at Berlin from the 1830s, and Wilhelm Wundt was teaching comparative ethnology at Heidelberg around 1860. See *Allgemeine Deutsche Biographie* 28:679–97; and Wundt *Erlebtes und Erkanntes*, p. 39.

8. On the origins of the Oriental Seminar, see Jake W. Spidle, Jr., "Colonial Studies in Imperial Germany," *History of Education Quarterly* 13, 3 (1973), pp. 231–47; and Max Lenz, *Geschichte der Königlichen Friedrich-Wilhelms-Universität zu Berlin*, 4 vols. (Halle, Ger. 1910), 3:239–47. Also, see chapter 9 herein.

9. The leaders of the *Berliner Gesellschaft*, especially Bastian, took the lead in organizing several societies for the exploration of inner Africa in the 1870s, including the one that sponsored the not fully successful Loango expedition. See Essner, *Deutsch Afrikareisende, sende*, pp. 24–33. On Schliemann and Virchow, see Ackerknecht, *Virchow*, pp. 224–29; and J. H. Ottaway, "Rudolf Virchow: An Appreciation," *Antiquity* 47, 186 (1973), pp. 101–8.

10. Ackerknecht, *Virchow*, p. 229.

11. Ibid., pp. 207–19; Virchow, "Rassenbildung und Erblichkeit," in *Festschrift für Adolf Bastian*, pp. 1–43.

12. Virchow, "Rassenbildung," pp. 1–43.

13. Koepping, *Bastian*, pp. 215–19.

14. Ibid. See also Adolf Bastian, *Der Mensch in der Geschichte: Zur Bergründung einer psychologischen Weltanschauung*, vol. 3, *Politische Pyschologie* (Leipzig, 1860), pp. 233–42.

15. The involvement of the Berlin anthropological establishment in the early years of German colonialism is discussed in chapter 9.

16. Koepping, *Bastian*, pp. 7–27.

17. Fritz Graebner and Wilhelm Schmidt, for example, did not engage directly in field research and yet were the leaders of ethnological thinking in the German-speaking world during the first quarter of the twentieth century. On Graebner, see Lowie, *History of Ethnological Theory*, pp. 177–95; on Schmidt, see his obituary by Martin Gusinde in *American Anthropologist* 56 (1954), pp. 869–70.

18. See the exchange of correspondence between Bastian and Boas, 1884–1888, *Microfilm Collection . . . Boas*.

19. *Neue Deutsche Biographie* 1:530–31.

20. *Festschrift . . . Berliner Gesellschaft*, pp. 9–20.

21. Virchow, "Rassenbildung," esp. pp. 5–6, 14–15, 37–40; Ackerknecht, *Virchow*, p. 235.

22. Adolf Bastian, *Der Völkergedanke, im Aufbau einer Wissenschaft vom Menschen und seine Begründung auf ethnologischen Sammlungen* (Berlin, 1881); idem, *Die Völkerkunde und der Völkerverkehr unter seiner Rückwirkung auf die Volksgeschichte* (Berlin, 1900), pp. 5–34.

23. Virchow, "Rassenbildung."

24. Ibid., pp. 14–15; Rudolf Virchow, "Acclimatisation," *Verhandlungen der Berliner Gesellschaft für Anthropologie, Ethnologie und Urgeschichte*, 1885, pp. 202–14.

25. *Festschrift . . . Berliner Gesellschaft*, p. 28.

26. Virchow, *Disease, Life, and Man*, pp. 120–41.

27. Adolf Bastian, *Zur Lehre von den geographischen Provinzen* (Berlin, 1886), p. 4–8.

28. Bastian, *Völkerkunde* p. 5; Virchow, *Disease, Life, and Man*, pp. 120–41.

29. Ackerknecht, *Virchow*, pp. 229–36.

30. Ibid., pp. 181–91.

31. Bastian, *Völkerkunde*, pp. 15–34.

32. Burrow, *Evolution and Society*, pp. 246–51.

33. Koepping, *Bastian*, pp. 126–27.

34. This point will be discussed in greater detail in chapter 10. For the impact of German historical thinking on British anthropology, see Stocking, *Victorian Anthropology*, pp. 20–25, 111.

35. Mühlmann, *Geschichte der Anthropologie*, pp. 122–29.

36. Burrow, *Evolution and Society*, pp. 101–36.

37. Stocking, *Victorian Anthropology*, pp. 144–85, 238–73.

38. This can be seen in Britain especially in the work of Sir Henry Maine. See Stocking, *Victorian Anthropology*, pp. 117–28; and Burrow, *Evolution and Society*, pp. 137–78. For Germany, see Virchow, "Freiheit der Wissenschaft."

39. Bastian, *Völkerkunde*, pp. 15–16.

40. Rickman, *Dilthey*, pp. 58–87, 123–62.

41. Virchow, "Rassenbildung."

42. See Bastian, *Der Mensch in der Geschichte*, pp. 233–42.

43. Koepping, *Bastian*, pp. 23, 118–26.

44. These matters will be discussed more fully in chapter 9.

45. Koepping, *Bastian* p. 23. For an idea of the place of anthropology and anthropologists in the Berlin curriculum, see *Verzeichnis der Vorlesungen an der Friedrich-Wilhelms-Universität zu Berlin im Winter-Semester 1907/8* (Berlin, 1907), esp. p. 55. Luschan was then one of two associate professors of anthropology on the philosophical faculty.

46. See *Festschrift . . . Berliner Gesellschaft*, pp. 93–113.

47. Bernhard Ankermann, "Kulturkreise und Kulturschichten in Afrika," *Zeitschrift für Ethnology* 37 (1905), pp. 54–84; Fritz Graebner, "Kulturkreise und Kulturschichten in Ozeanien," *Zeitschrift für Ethnology*, 37 (1905), pp. 28–53.

48. Adolf E. Jensen, "Kulturkreiselehre als Grundlage der Kulturgeschichte," in *Leo Frobenius: Ein Lebenswerk aus der Zeit der Kulturwende* (Leipzig, 1933), pp. 73–95.

49. Mühlmann, *Geschichte der Anthropology*, 2nd ed., pp. 122–29.

50. Boas's intellectual background is discussed in Stocking, *Race, Culture, and Evolution*, pp. 133–60.

51. Ibid., pp. 161–94; Franz Boas, *Race and Democratic Society* (New York, 1945).

Chapter 6

1. Herman K. Haeberlin, "The Theoretical Foundations of Wundt's Folk Psychology," in Rieber, *Wilhelm Wundt*, pp. 229–49. (Repr. of a 1916 article.)

2. Boring, *History of Experimental Psychology*, 2nd ed., pp. 326–27, 333. Boring's interpretation of Wundt is challenged by Arthur L. Blumenthal, "Wilhelm Wundt: Problems of Interpretation," in Wolfgang G. Bringmann and Ryan D. Tweney, eds., *Wundt Studies: A Centennial Collection* (Toronto, 1980), pp. 435–45.

3. For this, see Beuchelt, *Ideengeschichte der Völkerpsychologie*.

4. Wundt, *Erlebtes und Erkanntes*, p. 39; Diamond, "Wundt Before Leipzig," in Rieber, *Wilhelm Wundt*, p. 45.

5. Gebhardt, *Waitz' Allgemeine Pädogogik*, pp. xxiv–lvii.

6. Koepping, *Bastian*, pp. 140–46.

7. Ibid., pp. 7–27, for Bastian's biography.

8. Ibid., pp. 117–46.

9. On Bastian's liberalism, see Koepping, *Bastian*, pp. 69–76. Bastian's liberalism is most clearly seen in his arguments against colonialism. See Adolf Bastian, *Geographische und Ethnographische Bilder* (Jena, 1873), pp. 307–21; and idem., *Zwei Wörte über Colonial-Weisheit* (Berlin, 1883). See also chapter 5.

10. Bastian's *Völkerpsychologie* is summarized in Beuchelt, *Ideengeschicte der Völkerpsychologie*, pp. 16–23.

11. Koepping, *Bastian*, pp. 69–76; Adolf Bastian, *Controversen in der Ethnologie*, 4 vols. in 1 vol. (Berlin, 1893), 1:7–53.

12. Bastian, *Völkerkunde*, pp. 5–13.

13. Bastian, *Controversen*, 1:53–55; Bastian, *Völkerkunde*, p. 18.

14. Koepping, *Bastian*, pp. 104–16; Bastian, *Controversen*, pp. 8–55.

15. See Beuchelt, *Ideengeschicte der Völkerpsychologie*, pp. 16–23.

16. See, for example, Bastian, *Der Mensch in der Geschichte*, pp. 217–427.

17. Material on Wundt's life can be found in his autobiography, *Erlebtes und Erkanntes*, and in Diamond, "Wundt Before Leipzig," in Rieber, *Wilhelm Wundt*, pp. 3–70.

18. Haeberlin, "Theoretical Foundations," pp. 229–49; Beuchelt, *Ideengeschichte der Völkerpsychologie*, pp. 23–29.

19. Kurt Danziger, "Wundt and the Two Traditions of Psychology," in Rieber, *Wilhelm Wundt*, pp. 73–87. See Wundt's references in the introduction to Wilhelm Wundt, *Elemente der Völkerpsychologie: Grundlinien einer Entwicklungsgeschichte der Menschheit* (Leipzig, 1912), pp. 1–11. See also Wundt, *Erlebtes und Erkanntes*, pp. 52, 57.

20. Wundt, *Erlebtes und Erkanntes*, pp. 1–3, 8.

21. Ibid., pp. 3–30.

22. Ibid., pp. 9–13.

23. Ibid., pp. 6, 13–15.

24. Diamond, "Wundt Before Leipzig," in Rieber, *Wilhelm Wundt*, pp. 41–43.

25. Wundt, *Erlebtes und Erkanntes*, pp. 15–19.

26. Ibid., pp. 373–82.

27. Ibid., pp. 50–57.

28. Ibid., pp. 15–19; Beuchelt, *Ideengeschichte der Völkerpsychologie*, pp. 23–24.

29. Wundt, *Erlebtes und Erkanntes*, p. 57. Like Waitz, Wundt also wrote extensively on ethics and aesthetics.

30. Wilhelm Wundt, *Völkerpsychologie: Eine Untersuchung der Entwicklungsgeschichte von Sprache, Mythus und Sitte*, 10 vols. (Leipzig, 1900–1920).

31. Diamond, "Wundt Before Leipzig," in Rieber, *Wilhelm Wundt*, p. 45.

32. Summaries of Wundt's psychology are contained in Beuchelt, *Ideengeschichte der Völkerpsychologie*, pp. 23–29; Boring, *History of Experimental Psychology*, pp. 316–47; Kurt Danziger, "Wundt's Theory of Behavior and Volition," in Rieber, *Wilhelm Wundt*, pp. 89–115.

33. Wundt's *Völkerpsychologie* is summarized in Wundt, *Elemente*. See also Haeberlin, "Theoretical Foundations," pp. 229–49.

34. Wundt, *Elemente*, pp. 1–11.

35. Beuchelt, *Ideengeschichte der Völkerpsychologie*, pp. 23–29.

36. Wundt, *Elemente*, pp. 12–22, 116–23, 279–84, 465–73.

37. Haeberlin, "Theoretical Foundations," pp. 229–49; Boring, *History of Experimental Psychology*, pp. 326–33.

38. Wundt, *Elemente*, pp. 1–11.

39. This can be seen in Wilhelm Wundt, *Die Anfänge der Gesellschaft: Eine völkerpsychologische Studie* (Leipzig, 1907), pp. 1–9.

40. Beuchelt, *Ideengeschichte der Völkerpsychologie*, pp. 23–29.

41. Wundt, *Elemente*, pp. 12–115.

42. Ibid., pp. 116–278.

43. Ibid., pp. 279–443, 465–516.

44. Boring, *History of Experimental Psychology*, pp. 316–47; Sam Whimster, "Karl Lamprecht and Max Weber: Historical Sociology Within the Confines of a Historians' Controversy," in Mommsen and Osterhammel, *Max Weber*, pp. 268–83.

45. Ibid., pp. 327–28.

46. See Alfred Vierkandt, *Naturvölker und Kulturvölker: Ein Beitrag zur Sozialpsychologie* (Leipzig, 1896).

47. For an extreme example of the deviation of diffusionist ethnology from the traditions of neoliberal social science that affected Wundt up to the end, see Leo Frobenius, *Paideuma: Umrisse einer Kultur–und Seelenlehre* (Munich, 1921), pp. 1–13, 51–89.

Chapter 7

1. See Wilhelm Schmidt, "Die moderne Ethnologie," *Anthropos* 1 (1906), pp. 134–63, 318–88, 592–644, 950–97.

2. Friedrich Ratzel, *Völkerkunde*, 2nd rev. ed., 2 vols. (Berlin and Leipzig, 1894), 1:25; Heinrich Schurtz, *Völkerkunde* (Leipzig and Vienna, 1903), pp. 27–28.

3. Bergmann, *Agrarromantik*, pp. 33–69.

4. John G. Gagliardo, *From Pariah to Patriot: The Changing Image of the German Peasant 1770–1840* (Lexington, KY, 1969), pp. 211–83.

5. Ibid., pp. 136–210; Sheehan, *German Liberalism*, pp. 21–26, 29.

6. Gagliardo, *From Pariah to Patriot*, pp. 61–90, 253–83.

7. See Ellis, *One Fairy Story Too Many*.

8. On the relationship between Stein's reforms and early liberal economic thought, see Roscher, *Geschichte der National-Oekonomik in Deutschland,* pp. 702–32.

9. Sheehan, *German Liberalism,* pp. 24–25.

10. Hamerow, *Restoration, Revolution, Reaction,* pp. 156–72.

11. *"Ackerbau, Landwirtschaft"* in *SL,* 1:128–49.

12. Ibid., 129.

13. *"Bauer, Bauernstand,"* in SL, 2:371–80.

14. Ibid., 372.

15. Ibid., 373.

16. Ibid., 378.

17. We have already established Welcker's liberal credentials. If he is not a liberal, the term can mean nothing in Germany. The point is not that there was something flawed in Welcker's brand of liberalism (or in Germany's), but rather that many later conservative ideas arose from early liberal ones.

18. This ambiguity is also revealed in moderate liberal ideas about colonialism in the 1840s and 1850s. White settlement colonies were often looked upon as means whereby economic modernization in Germany and the protection of the peasantry (in colonies in America) could *both* be afforded. See W. D. Smith, *Ideological Origins,* pp. 21–30.

19. See Georg Friedrich Knapp, *Die Bauernbefreiung und der Ursprung der Landarbeiter in den älteren Theilen Preussens,* 2 vols. (Leipzig, 1887).

20. Adolf Wagner's agrarianism is summarized in his *Agrar- und Industriestaat,* 2nd ed. (Jena, 1902). See also Kenneth D. Barkin, *The Controversy over German Industrialization 1890–1902* (Chicago, 1970), pp. 138–47.

21. Bergmann, *Agrarromantik,* pp. 33–164.

22. Ratzel hardly mentions Riehl in the introductions to his major works where he discusses the people who have influenced him, despite the fact that Ratzel and Riehl lived in Munich throughout a large part of the 1870s and worked in similar fields. Buttmann, *Ratzel,* pp. 37–42, 51–60; Ratzel, *Erde und das Leben,* 1:3–66; Friedrich Ratzel, *Politische Geographie,* 3rd ed. (Munich and Berlin, 1923), pp. 7–8. In Ratzel, *Glückinseln,* pp. 261–92, 339–90, there are two very Riehl-like pieces about Ratzel's wanderings in Bavaria and southwestern Germany, but Riehl is not mentioned.

23. Riehl, *Bürgerliche Gesellschaft,* pp. 3–19 and passim.

24. Ibid., pp. 20–35.

25. Ibid.

26. Ibid., p. 151.

27. Ibid., pp. 152–242.

28. Ibid., pp. 245–341.

29. Ibid., pp. 342–66.

30. Ibid., pp. 51–81 ("good sort") and 82–107 ("degenerates").

31. Ibid., pp. 108–35.

32. Ibid., p. 47.

33. Ratzel, *Glückinseln,* pp. 1–13, 68–95.

34. Buttmann, *Ratzel,* pp. 14–19; Wanklyn, *Ratzel,* pp. 5–6.

35. Buttmann, *Ratzel,* pp. 14–19.

36. Ibid., pp. 20–29.

37. James M. Hunter, *Perspectives on Ratzel's Political Geography* (Lanham, MD, 1983), pp. 28–41, emphasizes Ratzel's social insecurity.

38. Ratzel, *Glückinseln,* pp. 96–113.

39. A juvenile taste for adventure fiction maintained into adult life was not uncommon

among the leaders of European imperialism. See L. H. Gann and Peter Duignan, *The Rulers of German Africa 1884–1914* (Standford, 1977), pp. 42–43.

40. Ratzel, *Sein und Werden*.

41. Buttmann, *Ratzel*, pp. 30–42; Ratzel, *Glückinseln,* pp. 115–260 (on Ratzel's experiences in the Franco-German War).

42. Buttmann, *Ratzel*, pp. 20–29; Ratzel, *Sein und Werden*, p. v.

43. Buttmann, *Ratzel*, pp. 35–36; Ratzel, *Glückinseln,* pp. 115–260.

44. Bruch, *Wissenschaft*, pp. 32–56, esp. 33, 37–38; Buttmann, *Ratzel*, pp. 30–33. On the *Grenzboten*, see Sheehan, *German Liberalism*, pp. 195–96. On Freytag, see chapter 10 herein.

45. Unsigned (F. Ratzel), "Die Beurteilung der Völker," *Nord und Süd* 6 (1878), pp. 177–200; Daniel Gasman, *The Scientific Origins of National Socialism: Social Darwinism in Ernst Haeckel and the German Monist League* (London and New York, 1971), pp. 120–22; Heinrich von Treitschke, *Politics*, trans. B. Dugdale and T. de Bille, 2 vols. (New York, 1916), 1:216–17.

46. For the situation of the National Liberals in the 1870s and 1880s, see Sheehan, *German Liberalism*, pp. 189–203.

47. See Ratzel's contribution to the National Liberals' position on colonialism: Friedrich Ratzel, *Wider die Reichsnörgler: Ein Wort zur Kolonialfrage aus Wählerkreisen* (Munich, 1884).

48. Sheehan, *German Liberalism*, pp. 189–203.

49. Hartmut Pogge von Strandmann, "Domestic Origins of Germany's Colonial Expansion Under Bismarck," *Past and Present* 42 (1969), pp. 140–59, esp. 144–45.

50. On the National Liberals in the 1880s, see Ludwig Bergsträsser, *Geschichte der politischen Parteien in Deutschland*, 8th/9th ed. (Munich, 1955), pp. 180–88; and Sheehan, *German Liberalism*, pp. 189–203. See also Ratzel, *Wider die Reichsnörgler*.

51. Barkin, *Controversy*, pp. 131–85; Volkov, *Rise of Popular Antimodernism,* pp. 172–91, 215–36.

52. Buttmann, *Ratzel*, pp. 51–60; Ratzel, "Beurteilungen," pp. 177–200; Friedrich Ratzel, "Über geographische Bedingungen und ethnographischen Folgen der Völkerwanderungen," *Verhandlungen der Gesellschaft für Erdkunde zu Berlin* 7 (1880), pp. 295–324.

53. Ratzel, *Glückinseln* p. 87.

54. Ibid., p. 93.

55. Friedrich Ratzel, "In Welcher Richtung beeinflussen die afrikanischen Ereignisse die Tätigkeit des Kolonialvereins?" *Deutsche Kolonialzeitung* 15 January 1885, pp. 38–44.

56. See chapters 7 and 12 for specifics. For the general point, see Ratzel, *Politische Geographie*, 3rd ed., pp. 17–32.

57. Trietschke, *Politics,* 1:216–17.

58. See, for example, the very similar analysis in Schurtz, *Völkerkunde*, pp. 25–28.

Chapter 8

1. Buttmann, *Ratzel*, pp. 32–35.

2. Mühlmann, *Geschichte der Anthropologie*, pp. 124–27.

3. Hermann Baumann, "Die afrikanischen Kulturkreise," *Africa* 7, 2 (1934), pp. 129–39, esp. 130–31.

4. Bastian, *Zur Lehre von den geographischen Provinzen*. For a detailed analysis of Bastian's theory of geographical provinces and its relationship to diffusionism, see Annemarie

Fiedermutz-Laun, *Der kulturhistorische Gedanke bei Adolf Bastian* (Wiesbaden, 1970), esp. pp. 148–255.

5. Fiedermutz-Laun, *Kulturhistorische Gedanke*, pp. 256–70.

6. Wanklyn, *Ratzel*, pp. 22–24.

7. Friedrich Ratzel, *Anthropo-Geographie*, 2 vols. (Stuttgart, 1882), esp. 1:7–17.

8. On M. Wagner, see H. Ganslmyer, "Moritz Wagner und seine Bedeutung für die Ethnologie," in *Verhandlungen des XXXVIII. internationalen Amerikanistenkongresses . . . 1968* (Munich, 1969), 4:459–70. Ratzel dedicated *Anthropo-Geographie* to Moritz Wagner: 1:xv–xviii. See also Ratzel, *Erde und das Leben*, 2:584–85.

9. Buttmann, *Ratzel*, pp. 37–42, 61–72.

10. Moritz Wagner, *Die Darwin'sche Theorie und das Migrationsgesetz der Organismen* (Leipzig, 1868). See also idem, *Entstehung der Arten durch räumliche Sonderung: Gesammelte Aufsätze* (Basel, 1889).

11. Buttmann, *Ratzel*, pp. 51–60.

12. Ratzel, *Völkerkunde*, p. 9. See also idem, *Anthropo-Geographie*, 1:460–64.

13. The 1887 article is summarized in the more complete 1893 one: Friedrich Ratzel, "Beiträge zur Kenntnis der Verbreitung des Bogens und des Speeres in indo-afrikanischen Völkerkreis," *Berichten des Königl. Sächs. Gesellschaft der Wissenschaften* (1893), pp. 147–82.

14. Ratzel, *Anthropo-Geographie*, 1:23–40; idem, *Völkerkunde*, 1:3–5.

15. Ratzel, *Anthropo-Geographie*, 1:7–17; idem, *Völkerkunde*, 1:5–18.

16. Ratzel, "Beiträge zur Kenntnis," pp. 148–50; idem, *Anthropo-Geographie*, 2:577–630.

17. Ratzel, *Anthropo-Geographie*, 2:631–48; idem, *Völkerkunde*, 1:5–13.

18. Ratzel, "Beiträge zur Kenntnis," pp. 148–52.

19. Ibid.; Ratzel, *Völkerkunde*, 1:19–28; idem, *Anthropo-Geographie*, 1:384–434.

20. Ratzel, *Völkerkunde*, 1:5, 8.

21. Ratzel, *Erde und das Leben*, 2:571–677; idem, *Anthropo-Geographie*, 1:41–87; 2:xxx–xxxvi.

22. Mühlmann, *Geschichte der Anthropologie*, 2nd ed., pp. 124–27.

23. Ratzel, *Völkerkunde*, 1:19–28; idem, *Anthropo-Geographie*, 1:384–434.

24. Ratzel, *Völkerkunde*, 1:71–81.

25. Ibid., 1:24–25, 82–132.

26. Hence, perhaps, Ratzel's fascination with Gustav Fechner's scientific animism: Ratzel, *Glückinseln*, pp. 497–509. See also Ratzel, *Anthropo-Geographie*, 1:384–434.

27. Mühlmann, *Geschichte der Anthropologie*, 2nd ed., pp. 126–27.

28. Ratzel, *Erde und das Leben*, 1:43–66; idem, *Anthropo-Geographie*, 1:3–40.

29. Ratzel, *Anthropo-Geographie*, 1:7–17.

30. Mühlmann, *Geschichte der Anthropologie*, 2nd ed., pp. 124–27, emphasizes Ratzel's positivism.

31. Ibid.

32. There is, however, an indication that toward the end of his life, Ratzel was groping toward a new conception of methodology. This arises in Ratzel's fascination with Fechner's idea that nature external to the individual and the individual's psychological states vary interactively. See Ratzel, *Glückinseln*, pp. 497–509.

33. Fiedermutz-Laun, *Kulturhistorische Gedanke*, pp. 256–70; Koepping, *Bastian*, pp. 60–69, 118–26.

34. Ratzel, *Völkerkunde*, 1:10, 23–24, 71–81.

35. Ibid., 1:5–13; Ratzel, *Erde und das Leben*, 2:632–34.

36. Ratzel, *Völkerkunde*, 1:26; 2:383–95; idem, *Erde und das Leben*, 2:671–77; Fried-

rich Ratzel, "Geschichte, Völkerkunde und historische Perspektive," *Historische Zeitschrift* 93, 1 (1904), pp. 1–46; idem, *Politische Geographie*, pp. 33–59.

37. Ratzel, *Völkerkunde*, 1:25–26, 82–87; 2:368, 370–83; idem, *Erde und das Leben*, 2:578–82. (The last citation shows Ratzel making his point about colonization in reference to all living nature. We shall come back to the broad version of colonization when we discuss *Lebensraum* in chapter 13.)

38. Ratzel, *Völkerkunde*, 1:71–81.

39. See, for instance, Bernhard Ankermann, "Die Lehre von den Kulturkreisen," *Korrespondenzblatt, Gesellschaft für Anthropologie Ethnologie und Urgeschichte* 42 (1911), pp. 156–62.

40. Ratzel, *Völkerkunde*, 2:370–83; idem, *Anthropo-Geographie*, 2:631–48.

41. Ratzel, *Völkerkunde*, 1:5–18; idem, *Erde und das Leben*, 2:530–35; idem, "Geschichte, Völkerkunde . . . Perspective" pp. 10–12.

42. Ratzel, *Völkerkunde*, 1:13–18.

43. Ibid., 1:3–5; Ratzel, "Geschichte, Völkerkunde . . . Perspective" pp. 12–13; idem, *Anthropo-Geographie*, 1:23–40; 2:577–630.

44. Ratzel, *Völkerkunde*, 2:367–70.

45. Hunter, *Perspectives*, pp. 28–41.

46. Ratzel, *Völkerkunde*, 1:3–5; idem, "Geschichte, Völkerkunde . . . Perspective" pp. 1–46; Berding, "Ranke," in Wehler, *Deutsche Historiker I*, pp. 7–24; Iggers, *German Conception of History*, pp. 63–123.

47. See Mühlmann, *Geschichte der Anthropologie*, 2nd ed., pp. 124–27; Ankermann, "Lehre," p. 160 (and M. Haberlandt's response on pp. 162–65); Baumann, "Afrikanischen Kulturkreise," p. 139; and Fritz Graebner, *Methode der Ethnologie* (Heidelberg, 1911), pp. 92–93, 104–25.

48. Mühlmann, *Geschichte der Anthropologie*, 2nd ed. pp. 124–27; Buttmann, *Ratzel*, pp. 84–88.

49. Baumann, "Afrikanischen Kulturkreise," pp. 129–39; Graebner, *Methode*, pp. 92–98, 125–51.

50. Ankermann, "Lehre," pp. 156–62; Graebner, *Methode*, pp. 91–104 (although Graebner tended to emphasize migration as well).

51. Ratzel, *Politische Geographie*, pp. 35–59, 90–121.

52. Ratzel, *Glückinseln*, pp. 391–477.

53. Friedrich Ratzel, *Die chinesische Auswanderung: Ein Beitrag zur Kultur- und Handelsgeographie* (Breslau, 1876).

54. Buttmann, *Ratzel*, pp. 37–42, 54–55; Ganslmayr, "Moritz Wagner," 4:459–70; Moritz Wagner and Carl Scherzer, *Die Republik Costa Rica in Centralamerika* (Leipzig, 1856).

55. W. D. Smith, *Ideological Origins*, pp. 21–30.

56. See Ganslmayr, "Moritz Wagner," and Karl von Scherzer's introduction to Wagner's *Entstehung der Arten*.

57. Buttmann, *Ratzel*, pp. 51–60; Wanklyn, *Ratzel*, pp. 22–23; Ratzel, *Wider die Reichsnörgler*.

58. Smith, W. D. *Ideological Origins*, pp. 32–40.

59. Ibid., pp. 84–85.

60. See Ratzel's anonymous defense of the disgraced Peters in *Die Grenzboten* 56, 18 (1897), pp. 252–56.

61. Ratzel, "In welcher Richtung."

62. Ernst Hasse, "Was können und sollen wir jetzt für die deutsche Auswanderung thun?" *Deutsche Kolonialzeitung*, 15 December 1884.

63. [Friedrich Ratzel], "Ein Beitrag zu den Anfangen der deutschen Kolonialpolitik," *Die Grenzboten* 62, 2 (1903), pp. 115–16.

64. W. D. Smith, *Ideological Origins*, pp. 21–40.

65. See, for example, Friedrich Ratzel, *Das Meer als Quelle der Völkergrösse: Ein politisch-geographische Studie* (Munich, 1900). See also Ratzel, *Politische Geographie*, pp. 17–32.

66. In the 1870s, Bastian and Virchow had involved themselves in encouraging government sponsorship of trade expansion in Africa and elsewhere. See Essner, *Deutsche Afrikareisende*, pp. 24–30. As we shall see in chapter 9, both made their peace later with the fact of a colonial empire. But before and during the period of colonial enthusiasm in the late 1870s and 1880s, Bastian and Virchow were both prominent anticolonialists—whereas some of their younger protégés figured in the ranks of the procolonialists. See Bastian, *Zwei Wörte*.

67. Virchow, "Acclimatisation," pp. 202–14.

68. Ratzel, *Politische Geographie*, pp. 17–32; idem, *Erde und das Leben*, 2:571–82.

69. Ratzel, *Erde und das Leben*, 2:530–46.

70. Bastian, *Zwei Wörte*; Hans Spellmeyer, *Deutsche Kolonialpolitik im Reichstage* (Stuttgart, 1931), p. 22.

71. Spellmeyer, *Deutsche Kolonialpolitik*, p. 22; Pogge von Strandmann, "Germany's Colonial Expansion," pp. 140–59.

72. Rudolf Virchow, "Die Deutschen und die Germanen," *Verhandlungen der Berliner Gesellschaft für Anthropologie, Ethnologie und Urgeschichte 1881*, pp. 68–75.

73. Ratzel, *Wider die Reichsnörgler*; Dietrich Schäfer, *Mein Leben* (Berlin and Leipzig, 1926), pp. 135–36.

74. See chapter 4 herein.

75. See Georg W. Stocking, Jr., ed., *The Shaping of American Anthropology 1883–1911: A Franz Boas Reader* (New York, 1974), p. 30.

76. See Ratzel's obituary of Schurtz in *Deutsche Monatshefte* 2, 11 (1903), pp. 673–74. See also Schurtz, *Völkerkunde*, pp. 24–32, 71–73; and Heinrich Schurtz, *Urgeschichte der Kultur* (Leipzig and Vienna, 1900), pp. 26–63.

77. Frobenius never completed the requirements for an earned doctorate. Much of his following consisted of laypeople rather than scholars. Until he established himself at the new University of Frankfurt in the 1920s, he was very much an outsider. See *Leo Frobenius*, esp. pp. 8–24.

78. Baumann, "Afrikanischen Kulturkreise," p. 131; Graebner, "Kulturkreise und Kulturschichten in Ozeanien," pp. 28–53; Ankermann, "Kulturkreise und Kulturschichten in Afrika," pp. 54–84.

79. Lowie, *History of Ethnological Theory*, pp. 177–95.

80. Mühlmann, *Geschichte der Anthropologie*, 2nd ed., pp. 126–28; Ankermann, "Lehre," pp. 156–62; Baumann, "Afrikanischen Kulturkreise," pp. 129–39.

81. See Graebner, "Kulturkreise . . . in Ozeanien," p. 29, and Graebner, *Methode*, pp. 98–99 (on Frobenius).

82. Graebner, *Methode*, esp. pp. 104–70.

83. Baumann, "Afrikanischen Kulturkreise," pp. 129–39.

84. See Ankermann, "Lehre," pp. 156–62; Bernhard Ankermann, "Die Entwicklung der Ethnologie seit Adolf Bastian," *Zeitschrift für Ethnologie* 58 (1926), pp. 221–30; Schmidt, "Moderne Ethnologie," pp. 134–63, 318–88, 592–644, 950–97; Fritz Graebner, *Das Weltbild der Primitiven: Eine Unterschung der Unformen weltanschaulichen Denkens bei Naturvölkern* (Munich, 1924), pp. 9–13; Graebner, *Methode*, pp. 91–104.

85. *Leo Frobenius*, pp. 8–24.

86. See Martin Gusinde's obituary of Schmidt in *American Anthropologist* 56 (1954), pp. 868–70.

87. This characteristic of diffusionism is remarked in Mühlmann, *Geschichte der Anthropologie*, pp. 127–28. See also Graebner, *Methode*, pp. 7–54.

88. L. Frobenius, *Paideuma*, pp. 3–4, 14–18.

89. Ankermann, "Lehre," pp. 156–57. Graebner, *Methode*, pp. 169–70, argues that psychological factors are important, but he then goes on to say that the main use of psychology for the ethnologist is to provide an "insight" that will aid in choosing between two or more hypotheses in cultural history when the decision cannot be clearly based on trait analysis. Individual psychology is thus no more than a platform for a theoretical leap in the dark when such a leap is unavoidable.

90. Ankermann, "Lehre," pp. 156–62; Graebner, *Methode*, pp. iii–xvii (introduction by William Foy); and idem, "Kulturkreise . . . in Ozeanien," pp. 28–53.

91. See Wilhelm Schmidt and Wilhelm Koppers, *Völker und Kulturleben. Erster Teil: Gesellschaft und Wirtschaft der Völker* (Regensburg, 1924), pp. 70–111; Wilhelm Schmidt, *Rasse und Volk: Eine Untersuchung zur Bestimmung ihrer Grenzen und zur Erfassung ihrer Beziehungen* (Munich, 1927), pp. 27–40.

92. Ankermann, "Lehre," pp. 158–60; Graebner, *Methode*, pp. 91–125.

93. Ankermann, "Lehre," pp. 158–59. See also Schurtz, *Urgeschichte*, p. 57, for an early version of the diffusionist idea of borrowing as a response to the difficulties of Ratzel's analysis.

94. Ratzel did not entirely neglect other media besides migration and colonization, but he downplayed their importance in trait transfer more than his successors did: Ratzel, *Völkerkunde*, 1:71–81; Ankermann, "Entwicklung," pp. 229–30; idem, "Lehre," pp. 158–59, and M. Haberlandt's response, pp. 162–65.

95. Baumann, "Afrikanischen Kulturkreise," pp. 129–39; Ankermann, "Lehre," pp. 156–62; Graebner, "Kulturkreise . . . in Ozeanien," pp. 28–53; idem, *Methode*, pp. 125–51.

96. Leo Frobenius, *Ursprung der afrikanischen Kulturen* (Berlin 1898), p. 9; Ankermann, "Kulturkreise . . . in Afrika," pp. 72–75.

97. Many diffusionists were quite aware of this problem. Ankermann, "Lehre," pp. 156–62, shows his awareness; Graebner, in *Methode*, pp. 104–70, tries to argue around it.

98. Baumann, "Afrikanischen Kulturkreise," p. 139; Mühlmann, *Geschichte der Anthropologie*, 2nd ed., pp. 126–27.

99. Frobenius largely admits this (in *Paideuma*, pp. 9–13) when he discusses the differences between "man," and "culture" that became evident to him on his expeditions.

100. Schmidt, "Moderne Ethnologie," pp. 356–57; Graebner, *Weltbild*, pp. 9–13; L. Frobenius, *Paideuma*, pp. 29–50.

101. Some diffusionists did specialize in tracing material traits. One of these was the American Berthold Laufer. See Kenneth S. Latourette, *Biographical Memoir of Berthold Laufer, 1874–1934* (Washington, DC, 1938).

102. L. Frobenius, *Ursprung*, p. 6; idem, *Paideuma*, pp. 51–89.

103. Graebner, *Methode*, pp. 123–25; Ankermann, "Entwicklung," pp. 224–25, 229; Schmidt, "Moderne Ethnologie," pp. 352–57. Frobenius did eventually come to the conclusion that anthropology could not follow the forms of "positivist" science. He presented it as an elaborate morphology—from which, however, he claimed to derive universal regularities. See L. Frobenius, *Paideuma*, pp. 7–9.

104. Baumann, "Afrikanischen Kulturkreise," pp. 131–34; Graebner, *Methode*, pp. 123–25.

105. Schmidt, "Moderne Ethnologie," pp. 600–601.

106. Baumann, "Afrikanischen Kulturkreise," pp. 129–39; Graebner, *Methode*, pp. iii–xviii (Foy's introduction). This idea is less pronounced in Graebner's main text.

107. Graebner, "Kulturkreise . . . in Ozeanien," pp. 28–53; Ankermann, "Kulturkreise . . . in Afrika," pp. 54–84.

108. See Max Weiss, *Die Völkerstämme im Norden Deutsch-Ostafrikas* (Berlin, 1910; repr. 1971), pp. 1–128.

109. L. Frobenius, *Paideuma*, pp. 29–42.

110. This is the theme of L. Frobenius's *Paideuma*. For a summary of Frobenius's argument, see Hellmut Wohlenberg, "Die Paideumalehre als Kulturphilosophie," in *Leo Frobenius*, pp. 32–56. On Frobenius's life and thought in general, see Jahnheinz Jahn, *Leo Frobenius: The Demonic Child* (Austin, 1972).

111. See, for example, the justification of militarism in Leo Frobenius, D. H. Frobenius, and D. E. Kohlhammer, *Menschenjagden und Zweikämpfe* (Jena, n.d.), pp. 4, 190.

112. See *Verhandlungen des Deutschen Kolonialkongresses 1902* (Berlin, 1903), pp. 148–74 (speeches by Wilhelm Schmidt and Felix von Luschan.)

113. See Friedrich von Bernhardi, *Deutschland und der nächste Krieg* (Stuttgart and Berlin, 1912), pp. 15, 74–88, 89, 115.

114. For an example of this, see the ways in which the contributors to *Leo Frobenius* attempted (without much difficulty) to associate Frobenius's theories with the prevailing politics of 1933 (pp. 8–11, 25–31.)

Chapter 9

1. See Stocking, *Shaping of American Anthropology,* pp. 24–26 (from an article by Boas on the history of anthropology).

2. On anthropology as a colonial venture, see Talal Asad, ed., *Anthropology and the Colonial Encounter* (New York, 1973). See also Henrika Kuklick, "The Sins of the Fathers: British Anthropology and African Colonial Administration," *Research in Sociology of Knowledge, Sciences and Art* 1 (1978), pp. 93–119.

3. Marshal Sahlins, *Culture and Practical Reason* (Chicago and London, 1976), p. 54.

4. A good general summary of German exploration, concentrating on Africa, is Essner, *Deutsche Afrikareisende*, which is much more than a narrative. See Essner's discussion of her use of the term *travellers* (*Reisende*) rather than *explorers* on p. 9. For convenience, the terms are used interchangeably in this chapter.

5. See ibid., pp. 16–24, on the organizational structure of German exploration and its ties to wider structures.

6. See Hans-Ulrich Wehler, *Bismarck und der Imperialismus* (Cologne, 1969), pp. 112–55, 158–68.

7. Essner, *Deutsche Afrikareisende,* pp. 24–36.

8. W. D. Smith, *Ideological Origins,* pp. 32–40.

9. Essner, *Deutsche Afrikareisende*, pp. 93–100.

10. See G. A. Schweinfurth, *Im Herzen von Afrika: Reisen und Entdeckungen im centralen Äquatorial-Afrika während der Jahre 1868–1871* (Leipzig, 1874); Gustav Nachtigal, *Sahara und Sudan: Ergebnisse sechsjähriger Reisen in Afrika*, 3 vols. (Leipzig, 1879–1889); Gerhard Rohlfs, *Quer durch Afrika* (Leipzig, 1874).

11. Essner, *Deutsche Afrikareisende*, p. 81.

12. Ibid., p. 187; Max Buchner, *Aurora colonialis . . .* (Munich, 1914).

13. See Bastian, *Völkergedanke.*

14. Hunter, *Perspectives,* pp. 28–41.

15. Klaus J. Bade, *Friedrich Fabri und der Imperialismus in der Bismarckzeit* (Freiburg,

1975), pp. 190–220; Wolfe W. Schmokel, "Gerhard Rohlfs: The Lonely Explorer," in Robert I. Rotberg, ed. *Africa and Its Explorers: Motives, Methods, and Impact* (Cambridge, MA, 1970), pp. 175–221; Buchner, *Aurora colonialis* . . . .

16. Essner, *Deutsche Afrikareisende*, pp. 89–93; Carl Peters, *Die deutsche Emin-Pascha Expedition* (Munich, 1891).

17. The leading early colonialist organization in Saxony was the Leipzig *Verein für Handelsgeographie und Förderung deutscher Interessen im Ausland*, founded in 1879 by Ernst Hasse. In response to the economic motives of its backers, the *Verein* focused part of its attention on trading colonies, but its predominantly academic and professional leaders were clearly most interested in settlement colonies. See Bade, *Fabri*, p. 105.

18. See chapter 8 herein. This point of view was summarized in an attack on the colonial enthusiasts launched in 1880 by the Berlin economist and businessman F. C. Philippsohn and the left liberal politician Friedrich Kapp (leader of the secessionist National Liberals). See, Bade, *Fabri* pp. 112–20.

19. Essner, *Deutsche Afrikareisende*, pp. 33–36.

20. Bastian, *Zwei Wörte*; Spellmeyer, *Deutsche Kolonialpolitik*, p. 22.

21. Bastian was already busy in 1885 pointing out to the Foreign Office the political and commercial advantages that might follow from an expedition the Royal Museum was fitting out for East Africa: *Bundesarchiv* Koblenz, *Nachlass* Walter Frank, no. 18 (letter from Bastian to Foreign Office, 3 April 1885).

22. On the establishment of a colonial administration, see W. D. Smith, *German Colonial Empire*, pp. 42–47.

23. Gann and Duignan, *Rulers of German Africa*, pp. 45–53.

24. Spidle, "Colonial Studies," pp. 231–47, esp. pp. 235–36; Lenz, *Universität zu Berlin*, 3:239–47.

25. Spidle, "Colonial Studies," pp. 241–43; Gann and Duignan, *Rulers of German Africa*, pp. 54–55.

26. Spidle, "Colonial Studies," pp. 241–43; Gann and Duignan, *Rulers of German Africa*, pp. 47–48.

27. See Richard Kandt, *Caput Nili: Eine empfindsame Reise zu den Quellen des Nils*, 4th ed. (Berlin, 1919).

28. L. H. Gann, "Heinrich Schnee (1871–1949)," in L. H. Gann and Peter Duignan, eds., *African Proconsuls: European Governors in Africa* (New York, 1978), pp. 492–522.

29. Woodruff D. Smith, "Julius Graf Zech auf Neuhofen (1868–1914)," in Gann and Duignan, *African Proconsuls*, pp. 473–91; Julius Graf Zech, "Vermischte Notizen über Togo und das Togohinterland," *Mitteilungen aus den deutschen Schutzgebieten* 11, 2 (1898); idem "Land und Leute an der Nordwestgrenze von Togo," *Mitteilungen aus den deutschen Schutzgebieten* 17, 3 (1904).

30. Franz Stuhlmann, *Beiträge zur Kulturgeschichte von Ostafrika* (Berlin, 1909).

31. Werner Schieffel, *Bernhard Dernburg 1865–1937: Kolonialpolitiker und Bankier in wilhelmischen Deutschland* (Zurich and Freiburg, 1974), pp. 62–66, 89–90.

32. In 1902, Felix von Luschan, soon to be professor of anthropology at Berlin, attempted (without great success) to elaborate on the utility of ethnology for colonial rule in an address to the first German Colonial Congress: *Kolonialkongress 1902*, pp. 163–74.

33. Geo A. Schmidt, *Das Kolonial-Wirtschaftliche Komitee* (Berlin, 1934).

34. See Gann, "Schnee," p. 499; Erich Schultz-Ewerth and Leonhard Adam, eds., *Das Eingeborenenrecht: Sitte und Gewohnheitsrechte der Eingeborenen der ehemaligen deutschen Kolonien*, 2 vols. (Stuttgart, 1930); *Kolonialkongress 1902*, pp. 377–89. Mention should also be made of Günter Tessmann, who was employed both by the Lübeck Ethnological Museum and by the German government to do research in Cameroon between 1904 and

1909. See Günter Tessmann, *Die Pangwe: Völkerkundliche Monographie eines westafri-kanischen Negerstammes,* 2 vols. (Berlin, 1913).

35. Gustav Adolf, Graf von Götzen, *Deutsch-Ostafrika im Aufstand 1905/6* (Berlin, 1909), esp. pp. 42–48; Theodor Leutwein, *Elf Jahre Gouverneur in Deutsch-Südwestafrika* (Berlin, 1908), pp. 428–525.

36. Klaus J. Bade, ed., *Imperialismus und Kolonialmission: Kaiserliches Deutschland und koloniales Imperium* (Wiesbaden, 1982), pp. 29–50, 79–102.

37. Lowie, *History of Ethnological Theory,* pp. 177–95; *American Anthropologist* 56 (1954), pp. 268–70.

38. See Father Schmidt's speech at the Colonial Congress in *Kolonialkongress 1902,* pp. 148–63.

39. See Bade, *Imperialismus und Kolonialmission,* pp. 51–67, 68–79, 165–88, 189–204, 205–25.

40. On Westermann, see Arthur J. Knoll, *Togo Under Imperial Germany 1884–1914: A Case Study in Imperial Rule* (Stanford, 1978), pp. 98–99. On Westermann's views, see Diedrich Westermann, *Afrika als europäische Aufgabe* (Berlin, 1941), pp. 103–9.

41. W. D. Smith, *Ideological Origins,* p. 144.

Chapter 10

1. The standard discussion of the "older" school of historical economics (Roscher, Hildebrand, and Knies) is Gottfried Eisermann, *Die Grundlagen des Historismus in der deutschen Nationalökonomie* (Stuttgart, 1956).

2. Ibid., pp. 120–26.

3. Ibid., pp. 125–26, 130–32.

4. Ibid., pp. 130–32; Roscher, *Geschichte der National-Oekonomik in Deutschland,* pp. 843–94.

5. Eisermann, *Grundlagen,* pp. 161–62; Rohr, *Social Liberalism,* pp. 154–66.

6. Wilhelm Roscher, *Kolonien, Kolonialpolitik, und Auswanderung,* 2nd ed. (Leipzig and Heidelberg, 1856).

7. Jürgen Reulecke, "Die Anfänge der organisierten Sozialreform in Deutschland," in Rüdiger vom Bruch, ed., *'Weder Kommunismus noch Kapitalismus': Bürgerliche Sozialreform in Deutschland vom Vormärz zum Ära Adenauer* (Munich, 1985), pp. 21–59.

8. See Moritz Wirth, ed. *Kleine Schriften von Dr. Carl Rodbertus-Jagetzow* (Berlin, 1890), esp. pp. 269–72, 307–8, 333–335.

9. Rochau, *Realpolitik;* Krieger, *German Idea of Freedom,* pp. 310–14, 353–56.

10. Rohr, *Social Liberalism,* pp. 85–91; Brentano, *Mein Leben,* pp. 72–73.

11. See Roscher, *Geschichte der National-Oekonomik in Deutschland,* pp. 912–48, 1007–11, 1032–45.

12. Eisermann, *Grundlagen,* pp. 158–88.

13. Wilhelm Roscher, *Ansichten der Volkswirtschaft aus dem geschichtlichen Stand-punkte,* 2nd ed. (Leipzig and Heidelberg, 1861), pp. 1–46, 399–495.

14. Eisermann, *Grundlagen,* pp. 120–23, 130–37, 170–72, 207–11.

15. This aspect of Roscher's thought was one of those particularly attacked by Max Weber in *Roscher and Knies,* pp. 55–91.

16. Roscher, *Ansichten,* pp. 173–278; Eisermann, *Grundlagen,* pp. 130–32.

17. Eisermann, *Grundlagen,* pp. 170–72.

18. Ibid., pp. 136–37, 207–11.

19. Ibid., pp. 192–211.

20. Ibid., p. 155; Roscher, *Geschichte der National-Oekonomik in Deutschland,* pp. 1032–45.

21. Eisermann, *Grundlagen*, p. 172.
22. Ibid., pp. 142, 155; Roscher, *Ansichten*, pp. 1–46.
23. Lindenlaub, *Richtungskämpfe*, 52:96–141.
24. Brentano, *Mein Leben*, pp. 72–73; Roscher, *Geschichte der National-Oekonomik in Deutschland*, pp. 1032–45.
25. Eisermann, *Grundlagen*, pp. 1–118.
26. Ibid., pp. 154–55; Roscher, *Ansichten*, pp. 1–46.
27. On the political, social, and intellectual effects of the depression, see Rosenberg, *Grosse Depression*.
28. Lindenlaub, *Richtungskämpfe*, 52:1–43; Bruch, '*Weder Kommunismus noch Kapitalismus*,' pp. 72–81.
29. Lindenlaub, *Richtungskämpfe*, 52:84–96.
30. Ibid., 52:1–10.
31. Bruch, '*Weder Kommunismus noch Kapitalismus*,' pp. 61–179. It should be noted that several important members of the *Verein*, even in its early years, did not fully agree with Schmoller about the need to accept the Bismarckian state. Brentano, for instance, thought that substantial political reform was needed.
32. Lindenlaub, *Richtungskämpfe*, 52:9.
33. Ibid., 52:141–53; Bruch, '*Weder Kommunismus noch Kapitalismus*', pp. 66–69, 72–75; Bruch, *Wissenschaft*, pp. 92–112, 157–64, 280–82, 320–63.
34. On Schmoller's theoretical outlook, see Gustav Schmoller, "Zur Methodologie der Staats- und Sozialwissenschaften," *Jahrbuch für Gesetzgebung, Verwaltung und Volkswirtschaft im Deutschen Reiche* n.F. 7 (1883), pp. 239–58; Lindenlaub, *Richtungskämpfe*, 52:96–153; *International Encyclopedia of the Social Sciences* 14, pp. 60–63.
35. Brentano, *Mein Leben*, pp. 63–67, 100–106; Sheehan, *Career of Lujo Brentano*; Lindenlaub, *Richtungskämpfe*, 52:84–95, 184–87.
36. A. Wagner, *Agrar- und Industriestaat*; Brentano, *Mein Leben*, pp. 63–67, 71–72; Lindenlaub, *Richtungskämpfe*, 52:96–141.
37. Lindenlaub, *Richtungskämpfe*, 53:272–384; Weber, *Roscher and Knies*; Mommsen and Osterhammel, *Max Weber*, pp. 25–98.
38. See, for example, Iggers, *German Conception of History*.
39. Rickman, *Dilthey*, pp. 123–44.
40. On Burckhardt and his thought, see Hardtwig, *Geschichtsschreibung*; and Karl J. Weintraub, *Visions of Culture* (Chicago and London, 1966), pp. 115–60.
41. Hardtwig, *Geschichtsschreibung*, pp. 290–92.
42. Ibid., pp. 290–98.
43. Ibid., pp. 273–98; Weintraub, *Visions*, pp. 148–50.
44. Hardtwig, *Geschichtsschreibung*, p. 292.
45. Ibid., pp. 51–69, 165–81.
46. Ibid., pp. 33–36, 44–50.
47. Jacob Burckhardt, *The Civilization of the Renaissance in Italy* (New York, 1954), pp. 3–99.
48. Hardtwig, *Geschichtsschreibung*, pp. 31–36.
49. Ibid., pp. 202–7, 213–16.
50. On Mommsen, see Albert Wucher, *Theodor Mommsen: Geschichtsschreibung und Politik* (Göttingen, 1956).
51. On Freytag, see Gabriele Büchler-Hauschild, *Erzählte Arbeit: Gustav Freytag und die soziale Prosa der Vor- und Nachmärz* (Paderborn, 1987).
52. Bruch, *Wissenschaft*, pp. 37–38.
53. Büchler-Hauschild, *Erzählte Arbeit*, pp. 83–95.

54. On Diederichs, see Mosse, *Crisis of German Ideology*, pp. 52–63.

55. Georg Steinhausen, ed., *Monographien zur deutschen Kulturgeschichte*, 12 vols. (Leipzig and Jena, 1899–1905).

56. Georg Liebe, *Der Soldat in der deutschen Vergangenheit* (Leipzig, 1899); Adolf Bartels, *Der Bauer in der deutschen Vergangenheit* (Leipzig, 1900); Georg Liebe, *Der Judentum* (Leipzig, 1903). These are, respectively, volumes 1, 6, and 11 in the Steinhausen series.

57. Bruch, *Weltpolitik*, pp. 44–46.

58. On Lamprecht's personal and intellectual background and his early education, see Chickering, "Young Lamprecht," pp. 198–214.

59. Ibid.

60. Bruch, *Wissenschaft*, pp. 367–76; Bruch, *Weltpolitik*, pp. 44–46, 91–122.

61. This effort resulted in Lamprecht's monumental (and controversial) *Deutsche Geschichte*, 12 vols. (Berlin, 1891–1909). For an analysis of Lamprecht's approach to cultural history, see Weintraub, *Visions*, pp. 161–207. For his own exposition of his approach, see Karl Lamprecht, *Die kulturhistorische Methode* (Berlin, 1900), and idem, *What Is History? Five Lectures on the Modern Science of History*, trans. E. A. Andrews (New York, 1905).

62. Lamprecht, *Kulturhistorische Methode*, pp. 44–46; Weintraub, *Visions*, pp. 63–65.

63. Chickering, "Young Lamprecht," pp. 211–13.

64. Lamprecht, *Kulturhistorische Methode*, p. 44; Ernst Engelberg, "Zum Methodenstreit um Karl Lamprecht," in Ernst Engelberg, ed., *Karl-Marx-Universität Leipzig 1409–1959: Beiträge zur Universitätsgeschichte*, 2 vols. (Leipzig, 1959), 2:23–38; Weintraub, *Visions*, pp. 183–86.

65. For a severe criticism of Lamprecht's use of Wundt's idea, see Weber, *Roscher and Knies*, pp. 101–20.

66. Whimster, "Lamprecht and Weber," pp. 268–83; Engelberg, "Methodenstreit," pp. 183–86; Bruch, *Wissenschaft*, pp. 367–76.

67. Weintraub, *Visions*, pp. 164–65, 175–76.

68. Lamprecht, *What Is History?* pp. 135–79; Weintraub, *Visions*, pp. 183–207.

69. Weber, *Roscher and Knies*, pp. 101–20.

70. Bruch, *Wissenschaft*, pp. 370–76; Bruch, *Weltpolitik*, pp. 44–46, 91–122.

71. Engelberg, "Methodenstreit," 2: pp. 23–38.

72. Whimster, "Lamprecht and Weber," pp. 268–83.

73. Ibid.

74. Bruch, *Weltpolitik*, pp. 46–47.

Chapter 11

1. Bruch, *Wissenschaft*, pp. 19–26.

2. W. D. Smith, *Ideological Origins*, pp. 41–51.

3. See, for example, Stern, *Politics of Cultural Despair*, pp. 5–15, 102–13; Ringer, *German Mandarins*, pp. 128–99.

4. Lindenlaub, *Richtungskämpfe*, 52:11–13; 53:385–432; Mitzman, *Iron Cage*, pp. 3–12.

5. Chickering, *We Men Who Feel Most German*; Eley, *Reshaping the German Right*, pp. 160–205.

6. Bruch, *Wissenschaft*, pp. 138–85.

7. For a comprehensive analysis by a contemporary, see Paul Rohrbach, *Der deutsche Gedanke in der Welt* (Düsseldorf and Leipzig, 1912). See also W. D. Smith, *Ideological Origins*, pp. 41–51.

8. Sheehan, *German Liberalism,* pp. 242, 252, 266–67; Eley, *Reshaping the German Right,* pp. 19–40; White, *Splintered Party.*

9. Eley, *Reshaping the German Right,* pp. 184–235; Blackbourn and Eley, *Peculiarities of German History,* pp. 118–26, 159–297; Manfred Rauh, *Die Parlamentarisierung des Deutschen Reiches* (Düsseldorf, 1977).

10. This problem arises, for example, with Ringer's classification of modernist and orthodox academics (Ringer, *German Mandarins,* pp. 128–43) and with Fritz Stern's categories of liberal and illiberal intellectuals in *The Failure of Illiberalism* (New York, 1972).

11. I must apologize for adding yet another analytical term to the discussion at this point, but it appears to be unavoidable because the intellectual politics of the first half of the Wilhelmian period cannot be readily examined with the terminology employed thus far. By a *community of political discourse,* I mean a group of intellectuals who define, analyze, and discuss political issues using a particular vocabulary, set of aims and attitudes. The term also encompasses the distinctive array of concepts that sets the groups off from other intellectuals who discuss the same issues. As we shall see, such communities are quite transitory.

12. This overview was suggested by, and is, I think, generally consistent with Bruch's analysis of Wilhelmian intellectual politics (in *Wissenschaft*), Chickering's study of radicalism in the Pan-German League (*We Men Who Feel Most German*), and Eley's investigation of the Navy League (*Reshaping the German Right*). All of these authors perceive a fluidity in intellectual politics in the early and mid-Wilhelmian periods that is later replaced by a growing tendency to align with parties and interest groups. None, however, employs the idea of a "community of political discourse."

13. See Arthur Mitzman, *Sociology and Estrangement: Three Sociologists of Imperial Germany,* pp. 135–264, and Mitzman, *Iron Cage,* passim.

14. For discussions of the posture that is here called apolitical, see Lindenlaub, *Richtungskämpfe,* 52:85, 141–53; and Bruch, *Wissenschaft,* pp. 185–89, 200–205, 249–78.

15. Eisermann, *Grundlagen,* pp. 143–44.

16. Lindenlaub, *Richtungskämpfe,* 52:9.

17. Ibid., 52:141–53; Bruch, *Wissenschaft,* pp. 249–82.

18. Lindenlaub, *Richtungskämpfe,* 53:385–432; Bruch, *Wissenschaft,* pp. 195–205.

19. Jacques Kornberg, "Dilthey's Introduction to the Human Sciences: Liberal Social Thought in the Second Reich," in Modris Ecksteins and Hildegard Hammerschmidt, eds., *Nineteenth-Century Germany* (Tübingen, 1983), pp. 78–105; Manfred Schön, "Gustav Schmoller and Max Weber," in Mommsen and Osterhammel, *Max Weber,* pp. 59–70.

20. Allan M. Sharlin, "Max Weber and the Origins of the Idea of Value-Free Social Science," *Archives européenes de sociologie* 15 (1974), pp. 337–53; Bruch, *Wissenschaft,* pp. 294–320.

21. On apolitical ideas of *Kulturpolitik,* see Bruch, *Wissenschaft,* pp. 320–63.

22. For a manifestation of older neoliberalism, see Virchow, *Sozialismus und Reaktion.* For discussions of the Wilhelmian version of neoliberalism, see the treatments of the *Freisinnige Vereinigung* in Beverly Heckart, *From Bassermann to Bebel: The Grand Bloc's Quest for Reform in the Kaiserreich, 1900–1914* (New Haven, CT, 1974), pp. 26–33; and Konstanze Wegner, *Theodor Barth und die Freisinnige Vereinigung: Studie zur Geschichte des Linksliberalismus im wilhelmischen Deutschland, 1893–1910* (Tübingen, 1968).

23. Bruch, ed., *'Weder Kommunismus noch Kapitalismus',* pp. 82–179.

24. See Marianne Weber, *Max Weber: A Biography,* trans. Harry Zohn (New York, 1975) pp. 399–415.

25. Bruch, *Wissenschaft,* pp. 282–90; Roland Eckert, *Kultur Zivilisation und Gesellschaft: Die Geschichtstheorie Alfred Webers, eine Studie zur Geschichte der deutschen Soziologie* (Tübingen, 1970), pp. 65–144.

26. On Bücher, see Heinz Barthel et al., "Karl Bücher: Seine politische und wissenschaftliche Stellung," in Engelberg, *Universität Leipzig*, 2:78–91; and *International Encyclopedia of the Social Sciences*, 2:163–65.

27. Bücher's major work was Carl Bücher, *Industrial Evolution*, trans. S. Morley Wickett (New York, 1901; repr. 1968).

28. Ibid., pp. 150–84, 283–314.

29. Barthel et al., "Bücher;" Franz Knipping, "Karl Bücher und das erste deutsche Universitätsinstitut für Zeitungskunde," in Engelberg, *Universität Leipzig*, 2:57–77.

30. See, for example, Stern, *Politics of Cultural Despair*, esp. pp. 213–16; and Mosse, *Crisis of German Ideology*, pp. 218–25.

31. See Chickering, *We Men Who Feel Most German*; and Eley, *Reshaping the German Right*.

32. Chickering, *We Men Who Feel Most German*, pp. 44–73; Eley, *Reshaping the German Right*, pp. 200–201.

33. On the Pan-German and other radical connections of these individuals, see Marianne Weber, *Max Weber*, pp. 202, 224–25; Mommsen, *Weber und die deutsche Politik*, 58–59; on Ratzel, see notes on the founding of the *Allgemeine Deutsche Verein*, 9 August 1891, in *Bundesarchiv* Koblenz, *Nachlass* Walter Frank, no. 23; Hans-Josef Steinberg, "Karl Lamprecht," in Wehler, *Deutsche Historiker I*, pp. 58–68.

34. Chickering, *We Men Who Feel Most German*, pp. 81–86, 122–32.

35. For a synopsis of radical attitudes within the Pan-German League, see Pan-German League (*Alldeutscher Verband*), *Zwanzig Jahre alldeutscher Arbeit und Kämpfe* (Berlin, 1910), esp. pp. 11–13, 157–89.

36. Marianne Weber, *Max Weber*, pp. 404–6.

37. See ibid., pp. 125, 128; Lindenlaub, *Richtungskämpfe*, 53:385–92; Pan-German League, *Zwanzig Jahre*, pp. 62–67 (1899 article by Ernst Hasse on economic policy), and pp. 157–89 (1903 speech by Heinrich Class).

38. Pan German League, *Zwanzig Jahre*, pp. 68–71.

39. W. D. Smith, *Ideological Origins*, pp. 104–5; Chickering, *We Men Who Feel Most German*, pp. 108–18.

40. See Max Weber's famous Freiburg inaugural address in Max Weber, *Gesammelte politische Schriften*, 3rd ed., Johannes Winckelmann, ed. (Tübingen, 1971), pp. 1–25.

41. Bruch, *Weltpolitik*, pp. 44–46, 91–122.

42. Pan-German League, *Zwanzig Jahre*, pp. 62–68, 314–29; R. W. Tims, *Germanizing Prussian Poland: The H-K-T Society and the Struggle for the Eastern Marches in the German Empire 1894–1919* (New York, 1941).

43. See Frobenius et al., *Menschenjagden und Zweikämpfe*, esp. pp. 187–90.

44. Eduard Hahn, *Die Entstehung der wirtschaftlichen Arbeit* (Heidelberg, 1908), pp. 1–4, 30–33, 102–4.

45. See, for example, Marianne Weber, *Max Weber*, pp. 218, 220–25, 402. See also the discussion of the motives of early academic members of the Pan-German League in Chickering, *We Men Who Feel Most German*, pp. 44–101.

46. Bruch, *Weltpolitik*, pp. 48–55.

47. This was what happened to the Webers and their associate Friedrich Naumann. Bruch, *Wissenschaft*, pp. 282–90.

48. Chickering, *We Men Who Feel Most German*, pp. 213–52; Eley, *Reshaping the German Right*, pp. 316–34. See also Daniel Frymann (Heinrich Class), *Wenn ich der Kaiser wär: Von den Grundzügen deutscher Machtpolitik*, 5th ed. (Leipzig, 1914).

49. The term *Leipzig Circle* is used by Hunter in *Perspectives*, pp. 41–48.

50. Bruch, *Wissenschaft*, pp. 92–112.

51. Buttmann *Ratzel*, pp. 73–83; Wanklyn, *Ratzel*, pp. 27–33; Brentano, *Mein Leben*, pp. 147–65; Engelberg, *Universität Leipzig*, 2:23–38, 78–91; *Bedeutende Gelehrte in Leipzig*, 2 vols. (Leipzig, 1965), 2:51–62 (on Ostwald); Wilhelm Ostwald, *Lebenslinien*, 3 vols. (Berlin, 1926), 2:90. See also the articles in the *International Encyclopedia of the Social Sciences* on Bücher (2:163–65) and on Lamprecht (8:544–50).

52. See Bruch, *Wissenschaft*, pp. 195–200. Bruch's discussion of this outlook is formulated in terms of the position of outsiders throughout academia, but he focuses on Lamprecht, who taught at a university (Leipzig) at which the point of view he describes was characteristic of the local academic establishment—more or less by definition an establishment of outsiders in relation to Berlin.

53. The situation of Saxony at the turn of the century is nicely summarized in Donald Warren, Jr., *The Red Kingdom of Saxony: Lobbying Grounds for Gustav Stresemann, 1901–1909* (The Hague, 1964), pp. ix–xii, 1–24.

54. Rudolf Kittel, *Die Universität Leipzig und ihre Stellung im Kulturleben* (Dresden, 1924), pp. 22–25, 29, 34. (Kittel was a secondary member of the Leipzig Circle.)

55. Ibid., pp. 29–37; Brentano, *Mein Leben*, pp. 147–65.

56. Buttmann, *Ratzel*, pp. 73–74.

57. Warren, *Red Kingdom*, pp. 12–18; Brentano, *Mein Leben*, pp. 148–49.

58. See the summary of Roscher's thought in Roscher, *Ansichten*, esp. pp. 1–46, 173–278.

59. Warren, *Red Kingdom*, pp. 3–9; Brentano, *Mein Leben*, pp. 147–65.

60. On Fechner, see *International Encyclopedia of the Social Sciences*, 5:350–52; the biographical portion of Gustav Fechner, *Religion of a Scientist*, ed. and trans. Walter Lowrie (New York, 1946), pp. 23–46; Ratzel, *Glückinseln*, pp. 497–509; and Boring, *History of Experimental Psychology*, pp. 275–96.

61. Ratzel, *Glückinseln*, pp. 497–509; Buttmann, *Ratzel*, pp. 100–15.

62. Kelly, *Descent of Darwin*, pp. 40–42; Gasman, *Scientific Origins*, pp. 140–42.

63. Buttmann, *Ratzel*, pp. 73–83, 100–15; Ostwald, *Lebenslinien*, 2:90; Engelberg, *Universität Leipzig*, 2:23–38, 78–91.

64. Kittel, *Universität Leipzig . . . Kulturleben*, pp. 29, 34; Knipping, "Bücher," 2:57–77.

65. See Kittel, *Universität Leipzig . . . Kulturleben*, p. 44; Ratzel, *Erde und das Leben*, 2:530–46; Lamprecht, *What Is History?*

66. Again, see Bruch, *Weltpolitik*, pp. 41–57. Bruch's focus is broader than the Leipzig academics and he is more interested in *Kulturpolitik* than in cultural science, but he describes essentially similar phenomena.

67. Bücher et al., *Grossstadt*, preface; Schäfer, *Mein Leben*, pp. 140–41.

68. See Woodruff D. Smith, "The Emergence of German Urban Sociology, 1900–1910," *Journal of the History of Sociology*, 1, 2 (1979), pp. 1–16.

69. Ibid.

70. On the tariff issue, its generalization, and its effects on Wilhelmian political and social life, see Barkin, *Controversy*; Puhle, *Agrarische Interessenpolitik*; and (emphasizing the broad basis of anti-Caprivi sentiment) Blackbourn, *Populists and Patricians*, pp. 114–39.

71. Barkin, *Controversy*, pp. 138–85.

72. Mommsen, *Weber und die deutsche Politik*, p. 59; W. D. Smith, *Ideological Origins*, p. 101.

73. W. D. Smith, "Urban Sociology," pp. 1–16; Max Weber, *The City*, trans. D. Martindale and G. Neuwirth (New York, 1958); Bergmann, *Agrarromantik*, pp. 33–85.

74. Bücher et al., *Grossstadt*, pp. 1–32.

75. Ibid., pp. 16–17, 20–21.

76. Ibid., pp. 24–28.

77. Ibid., p. 31.

78. Ibid., pp. 33–72; Buttmann, *Ratzel,* pp. 69–72.

79. Bücher et al., *Grossstadt,* pp. 35–37.

80. Ibid., pp. 42–45.

81. Ibid., pp. 65–72.

82. Ibid., p. 72.

83. Ibid., pp. 73–146.

84. Ibid., pp. 147–84.

85. Schäfer, *Mein Leben,* esp. pp. 129–36, 140–41, 151–54; Roger Chickering, "Dietrich Schäfer and Max Weber," in Mommsen and Osterhammel, *Max Weber,* pp. 334–44.

86. Bücher et al., *Grossstadt,* pp. 231–82.

87. Ibid., pp. 257–67.

88. Ibid., pp. 279–82.

89. Ibid., pp. 185–206. On Simmel's thought in general, see Lewis A. Coser, ed., *Georg Simmel* (Englewood Cliffs, NJ, 1965), pp. 4–23.

90. Coser, *Simmel,* pp. 37–39; Schäfer, *Mein Leben,* pp. 140–41.

91. See Georg Simmel, *Brücke und Tür: Essays des Philosophen zur Geschichte, Religion, Kunst und Gesellschaft,* ed. Michael Landmann (Stuttgart, 1957), pp. 95–97, 208–70 (including the *Grossstadt* piece on pp. 227–42.)

92. Coser, *Simmel,* pp. 4–23.

93. Bücher et al., *Grossstadt,* pp. 207–30.

94. Bruch, *Weltpolitik,* pp. 41–57, 91–122.

95. Ibid., pp. 41–44, 48–49.

96. Ibid., pp. 46–47; Bruch, *Wissenschaft,* pp. 367–79.

Chapter 12

1. H. W. Koch, *Der Sozialdarwinismus: Seine Genese und sein Einfluss auf das imperialistischen Denken* (Munich, 1973).

2. The discussion in this chapter is built on those found in Woodruff D. Smith, "Ratzel," pp. 51–68; and idem, *Ideological Origins,* pp. 146–52.

3. For example, War Minister Roon's sponsorship of strategic geography in the Prussian military: Roon, *Denkwürdigkeiten,* 1:55, 57–59, 61–62, 91.

4. See Erich von Drygalski, *Ferdinand Freiherr von Richthofen* (Leipzig, 1906), pp. 11–15.

5. Ratzel, *Anthropo-Geographie,* 2:384–434; idem, *Erde und das Leben,* 2:530–46, 617–77; idem, *Völkerkunde,* 1:19–28.

6. This need can be seen in Ratzel, *Anthropo-Geographie,* 2:3–142. The political implications of culture and geography are the main focus of Ratzel's *Politische Geographie.* See Hunter, *Perspectives,* specifically on Ratzel's political geography, and Buttmann, *Ratzel,* pp. 88–95.

7. Ratzel, *Anthropo-Geographie,* 1:460–64.

8. Ratzel, *Völkerkunde,* 1:13–28; idem, "Geschichte, Völkerkunde und historische Perspektive," pp. 1–46.

9. Ratzel, *Anthropo-Geographie,* 1:23–87; Buttmann, *Ratzel,* p. 72.

10. Buttmann, *Ratzel,* pp. 84–99; Hunter, *Perspectives,* pp. 28–48.

11. See, for instance, Ratzel, *Erde und das Leben,* 2:578–82.

12. For Ratzel's involvement in colonialism, imperialism, and radical nationalism, see Buttmann, *Ratzel,* pp. 80–83, 92–95; Ratzel [Anon.], "Beitrag zu den Anfangen"; idem,

"In welcher Richtung"; idem, "Die Maske ab!" *Grenzboten* 53, 21 (1894), pp. 337–40; "Dr. Karl Peters," pp. 252–56. See also *Bundesarchiv* Koblenz, *Nachlass* Walter Frank, no. 8 (letter of Ratzel to Peters, 28 August 1890).

13. Friedrich Ratzel, *Das Meer als Quelle der Völkergrösse: Eine politisch-geographisch Studie* (Munich, 1900).

14. Buttmann, *Ratzel,* pp. 88–94; Wanklyn, *Ratzel,* pp. 37–40.

15. Wanklyn, *Ratzel,* p. 38.

16. Friedrich Ratzel, "Der Lebensraum: Eine biogeographische Studie," in K. Bücher, K. V. Fricker, et al., *Festgaben für Albert Schäffle zur siebenzigsten Widerkehr seines Geburtstages am 24. Februar 1901* (Tübingen, 1901), pp. 101–89. See also idem, *Erde und das Leben,* 2:590–606.

17. Ratzel, "Lebensraum," pp. 139–40; idem, *Erde und das Leben,* 2:630–52; idem, "Die Gesetze des räumlichen Wachstums der Staaten," *Petermanns Mitteilungen* 42 (1896), pp. 97–107.

18. Ratzel, "Lebensraum," pp. 126–37; idem, *Erde und das Leben,* 2:571–82.

19. See chapter 8 herein.

20. See Ratzel, *Erde und das Leben,* esp. 2:502–3, 530–39, 590–606.

21. Ibid., 2:590–677.

22. Ratzel, "Gesetze"; idem, "Geschichte, Völkerkunde . . . Perspektive," p. 21.

23. Ratzel, *Erde und das Leben,* 2:590–677.

24. Ratzel, "Geschichte, Völkerkunde . . . Perspektive."

25. Ratzel, "Lebensraum," pp. 114–26, 169–73.

26. See W. D. Smith, "Ratzel."

27. Ratzel, *Politische Geographie,* pp. 90–121, 276–300; idem, "Gesetze," pp. 100–3, 106–7.

28. Ratzel, *Meer als Quelle.*

29. On the *Mitteleuropa* idea, see W. D. Smith, *Ideological Origins,* pp. 78–79, 109–11; and Henry Cord Meyer, *Mitteleuropa in German Thought and Action, 1815–1945* (The Hague, 1955).

30. On Julius Wolf, see Lindenlaub, *Richtungskämpfe,* 52:178–80. See also Chickering, *We Men Who Feel Most German,* pp. 78–79.

31. Friedrich Ratzel, "Die mitteleuropäische Wirtschaftsverein," *Grenzboten* 63, 5 (1904), pp. 253–59; idem, *Glückinseln,* p. 477.

32. Ratzel, *Politische Geographie,* pp. 17–32; idem, *Völkerkunde,* 2:370–83.

33. On the inner colonization idea, see W. D. Smith, *Ideological Origins,* pp. 106–8. See also Max Sering, *Die innere Kolonisation in östlichen Deutschland* (Leipzig, 1893), and Ratzel, *Glückinseln,* pp. 470–75.

34. Ratzel, *Glückinseln,* pp. 470–77; W. D. Smith, *Ideological Origins,* pp. 153–55.

35. Ratzel, *Erde und das Leben,* 2:617–30; idem, *Völkerkunde,* 1:13–18.

36. Mühlmann, *Geschichte der Anthropologie,* pp. 124–27.

37. Appleman, *Darwin,* pp. 211–19.

38. Ratzel, "Lebensraum," pp. 171–73.

39. As, for example, Ratzel does in "Gesetze."

40. Ibid.

41. See the editor's supplement to the 1923 edition of Ratzel, *Politische Geographie,* pp. 597–618. See also Rudolf Kjellén, *Der Staat als Lebensform,* 4th ed., trans. J. Sandmeier (Berlin, 1924), pp. 25–26.

42. See Eley, *Reshaping the German Right,* pp. 316–34.

43. Bernhardi, *Deutschland,* pp. 9–55, 82.

44. Ibid., pp. 89–124.

278 *Notes*

45. See W. D. Smith, *Ideological Origins,* pp. 129–40, 152–65.
46. Bernhardi, *Deutschland,* pp. 74–88.
47. W. D. Smith, *Ideological Origins,* pp. 166–95.
48. Ibid., pp. 187–95.
49. Ibid., pp. 203–13, 218–23.
50. *Bundesarchiv* Koblenz, *Nachlass* Haushofer, No. HC 834 (essay "Was ist Geopolitik?" 28 May 1929); Karl Haushofer, *Weltpolitik von heute* (Berlin, 1936), pp. 22–50.
51. Hans Grimm, *Volk ohne Raum* (Munich, 1932), pp. 958–63, 989–1007; Woodruff D. Smith, "The Colonial Novel as Political Propaganda: Hans Grimm's *Volk ohne Raum,*" *German Studies Review* 6 (1983), pp. 215–35.
52. This discussion summarizes one given at greater length in W. D. Smith, *Ideological Origins,* pp. 231–58.

Chapter 13
1. See Lowie, *History of Ethnological Theory,* pp. 177–95; and James, *All Possible Worlds,* pp. 518–22.
2. Harris, *Rise of Anthropological Theory,* pp. 250–89.
3. W. D. Smith, *Ideological Origins,* pp. 166–95; Leo Frobenius, *Deutschlands Gegner im Weltkrieg* (Berlin, n.d.)
4. *Festschrift . . . Berliner Gesellschaft,* pp. 100–30.
5. R. W. Darré, *Bauerntum als Lebensquell der nordischen Rasse* (Munich, 1929) See also Erwin Baur, *Der Untergang der Kulturvölker im Lichte der Biologie* (Munich, 1932), pp. 3–19.
6. Harris, *Rise of Anthropological Theory,* pp. 250–89.
7. James, *All Possible Worlds,* pp. 518–22.
8. This view is best expounded in Wehler, *German Empire.*
9. See Blackbourn and Eley, *Peculiarities of German History.*

Bibliography

Archival sources:
Bundesarchiv Koblenz
Bestand R13I (*Wirtschaftsgruppe Eisenschaffende Industrie*)
Walter Frank papers
Karl Haushofer papers
Microfilm Collection of the Professional Papers of Franz Boas. Philadelphia: American Philosophical Society.

Primary periodical sources:
Africa
American Anthropologist
Anthropological Review
Anthropos
Berichten des Königl. Sächs. Gesellschaft der Wissenschaften
Deutsche Kolonialzeitung
Deutsche Monatshefte
Globus
Die Grenzboten
Historische Zeitschrift
Jahrbuch für Gesetzgebung, Verwaltung und Volkswirtschaft im Deutschen Reiche
Korrespondenzblatt, Gesellschaft für Anthropologie, Ethnologie und Urgeschichte
Mitteilungen aus den deutschen Schutzgebieten
Nord und Süd
Petermanns Mitteilungen
Verhandlungen der Berliner Gesellschaft für Anthropologie, Ethnologie und Urgeschichte
Verhandlungen der Gesellschaft für Erdkunde zu Berlin
Zeitschrift für Ethnologie
Zeitschrift für Geopolitik

Published works cited:
Ackerknecht, Erwin H. *Rudolf Virchow: Doctor Statesman Anthropologist*. Madison, WI, 1953.
Allegemeine Deutsche Biographie. 56 vols. Berlin, 1967–1971. Reprint of 1875–1912 ed.
Andree, Carl Theodor. *Geographische Wanderungen*. 2 vols. Dresden, 1859.
Andree, Christian. ''Geschichte der Berliner Gesellschaft für Anthropologie, Ethnologie und Urgeschichte.'' In *Festschrift zum hundertjährige Bestehen der Berliner Gesellschaft für Anthropologie, Ethnologie und Urgeschichte 1869–1969*. Part 1. Berlin, 1969. Pp. 9–140.

Ankermann, Bernhard. "Die Entwicklung der Ethnologie seit Adolf Bastian." *Zeitschrift für Ethnologie* 58 (1926). Pp. 221–30.

———. "Kulturkreise und Kulturschichten in Afrika." *Zeitschrift für Ethnologie* 37 (1905). Pp. 54–84.

———. "Die Lehre von den Kulturkreisen." *Korrespondenzblatt, Gesellschaft für Anthropologie, Ethnologie und Urgeschichte* 42 (1911). Pp. 156–62.

Appleman, Philip. Ed. *Darwin: A Norton Critical Edition*, 2nd ed. New York, 1979.

Asad, Talal. Ed. *Anthropology and the Colonial Encounter*. New York, 1973.

Bade, Klaus J. *Friedrich Fabri und der Imperialismus in der Bismarckzeit*. Freiburg, 1975.

———. Ed. *Imperialismus und Kolonialmission: Kaiserliche Deutschland und koloniales Imperium*. Wiesbaden, 1982.

Barkin, Kenneth D. *The Controversy over German Industrialization 1890–1902*. Chicago, 1970.

Barnes, Barry. "Thomas Kuhn." In Quentin Skinner, ed., *The Return of Grand Theory in the Human Sciences*. Cambridge, 1985. Pp. 83–100.

Bartels, Adolf. *Der Bauer in der deutschen Vergangenheit*. Leipzig 1900. Vol. 6 of Georg Steinhausen, ed., *Monographien zur deutschen Kulturgeschichte*.

Barthel, Heinz, et al. "Karl Bücher: Seine politische und wissenschaftliche Stellung." In Ernst Engelberg, ed., *Karl Marx-Universität Leipzig, 1409–1959: Beiträge zur Universitätsgeschichte*. 2 vols. Leipzig, 1959. 2:78–91.

Bastian, Adolf. *Controversen in der Ethnologie*. 4 vols. in one vol. Berlin, 1893.

———. *Geographische und Ethnographische Bilder*. Jena, 1873.

———. *Zur Lehre von den geographischen Provinzen*. Berlin, 1886.

———. *Der Mensch in der Geschichte: Zur Begründung einer psychologischen Weltanschauung*. vol. 3, *Politische Psychologie*. Leipzig, 1860.

———. *Der Völkergedanke, im Aufbau einer Wissenschaft vom Menschen und seine Begründung auf ethnologischen Sammlungen*. Berlin, 1881.

———. *Die Völkerkunde und der Völkerverkehr unter seiner Rückwirkung auf die Volksgeschichte*. Berlin, 1900.

———. *Zwei Wörte über Colonial-Weisheit*. Berlin, 1883.

Baumann, Hermann. "Die afrikanischen Kulturkreise." *Africa* 7, 2 (1934). Pp. 129–39.

Baur, Erwin. *Der Untergang der Kulturvölker im Lichte der Biologie*. Munich, 1932.

Beck, Hanno. *Alexander von Humboldt*. 2 vols. Wiesbaden, 1959.

———. "Geography and Travel in the Nineteenth Century: Prolegomena to a General History of Travel." In Gary S. Dunbar, ed., *The History of Geography: Translations of Some French and German Essays*. Malibu, CA, 1983.

Bedeutende Gelehrte in Leipzig. 2 vols. Leipzig, 1965.

Berding, Helmut. "Leopold Ranke." In H. U. Wehler, ed., *Deutsche Historiker I*. Pp. 7–24.

Bergmann, Klaus. *Agrarromantik und Grossstadtfeindschaft*. Meisenheim am Glan, 1970.

Bergmann, Peter. *Nietzsche: "The Last Antipolitical German."* Bloomington and Indianapolis, 1987.

Bergsträsser, Ludwig. *Geschichte der politischen Parteien in Deutschland*. 8th/9th ed. Munich, 1955.

Bernhardi, Friedrich von. *Deutschland und der nächste Krieg*. Stuttgart and Berlin, 1912.

Beuchelt, Eno. *Ideengeschichte der Völkerpsychologie*. Meisenheim am Glan, 1974.

Birtsch, Günter. *Die Nation als sittliche Idee*. Cologne, 1964.

Blackbourn, David. *Populists and Patricians: Essays in Modern German History*. London, 1987.

Blackbourn, David, and Eley, Geoff. *The Peculiarities of German History: Bourgeois Society and Politics in Nineteenth-Century Germany*. New York, 1984.

Blumenthal, Arthur L. "Wilhelm Wundt: Problems of Interpretation." In Wolfgang G. Bringmann and Ryan D. Tweney, eds., *Wundt Studies: A Centennial Collection*. Toronto, 1980. Pp. 435–45.

Boas, Franz. *Anthropology and Modern Life*. New York, 1928.

———. *Race and Democratic Society*. New York, 1945.

Böhme, Helmut. *Deutschlands Weg zur Grossmacht: Studien zum Verhältnis von Wirtschaft und Staat während der Reichsgründungszeit 1848–1881*. Cologne, 1966.

———. *An Introduction to the Social and Economic History of Germany: Politics and Economic Change in the Nineteenth and Twentieth Centuries*. Trans. W. R. Lee. New York, 1978.

Boring, Edwin G. *A History of Experimental Psychology*, 2nd ed. New York, 1950.

Brentano, Lujo. *Mein Leben im Kampf um die soziale Entwicklung Deutschlands*. Jena, 1931.

Broce, Gerald. "Herder and Ethnography." *Journal of the History of the Behavioral Sciences* 22 (1986). Pp. 150–70.

Brown, Richard Harvey. "Postivism, Relativism, and Narrative in the Logic of the Historical Sciences." *American Historical Review* 92, 4 (1987). Pp. 908–20.

Bruch, Rüdiger vom. Ed. *'Weder Kommunismus noch Kapitalismus': Bürgerliche Sozialreform in Deutschland vom Vormärz zum Ära Adenauer*. Munich, 1985.

———. *Weltpolitik als Kulturmission: Auswärtige Kulturpolitik und Bildungsbürgertum in Deutschland am Vorabend des Ersten Weltkrieges*. Paderborn, 1982.

———. *Wissenschaft, Politik und öffentliche Meinung: Gelehrtenpolitik im Wilhelmischen Deutschland (1890–1914)*. Husum, Ger., 1980.

Buchner, Max. *Aurora colonialis . . . .* Munich, 1914.

Bücher, Carl [Karl]. *Industrial Evolution*. Trans. S. Morley Wickett. New York, 1901. Repr. 1968.

Bücher, Karl et al. *Die Grossstadt*. Dresden, 1903.

Büchler-Hauschild, Gabriele. *Erzählte Arbeit: Gustav Freytag und die soziale Prosa der Vor- und Nachmärz*. Paderborn, 1987.

Burckhardt, Jacob. *The Civilization of the Renaissance in Italy*. New York, 1954.

Burrow, J. W. *Evolution and Society: A Study in Victorian Social Theory*. Cambridge, 1966.

Buttmann, Günther. *Friedrich Ratzel: Leben und Werk eines deutschen Geographen*. Stuttgart, 1977.

Caton, Hiram. "The Preindustrial Economics of Adam Smith." *Journal of Economic History* 45, 4 (1985). Pp. 833–53.

Chickering, Roger. "Dietrich Schäfer and Max Weber." In Wolfgang J. Mommsen and Jürgen Osterhammel, eds., *Max Weber and His Contemporaries*. Pp. 334–44.

———. *We Men Who Feel Most German: A Cultural Study of the Pan-German League, 1886–1914*. Boston, 1984.

———. "Young Lamprecht: An Essay in Biography and Historiography." *History and Theory* 28, 2 (1989). Pp. 198–214.

Coser, Lewis A. Ed. *Georg Simmel*. Englewood Cliffs, NJ, 1965.

Danziger, Kurt. "Wundt and the Two Traditions of Psychology." In R. W. Rieber, ed., *Wilhelm Wundt and the Making of a Scientific Psychology*. New York and London 1980. Pp. 73–87.

———. "Wundt's Theory of Behavior and Volition." In R. W. Rieber, ed., *Wilhelm Wundt and the Making of a Scientific Psychology*. New York and London, 1980. Pp. 89–115.

Darré, R. W. *Das Bauerntum als Lebensquell der nordischen Rasse*. Munich, 1929.

Diamond, Solomon. "Wundt Before Leipzig." In R. W. Rieber, ed., *Wilhelm Wundt and the Making of a Scientific Psychology*. New York and London, 1980. Pp. 3–70.

Drygalski, Erich von. *Ferdinand Freiherr von Richthofen.* Leipzig, 1906.

Eckert, Roland. *Kultur Zivilisation und Gesellschaft: Die Geschichtstheorie Alfred Webers, eine Studie zur Geschichte der deutschen Soziologie.* Tübingen, 1970.

Eisermann, Gottfried. *Die Grundlagen des Historismus in der deutschen Nationalökonomie.* Stuttgart, 1956.

Ellis, John M. *One Fairy Story Too Many: The Brothers Grimm and Their Tales.* Chicago, 1983.

Eley, Geoff. *Reshaping the German Right: Radical Nationalism and Political Change After Bismarck.* New Haven, CT, and London, 1980.

Engleberg, Ernst. Ed. *Karl-Marx-Universität Leipzig 1409–1959: Beiträge zur Universitätsgeschichte.* 2 vols. Leipzig, 1959.

———. "Zum Methodenstreit um Karl Lamprecht." In Ernst Engelberg, ed., *Karl-Marx-Universität Leipzig 1409–1959: Beiträge zur Universitätsgeschichte.* 2 vols. Leipzig, 1959. 2:23–38.

Epstein, Klaus. *The Genesis of German Conservatism.* Princeton, NJ, 1966.

Essner, Cornelia. *Deutsche Afrikareisende im neunzehnten Jahrhundert.* Stuttgart, 1985.

Eyck, Frank. *The Frankfurt Parliament 1848–1849.* London, 1968.

Fechner, Gustav. *The Religion of a Scientist.* Ed. and trans. Walter Lowrie. New York, 1946.

Festschrift für Adolf Bastian zu seinem 70. Geburtstage 26. Juni 1896. Berlin, 1896.

Festschrift zum hundertjährige Bestehen der Berliner Gesellschaft für Anthropologie, Ethnologie und Urgeschichte 1869–1969. Pt. 1. Berlin, 1969.

Fiedermutz-Laun, Annemarie. *Die kulturhistorische Gedanke bei Adolf Bastian.* Wiesbaden, 1970.

Fischer, Hans, and Müller-Wille, Ludger. *Ethnologen-Verzeichnis.* Bonn, 1977.

Foucault, Michel. *The Order of Things: An Archaeology of the Human Sciences.* New York, 1970.

Frobenius, Leo. *Deutschlands Gegner im Weltkrieg.* Berlin, n.d.

———. *Paideuma: Umrisse einer Kultur- und Seelenlehre.* Munich, 1921.

———. *Ursprung der afrikanischen Kulturen.* Berlin, 1898.

Frobenius, Leo, Frobenius, D. H., and Kohlhammer, D. E. *Menschenjagden und Zweikämpfe.* Jena, n.d.

Frymann, Daniel [Heinrich Class]. *Wenn ich der Kaiser wär: Von den Grundzügen deutscher Machtpolitik,* 5th ed. Leipzig, 1914.

Gädecke, Hannah. *Wilhelm Heinrich Riehls Gedanken über Volk und Staat.* Heidelberg, 1935. Inaugural dissertation.

Gagliardo, John G. *From Pariah to Patriot: The Changing Image of the German Peasant 1770–1840.* Lexington, KY, 1969.

Gall, Bernd. *Die individuelle Anerkennungstheorie von Karl Theodor Welcker.* Bonn, 1972.

Gann, L. H. "Heinrich Schnee (1871–1949)." In L. H. Gann and Peter Duignan, eds., *African Proconsuls: European Governors in Africa.* New York, 1978. Pp. 492–522.

Gann, L. H., and Duignan, Peter. Eds. *African Proconsuls: European Governors in Africa.* New York, 1978.

———. *The Rulers of German Africa 1884–1914.* Stanford, 1977.

Ganslmyer, H. "Moritz Wagner und seine Bedeutung für die Ethnologie" in *Verhandlungen des XXXVIII. internationalen Amerikanistenkongresses . . . 1968.* Munich, 1969. 4:459–70.

Gasman, Daniel. *The Scientific Origins of National Socialism: Social Darwinism in Ernst Haeckel and the German Monist League.* London and New York, 1971.

Gebhardt, Otto. Ed. *Theodor Waitz' Allgemeine Pädogogik und kleinere pädogogische Schriften.* Langensalza, Ger., 1910.

Geramb, Viktor von. *Wilhelm Heinrich Riehl: Leben und Wirken (1823–1897).* Salzburg, 1954.

Gipper, Helmut, and Schmitter, Peter. *Sprachwissenschaft und Sprachphilosophie im Zeitalter der Romantik: Ein Beitrag zur Historiographie der Linguistik.* Tübingen, 1979.

Gneist, Rudolf. *The History of the English Constitution.* Trans. P. Ashworth. 2 vols. New York, 1886.

Götzen, Gustav Adolf, Graf von. *Deutsch-Ostafrika im Aufstand 1905/6.* Berlin, 1909.

Gollwitzer, Heinz. *Die gelbe Gefahr.* Göttingen, 1962.

Graebner, Fritz. "Kulturkreise und Kulturschichten in Ozeanien." *Zeitschrift für Ethnologie* 37 (1905). Pp. 28–53.

———. *Methode der Ethnologie.* Heidelberg, 1911.

———. *Das Weltbild der Primitiven: Eine Untersuchung der Urformen weltanschaulichen Denkens bei Naturvölkern.* Munich, 1924.

Gregory, Frederick. *Scientific Materialism in Nineteenth Century Germany.* Dordrecht and Boston, 1977.

Grimm, Hans. *Volk ohne Raum.* Munich, 1932.

Haeberlin, Herman K. "The Theoretical Foundations of Wundt's Folk Psychology." In R. W. Rieber, ed., *Wilhelm Wundt and the Making of a Scientific Psychology.* New York and London, 1980. Pp. 22–49.

Haeckel, Ernst. *Freie Wissenschaft und freie Lehre.* Stuttgart, 1878.

Hahn, Eduard. *Die Entstehung der wirtschaftlichen Arbeit.* Heidelberg, 1908.

Hamerow, Theodore S. *Restoration, Revolution, Reaction: Economics and Politics in Germany, 1815–1871.* Princeton, NJ, 1958.

———. *The Social Foundations of German Unification, 1858–71,* 2 vols. Princeton, NJ, 1969, 1972.

Hardtwig, Wolfgang. *Geschichtsschreibung zwischen Alteuropa und moderner Welt: Jacob Burckhardt in seiner Zeit.* Göttingen, 1974.

Harris, Marvin. *The Rise of Anthropological Theory: A History of Theories of Culture.* New York, 1968.

Haskell, Thomas L. *The Emergence of Professional Social Science: The American Social Science Association and the Nineteenth-Century Crisis of Authority.* Urbana, IL, 1977.

Hasse, Ernst. "Was können und sollen wir jetzt für die deutsche Auswanderung thun?" *Deutsche Kolonialzeitung,* 15 December 1884.

Haushofer, Karl. *Weltpolitik von heute.* Berlin, 1936.

Heckart, Beverly. *From Bassermann to Bebel: The Grand Bloc's Quest for Reform in the Kaiserreich, 1900–1914.* New Haven, CT, 1974.

Hegel, Georg Wilhelm Friedrich. *The Philosophy of History.* New York, 1956.

Helmholtz, Hermann. "On the Relation of Natural Science to General Science." In H. Helmholtz, *Popular Lectures on Scientific Subjects.* Trans. E. Atkinson. New York, 1873. Pp. 1–32.

Herder, Johann Gottfried von. *Ideen zur Philosophie der Geschichte der Menschheit.* Berlin, 1879.

Holborn, Hajo. *A History of Modern Germany 1840–1945.* New York, 1973.

Hothersall, David. *History of Psychology.* Philadelphia, 1984.

Hübbe-Schleiden, Wilhelm. *Deutsche Colonisation.* Hamburg, 1881.

Humboldt, Alexander von. *Kosmos: Entwurf einer physischen Weltbeschreibung.* 4 vols. Stuttgart, 1845–1858.

Humboldt, Wilhelm von. *Humanist Without Portfolio.* Trans. Marianne Cowan. Detroit, 1963.

———. *Schulpläne des Jahres 1809: "Über die innere und äussere Organisation der höheren wissenschaftlichen Anstalten in Berlin," 1810.* Hamburg, 1946.

Hunt, James. "On the Study of Anthropology." *Anthropological Review* 1 (1863). Pp. 1–20.

Hunter, James M. *Perspectives on Ratzel's Political Geography.* Lanham, MD, 1983.

Iggers, Georg G. *The German Conception of History: The National Tradition of Historical Thought from Herder to the Present.* Middletown, CT, 1968.

International Encyclopedia of the Social Sciences. 18 vols. New York, 1968.

Jacob und Wilhelm Grimm als Sprachwissenschaftler: Geschichtlichkeit und Aktualität ihres Wirkens. Berlin, 1985.

Jahn, Jahnheinz. *Leo Frobenius: The Demonic Child.* Austin, 1972.

James, Preston E. *All Possible Worlds: A History of Geographical Ideas.* Indianapolis and New York, 1972.

Jarausch, Konrad. *Students, Society, and Politics in Imperial Germany: The Rise of Academic Illiberalism.* Princeton, NJ, 1982.

Jensen, Adolf E. "Kulturkreislehre als Grundlage der Kulturgeschichte." In *Leo Frobenius: Ein Lebenswerk aus der Zeit der Kulturwende.* Leipzig, 1933. Pp. 73–95.

Jones, Greta. *Social Darwinism and English Thought: The Interaction Between Biological and Social Theory.* Brighton, Eng., 1980.

Kandt, Richard. *Caput Nili: Eine empfindsame Reise zu den Quellen des Nils,* 4th ed. Berlin, 1919.

Kelly, Alfred. *The Descent of Darwin: The Popularization of Darwin in Germany, 1860–1914.* Chapel Hill, NC, 1981.

Kennedy, Kenneth R. *Neanderthal Man.* Minneapolis, 1975.

Kittel, Rudolf. *Die Universität Leipzig und ihre Stellung in Kulturleben.* Dresden, 1924.

Kjellén, Rudolf. *Der Staat als Lebensform,* 4th ed. Trans. J. Sandmeier. Berlin, 1924.

Klemm, Gustav. *Allgemeine Cultur-Geschichte der Menschheit.* Vol. 1. Leipzig, 1843.

Kluckhorn, Clyde, and Prufer, Olof. "Influences During the Formative Years." In Walter Goldschmidt, ed., *The Anthropology of Franz Boas. American Anthropologist* 61, 5, p. 2: Memoir No. 89 (1959). Pp. 4–28.

Knapp, Georg Friedrich. *Die Bauernbefreiung und der Ursprung der Landarbeiter in den älteren Theilen Preussens.* 2 vols. Leipzig, 1887.

Knipping, Franz. "Karl Bücher und das erste deutsche Universitätsinstitut für Zeitungskunde." In Ernst Engelberg, ed., *Karl-Marx-Universität Leipzig 1409–1959: Beiträge zur Universitätsgeschichte,* 2 vols. Leipzig, 1959. Pp. 57–77.

Knoll, Arthur J. *Togo under Imperial Germany 1884–1914: A Case Study in Imperial Rule.* Stanford, 1978.

Knudsen, Jonathan B. *Justus Möser and the German Enlightenment.* Cambridge, 1986.

Koch, H. W. *Der Sozialdarwinismus: Seine Genese und sein Einfluss auf das imperialistischen Denken.* Munich, 1973.

Koepke, Wulf. *Johann Gottfried Herder.* Boston, 1987.

Koepping, Klaus-Peter. *Adolf Bastian and the Psychic Unity of Mankind: The Foundations of Anthropology in Nineteenth Century Germany.* Saint Lucia, Queensland, Austral., 1983.

Kohl, Ernst Werner. *Virchow in Würzburg.* Hanover, 1976.

Kornberg, Jacques. "Dilthey's Introduction to the Human Sciences: Liberal Social Thought in the Second Reich." In Modris Ecksteins and Hildegard Hammerschmidt, eds., *Nineteenth-Century Germany.* Tübingen, 1983. Pp. 78–105.

Koszyk, Kurt. *Die deutsche Presse im 19. Jahrhundert.* Berlin, 1966.

Krieger, Leonard. *The German Idea of Freedom. History of a Political Tradition*. Boston, 1957.

Kuhn, Thomas S. *The Essential Tension: Selected Studies in Scientific Tradition and Change*. Chicago and London, 1977.

———. *The Structure of Scientific Revolutions*, 2nd ed. Chicago, 1970.

Kuklick, Henrika. "The Sins of the Fathers: British Anthropology and African Colonial Administration." *Research in the Sociology of Knowledge, Sciences and Art* 1 (1978). Pp. 93–119.

Lamprecht, Karl. *Deutsche Geschichte*. 12 vols. Berlin, 1891–1909.

———. *Die kulturhistorische Methode*. Berlin, 1900.

———. *What Is History? Five Lectures on the Modern Science of History*. Trans. E. A. Andrews. New York, 1905.

Latourette, Kenneth S. *Biographical Memoir of Berthold Laufer, 1874–1934*. Washington, DC, 1938.

Lemmer, Adolf. *Der Begriff des Gemütes bei Waitz und Hildebrand*. Cologne, 1927. Inaugural dissertation.

Lenz, Max. *Geschichte der Königlichen Friedrich-Wilhelms-Universität zu Berlin*. 4 vols. Halle, Ger., 1910.

Leo Frobenius: Ein Lebenswerk aus der Zeit der Kulturwende. Leipzig, 1933.

Leutwein, Theodor. *Elf Jahre Gouverneur in Deutsch-Südwestafrika*. Berlin, 1908.

Liebe, Georg. *Der Judentum*. Leipzig, 1903. Vol. 11 of Georg Steinhausen, ed., *Monographien zur deutschen Kulturgeschichte*.

———. *Der Soldat in der deutschen Vergangenheit*. Leipzig, 1899. Vol. 1 of Georg Steinhausen, ed., *Monographien zur deutschen Kulturgeschichte*.

Lindenlaub, Dieter. *Richtungskämpfe im Verein für Sozialpolitik*. Supp. 52 and 53 of *Vierteljahrshefte für Sozial- und Wirtschaftsgeschichte*. Wiesbaden, 1967.

List, Friedrich. *The National System of Political Economy*. Trans. G. A. Matile. Philadelphia, 1856.

Lowe, Adolph. "The Classical Theory of Economic Growth." *Social Research* 51, 1 and 2 (1984). Pp. 111–42. (Orig. published 1954.)

Lowie, Robert H. *The History of Ethnological Theory*. New York, 1937.

Manicas, Peter T. *A History and Philosophy of the Social Sciences*. Oxford, 1987.

Marcuse, Herbert. *Reason and Revolution: Hegel and the Rise of Social Theory*, 2nd ed. Boston, 1960.

McClelland, Charles E. *State, Society, and University in Germany 1700–1914*. Cambridge, 1980.

Meiners, Christoph. *Grundriss der Geschichte der Menschheit*. Lemgo, Ger., 1785.

Meyer, Henry Cord. *Mitteleuropa in German Thought and Action, 1815–1945*. The Hague, 1955.

Mitchell, B. R. *European Historical Statistics, 1750–1975*, 2nd ed. New York, 1981.

Mitzman, Arthur. *The Iron Cage: An Historical Interpretation of Max Weber*. New York, 1969.

———. *Sociology and Estrangement: Three Sociologists of Imperial Germany*. New York, 1973.

Mommsen, Wolfgang J. *Max Weber und die deutsche Politik*, 2nd rev. ed. Tübingen, 1974.

Mommsen, Wolfgang J., and Osterhammel, Jürgen. Eds. *Max Weber and His Contemporaries*. London, 1987.

Montesquieu. *Oeuvres complètes*. 2 vols. Paris, 1951.

Mosse, George L. *The Crisis of German Ideology: Intellectual Origins of the Third Reich*. New York, 1964.

———. *Toward the Final Solution: A History of European Racism*. New York, 1978.

Mueller-Vollmer, Kurt. Ed. *The Hermeneutics Reader: Texts of the German Tradition from the Enlightenment to the Present*. New York, 1985.

Mühlmann, Wilhelm E. *Geschichte der Anthropologie*, 2nd ed. Frankfurt am Main and Bonn, 1968.

Müller, Friedrich. *Allgemeine Ethnographie*. Vienna, 1873.

Nachtigal, Gustav. *Sahara und Sudan: Ergebnisse sechsjähriger Reisen in Afrika*. 3 vols. Leipzig, 1879–1889.

Neue Deutsche Biographie. 15 vols. Berlin, 1971–1987.

Oakes, Guy. "Weber and the Southwest German School: The Genesis of the Concept of the Historical Individual." In Wolfgang J. Mommsen and Jürgen Osterhammel, eds., *Max Weber and His Contemporaries*. London 1987. Pp. 434–46.

Oberschall, Anthony. *Empirical Social Research in Germany 1848–1914*. Paris and The Hague, 1965.

Ostwald, Wilhelm. *Lebenslinien*. 3 vols. Leipzig, 1926.

Ottaway, J. H. "Rudolf Virchow: An Appreciation." *Antiquity* 47 (1973). Pp. 101–8.

Pan-German League (*Alldeutscher Verband*). *Zwanzig Jahre alldeutscher Arbeit und Kämpfe*. Berlin, 1910.

Peschel, Oscar. *Völkerkunde*, 4th ed. Leipzig, 1877.

Peters, Carl. *Die deutsche Emin-Pascha Expedition*. Munich, 1891.

Pinney, Thomas. Ed. *Essays of George Eliot*. New York, 1963.

Pinson, Koppel S. *Modern Germany: Its History and Civilization*, 2nd ed. New York, 1966.

Pogge von Strandmann, Hartmut. "Domestic Origins of Germany's Colonial Expansion Under Bismarck." *Past and Present* 42 (1969). Pp. 140–59.

Pohle, Hermann. "Der Vorstand der Berliner Gesellschaft für Anthropologie, Ethnologie und Urgeschichte." In *Festschrift zum hundertjährige Bestehen der Berliner Gesellschaft für Anthropologie, Ethnologie und Urgeschichte 1869–1969*. Part 1. Berlin, 1969. Pp. 141–42.

Poliakov, Leon. *Le Mythe aryen*. Paris, 1971.

Puhle, Hans-Jürgen. *Agrarische Interessenpolitik und preussischer Konservatismus im Wilhelmischen Reich, 1893–1914*. Hanover, 1966.

Quatrefages, Armand de. *La Race prussienne*. Paris, 1871.

Ranke, Leopold von. *The Secret of World History*. Trans. and ed. Roger Wines. New York, 1981.

Ratzel, Friedrich. *Anthropo-Geographie*. 2 vols. Stuttgart, 1882.

———. [Anon.] "Ein Beitrag zu den Anfangen der deutschen Kolonialpolitik." *Grenzboten* 62, 2 (1903). Pp. 115–16.

———. "Beiträge zur Kenntnis der Verbreitung des Bogens und des Speeres in indo-afrikanischen Völkerkreis." *Berichten des Königl. Sächs. Gesellschaft der Wissenschaften* (1893). Pp. 147–82.

———. "Die Beurteilungen der Völker." *Nord und Süd* 6 (1878). Pp. 177–200.

———. *Die chinesische Auswanderung: Ein Beitrag zur Kultur-und Handelsgeographie*. Breslau, 1876.

———. [Anon.] "Dr. Karl Peters." *Grenzboten* 56, 18 (1897). Pp. 252–56.

———. *Die Erde und das Leben: Eine vergleichende Erdkunde*. 2 vols. Leipzig and Vienna, 1901.

———. "Über geographische Bedingungen und ethnographischen Folgen der Völkerwanderungen." *Verhandlungen der Gesellschaft für Erdkunde zu Berlin* 7 (1880). Pp. 295–324.

———. "Geschichte, Völkerkunde und historische Perspektive." *Historische Zeitschrift* 93, 1 (1904). Pp. 1–46.

————. "Die Gesetze des räumlichen Wachstums der Staaten." *Petermanns Mitteilungen* 42 (1896). Pp. 97–107.

————. *Glückinseln und Träume: Gesammelte Aufsätze aus den Grenzboten.* Leipzig, 1905.

————. "Der Lebensraum: Eine biogeographische Studie." In K. Bücher, K. V. Fricker, et al., *Festgaben für Albert Schäffle zur siebenzigsten Widerkehr seines Geburtstages am 24. Februar 1901.* Tübingen, 1901. Pp. 101–89.

————. "Die Maske ab!" *Grenzboten* 53, 21 (1894). Pp. 337–40.

————. *Das Meer als Quelle der Völkergrösse: Ein politisch-geographische Studie.* Munich, 1900.

————. "Die mitteleuropäische Wirtschaftsverein." *Grenzboten* 63, 5 (1904). Pp. 253–59.

————. *Politische Geographie,* 3rd ed. Munich and Berlin, 1923.

————. *Sein und Werden der organischen Welt: Eine populäre Schöpfungsgeschichte.* Leipzig, 1869.

————. *Völkerkunde,* 2nd rev. ed. 2 vols. Berlin and Leipzig, 1894.

————. "In welcher Richtung beeinflussen die afrikanischen Ereignisse die Thätigkeit des Kolonialvereins?" *Deutsche Kolonialzeitung,* 15 January 1885. Pp. 38–44.

————. *Wider die Reichsnörgler: Ein Wort zur Kolonialfrage aus Wählerkreisen.* Munich, 1884.

Rauh, Manfred. *Die Parlamentarisierung des Deutschen Reiches.* Düsseldorf, 1977.

Reddy, William M. *Money and Liberty in Europe: A Critique of Historical Understanding.* Cambridge, 1987.

Reill, Peter Hanns. *The German Enlightenment and the Rise of Historicism.* Berkeley, CA, 1975.

Reulecke, Jürgen. "Die Anfänge der organisierten Sozialreform in Deutschland." In Rüdiger vom Bruch, ed. *'Weder Kommunismus noch Kapitalismus': Bürgerliche Sozialreform in Deutschland vom Vomärz zum Ära Adenauer.* Pp. 21–59.

Rickman, H. P. *Wilhelm Dilthey: Pioneer of the Human Studies.* Berkeley, 1979.

Rieber, R. W. Ed. *Wilhelm Wundt and the Making of a Scientific Psychology.* New York and London, 1980.

Riehl, Wilhelm Heinrich. *Die bürgerliche Gesellschaft.* Stuttgart, 1861.

————. *Die Naturgeschichte des Volkes als Grundlage einer deutschen Social-Politik.* 4 vols. Stuttgart, 1862–1869.

————. *Religiöse Studien eines Weltkindes.* Stuttgart, 1894.

————. *Die Volkskunde als Wissenschaft.* Berlin and Leipzig, 1935.

Ringer, Fritz K. *The Decline of the German Mandarins: The German Academic Community, 1890–1933.* Cambridge, MA, 1969.

Rochau, August Ludwig von. *Grundsätze der Realpolitik, angewendet auf die staatlichen Zustände Deutschlands.* Stuttgart, 1853.

Rodbertus-Jagetzow, Carl. *Zur Beleuchtung der socialen Frage.* Ed. A. Wagner and T. Kozak. Berlin, 1875.

Roessler, Wilhelm. *Die Entstehung des modernen Erziehungswesens in Deutschland.* Stuttgart, 1961.

Rohlfs, Gerhard. *Quer durch Afrika.* Leipzig, 1874.

Rohr, Donald G. *The Origins of Social Liberalism in Germany.* Chicago, 1963.

Rohrbach, Paul. *Der deutsche Gedanke in der Welt.* Düsseldorf and Leipzig, 1912.

Roon, Waldemar Graf von. *Denkwürdigkeiten aus dem Leben des Generalfeldmarschalls Kriegsministers Grafen von Roon,* 5th ed. 3 vols. Berlin, 1905.

Roscher, Wilhelm. *Ansichten der Volkswirtschaft aus dem geschichtlichen Standpunkte,* 2nd ed. Leipzig and Heidelberg, 1861.

————. *Geschichte der National-Oekonomik in Deutschland*, 2nd ed. Munich and Berlin, 1924.

————. *Kolonien, Kolonialpolitik und Auswanderung*, 2nd ed. Leipzig and Heidelberg, 1856.

Rosenberg, Hans. *Grosse Depression und Bismarckzeit: Wirtschaftsablauf, Gesellschaft und Politik in Mitteleuropa*. Berlin, 1967.

Rotteck, Karl von and Welcker, Karl. Eds. *Das Staats-Lexikon. Encyklopädie der sammtlichen Staatswissenschaft für alle Stände*, 3rd ed. 14 vols. Leipzig, 1856ff.

Rüsen, Jörn. "Jacob Burckhardt." In Hans-Ulrich Wehler, ed., *Deutsche Historiker III*. Pp. 5–28.

Ruggiero, Guido de. *The History of European Liberalism*. Trans. R. G. Collingwood. Boston, 1959.

Sahlins, Marshal. *Culture and Practical Reason*. Chicago and London, 1976.

Schäfer, Dietrich. *Mein Leben*. Berlin and Leipzig, 1926.

Schieffel, Werner. *Bernhard Dernburg 1865–1937: Kolonialpolitiker und Bankier in wilhelmischen Deutschland*. Zurich and Freiburg, 1974.

Schmidt, Geo A. *Das Kolonial-Wirtschaftliche Komitee*. Berlin, 1934.

Schmidt, Wilhelm. "Die moderne Ethnologie." *Anthropos* 1 (1906). Pp. 134–63, 318–88, 592–644, 950–97.

————. *Rasse und Volk: Eine Untersuchung zur Bestimmung ihrer Grenzen und zur Erfassung ihrer Beziehungen*. Munich, 1927.

Schmidt, Wilhelm, and Koppers, Wilhelm. *Völker und Kulturleben. Erster Teil: Gesellschaft und Wirtschaft der Völker*. Regensburg, 1924.

Schmokel, Wolfe W. "Gerhard Rohlfs: The Lonely Explorer." In Robert I. Rotberg, ed. *Africa and Its Explorers: Motives, Methods, and Impact*. Cambridge, MA, 1970.

Schmoller, Gustav. "Zur Methodologie der Staats- und Sozialwissenschaften." *Jahrbuch für Gesetzgebung, Verwaltung und Volkswirtschaft im Deutschen Reiche* n.F. 7 (1883). Pp. 96–153.

Schön, Manfred. "Gustav Schmoller and Max Weber." In Wolfgang J. Mommsen and Jürgen Osterhammel, *Max Weber and His Contemporaries*. London, 1989. Pp. 59–70.

Schultz, Hans-Dietrich. *Die deutschsprachige Geographie von 1800 bis 1970: Ein Beitrag zur Geschichte ihrer Methodologie*. Berlin, 1980.

Schultz-Ewerth, Erich, and Adam, Leonhard. Eds. *Das Eingeborenenrecht: Sitte und Gewohnheitsrechte der Eingeborenen der ehemaligen deutschen Kolonien*. 2 vols. Stuttgart, 1930.

Schurtz, Heinrich. *Urgeschichte der Kultur*. Leipzig and Vienna, 1900.

————. *Völkerkunde*. Leipzig and Vienna, 1903.

Schweinfurth, G. A. *Im Herzen von Afrika: Reisen und Entdeckungen im centralen Äquatorial-Afrika während der Jahre 1868–1871*. Leipzig, 1874.

Sering, Max. *Die innere Kolonisation in östlichen Deutschland*. Leipzig, 1893.

Sharlin, Allan M. "Max Weber and the Origins of the Idea of Value-Free Social Science." *Archives européenes de sociologie* 15 (1974). Pp. 337–53.

Sheehan, James J. *The Career of Lujo Brentano: A Study of Liberalism and Social Reform in Imperial Germany*. Chicago and London, 1966.

————. *German Liberalism in the Nineteenth Century*. Chicago and London, 1978.

Simmel, Georg. *Brücke und Tür: Essays des Philosophen zur Geschichte, Religion, Kunst und Gesellschaft*. Ed. Michael Landmann. Stuttgart, 1957.

Skinner, Quentin. Ed. *The Return of Grand Theory in the Human Sciences*. Cambridge, 1985.

Smith, Anthony. *The Newspaper: An International History*. London, 1979.

Smith, Woodruff D. "The Colonial Novel as Political Propaganda: Hans Grimm's *Volk ohne Raum*." *German Studies Review* 6 (1983). Pp. 215–35.

———. "The Emergence of German Urban Sociology, 1900–1910." *Journal of the History of Sociology* 1, 2 (1979). Pp. 1–16.

———. "Friedrich Ratzel and the Origins of *Lebensraum*." *German Studies Review* 3 (1980). Pp. 51–68.

———. *The German Colonial Empire*. Chapel Hill, NC, 1978.

———. *The Ideological Origins of Nazi Imperialism*. New York, 1986.

———. "Julius Graf Zech auf Neuhofen (1868–1914)." In L. H. Gann and Peter Duignan, eds., *African Proconsuls: European Governors in Africa*. New York, 1978. Pp. 473–91.

———. "The Social and Political Origins of German Diffusionist Ethnology." *Journal of the History of the Behavioral Sciences* 14 (1978). Pp. 103–12.

Smith, Woodruff D., and Turner, Sharon A. "Legislative Behavior in the German Reichstag, 1898–1906." *Central European History* 14 (1981). Pp. 3–29.

Spellmeyer, Hans. *Deutsche Kolonialpolitik im Reichstage*. Stuttgart, 1931.

Spidle, Jake W., Jr. "Colonial Studies in Imperial Germany." *History of Education Quarterly* 13, 3 (1973). Pp. 231–47.

Stannard, David E. *Shrinking History: On Freud and the Failure of Psychohistory*. New York, 1982.

Stauffer, R. C. Ed. *Science and Civilization*. Madison, WI, 1949.

Steinberg, Hans-Josef. "Karl Lamprecht." In Hans-Ulrich Wehler, ed., *Deutsche Historiker I*. Pp. 58–68.

Steinhausen, Georg. Ed. *Monographien zur deutschen Kulturgeschichte*. 12 vols. Leipzig and Jena, 1899–1905.

Stern, Fritz. *The Failure of Illiberalism*. New York, 1972.

———. *The Politics of Cultural Despair: A Study in the Rise of the Germanic Ideology*. Garden City, NY, 1965.

Stocking, George W., Jr. Ed. *Functionalism Historicized: Essays on British Social Anthropology*. Madison, WI, 1984.

———. *Race, Culture, and Evolution: Essays in the History of Anthropology*. New York, 1968.

———. Ed. *The Shaping of American Anthropology 1883–1911: A Franz Boas Reader*. New York, 1974.

———. *Victorian Anthropology*. New York, 1987.

Stuhlmann, Franz. *Beiträge zur Kulturgeschichte von Ostafrika*. Berlin, 1909.

Temkin, Owsei. "Metaphors of Human Biology." In R. C. Stauffer, ed., *Science and Civilization*. Madison, WI, 1949. Pp. 169–94.

Tessmann, Günter. *Die Pangwe: Völkerkundliche Monographie eines westafrikanischen Negerstammes*, 2 vols. Berlin, 1913.

Tims, R. W. *Germanizing Prussian Poland: The H-K-T Society and the Struggle for the Eastern Marches in the German Empire 1894–1919*. New York, 1941.

Toews, John E. "Intellectual History After the Linguistic Turn: The Autonomy of Meaning and the Irreducibility of Experience." *American Historical Review* 92, 4 (1987). Pp. 879–907.

Treitschke, Heinrich von. *History of Germany in the Nineteenth Century*. Ed. Gordon Craig. Chicago, 1975.

———. *Politics*. Trans. B. Dugdale and T. de Bille. 2 vols. New York, 1916.

Tucker, Robert C. Ed. *The Marx-Engels Reader*, 2nd ed. New York, 1978.

Tylor, Edward B. *Primitive Culture*. 2 vols. New York, 1977.

Valjavec, Fritz. *Die Entstehung der politischen Strömungen in Deutschland, 1770–1815*. Munich, 1951.

Verhandlungen des Deutschen Kolonialkongresses 1902. Berlin, 1903.

Verzeichnis der Vorlesungen an der Friedrich-Wilhelms-Universität zu Berlin im Winter-Semester 1907/8. Berlin, 1907.

Vierkandt, Alfred. *Naturvölker und Kulturvölker: Ein Beitrag zur Sozialpsychologie*. Leipzig, 1896.

Virchow, Rudolf. "Acclimatisation." *Verhandlungen der Berliner Gesellschaft für Anthropologie, Ethnologie und Urgeschichte*. 1885. Pp. 202–14.

———. *Briefe an seine Eltern 1839 bis 1864*. Ed. Marie Rabl. Leipzig, 1907.

———. "Die Deutschen und die Germanen." *Verhandlungen der Berliner Gesellschaft für Anthropologie, Ethnologie und Urgeschichte*. 1881. Pp. 68–75.

———. *Disease, Life, and Man: Selected Essays*. Trans. L. J. Rather. Stanford, CA, 1958.

———. "Die Freiheit der Wissenschaft im modernen Staat." *Amtlicher Bericht der Gesellschaft deutscher Naturforscher und Aertze, 75. Versammlung* . . . . Munich, 1877. Pp. 65–77.

———. *Die Not im Spessart. Mitteilungen über die im Oberschlesien herrschende Typhus-Epidemie*. Hildesheim, 1968.

———. "Rassenbildung und Erblichkeit." In *Festschrift für Adolf Bastian zu seinem 70. Geburtstage 26. Juni 1896*. Berlin, 1896. Pp. 1–43.

———. *Sozialismus und Reaktion*. Berlin, 1878.

Volkov, Shulamit. *The Rise of Popular Antimodernism in Germany: The Urban Master Artisans, 1873–1896*. Princeton, NJ, 1978.

Wagner, Adolf. *Agrar- und Industriestaat*, 2nd ed. Jena, 1902.

Wagner, Moritz. *Die Darwin'sche Theorie und das Migrationsgesetz der Organismen*. Leipzig, 1868.

———. *Entstehung der Arten durch räumliche Sonderung: Gesammelte Aufsätze*. Basel, 1889.

———, and Scherzer, Carl. *Die Republik Costa Rica in Centralamerika*. Leipzig, 1856.

Waitz, Theodor. *Anthropologie der Naturvölker*. 6 vols. Leipzig, 1859–1872.

———. *Introduction to Anthropology*. Ed. and trans. J. Frederick Collingwood. London, 1863.

Wanklyn, Harriet. *Friedrich Ratzel. A Biographical Memoir and Bibliography*. Cambridge, 1961.

Warren, Donald, Jr. *The Red Kingdom of Saxony: Lobbying Grounds for Gustav Stresemann, 1901–1909*. The Hague, 1964.

Weber, Marianne. *Max Weber: A Biography*. Trans. Harry Zohn. New York, 1975.

Weber, Max. *The City*. Trans. D. Martindale and G. Neuwirth. New York, 1958.

———. *Gesammelte politische Schriften*, 3rd ed. Ed. Johannes Winckelmann. Tübingen, 1971.

———. *Roscher and Knies: The Logical Problems of Historical Economics*. Trans. Guy Oakes. New York, 1975.

Weber, Wolfgang. *Priester der Klio. Historisch-sozialwissenschaftliche Studien zur Herkunft und Karriere deutscher Historiker und zur Geschichte der Geschichtswissenschaft 1800–1970*, 2nd ed. Frankfurt am Main, 1987.

Wegner, Konstanze. *Theodor Barth und die Freisinnige Vereinigung: Studie zur Geschichte des Linksliberalismus im wilhelmischen Deutschland, 1893–1910*. Tübingen, 1968.

Wehler, Hans-Ulrich. "Bismarck's Imperialism, 1862–1890." In James J. Sheehan, ed., *Imperial Germany*. New York, 1976.

———. *Bismarck und der Imperialismus.* Cologne, 1969.

———. Ed. *Deutsche Historiker I.* Göttingen, 1971.

———. Ed. *Deutsche Historiker III.* Göttingen, 1972.

———. *The German Empire 1871–1918.* Trans. Kim Traynor. Leamington Spa, Eng., 1985.

Weintraub, Karl J. *Visions of Culture.* Chicago and London, 1966.

Weiss, Max. *Die Völkerstämme im Norden Deutsch-Ostafrikas.* Berlin, 1910. Repr. 1971.

Wer Ist's? 10th ed. Berlin, 1914.

Westermann, Diedrich. *Afrika als europäische Aufgabe.* Berlin, 1914.

Westphal-Hellbusch, Sigrid. "Hundert Jahre Ethnologie in Berlin, unter besonderer Berücksichtigung ihrer Entwicklung an der Universität." In *Festschrift zum hundertjährigen Bestehen der Berliner Gesellschaft für Anthropologie, Ethnologie und Urgeschichte 1869–1969.* Part 1. Berlin, 1969.

Whimster, Sam. "Karl Lamprecht and Max Weber: Historical Sociology Within the Confines of a Historians' Controversy." In Wolfgang J. Mommsen and Jürgen Osterhammel, eds., *Max Weber and His Contemporaries.* London, 1987. Pp. 268–83.

White, Dan S. *The Splintered Party: National Liberalism in Hessen and the Reich, 1867–1918.* Cambridge, MA, 1976.

Whitman, James. "From Philology to Anthropology in Mid-Nineteenth-Century Germany." In George W. Stocking, Jr., ed., *Functionalism Historicized: Essays On British Social Anthropology.* Madison, WI. Pp. 214–29.

Wild, Karl. *Karl Theodor Welcker, ein Vorkämpfer des älteren Liberalismus.* Heidelberg, 1913.

Wirth, Moritz. Ed. *Kleine Schriften von Dr. Carl Rodbertus-Jagetzow.* Berlin, 1890.

Wohlenberg, Hellmut. "Die Paideumalehre als Kulturphilosophie." In *Leo Frobenius: Ein Lebenswerk aus der Zeit der Kulturwende.* Leipzig, 1933. Pp. 32–56.

Wucher, Albert. *Theodor Mommsen: Geschichtsschreibung und Politik.* Göttingen, 1956.

Wundt, Wilhelm. *Die Anfänge der Gesellschaft: Eine völkerpsychologische Studie.* Leipzig, 1907.

———. *Elemente der Völkerpsychologie: Grundlinien einer Entwicklungsgeschichte der Menschheit.* Leipzig, 1912.

———. *Erlebtes und Erkanntes.* Stuttgart, 1920.

———. *Völkerpsychologie: Eine Untersuchung der Entwicklungsgeschichte von Sprache, Mythus und Sitte.* 10 vols. Leipzig, 1900–1920.

Zech, Julius Graf. "Land und Leute an der Nordwestgrenze von Togo." *Mitteilungen aus den deutschen Schutzgebieten* 17, 3 (1904).

———. "Vermischte Notizen über Togo und das Togohinterland." *Mitteilungen aus den deutschen Schutzgebieten* 11, 2 (1898).

Index